FORTRESS
MALTA

FORTRESS MALTA

AN ISLAND UNDER SIEGE
1940-1943

JAMES HOLLAND

ORION

First published in Great Britain in 2003 by
Orion Books Ltd
Orion House, 5 Upper St Martin's Lane, London WC2H 9EA

Copyright © James Holland 2003

A CIP catalogue record for this book is available
from the British Library.

ISBN: 0 75286 0380 (trade paperback)
ISBN: 0 75285 2884 (hardback)

Typeset by Selwood Systems,
Midsomer Norton

Printed by Butler & Tanner Ltd,
Frome and London

Indexing by Indexing Specialists Ltd

CONTENTS

ILLUSTRATIONS

Endpapers   A Maltese, with his mule and cart, stands beside a Spitfire in its blast pen.

1. Admiral Cunningham – determined, bullish, but with a hint of the humour that was never far away.
2. Meme Cortis flanked by two other VAD nurses outside the 90th General Hospital at Imtarfa.
3. George Burges leaning against one of the many dry-stone walls that made crash-landing on the Island so hazardous.
4. Frank Rixon in boxing mode.
5. Suzanne Parlby. Young English women were few and far between on Malta.
6. John Agius outside the RAF Headquarters at Scots Street, Valletta, where he worked as a civilian clerk.
7. George Burges strapped into one of the Gloster Gladiator biplanes, ready to go at a moment's notice.
8. The Whizz-Bangs, the travelling cabaret show that brought much welcome relief to the troops around the Island.
9. General Sir William Dobbie, Acting Governor, then later Governor of Malta.
10. Warby. Cigarette in hand, battered cap perched on his head, grey slacks and the favoured battle-blouse.
11. An Italian Savoia-Marchetti S.M. 79 bomber plunges towards Grand Harbour on 10 July 1940.
12. Warby's battle-scarred Glenn Martin Maryland at Luqa.
13. Bombs falling on Grand Harbour and the Three Cities in January 1941.
14. Nat Gold. He looks cheerful enough here, but he discovered there was little to smile about during his year on Malta serving with 830 Fleet Air Arm Squadron.

15. A Fairey Swordfish at Hal Far. The 'Stringbag' is loaded with a torpedo.
16. The remains of a Swordfish at Hal Far.
17. Shrimp Simpson, the indefatigable and inspirational commander of the Tenth Submarine Flotilla.
18. The crew of HMS/S *Upholder*, the most successful Allied submarine of the war.
19. Tommy Thompson, who volunteered to join the fledgling Malta Night Fighter Unit.
20. Tom Neil of 249 Squadron.
21. Hurricanes burning at Takali after Müncheberg's attack on 25 May.
22. Lazzaretto and Manoel Island, home to the Malta-based submarines.
23 & 24. The control room of a U-class submarine such as *Upholder*. Almost every inch is covered in pipes, dials and other bits of equipment.
25. 'Pop' Giddings with Mary and Annie, two of the submariners' pigs.
26. Soldiers cycling across the Maltese countryside. Accidents were fairly frequent, as Frank Rixon discovered.
27. Takali some time in 1941. There are no blast pens yet, the Hurricanes lined up on the far side are an easy target for any would-be attackers.
28. Ken Griffiths on the motorcycle he was taught to ride on the Island.
29. A six-man Bofors gun crew, like the one to which Ken Griffiths belonged.
30. The dispersal hut at Takali, built by Maltese labourers in 1941.
31. Ghajn Tuffieha, a bay on the north-west of the Island and a favoured rest-camp for the submariners.
32. Digging shelters.
33. The Control Room at Lascaris, where Christina Ratcliffe worked as a civilian plotter for the RAF.
34. Peter Rothwell who, at just twenty-one, took over command of the Special Duties Flight.
35. Bombs explode on Malta, while the anti-aircraft barrage bursts above.
36. Ken Griffiths and his company of the 32nd Light Anti-Aircraft Regiment.
37. Raoul Daddo-Langlois, the young Spitfire pilot who, in England,

had craved action and excitement and found it in spades during his time on Malta.

38. A German reconnaissance photograph of Takali airfield.

39. Takali airfield again after the bombing raids. The white dots and patches are bomb craters.

40. HMS *Talabot* burning. This picture is taken from Castille Square looking across Grand Harbour towards the Corradino Heights.

41. The remains of the Royal Opera House after the raids of 7 April 1942.

42. A dilapidated bus, very much like the one that greeted Raoul Daddo-Langlois and Denis Barnham on their arrival on the Island.

43. A Spitfire Mark V on Malta.

44. An aerial photograph of a raid on Grand Harbour taken from a German Junkers 88.

45. Carnage in Grand Harbour.

46. Pete Watson (far right) and colleagues outside their billet in Rabat.

47. The tough twenty-two-year-old Canadian Buck McNair.

48. HMS *Penelope*. No wonder she was nicknamed HMS '*Pepperpot*'.

49. Takali under attack and completely covered by dust and smoke.

50. A Bofors gun crew.

51. Cartoon from the *Times of Malta*, 7 May 1942.

52. The future? What? Denis Barnham's self-portrait of 16 May 1942.

53. Maltese amongst the ruins.

54. Denis Barnham in his Spitfire at Luqa.

55. A Maltese, with his mule and cart, stands beside a Spitfire in its blast pen.

56. Christina Ratcliffe in a publicity shot for the Victory Kitchens.

57. Denis Barnham's painting of the Air Battle for Malta. The underbelly of a Messerschmitt 109 flashes past a Spitfire.

58. Warby, wearing his white scarf, grey baggy slacks and desert boots. Attitudes to dress were relaxed on Malta.

59. An aerial reconnaissance photograph of Tripoli Harbour taken by Warby.

60. Denis Barnham. By the time this photograph was taken, Denis had the necessary five kills that made him an 'ace' – four German and one Italian, painted on the side of his Spitfire.

61. A page from Denis's diary, 14 June 1942, and his sketch of the ruins of Sliema, home of John Agius and Meme Cortis.

62. Frank and Mary Rixon with their baby daughter, Betty.

PHOTOGRAPHIC ACKNOWLEDGEMENTS

John Agius: 6
Diana Barnham: 52, 61
Fraser Carlisle-Brown: 77, 82
Capt M.L.C. Crawford: 18, 79, 81, 83
W.R. Daddo-Langlois: 68
Keith Durbridge: 10
Ken Fielder: 12
H.W. Gold: 14
Ken Griffiths: 28, 36
James Holland: 84
Fred Jewett: 69
Suzanne Kyrle-Pope: 5
Imperial War Museum, London: 1, 17, 23, 24, 25, 26, 29, 31, 32, 33, 43, 55, 57, 60, 80
Laddie Lucas: 47

Joseph McCarthy: 73, 78
Wing Commander T.F. Neil: 19, 20
Frederick Treves: 67
Meme Turner: 2, 66
National War Museum Archive, Malta: 3, 7, 8, 9, 11, 13, 21, 22, 27, 39, 40, 41, 42, 45, 48, 50, 53, 54, 56, 58, 59, 65, 70, 71, 72, 74, 75, 76
Frank Rixon: 4, 62
Peter Rothwell: 34
Signal Magazine: 38, 44
Zoë Thomas: 37
Times of Malta: 51
Peter Watson: 15, 16, 30, 35, 46, 49, 63, 64

Every effort has been made to contact the copyright holders, but if any have been inadvertently overlooked, the publishers will be pleased to make the necessary arrangements at the first opportunity.

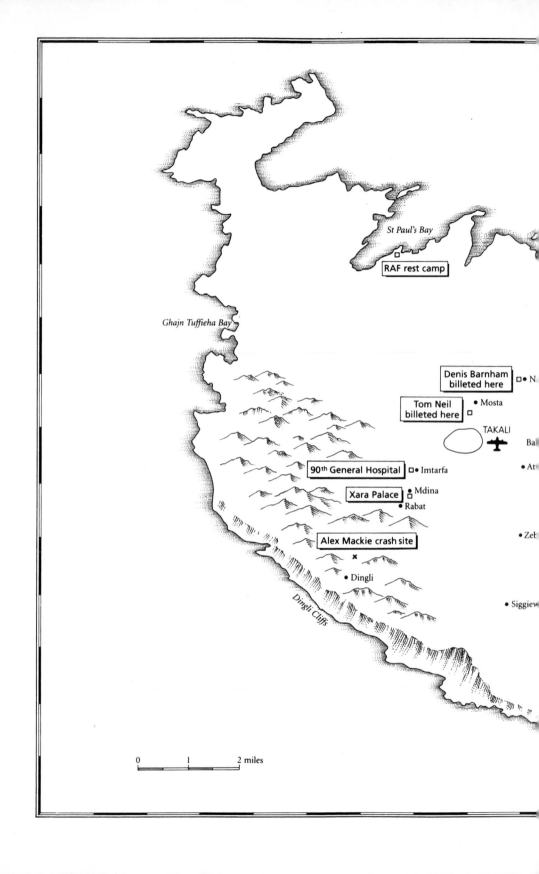

St Paul's Bay

RAF rest camp

Ghajn Tuffieha Bay

Denis Barnham billeted here ☐● N

Tom Neil billeted here ☐ ● Mosta

TAKALI

Ba

90th General Hospital ☐● Imtarfa

● At

Xara Palace ☐ ● Mdina
● Rabat

● Zeb

Alex Mackie crash site
✕

● Dingli

Dingli Cliffs

● Siggiew

0   1   2 miles

MALTA

Mediterranean Sea

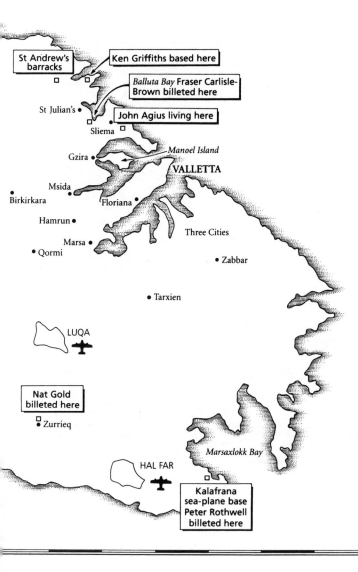

St Andrew's barracks

Ken Griffiths based here

Balluta Bay Fraser Carlisle-Brown billeted here

St Julian's

John Agius living here

Sliema

Gzira

Manoel Island

VALLETTA

Msida

Birkirkara

Floriana

Hamrun

Three Cities

Marsa

Qormi

Zabbar

Tarxien

LUQA

Nat Gold billeted here

Zurrieq

Marsaxlokk Bay

HAL FAR

Kalafrana sea-plane base
Peter Rothwell billeted here

Malta and Gozo looking north.

Valletta, Grand Harbour and the south-east of the Island.

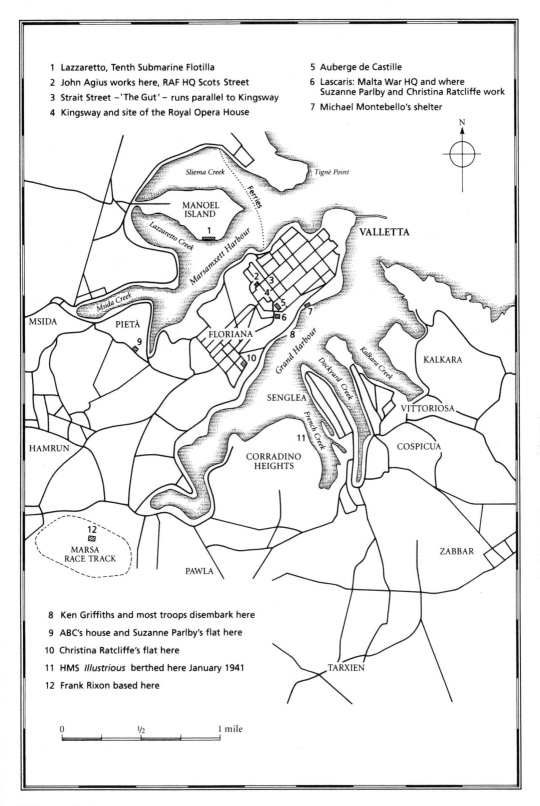

1 Lazzaretto, Tenth Submarine Flotilla
2 John Agius works here, RAF HQ Scots Street
3 Strait Street –'The Gut' – runs parallel to Kingsway
4 Kingsway and site of the Royal Opera House

5 Auberge de Castille
6 Lascaris: Malta War HQ and where Suzanne Parlby and Christina Ratcliffe work
7 Michael Montebello's shelter

N

Sliema Creek
Tignè Point
Ferries
MANOEL ISLAND
1
Lazzaretto Creek
Marsamxett Harbour
VALLETTA
Msida Creek
MSIDA
PIETÀ
2 3
4
5
6 7
9
FLORIANA
8
10
Grand Harbour
Dockyard Creek
Kalkara Creek
KALKARA
SENGLEA
French Creek
VITTORIOSA
HAMRUN
11
CORRADINO HEIGHTS
COSPICUA
12
MARSA RACE TRACK
ZABBAR
PAWLA
TARXIEN

8 Ken Griffiths and most troops disembark here
9 ABC's house and Suzanne Parlby's flat here
10 Christina Ratcliffe's flat here
11 HMS *Illustrious* berthed here January 1941
12 Frank Rixon based here

0   1/2   1 mile

Valletta and harbour areas.

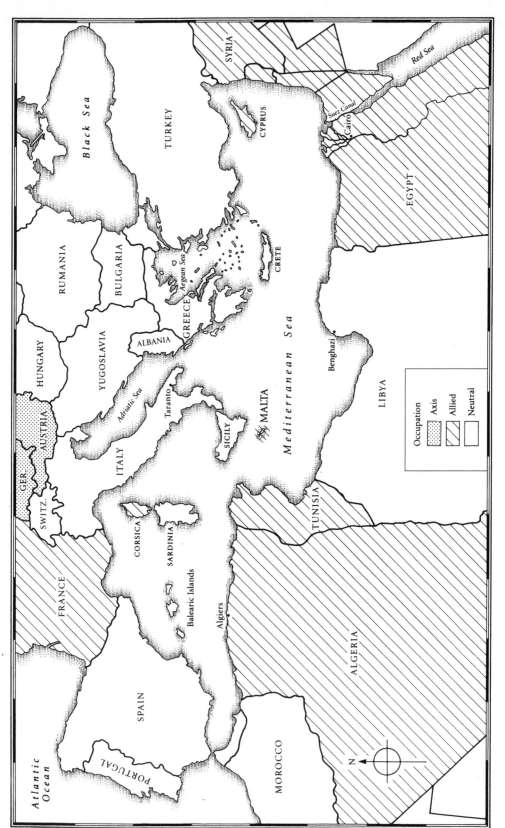

Mediterranean in 1939.

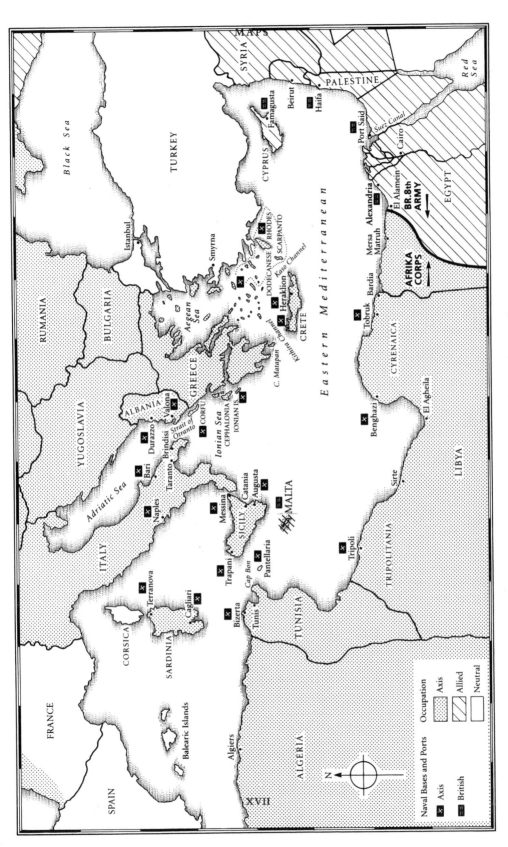

Mediterranean June 1941–November 1942. (Algeria and Tunisia were Vichy until the end of November 1942.)

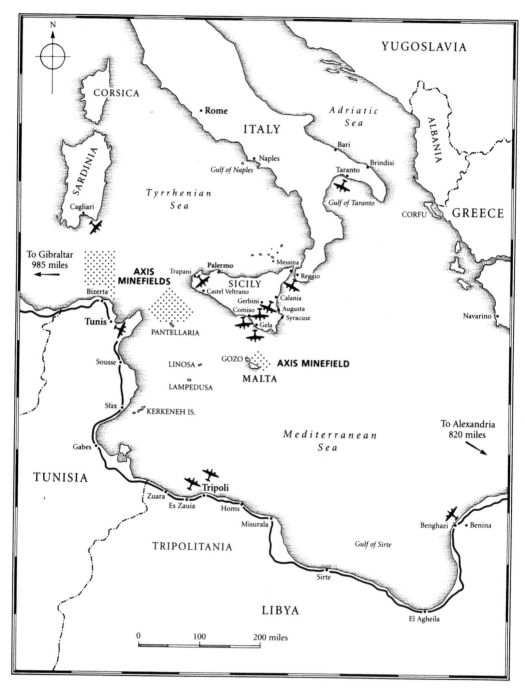

Surrounded by the enemy. During the siege, Malta was walled to the north and south by Axis territory and to the west by Vichy-controlled Tunisia. Enemy minefields and air fleets had her trapped.

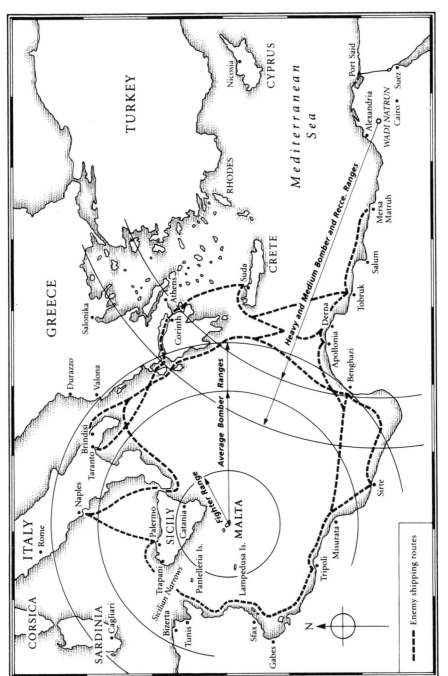

Allied aircraft range from Malta and Axis shipping routes.

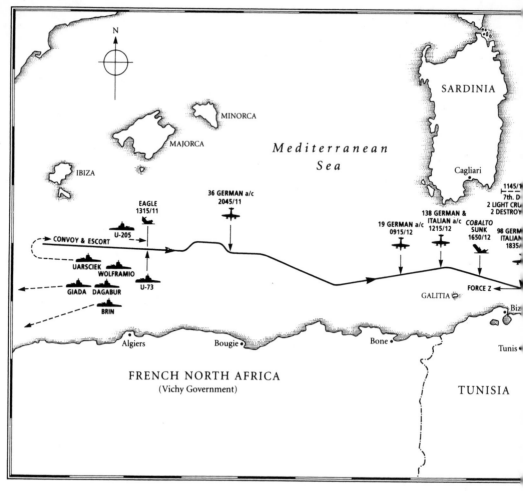
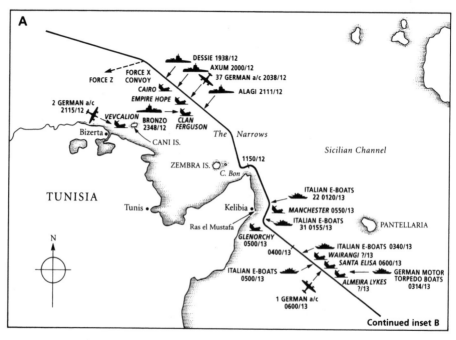

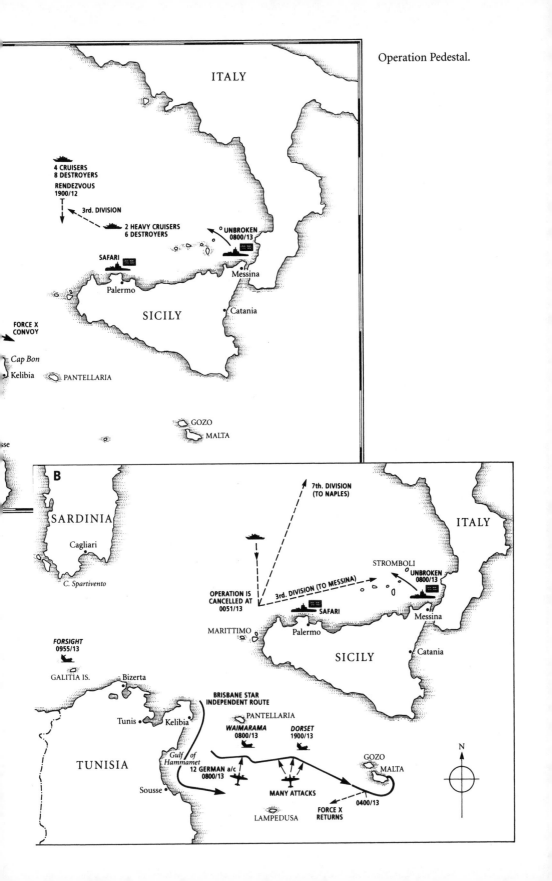

Operation Pedestal.

Map A (top):

ITALY

4 CRUISERS
8 DESTROYERS
RENDEZVOUS
1900/12

3rd. DIVISION

2 HEAVY CRUISERS
6 DESTROYERS

UNBROKEN
0800/13

SAFARI

Messina

Palermo

SICILY

Catania

FORCE X
CONVOY

Cap Bon

Kelibia   PANTELLARIA

GOZO
MALTA

Map B (bottom):

B

SARDINIA

Cagliari

C. Spartivento

7th. DIVISION
(TO NAPLES)

STROMBOLI

UNBROKEN
0800/13

OPERATION IS
CANCELLED AT
0051/13

3rd. DIVISION (TO MESSINA)

SAFARI

Messina

MARITTIMO

Palermo

SICILY

Catania

FORSIGHT
0955/13

GALITIA IS.   Bizerta

Tunis   Kelibia

BRISBANE STAR
INDEPENDENT ROUTE

PANTELLARIA

WAIMARAMA
0800/13

DORSET
1900/13

TUNISIA

Gulf of
Hammamet

12 GERMAN a/c
0800/13

MANY ATTACKS

GOZO
MALTA

Sousse

0400/13

LAMPEDUSA   FORCE X
RETURNS

N

LETTER FROM DOROTHY MACKIE TO PRINCIPAL MATRON MAUD BUCKINGHAM, 90TH GENERAL HOSPITAL, IMTARFA, MALTA

March 10 1942

Dear Matron,

I thank you so very much for writing to me about my son's death. I was so thankful to know that he never regained consciousness after his crash, and so *did not endure any terrible suffering*. He was always such a splendid brave boy – and I am proud to know that he has been one of the defenders of Malta.

You must have seen so many sad cases – and we all think your island is simply *wonderful* withstanding all the continuing air attacks.

I shall hope, one day, when this cruel War is over, to visit Malta – and see where my boy is buried. My husband is in Hospital in Durban – suffering from shell shock. He was bombed in Singapore.

Again with so many thanks for your kind letter and sympathy.

From yours sincerely,
Dorothy Mackie

A Brief Engagement over Malta

ROUND 5 P.M. on Sunday 25 January 1942. Six German fighter planes are taking off from their airfield in Sicily and heading south towards the tiny Island of Malta, just sixty miles away. Led by Oberleutnant Otto Belser, they are all flying the Messerschmitt 109F: fast, agile, highly manœuvrable and a cut above the Royal Air Force Hurricanes they are flying against. The light is already fading, but they won't need long. A little under a quarter of an hour to get there, a few minutes' shooting up anything they can see – planes on the ground, buildings, service personnel, that sort of thing – then nip back in time for a drink and some dinner. And by flying low, speeding at nearly three hundred miles an hour just fifty feet above the dark blue Mediterranean, they will never be picked up by radar, nor spotted in the failing light. They can sweep in over St Paul's Bay in the north and up over the ridge of the Victoria Lines and strafe one of the airfields before anyone even realizes they are there.

It is also at about five o'clock that twenty-year-old Alex Mackie picks up his flying helmet and goggles from the crew room and takes his parachute out from open-faced lockers screwed roughly onto one side of the walls. Short, with dark hair and boyish looks, he could pass for even younger. He is wearing blue serge trousers, and a pullover underneath his RAF battledress-blouse. Strapped around his neck and waist is his pale yellow Mae West lifejacket. He and the other pilots of the Malta Night Fighter Unit have come down from their Mess in Mdina to the airfield at Takali a short while before. Glancing up at the ancient citadel, he can see his window now, and above it the roof balcony with its bar and mounted twin-Browning machine-guns. They've been lucky all right, with their Mess – after all, it is not everyone who gets to live in a palace, however down-at-heel. He looks up again – at the cathedral with its high cupola, and the imposing walls of pale limestone that remind him of his home in Edinburgh.

Eight of them are going out tonight – for an intruder patrol over Sicily. For the first time since the unit was formed the previous August, they are taking the attack to the enemy. An air of excited anticipation has surrounded the small band of pilots that make up the Night Fighter Unit. For the past few days they have been practising with forty-four gallon long-range fuel tanks saddled under each wing. So far they seem to have done their job pretty well, but Alex offers a silent prayer that the electric pumps feeding petrol from the overload to the main tanks will work without any hitches. They've all heard stories of pilots ditching into the sea, lost for ever, because of fuel supply failure.

Nor will they fly together. The Night Fighters do things differently at the best of times, and tonight they will head off one by one, at intervals. Alex is to be first off. He breathes deeply, aware of feeling more apprehensive than usual. His air test is essential, because if anything goes wrong with his Hurricane at night, the chances are he will have had it. Their daily practice flight used to be nothing more than a quick circuit around the airfield. Now they need to be a bit longer, twenty-minute flights instead of ten – time to ensure that the tanks are working properly.

He walks towards his Hurricane – a Mark IIC, armed with four cannons, but no match for the 109s. Another advantage of night flying: not so many of those about. The Germans have only recently reappeared, but already their presence has been felt. No half-hearted raids from them – their bombing is more intense, determined and destructive, as he discovered during his first few weeks on the Island the previous May. Then suddenly they were gone, off to the Russian front, he'd found out later, leaving the Italians on their own. The relief at Takali had been palpable.

It had been hot back then. And then it became hotter. July and August had been almost unbearable. Mosquitoes everywhere, too. He'd almost been eaten alive. And the heat did strange things to the air, making flying conditions very different from those back home in Britain. Pockets of heat seemed to bounce off the Island. He'd be coming into land and suddenly his plane would be buffeted and bumped all over the place –

the worse kind of turbulence. It had been quite a shock the first time. Strictly tropical kit back then – sand-coloured shirts and shorts – and only once airborne was he ever cool enough. On the ground the Hurricanes were baked, the metal so hot it could burn. Alex had discovered this a number of times. He still had the faint scars on his arms and legs.

But this winter has been filthy. At the end of December there were terrific storms. A week ago, the rain was so bad all flying from Takali had to cease. This was the problem with makeshift airfields like these – only Luqa had proper runways, and even then only an inch or so of tarmac on top. Takali was nothing but a dried-out lake. Dust and baked mud in summer quickly turned into a quagmire the moment it pelted down with rain, as it has been doing recently.

The past few days have been drier, though, and the place has once again become fit enough to fly from.

Alex Mackie reaches his plane, lined up at the edge of the airfield with the other Hurricanes of the Malta Night Fighter Unit, distinguishable by the letter 'J' painted either side of the fuselage. They have begun building blast pens around the perimeter from sandbags and old four-gallon petrol cans filled with sand – supposedly to protect the precious machines from shrapnel and indirect bomb damage – but there are not enough for their planes yet. Another difference: the Night Fighter Hurricanes are painted all black, with a long, narrow blinker sticking out of the engine cowling to hide the ends of the exhaust stubs; it's hard enough to see anything at night as it is, without exhaust sparks causing unnecessary glare. His fitter and rigger are there already. They have checked over the outside and even started her up once, making sure the magnetos are all working correctly. He puts one foot through the canvas loop of his parachute harness, then the other, and pulls the remaining straps over his shoulders until all four ends click together into the fastener at the front, leaving the parachute bag resting against his backside. This will be his cushion on the hard bucket seat of the Hurricane.

A nod, a few words, as Alex clambers onto the wing root. There is a strip of rough metal there for standing on, but the paint around it is chipped from use, revealing odd flecks of bare metal. Placing his hands either side of the canopy, he then lowers himself into the tight cockpit. That familiar smell of metal, oil and mustiness. More straps: the safety harness, like the parachute, brought over his shoulders and between his legs. The R/T – or radio – and oxygen leads are plugged in. Check the fuel gauge: full. Brake pressure: fine. Alex places his booted feet in the rudder pedals and looks up into the tiny mirror above the canopy. Rudder swinging nicely. Hand on the stick – pull left, then right. On the wings, the ailerons swing upwards then lower. All seems to be fine, so he prepares to start. Flaps at about fifteen degrees, airscrew full, fine pitch. He fastens his leather flying helmet, gives the thumbs up to his fitter and rigger who have brought round the starter trolley that will kick the engine into life. A word in his ear from Control: nothing stirring – he's got the Island to himself. Alex presses the starter button. Slowly, the propeller turns, chugging, once, twice, then with a few licks of orange flame from the exhaust stubs, the airscrew whirs into life with a roar. The whole plane shakes; the vibration runs through the seat and into his body. His fitter has pulled the starter trolley clear and so Alex releases the brakes, opens the throttle slightly and the machine begins to roll. Waving his rigger clear, he is now on his own, with the whole airfield to himself. Turning the plane north-west, towards the wind, he opens the throttle wide and surges off across the scrub surface. The plane jostles and bounces, rattling and jolting him, despite the tightness of his harness. Push the stick forward and the tail lifts so that at last he can see something in front of him other than the large engine cowling pointing skywards. Gathering speed – sixty, seventy, eighty, ninety miles an hour, then pull back the stick and suddenly the terrible rattling and jolting stops as the Hurricane lifts into the air. In seconds Takali is beneath him, despite the extra drag caused by the two fuel tanks under his wings. Mdina is away to his left, and there is the large hospital and clock tower of Imtarfa. A couple of circuits should do it: round behind those two promontories, over the quiet valley behind, and then, with the high village of Dingli on his right, he will swoop back in a wide arc to Takali, then round again, touch down, rest up for an hour or so, then take off for Sicily.

So far, everything is in order, just as he expects it to be: the plane gently curves to port, the mouth of the valley beneath him. Even from this low height he can see the entire Island and the little villages, each one dominated by a church. Then beyond, the Mediterranean, a vast expanse of deep blue. Even in January it looks warm, inviting.

Flashes of light pulsing across his wing catch his eye, then a loud crack and the plane reels as though punched by a giant fist. A lurch in his chest and a glance in the mirror – Messerschmitts, two of them, and his Hurricane has been badly hit. Where the hell did they come from? Alex flings the plane from side to side, but he simply doesn't have enough height or speed. A frantic glance behind: they're still there, still firing at him. Try not to panic, try not to panic. More bullets riddle his plane and now there's smoke, pouring from the engine and rapidly filling the cockpit. Fear – stark fear. So little time to think clearly. Another glance around and the planes have vanished – they know they've got him.

Miraculously, he himself is unhurt, but his Hurricane is in a terrible way. Bullets have torn into his elevators and the engine. The plane is coughing and grinding; its power – so vibrant only moments before – now all but gone. The controls are loose in his hands. He is drifting into the narrowing valley. Curse Malta, with its tiny fields and endless lines of stone walls – nowhere at all to crash-land, not like England. Perhaps if he can just stay high enough to skim over the end of the valley he can keep gliding round on the circuit, and then crash-land at Takali.

But the Hurricane is still losing height, the engine dying. Come on, come on, he urges, just clear the ridge.

What Alex Mackie must have been thinking in those final moments can only be imagined; but for several seconds, he would have known he was not going to clear the valley and that he would crash horrifically. In fact, his Hurricane, Z3571/J, hit a high stone wall built into the side of the hill – a wall protecting a small orchard – at an angle of about fifteen degrees, ripping off the starboard wing and causing the rest of the plane to crash to the ground. A large part of the wall collapsed on impact, Mackie's harness snapped and he was flung clear of the plane, landing at the foot of a tree some twenty metres away.

On the opposite side of the narrow valley lived Francis Borg, a farmer. It was a busy time for him: with the war on, they were now growing two crops a year, and so although it was January, there was wheat ripening in the fields below. He'd been working on the terraces above the valley and had watched the Hurricane desperately trying to evade the Messerschmitts, then seen the stricken plane – engine spluttering and pouring smoke – drift into the wall on the far side with a terrible crack that made his blood run cold. Running as fast as he could, he headed out of the field, across the track and down past some houses towards the smouldering wreckage. By the time he arrived, there were several people there, including the priest of the tiny St Katherine's Church, which stood overlooking the valley. To his amazement, Francis Borg saw the pilot was not only alive but also conscious and without any obvious injury. Someone had brought some whisky, and cradling the pilot's head, was trying to pour a few drops into his mouth. Having no stretcher, the farmer helped lay the boy on a ladder and carry him across the valley and up the track that wound its way to the church and a small cluster of buildings. There, while someone went to call for an ambulance, they covered him with blankets and waited for it to arrive. By this time, Alex Mackie had already slipped into unconsciousness. He was taken to the 90th General Hospital at Imtarfa, just a quarter of a mile away from his mess in Mdina.

Oberleutnant Otto Belser took the credit for shooting down Alex Mackie's plane. He and the five other German fighter pilots were back in Sicily long before the ambulance arrived to take the wounded pilot to the hospital.

That night seven Hurricane Night Fighters set off for Sicily. They patrolled a line between Catania and Comiso, as originally ordered. After about an hour they were heading for home when they saw the airfield at Comiso lit up. An aircraft was taking off with lights on, and Sergeant Wood closed in and shot it down, watching it crash in flames. 'Mac's revenge,' Wood noted in his logbook on his return.

Never regaining consciousness, Alex Mackie died of his wounds four days later.

PART I

Under Siege from the Italians

'It may be that hard times lie ahead...'

ACTING GOVERNOR-GENERAL SIR WILLIAM DOBBIE

CHAPTER I

The First Day of the Siege
11 JUNE 1940

JUST BEFORE SEVEN o'clock in the morning on Tuesday 11 June 1940, Meme Cortis was standing by her washstand, splashing her face with cold water, when she was startled by a loud and mournful drone from outside. Recognizing the air raid siren at once, she immediately dashed to the window. She barely noticed it was a beautifully clear summer's morning outside. Instead of looking across the familiar sweep of the Island, she lifted her face to the sky, craning to see any Italian planes. Mussolini had declared war the previous evening, but neither Meme nor the other nurses had any idea what to expect and could not quite believe Malta would ever be directly involved.

The VAD Mess of the 90th General Hospital, Imtarfa, was perched high on a promontory, and Meme believed it offered one of the very best views on the entire Island. Facing out west from her window she could see Malta stretch away beneath her. To her right was the ancient walled city of Mdina with its imposing cathedral; away to her left, like a giant beehive, Mosta's dome, one of the largest of its kind in the world. On a dried-up lake directly below her lay the little-used airfield of Takali, while the surrounding countryside spread out on all sides, a patchwork of fields outlined by silvery stone walls. And she could see, dotted across the Island, the distinct twin towers and domes of a number of churches, standing proud and high, the markers of Malta's towns and villages: Zebbug, Qormi, Birkirkara, Attard – where the Governor had his official residence – Hamrun and Tarxien. In the far distance she could even see Grand Harbour and Tigné Point in Sliema, close to where she'd been brought up; beyond that, some ten miles away, nothing but the dark blue Mediterranean.

Admittedly, the VAD Mess lay a small way from the main hospital, but Meme wasn't complaining. After all, when she'd first become a VAD – or Voluntary Aid Detachment – nurse the previous November, she'd never imagined for a minute she would be billeted in such a grand building.

The Cortis family was a large one; Meme was the eighth of nine. One brother had died after three months, and her older sister Victoria at fourteen. Then, when Meme was just seven, her mother died too. Her father did the best he could, but it was up to her oldest sister Antonia to look after Meme and the other children, while their father worked hard at his newsagent shop to provide for the family. Despite these losses, Meme was a happy child. Antonia made sure they never left the house in the morning hungry, and every evening, once their father had come home from work, they sat down all together at the table. 'She took mother's place at home,' says Meme. 'She was good to us.' By the age of eighteen, however, it was time for Meme to leave home. With dark, wavy hair, deep brown eyes and a mischievous, open face, she had grown into a young woman eager for some independence and adventure. Becoming a VAD and living her life at Imtarfa had provided her with just that, and in the nine months since joining, she'd not regretted the decision even once.

But now, with the wail of the siren ringing in her ears, she thought, 'This is it, then. This is war for real.' The Second World War had finally reached Malta. Moments later, she heard explosions over the south of the Island – a strange, chilling boom, that resounded eerily in the still morning air. Italy had always been their neighbour – Sicily was just sixty miles away – and the Italians their friends. But hard as it was to comprehend, they were now bombing her home.

Down at the Marsa Race Track, just south-west of the bottom tip of Grand Habour, 'C' Company of the 2nd Battalion Queen's Own Royal West Kent Regiment were getting ready to continue work on the defence posts they were building when the sirens rang out. Along with the three airfields on the Island, the United Services Sports Club at Marsa, with its racecourse, polo and cricket pitches, was seen as an obvious place for the enemy to attempt an air invasion.

As the sirens droned, nineteen-year-old Frank Rixon and the rest of

'C' Company left their work and hastily took cover in the number of slit trenches already dug around the sports ground. They had never been bombed before and had no idea how close the attackers might come. Moments later, they heard the first explosions directly to the south of them. Frank watched clouds of smoke and dust rise over Hal Far airfield, where the tiny Malta Fighter Flight was based. Shortly after, another wave of bombers appeared; at some 14,000 feet, the Italian planes looked innocuously small against the deep blue sky. Their target was not the airfields but Grand Harbour; in fact, it was the harbour's few anti-aircraft guns booming and the sight of black puffs of smoke as the shells exploded that alerted Frank to this new raid. Moments later he heard further explosions. He was not to know it, but at that moment, the first casualties of the siege were being blown to pieces. Buildings around the dockyard were hit, and a Maltese mother and her two sons, aged four and five, were killed. Another bomb landed directly on Upper Fort St Elmo, on the outermost tip of Valletta, where men of the Royal Malta Artillery were keeping watch for any attempted enemy landing. Six were killed there outright, including Philip Busuttil, the duty-telephonist, who was just sixteen.

Frank Rixon had arrived on Malta to join the 2nd Battalion two months before. Although only nineteen, he had far more experience of army life than most of his comrades, having joined as a boy soldier at fifteen and with a two-year stint with the regiment in India already behind him. Quite a few of the boys at the St Augustine's Waifs and Strays Home had joined one or other of the forces, and Frank had felt that was the best course of action for him too. Really, there had been little alternative – he had no home to go to, no skills and no family business where he could learn a trade. The Army, on the other hand, promised adventure, the chance to see the world and the kind of regimentation he'd become used to at the home. He'd written to his older sister, Irene, for her blessing, then joined the Royal West Kents, the local regiment for St Augustine's. It was a decision he'd never had cause to regret. And although he still wrote regularly to his sister, the Regiment was his family now.

As Italy had declared war the previous day, 'Stand To' that Tuesday morning had been fifteen minutes earlier than normal, at 4.15 a.m. Frank was able to get himself up fairly quickly. Although now some five feet ten inches high, he still barely needed to shave. A quick sluice of water over his face and comb of his short, light-brown hair and he was ready. He was in good physical shape too. The Army liked to keep its men fit, but Frank would also go running and box whenever he could. He enjoyed exercise and the competition sport provided.

Even so, getting up at that time made for a long day, and digging holes in the ground – especially when the soil was thin and most of the work involved hacking through limestone rock – was not everyone's idea of soldiering, but up until then, Frank had thought there were many worse places he could be. After all, most days it was warm and sunny, and they were surrounded by the twinkling blue sea.

Flight Lieutenant George Burges and the other fighter pilots had been at readiness to try to intercept any enemy bombers that might attack from 6.30 a.m. Or at least, they were at readiness in *theory*; Burges was, in fact, sitting on the lavatory as the first enemy plots were picked up. With the alarm bell ringing, he was frantically pulling up his trousers and rushing out to his aircraft, a former Royal Navy biplane. Soon after, he was speeding down the runway along with two of his colleagues, although it was not soon enough: they were still desperately climbing to meet the enemy bombers when they saw bombs bursting over Grand Harbour.

George Burges had originally arrived on the Island as a flying boat pilot at the sea plane base of Kalafrana in the south-east of the Island. With dark, Mediterranean good looks, he could have passed for a Maltese, despite having been born and brought up in Sheffield in the north of England. A product of the RAF Training College at Cranwell, he was a career officer and had considerable experience in the Middle East, having spent time at Mediterranean Headquarters in Cairo. On the arrival of Air Commodore F.H.M. Maynard in January, he'd become the new AOC's – Air Officer Commanding – personal assistant. Six weeks ago, however, at the end of April, Burges had volunteered to join the fledgling Malta Fighter Flight. Although none of the pilots had any experience of flying fighters, throughout May they had practised elementary tactics, and hoped they were now ready to put up some kind of a challenge.

By now, Burges could see their airfield, Hal Far, under a cloud of smoke from the first bombs to fall, although they had not, in fact, struck any important targets. Then he saw the second wave of bombers begin slowly arcing back towards Sicily, and, finally catching up with one, began firing his machine guns. But having never shot at another plane before, he misjudged the distance and was too far away for his bullets to have any effect. As soon as the Italians spotted them, they opened their throttles and sped away. 'The Gladiator just couldn't catch up,' said Burges.[1]

At seven that morning, Christina Ratcliffe was woken by her house-mates, Babs and Cecil Roche, banging on her door. Slowly, she lifted herself out of bed and, still half-asleep, felt for her slippers and dressing-gown. She wondered what the fuss was all about – she'd heard no siren. All seemed perfectly quiet. Perhaps there was some kind of practice going on. Sleepily she sat at her dressing-table and began to undo the curlers from her blonde hair – air raid or not, it would be embarrassing to be seen with a head full of curling pins.

The previous evening had been quiet at the Morning Star Club, and Christina, a dancer there, had been looking forward to finally heading back to England once her contract expired in a week's time. She had worked in shows and cabarets all round Europe and, with her large brown eyes, blonde hair and long, slender legs, was considered quite a beauty. Her wit and intelligence had also made her friends wherever she went, but especially in Malta where she'd been for a while. However, work had been slow in recent months and with everything that was happening in France, and the tragedy of Dunkirk, going home seemed the right thing to do. She was quietly talking to a Maltese friend when suddenly a radio in one of the bars across the street was turned up to full volume. A torrent of Italian rang out down the street. Christina's Italian was hardly fluent and she struggled to keep pace with the rapid ranting crackling across the airwaves, but even she could recognize Mussolini when she heard him, and was certainly able to understand the gist of his words. Even if she hadn't, the ghost-white face of her friend said it all.

'Have I understood properly?' she asked him. 'Is it really war for Malta?'[2]

It was. From midnight, Mussolini had said – that meant in just a couple of hours' time. Her friend left and Christina suddenly felt very lonely. Outside, a commotion started up – an irate crowd had gathered in front of an Italian barber's shop, and Christina feared for the Italian's safety. Then the police arrived, the man was taken into custody, and the mob dispersed. She couldn't help thinking about Spain, where she'd been caught up in the Civil War. She remembered how loving neigh-bours had turned to deadly enemies. It had seemed so senseless, as it did now.

Her boss told them they could all go home. After all, the place was now dead, so they might as well shut up shop. But should she turn up again tomorrow? she asked him. Her boss shrugged sadly.

Now, the following morning, she was still at her dressing-table when a thunderous crash brought her to her senses. The whole building shook as though it were about to collapse. Then another crash and overhead she heard the roar of aircraft, followed by a deafening explosion and the sound of gunfire. Curlers or no curlers, Christina ran down the stairs as quickly as she could, more explosions crashing around her. For some reason, the cellar seemed to be further down than normal, and she feared she would never reach it alive.[3]

Twenty minutes later the All Clear sounded and Christina rushed back up to her room and out on to the balcony to see the scale of destruction. The air was filled with dust and the smell of cordite, and broken glass covered the road, but much to her amazement, all the buildings around her still seemed to be standing. Her neighbours gradually came out on to the road. A hunchbacked old woman stood waving her fist at the sky and shouting abuse at Mussolini.

A mile north of Floriana, John Agius had been getting ready to leave for work when the air raid sirens began. His family lived at No. 39 Victoria Terrace, Sliema, not far from where Meme Cortis had been brought up. Always an early riser, John liked to leave the house promptly at 7 a.m. every morning to be at the RAF Headquarters in Scots Street, Valletta, for 7.30. A civilian clerk, he'd worked there since leaving school as a sixteen-year-old nearly four years before. Of slight build and with dark hair and glasses, he had something of a bookish appearance, in keeping with his punctilious and reliable nature. This had served him well at RAF HQ, where the staff had come to value him greatly.

It was no surprise to him that the bombers were now coming over. Before the war, Emanuel, one of his older brothers, had regularly travelled to and from England by train via Italy and had told him about the Italian propaganda – and how it was so overwhelming one could understand how most Italians had been taken in by it. Since the Italian invasion of Abyssinia in 1935, Mussolini had regularly claimed Malta should also become a part of Italy's overseas expansion. 'I listened to my brothers and I read the paper,' says John. 'We could see what was happening.' Furthermore, since the Abyssinian Crisis there had been periodic rehearsals of black-outs and mock air raids, and demonstrations of anti-gas precautions. As a Scout leader, John had latterly been involved in some of these preparations. Just two days before, on Sunday the 9th, he'd taken his Scout Troop to the town square in Gzira to give a demonstration of how to deal with any possible casualties in the event of war. They showed people how to create makeshift stretchers, and offered lessons in basic first aid. Now, with the first bombs falling, John was wondering whether he would soon be called upon to put his training into practice.

The RAF already had schemes in place for evacuating families of serving personnel and other civilians from the built-up areas around the harbour in the event of air raids, and John had volunteered to help with taking local British families to a designated house in Naxxar, a village north of Mosta in the middle of the Island. So, instead of heading for the ferry to take him across the harbour to work, he set off to round up the families under his care. To his surprise not one of them was there; they had already gone to Naxxar under their own steam.

After the first raids, people all around the harbour areas began rushing to the safety of the interior, including ten-year-old Michael Montebello and his family. Their home was in Senglea, one of the 'Three Cities', along with Cospicua and Vittoriosa, which surrounded the creeks along the southern side of Grand Harbour. News of Mussolini's declaration of war had quickly spread round their neighbourhood the previous evening. Many people had the Rediffusion system in their homes – a form of island radio service – but for those, like the Montebellos, who did not, there were also loudspeakers set up in many of the village and town squares. Michael's parents, along with many of their neighbours, had gathered in front of St Philip's Church to hear the news and to talk about Mussolini and what he might do. Little had they realized events would move so fast.

Elsewhere on the Island that evening, 10 June, regular programmes had been interrupted with 'special announcements', bearing the news and ordering all service personnel to report immediately for duty. In the cinemas, similar bulletins had been announced, while military police had cleared all the bars, restaurants and nightclubs in Valletta of those members of the Forces who had not heard the news.

Michael's father had already seen action. Like many Maltese men, he served with the Royal Navy, and at the outbreak of war the previous September his ship, HMS *Malaya*, had been sent to the Atlantic to escort convoys from Nova Scotia to England. Then tragedy befell the family: Michael's two-year-old sister became seriously ill and the Admiralty sent his father back home, only for him to arrive two days after his daughter died. He'd yet to rejoin his ship and so was there to help his wife and two sons hurry from Senglea and out into the countryside now that the bombs had already begun to fall.

There had been no specific plans for evacuation put in place by the Maltese Government, although as the German tanks had rolled into Belgium on 10 May, the Governor had advised people with friends in the countryside to move there straight away. Most had ignored the warning. Rather like the mass evacuations that occurred in England preceding the outbreak of war, the areas surrounding the harbours now descended into chaos with thousands of Maltese civilians trying to flee to the country. Unlike in England, however, where the majority of evacuations had occurred *before* war broke out, it was the sudden shock of seeing houses demolished and people actually killed that caused this panic. The Government had been trying to prepare people for war – along with the various blackouts and air raid practices, they had also set up ARP (Air Raid Precaution) centres and three weeks earlier had even imposed a night-time curfew between 11 p.m. and 5 a.m. The news-papers that morning carried more advice about carrying gas masks, and what to do in the event of an air raid. But the majority of Maltese were not as well briefed or pragmatic as the Agius family and had barely had time to get used to the idea that Italy had declared war. With the first Italian bombers arriving before most Maltese had left for work, many were shocked beyond belief to find themselves under attack so soon – and understandably so. Although the Island's history was littered with conflict, the Maltese were peace-loving people and had not come under fire in living memory. And while the aggressors of old had arrived by sea, their new enemy was now dropping his weapons of destruction from the sky. Even worse, they were Italians, neighbours a mere sixty miles away – the same distance as that between London and Oxford.

By the afternoon, trails of refugees began to litter the roads leading out of Sliema, Valletta, and the Three Cities. Men and women carrying cases and bundles trudged, heads hanging, along the dusty roads. Most only had a vague sense of where they were headed – perhaps to a second cousin in Zabbar, or an aunt's house in Birkirkara, relatives whom in many cases they barely knew. Even more hoped simply to rely on the pity of strangers. On that first day, and in the few days following, nearly

100,000 left the harbour areas from an entire island population of a quarter of a million. Four of those were Michael Montebello and his family.

Suzanne Parlby was unaware of the mayhem unfolding around Grand Harbour and unimpressed by the Italian bombing. A newly married woman of nineteen, she was billeted with other wives of her husband John's regiment at St Andrew's Barracks. She'd neither seen any bombers nor heard any bombs exploding, although the terrible and sudden din of the nearby anti-aircraft gun had made her jump out of her skin.

Suzanne's father had been a pioneering submariner who rose to the rank of Admiral when he was posted to Malta in 1937. A fierce man, he enjoyed humiliating his youngest daughter with repeated assurances that she was both stupid and useless. He had wanted a boy, a son to continue the family name and follow in his footsteps with an illustrious career in the Navy; and when Suzanne was born, eight years after the second of two older daughters, he never forgave her for being a girl.

The bullying did not stop even after Suzanne had left school and joined her father on Malta. She had to suffer his moods and outbursts of anger as well as regular humiliations. Never were these more keenly felt than on the tennis court, a sport her father loved, but Suzanne came to loathe. He would always insist she partnered him in doubles, then criticized her throughout the game. 'It was a nightmare,' she says, 'and not only for me: the other guests would be miserable with embarrassment and I would pray for the moment when I would be sent home in disgrace and floods of tears.' She knew she had to get away, and prayed someone would ask her to marry them. This, it seemed to her, was her only means of escape.

But despite such bruised confidence, she had much to offer. She might not have received the greatest of educations, but she was bright, possessed of a quick wit, and attractive too: tall, slim, and blessed with high cheekbones and an enchanting smile.

Her saviour came in the form of John Parlby, a young infantry officer in the Devonshire Regiment. When he asked her to marry him, Suzanne agreed without pausing for thought. Perhaps he was a bit immature, and maybe she didn't really know him all that well, but he was kind, a very good dancer, and, most important, offered escape from her father's tyranny. As soon as her father had agreed to the engagement, Suzanne came into the room where he and John were sitting and smashed her tennis racket over his chair, shouting, 'Never again! I will never play tennis again in my life!' Nor did she, for over twenty years.

She and John had been married just two months before on 12 April, in St Paul's Anglican cathedral in Valletta. Her father was not there, having already left for England, but had written urging them to agree a date so that there would still be time for her mother to safely travel back across Europe to England while the Phoney War still held. The product of a very Victorian upbringing, Suzanne went into marriage ignorant and lacking in confidence. Their three-day honeymoon on the neighbouring island of Gozo was not a success, and so it was almost a relief when a few weeks later, with the Italian situation looking ever more threatening, Suzanne was ordered into barracks with the other regimental families and John was sent to rejoin the coastal billet where his company of the Devons were now based.

St Andrew's was a sprawling barracks full of colonial limestone buildings neatly laid out along a stretch of the north coast. There were the various messes, depots, ammunition stores, parade grounds, regimental HQs and a large number of houses purpose-built for accommodating the British Army abroad and all that went with it. Suzanne found herself billeted with the regimental quartermaster's wife, Midge Labbett, and their two sons, Peter and Michael. Also staying there was Elisabeth Young, another army wife of similar age, and the two became great friends. Now, on that first day of the siege, all of them seemed to be spending the day dashing in and out of the nearby slit trench, as the All Clear signal was called only for another raid to appear soon after.

In the afternoon, the Italians attacked the other airfields of Luqa and Takali. Luqa was only a mile south of Marsa, where Frank Rixon was based with 'C' Company of the Royal West Kents. Frank had felt scared earlier in the day, but was now even more so as the bombs landed not only on Luqa but on Marsa too. He was amazed by the enormous amount of dust and debris caused by the explosions, but was relieved that, as he'd been trained to do, he'd remained cool and calm in the face of this danger, despite his fears.

The heaviest raid of the day was the last, in the evening, and, although the bombs were meant for the dockyard once more, most fell on Cospicua, killing 22 people. John Agius was on his way home when this final raid came over. Ignorant of the bombs falling two miles to the south of him, he stood in the middle of the street, open-mouthed, watching the anti-aircraft barrage going up over Grand Harbour. 'It was terrific. There were guns blazing all over,' he says. Over two hundred houses around Grand Harbour already lay in ruins.

That evening, along with hundreds of others with the same idea, Christina Ratcliffe trooped down to the old disused railway tunnel beneath Valletta. Old and young alike struggled there with bags, pillows and cushions, desperately craving safety from the bombs. Some even brought rolled-up mattresses on wheelbarrows and prams. Walking through the dimly lit cavern, Christina eventually spread out her blanket in a space near one of the entrances. Nearby were a family of four – husband, wife and two girls – huddled together on a mattress. Beyond them, a young mother sat leaning against the wall, feeding her tiny baby. On her other side an old man was fussing and muttering, preparing himself for the night by folding his shirt and trousers. In just his underpants and vest, he sank on to his knees and prayed, before lying down and pulling a rug over his shoulders.

Britain's Dilemma

THE BUILD-UP TO 11 JUNE

ADMIRAL SIR ANDREW Browne Cunningham had spent much of his professional life in the Mediterranean and knew it inside out: its coastline and ports, its strange and dangerous currents, and the khamsin and sirocco – capricious winds that swept across the sea from the North African desert. He knew how to fight on these waters too, and since May 1939 he had been, like Nelson more than a hundred years earlier, Commander-in-Chief of the Mediterranean Fleet. The post had been one of the most crucial and prestigious in the Royal Navy, ever since the trouncing of the French fleet at the Battle of the Nile. In Cunningham – or ABC as he was known to all – Britain had a leader of Nelson's cut.

Unlike his predecessor, Admiral Sir Dudley Pound – who was now First Sea Lord – Cunningham had little time for bureaucracy and paper work; he was a man of action, who liked to take on the enemy at sea whenever he could. Before the Battle of Trafalgar, Nelson told his captains that if smoke clouded his signals, they could do little wrong by placing their ships alongside the enemy; this was Cunningham's approach. His written orders tended to come in the form of single sentences, and he believed aggression and skilful manœuvring could often overcome superior numbers. Unlike most of his colleagues with Flag Rank, ABC's background lay firmly with the small, agile destroyer class of ship, rather than the much larger and heavily armoured battleships and heavy cruisers. He'd been captain of a destroyer in the Mediterranean during the First World War, then had commanded a destroyer flotilla during the 1920s, rising to become Rear-Admiral Destroyers in the Mediterranean in 1933. By the time war broke out, he had acquired a unique knowledge of the capabilities of these ships in narrow seas and the tactics required. And although he'd commanded large, heavily armed battleships too, he firmly believed that proper seamanship could only be acquired on the smaller, more manœuvrable destroyers where instantaneous decisions and ruthless determination were part and parcel of good leadership. 'The best officers to be found in big ships have come from submarines or destroyers,' he said. 'I have always maintained there is more real discipline in destroyers than big ships, and of course we are always in so much more touch with our men.'[1] ABC looked like a man who relished being on the open seas. At 56, he had a compact five-feet-ten-inch frame, and a face weather-beaten from years of standing in the sun and sea-spray. His thin mouth and slightly jutting chin perfectly complemented his determined and dogmatic nature. But it was his penetrating blue eyes, familiar to all who served him, that revealed not only his unwavering authority, but also his warm sense of humour, which, when combined with his reputation as a naval commander, ensured a devotion unequalled in the Navy.

Back in 1800, Nelson had been fully aware of the important role Malta would play in maintaining domination of the Mediterranean, and had declared, 'I hope we shall never give it up'[2]; it was a sentiment Cunningham echoed some 140 years later. To his mind, British domination of the Mediterranean was crucial. At its western mouth, there was the British port of Gibraltar, the gateway to the Atlantic; while at the eastern end was the Suez Canal, the narrow passage that led to India and the Far East, and the port of Alexandria. Malta, a tiny island just seventeen miles by nine and slightly smaller than the Isle of Wight, lay almost exactly in the middle, and between Italy and North Africa. Tactically, this gave Britain a unique footing from which to attack enemy shipping in the Central Mediterranean, and in turn protect interests in the Middle East and Egypt. But it wasn't just its geographical situation that made it so crucial. Malta was also blessed with a fine natural harbour. Valletta, the Island's capital, stretched out like a long finger in the middle of this port, in places three hundred feet high above the surrounding waters. On its southern side was Grand Harbour, eighty feet deep and nearly two miles long with four inlets with dockyards around the middle two – French Creek and Dockyard Creek. Crucially, by the late 1930s, Grand Harbour had facilities and the trained expertise to equip and repair any ship in the British fleets. On the other side of the Valletta finger, to the north, lay Marsamxett Harbour, seventy feet deep and divided from Sliema Creek by Manoel Island. Both harbours could house the biggest ships in the world and shield them from the fiercest storms. Overlooking them were the mighty bastions of Valletta and the Three Cities, enormous fortified walls built of creamy limestone blocks by the Knights of St John in the sixteenth century, from where defensive gun batteries could rain down their fire on any would-be attackers. Their potential as gun emplacements had not diminished during the ensuing centuries.

The French had taken over the Island in 1798, but following their defeat at the Battle of the Nile, their position in the Mediterranean was considerably weakened and, after an occupation of plunder and misrule, the Maltese took the opportunity to revolt. Besieged within the city walls of Valletta by the Maltese, and by the British out at sea, the French soon capitulated. Although the Island was still not formally under British jurisdiction, the Union Jack was run up over Valletta on 5 September 1800. In a Declaration of Rights, however, the Maltese people demanded to come 'under the protection and sovereignty of the King of the free people, His Majesty the King of the United Kingdom of Great Britain and Ireland.' They also demanded that 'His Majesty has no right to cede these Islands to any power … if he chooses to with-draw his protection, and abandon his sovereignty, the right of electing another sovereign, or of the governing of these islands, belongs to us, the inhabitants and aborigines alone, and without control.'[3] Under these unique circumstances, the close relationship between the British and Maltese began. It was, of course, a mutually beneficial arrangement: the Maltese now had a protector – one that just happened to have the most powerful navy in the world – and the British an island of immense strategic importance. The first British governor arrived in 1813 and the following year, under the Treaty of Paris, Malta was formally annexed to the British Crown.

The coming together of a northern European Protestant superpower and a devoutly Catholic Mediterranean population of around a quarter of a million might not have been an obviously harmonious union; but, despite a pro-Italian minority, the relationship worked well, and many Maltese served Britain loyally, particularly as dockworkers, and as merchant and naval sailors. VAD nurse Meme Cortis was also happy to do her bit for Britain's war effort. She was fiercely proud of being both Maltese and British. At school she was taught about Britain and her Empire, but she also learnt about Malta's incredibly rich prehistory and about the Knights of St John taking over the Island after leaving Rhodes; and how La Valette – the Grand Master – and the other knights managed to defeat the all-conquering Suleiman the Magnificent in the Great Siege of 1565. At home her family all spoke Maltese, but at school she was taught in English. As a young girl she liked speaking it and would stop people in the street and say, 'Hello, how are you?' and 'Good morning,' for the practice. She grew up with many British traditions: toast and marmalade for breakfast, tea, the National Anthem.

And yet despite this Anglicization, Meme was, like most Maltese, raised a devout Catholic. The church – her local church, the Sacred Heart of Our Lady in Sliema – was the focus of her social life, as it was for all the other Maltese of the surrounding neighbourhood. Nowhere in the world had a greater density of churches. From the magnificence of St John's Co-Cathedral in Valletta, to the smaller but no less imposing churches that dominated every town and village, they were at the heart of Maltese culture. Every parish had a brass band club and regardless of whether you played an instrument or not, the club and the church services brought everyone together. 'The club was really good,' says Meme, 'for everybody – families, old folk, and young. You would meet up, have a drink, play snooker or bowls. It was a club for the parish.' Everyone knew everyone. Meme went to Mass every Sunday, and sometimes every day. The focal point of the year was the parish *festa*, a church carnival that lasted several days: the streets were decorated with banners and bunting, statues of saints were put on display and processions with dressing up and music were followed by fireworks. Organized by the local church and clubs, it was for the people of the parish and everyone was, one way or another, involved.

In other words, Catholicism gave the Maltese a local focus; everyday life revolved around the parish church and the particular traditions and customs the Maltese attached to that. But it was to Britain that the vast majority of Maltese turned for national identity; after all, she was a global and military power of whom they could be proud to be a part. Consequently, when war broke out in 1939, although Meme never thought that Malta would be directly involved, she fully expected many of the Islanders to answer the call to arms.

Admiral Cunningham knew Malta well; he had spent a lot of time with the Mediterranean Fleet, which had been based there, so this was not surprising. And as Rear-Admiral Destroyers he'd lived with his wife

Nona in the Casa Pieta, in Guardamangia, on the hillside overlooking Marsamxett Harbour.

Those had been good times – and sociable times too. The house was big enough to hold dances, which he and his wife were glad to lay on quite regularly. Almost every night there were cocktail parties, receptions or dinners, either on the Island or on one of the ships lying at anchor. Valletta itself was a beautiful city, unlike any other in the Mediterranean. Although further south than much of the North African coastline, the Island and its capital betrayed little of its Arabic influences, largely because of the many great architects encouraged by the Knights of St John – not least Gerolamo Cassar, who was to Valletta what Christopher Wren was to London, building a large number of Italianate palaces and churches, all in the pale, bleached limestone carved from the Island's quarries. Valletta's magnificent Opera House attracted some of the finest voices and musicians in the world; the Manoel Theatre was home to amateur and professional productions, staging everything from Shakespeare to Noël Coward. At Marsa, a little way inland from Valletta, there was horse-racing, polo, tennis, golf and cricket. Around the Island lay the tiny beaches of Ghar Lapsi and Ghajn Tuffieha, and sheltered inlets such as the Blue Grotto on the south coast where one could swim and picnic. Malta was also rich in strange prehistoric megaliths and temples, popular and romantic places to visit; and criss-crossing the entire Island were endless tiny fields, divided by ancient dry-stone walls, and filled with crops and vines and an abundance of wild flowers.

For those who simply wanted to let their hair down, there were any number of restaurants, bars and nightclubs. Food and drink were cheap and plentiful. As cabaret dancer Christina Ratcliffe noted, Malta before the war was a 'boozer's paradise'. Spirits were sixpence a tot and beer fourpence a bottle.[4] Most servicemen made for Strait Street, as its name suggests, a long, narrow street in Valletta known to everyone as 'The Gut'. During the day it was dead, drab and dusty, working off the hangover of the previous evening, but by night it sprang into life, ablaze with colour and noise and teeming with soldiers and sailors surfeiting on cheap booze, girls and jazz. As the night progressed, so the din became louder – drunken servicemen singing raucously, shouting and brawling.

Whether permanently stationed on the Island or just passing through, servicemen found Malta had much to offer. And in turn, the British, with their Army and Navy, offered security and trade to the native Maltese.

So it was that ABC not only recognized the tactical and strategic advantages of Britain keeping Malta, but also understood the strange symbiotic relationship between the two. That Britain should abandon the Island was unthinkable, not just to him, but to the majority of Maltese as well. Even so, not everyone shared this opinion. During the war years, Cunningham would be repeatedly tested to the limit of his reserves, but well before the first bombs were ever dropped over the Island on 11 June, he found himself forced to fight an uphill battle much closer to home, one that could have lost Malta the war before it even started.

Despite his disdain for paper-pushing, Cunningham was appointed Deputy Chief of the Naval Staff of the Admiralty (DCNS) in October 1938, which meant being based at Chatham and working directly for the then new First Sea Lord, Admiral Sir Roger Backhouse. Perhaps in those times of frantic rearmament, Backhouse recognized that a no-nonsense battler like Cunningham would be a useful man to help him fight his corner; at any rate, ABC soon found himself up to his neck in trying to prepare the Royal Navy for war. It was an unenviable task and involved much lobbying to the Committee for Imperial Defence (CID). The task of bringing Britain's defences to a level where they could take on Germany was enormous – too enormous for the time and money available, and so prioritization was the byword. One of the big debates was over anti-aircraft defence posts. There was a severe shortage of anti-aircraft guns (and many were eventually bought from abroad, like the Bofors made in Sweden), and severe differences of opinion between the three services as to who should get the lion's share. Predictably, the Navy wanted fleet bases to be given the highest priority, and Malta became a major bone of contention. In 1935, the Island was served by just twelve anti-aircraft guns, increased to 24 – with search-lights – during the Abyssinian Crisis. However, these were of the old, increasingly obsolete three-inch variety and of limited value. Backhouse and Cunningham argued strongly that Malta should have brand-new, up-to-date anti-aircraft guns and plenty of them. But the RAF was working on the assumption that bombers would dominate any forth-coming war. The aerial pulverisation of Guernica, for example, during the Spanish Civil War, had only strengthened this opinion. From Sicily, it was argued, Malta would be indefensible against sustained bombing and therefore updating her anti-aircraft defences was a waste of resources.

The Army, to whom a tiny island in the middle of the Mediterranean was not a priority, sided with the RAF. And in this battle of priorities, the threat to, and from, various potential theatres had to be weighed up.

The situation with Italy was precarious, but not as great a threat as that developing from Germany. Since the Abyssinian Crisis of 1935, relations between Britain and Italy had been strained. These had been worsened by Italy's involvement in the Spanish Civil War and then, in April 1939, her invasion of Albania, with its implications regarding Italian intentions towards Greece. If Greece were in Italian hands and Britain at war with Italy, enemy forces would be dangerously close to British interests in the Middle East. However, Italy still had a severe lack of raw materials, and, despite a highly developed and modernized navy, lacked the kind of military hardware needed for long-term expansion of her territories. Britain could exacerbate this by blockading commodities destined for Italy that passed through British-occupied waters.

The playing field changed, however, when Mussolini and Hitler signed the 'Pact of Steel' in May 1939 that brought about the Berlin-Rome 'Axis'. As Lord Halifax, the Foreign Secretary, pointed out in the summer of 1939, war with Italy was a distinct possibility; in which case the effect of the British deserting Malta would, to his mind, be politically disastrous.

Such were the two sides of the coin, and consequently, the question of whether or not to improve Malta's defences was continually debated, although it was not until July 1939 – after Cunningham had left the Admiralty to return to the Mediterranean as Commander-in-Chief – that increased guns and fighter protection for Malta were finally approved. The Committee for Imperial Defence promised the Island 112 heavy and 60 light anti-aircraft guns, 24 searchlights, four squadrons of fighter aircraft and a number of barrage balloons, aerial mines and smoke producers – although even after agreeing this, there were still differences of opinion as to whether this would be sufficient to save the Island and the Fleet.

But promising them was one thing and delivery quite another. The debate turned out to have been an academic one: when Britain and France declared war on Germany in September 1939, Italy announced her neutrality and a policy of non-belligerency. For all Mussolini's ranting and raving, even he realized that coming into the war on the side of Germany in September 1939 would have been suicidal, especially with the combined naval might of France and Britain patrolling the Mediterranean. So, with France as an active ally and with the rest of the

Mediterranean coast neutral, it's easy to understand why Malta dropped off the map in terms of precedence for reinforcements. In a frustrating chicken-and-egg scenario, the Fleet was moved from Malta to Alexandria in April 1939, purely *because* of the lack of adequate defences on the Island, leaving only a few motor torpedo boats and submarines. Although ABC had based his headquarters on the Island since November 1939, he, too, moved to Egypt on 30 April 1940, so that when Italy did finally declare her hand in June, Malta had neither a navy based at Grand Harbour to defend, nor anything like the defences promised. And, although during the spring of 1940 the Maltese steve-dores had been busy unloading supplies, it was not just a case of too little too late, but those that arrived were not always of the most pressing variety: 145 bicycles were delivered in May, as were 400 tons of sandbags and a detachment of the Middle East Pigeon Section, made up of fifteen soldiers, 200 pigeons and eight rabbits – possibly not an integral part of Malta's war machine, or *quite* as important as the 78 heavy and 38 light anti-aircraft guns still needed to make up the quota promised the previous summer. In other words, Malta had just 34 heavy anti-aircraft guns to protect an entire island with its three airfields, a massive harbour complex and over 200 miles of coastline. To put this into some kind of perspective, Coventry, an industrial city in the British Midlands, had 44 heavy anti-aircraft guns at this time, and Tyneside in the north of England, 56.

Of the four squadrons of fighters there was no sign whatsoever. Air Commodore F.H.M. Maynard had been posted to Malta as Air Officer Commanding (AOC) in January 1940, although there was almost nothing for him to command: just a few Fairey Swordfish, old biplanes that were used by the Anti-Aircraft Co-operation Unit for target-towing duties, and a solitary radio-controlled De Havilland Queen Bee, used for very little. As far as he was aware, there were absolutely no other aircraft on the Island. Although there were three airfields, none of them was a fully functioning RAF station. Hal Far in the south, although equipped with hangars and other buildings, had no runway as such, and was principally used by the Royal Navy's Fleet Air Arm. A couple of miles north was Luqa, which had a couple of runways, but which was still being built and developed. Then there was Takali, further to the west, another rough field like Hal Far, laid out on a dried lake, but with no facilities whatsoever. It had been used as a civil airfield before the war. Finally, there was the seaplane base at Kalafrana, situated on the

edge of Marsaxlokk Bay in the south-east. The Island did possess RDF
– Radio Direction Finding, or radar – high on Dingli Cliffs in the south
of the Island; these systems were, admittedly, the only ones used by the
British outside Britain at this time, but with no planes they were of
limited use.

Maynard must have felt he'd been given the worst posting in the
RAF. And if things had looked bleak in January, they surely seemed even
worse by the middle of May: Britain had been humiliated in Norway,
and was being so again in Belgium and France, where the German
blitzkrieg was cutting a swathe through northern Europe with appalling
ease. It quickly became apparent that with the collapse of Holland,
Belgium – and, as looked increasingly likely, France – Britain herself
would be next for attack. Her immediate defence had to take priority.
The fighter squadrons, for the time being, would not be coming to
Malta, even though it was plain to all that with Hitler's lightning gains,
Mussolini was merely waiting for the right moment to strike.

It was Maynard's chief administrative officer who tipped him off
about the Sea Gladiators lying in crates at the RAF seaplane station of
Kalafrana. Twenty-four of these Royal Navy biplanes had arrived there
the previous March. For a variety of reasons, 18 of them were still there
the following spring, and it was agreed that they would be assembled
and eight of them flown to the aircraft carrier HMS *Glorious*, and ten
to HMS *Eagle*. The eight for *Glorious* were duly despatched, but it was the
ten for *Eagle* that Maynard was told about. Maynard asked Cunningham
if he could borrow them, to which the Admiral readily agreed. In early
April, the pre-war civil airfield of Hal Far, just a mile west of Kalafrana,
was given a Station Fighter Flight and four of the ten Gladiators were
finally transferred over to the RAF. On 23 April 1940 the Malta Fighter
Flight was born, even though Maynard had no trained fighter pilots on
the Island. Undeterred, he asked for volunteers, of which his Personal
Assistant, George Burges, was one. Within 24 hours, Maynard had his
eight new fighter pilots. Basic training began, but no sooner had it
started than they were told that a transport ship was coming to collect
the ten Gladiators after all. Just six days after the Malta Fighter Flight
had been formed, it was dissolved, and the planes dismantled and put
back in crates ready for shipping. The farce continued, when a few days
later the Navy decided they only needed three of the planes; on 4 May,
the Fighter Flight was reformed after all. The Gladiators were reassembled
and stripped of their naval modifications; armour plating was added,

along with a number of other improvements. The Fighter Flight was split into two flights of three so as to operate in shifts, with no more than two planes in the air at any given time. Enthusiastic and dedicated as the pilots were, however, bravado and courage were not enough to take on the might of the Italian air force, the Regia Aeronautica. The harsh reality was, they lacked any form of operational experience, were desperately short of supplies, and the Gladiators were virtually obsolete against the Italians' faster, more modern fighter aircraft.

And if the Italians did try to invade, there would be no huge ground force waiting to repel them. At the outbreak of war, there were only four trained infantry battalions on Malta: the 2nd Devons, with whom John Parlby, Suzanne's husband, was serving; the 1st Dorsets; the 2nd Royal Irish Fusiliers; and the 2nd Battalion of Frank Rixon's regiment, the Queen's Own Royal West Kents. In May the following year, the 8th Battalion of the Manchester Regiment arrived, but this still only made up a total of less than four thousand men. In addition there was the King's Own Malta Regiment, but these were entirely locally based territorials, and with one whole company of the 2nd Battalion made up of Boy Scouts, this hardly inspired confidence. In the case of the Royal West Kents, battalion strength on 10 June stood at 24 officers and 744 other ranks. These were divided into four companies – A, B, C and D – of just under 200 men each.

It was the task of these infantry battalions to build defence posts and make the Island as secure from invasion as they possibly could. In this, at least, Malta had some natural defensive advantages. Much of the south coast of Malta is made up of steep jagged cliffs, reaching up to 900 feet in places, making any enemy landing impossible. In the north of the Island, admittedly, there are a number of beaches, but a few miles inland are the Victoria Lines, a steep natural escarpment running north-east across the Island, which would prevent enemy tanks from driving across the Island from the north. At various places along the coast where landings might be possible, a number of concrete pill-boxes were built and wire laid down.

Malta's countryside also made large-scale air invasion difficult. The patchwork of tiny fields and terraces, all lined and criss-crossed with silvery-grey dry-stone walls, made landing impossible. The Island's airfields were obvious exceptions, as were the extensive playing fields and racecourse of the United Services Sports Club at Marsa, where Frank Rixon and the 2nd Battalion of the Royal West Kent Regiment had been based since arriving on the Island that April. On the other hand, with few trees, the land was exposed, giving any attacking forces little cover.

Ultimately, although Malta may have had a number of topographical characteristics to help her, neither these nor the troops on the ground would be anything like enough to prevent a large or concentrated attempt at invasion.

Naturally, since Malta was surrounded by sea, her naval strength was also critical. Cunningham might be a brilliant leader, but the ships under his command were behind the game in terms of modern naval technology. Many of the Italian navy's ships were new; and those which were not – principally her battleships – had been modernized far more effectively than those of the Royal Navy. British armoured steel was of particularly bad quality and many of the ships under Cunningham's command simply did not have sufficient armour plating. The Fleet Air Arm was also alarmingly backward. The aircraft carriers available to Cunningham were ageing, insufficiently protected and used aircraft that were largely obsolete. By 11 June, the only naval aircraft ABC had at his disposal were Gloster Gladiators and Fairey Swordfish, biplanes, which, in the age of the Stuka, Spitfire and Messerschmitt 109, were positively pre-historic in comparison. Nor was there much in the way of naval air intelligence; the best he could hope for were the efforts of a few flying boats, which again were, frankly, not good enough if the Mediterranean Fleet was to operate to its best ability.

The area in which the Navy was perhaps found most wanting was its submarine branch. Despite – or perhaps because of – her naval tradition, Britain had remained deeply mistrustful of the submarine as a potent weapon of war. Repeatedly, at the Washington Conference of 1922 and again in the 1930s, she had called for an international ban on submarines; but her demands were disdainfully brushed aside. Submarines, like all aspects of the armed services, suffered because of the lack of rearmament, but this was a part of the Royal Navy that was particularly neglected, and by the outbreak of war, most of her submarines were inferior in numbers and quality to those of her enemies. By May 1940, Britain had just 12 in the Mediterranean, four of which were out-of-date varieties recalled from the Far East in April, while Italy had 115 of the German-style U-boats. By the middle of 1940, the U-boats had already exacted a heavy toll on British shipping, including the battleship *Royal Oak*, sunk at Scapa Flow by a German U-boat in October 1939. Her loss had been keenly felt on Malta. She had been well known there in pre-war days, and many Maltese had been serving on board when she was hit. Yet despite such blatant demonstrations of their effectiveness, submarines were considered distinctly second-class citizens in comparison to the surface ships.

Malta was an obvious place from which they could operate in the Mediterranean. Not everyone in the Navy viewed submarines with suspicion, and in the 1930s plans had repeatedly been put forward for an underground base at Malta – a series of shelters, or pens, to be built under the bastions of Valletta. Construction of some pens was even begun, but then later abandoned. In June 1938, Captain Raw took over command of the First Flotilla and at once saw the potential of such a base. Making some modifications on the original plans to bring down costs, he proposed a plan for eight submarine shelters. As a further inducement to obtaining approval, the tunnels were to be slightly heightened in order to house, if need be, up to 10,000 civilians. The whole cost was estimated at around £340,000, roughly the same as one submarine. Yet even this comparatively small outlay was considered too great and the scheme was not taken up, despite repeated lobbying throughout 1939 and 1940. It was another example of Malta's low priority rating at the time.

What submarines the Navy possessed were needed closer to home. The only Flotilla in the Mediterranean was the First, based at Alexandria. Malta was little more than a place from which to refuel, rearm and repair. In a scenario more akin to *Dad's Army* than a front-line battle station, the man left running the show on the Island was a retired reserve officer called Lieutenant-Commander R.G. Giddings, known as 'Pop'. Nor was this even a full-time post; between preparations for war, he was also a sales representative for the wine company Saccone and Speed, and had just 35 Maltese sailors under his command.

Into this rapidly escalating crisis for the Island came another potential catastrophe. In the spring of 1940, the Governor and Commander-in-Chief, General Sir Charles Bonham-Carter, contracted pneumonia and after a brief spell in hospital, it became clear he was too unwell for an immediate return to office and so was sent back to England. The timing was terrible. Not only was the Island effectively defenceless, there were also rising political tensions. Head of the Constitutional pro-British party was Lord Strickland, since 1935 the owner of the *Times of Malta*, while Dr Enrico Mizzi was leader of the pro-Italian Nationalist Party. Strickland, with an English father and a Maltese mother, had dominated the pro-British political faction for many years, despite being something of a loose cannon. In 1930 he was responsible for one of the few occasions when British-Maltese relations were seriously impaired. By making some unnecessary and provocative criticisms of the Maltese church he committed a serious political *faux pas*. The British-Maltese relationship worked so well precisely because the Maltese church was respected; but, if this was undermined, then political turmoil would not be far away. In this instance, the Archbishop of Malta, Monsignor Caruana – despite being pro-British – forbade any Maltese to vote for Strickland in the forthcoming elections. Neither party would give way and so the British Government was forced to suspend the constitution that allowed self-government, a potentially dangerous move in itself. Eventually Strickland relented, apologizing for his remarks, and the crisis passed. With Italy waiting in the wings, however, the 1930s were no time to be jeopardizing British popularity. By 1940, Strickland was still leader of the Constitutionals and, although by then an old man, was every bit as volatile and unpredictable as he had been a decade before.

With Bonham-Carter ill, the British government had no option but to find a temporary replacement, and fast; but finding an Acting Governor who would hold the Island together and fight hard for Malta's needs in the ensuing crucial few weeks was a tall order.

Entering the breach at this critical time was Lieutenant-General William Dobbie. An engineer by training, Dobbie had been serving in Singapore when he was asked to take over from Bonham-Carter as Acting Governor. On paper this must have seemed like a brave move: Dobbie, a Scot, was as devoutly Protestant as most of his new subjects were Catholic. And as a member of the Plymouth Brethren, he believed that official priesthood was a denial of the spiritual priesthood of all believers. With priests at the very heart of everyday Maltese life, Dobbie's faith could have quickly been exposed as a major hindrance to his effectiveness as Governor.

Nonetheless, he started well enough. On Friday 10 May, the day that the German panzers began their blitzkrieg in the west, General Dobbie made his first broadcast to the people of Malta. His voice crackling over the Rediffusion system he spoke of defiance and the need for steady nerves in the days to come. 'The unsettlement caused by the war renders it all the more necessary to hold on with inflexible determination to the solid foundations on which our cause is based, the foundations of righteousness, truth and honour, which cannot be shaken.' He told the people that much had been done to improve the defensive measures of the Island, but was careful to add that 'these steps have been taken purely as a precautionary measure and for no other reason.' Even so, he said, 'not only are we confident in the righteousness of our cause, but that we have ample resources both of men and material, in quantity and in quality, to ensure that, with God's help, Victory will most certainly be achieved.'[5] Did this pious man suffer any moral qualms about telling the people such a whopping lie? One can only wonder, but at least when he exhorted them to put their trust in 'God's Good Hand' he was speaking a language the Maltese understood, even when he was standing at the opposite end of the Christian spectrum.

Dobbie was not the only man with a new job, however, and for all his talk of defiance on 10 May, Malta's position was soon to become far more precarious than he could ever have known. Back in Britain Chamberlain had resigned and Winston Churchill had taken over as Prime Minister. Lord Halifax had been expected to take the post, but had declined, leaving Churchill as the only choice. Viewed with suspicion by many, the new PM had a reputation as a maverick and for recklessness, and in the first few days of his office, as the situation went from bad to worse on the Continent, his survival was far from assured. From Malta's point of view, Churchill was definitely the best man for the job: despite the disaster of the Dardanelles in the First World War, he had never lost any of his enthusiasm for the Mediterranean and the Balkans as a route into Europe, and so regarded safeguarding British interests there as essential. He made it clear from the outset that he would rather go down fighting than give in to Fascism, whether it be the Nazi or Italian kind. Lord Halifax, now Foreign Minister, did not entirely agree with Churchill. Despite his stance the previous year, he was increasingly in favour of opening some kind of dialogue with the Italians with a view to possible concessions in return for their assurance of keeping out of the war. On Sunday 26 May, the French Prime Minister, Paul Reynaud, visited London to report on the dire French situation. He was unsure how long France would be able to hold out, but was anxious to buy off Italy, whose forces were assembling along the French border in the south. Malta was named as one of these concessions. The British War Cabinet was divided. Churchill, believing such a move to appease Italy would not only be pointless but also a clear demonstration of British weakness, was against the idea; but with the British Expeditionary Force in France beaten back to Dunkirk, and with the German war-machine apparently invincible, he needed to tread very carefully in order to bring the rest of the Cabinet round to his way of thinking. For two days the situation was touch and go, Churchill's defeat by his own cabinet a serious possibility. After all, the pressure to make the right decision was enormous. But by 5 p.m. on Tuesday 28 May, as the first British troops were being lifted from the beaches of Dunkirk, Winston had achieved his coup, having worn down Halifax and won over the former Prime Minister, Neville Chamberlain. There would be no concessions. Britain and her Empire would fight on, alone if need be. Malta would not be handed over without a fight.

The same day, Belgium capitulated and Mussolini told his inner circle that he intended to enter the war on 10 June. British Intelligence soon picked up decrypts to this effect. Acting on this information, Dobbie swiftly interned all those of known pro-Italian sympathies, including Enrico Mizzi, but not the Chief Justice, Sir Arturo Mercieca, even though he was a self-proclaimed Italianist. This caused considerable outrage from Lord Strickland, much to Dobbie's frustration. 'I think he must be senile,' wrote Dobbie to his friend Lord Lloyd, the Colonial Secretary;[6] Lloyd, who knew Strickland well, suggested caution. On 11 June, Mercieca was asked to see Dobbie at the Governor's Palace in Valletta to tender his resignation, which he did, and was then placed under house arrest. 'Sir Arturo Mercieca's resignation has been some-what tardy, for his pro-Italian proclivities and sympathies were only too well known among his fellow countrymen and public indignation was steadily rising at his continuance in office,' wrote the *Times of Malta* the following day.[7]

With his knowledge of Il Duce's plans from British Intelligence, General Dobbie addressed the people again on 29 May. There was no immediate danger, he warned them disingenuously, but, as a *precaution*, those who had families to go to in the interior were advised to go to them. Despite the clear implications, few followed his advice, although most seemed to have taken heart from his words of defiance and assurance again that, 'we will endure to the end and we WILL win through.'

But successful management of propaganda was hiding the truth. By 10 June, Malta was in no position to take on a determined enemy.

Severely under-armed, the entire Island – with its three airfields and extensive harbours – had just 34 heavy and 22 light anti-aircraft guns; on the ground her beaches were inadequately defended with no reserves for counter-attack worth speaking of; there were a mere four obsolete fighter aircraft, four submarines and a few other light surface vessels. Tucked away in Alexandria, ABC's Mediterranean Fleet was now not only outnumbered, but also outgunned by the Italians; furthermore, her ships lacked the kind of armour plating and aircraft needed for the role she wished to play. In charge of the Island was a new Acting Governor, who, despite a promising start, was largely unfamiliar with the ways of the Maltese and only there because the official Governor was ill. On top of all that, Britain, so long her guardian and champion, had, in France, just suffered the greatest military defeat of her history and was looking down the barrel of a German invasion.

Malta was alone, sandwiched to the north and south by her enemy and almost defenceless.

Not that Frank Rixon knew any of this as he dived into his slit trench at the Marsa Race Track. 'We knew were getting ready for war and had every confidence that all was in hand. I didn't know what to expect, to be honest,' says Frank. 'I was only nineteen.' Was John Agius aware of the shortage of guns on the Island? 'No. We knew we were up to scratch.' After all, Cunningham, the greatest British admiral since Nelson, was in charge of the Mediterranean Fleet, and large numbers of Maltese were answering the call to arms.

With a large anti-aircraft gun right outside her billet, Suzanne Parlby also had complete faith that an enemy attack would be seen off. Mussolini was a bit of a joke anyway. She could not see how the Italians could possibly pose a major threat. And although she'd been a bit put out at having to move to barracks, she was now rather enjoying living with Midge, Elisabeth and the two children.

CHAPTER 3

Faith, Hope and Charity

JUNE–AUGUST 1940

AFTER THE INITIAL onslaught, the raids lessened over the ensuing days. The weather was fine and sunny on 12 June, but although the Italians sent over a reconnaissance plane to assess the damage, they did not bother with any further incursions that day. Then the weather turned and for the next three days low cloud provided the Island with some shelter from the attackers.

If Suzanne Parlby had been unimpressed by the Italians on the first day, her opinion of them was further lowered during the days that followed. Every time the air raid warning sounded, she, Elisabeth, Midge and the two boys would dash over to the slit-trench outside the house and wait for explosions that never came. Occasionally, the ack-ack gun would blast its charge into the sky, but Suzanne never saw a thing. It seemed the Italians could barely hit the Island. They were also amused to read in the paper about Italian radio bulletins claiming their bombers had hit the non-existent railway station and sunk the equally mythical ship HMS *St Angelo* in Valletta Harbour. Suzanne was torn between laughing and utter contempt.

Still, orders were orders and, despite the seemingly ineffectual bombing, they continued, as instructed, to make for the trench every time the siren wailed, waiting obediently until the All Clear was sounded. Soon they brought deckchairs, rugs and cushions into the slit-trench, and biscuits, water and insect repellent. Sandflies lived in the rock and soon became a source of considerable irritation. The odd bite, rather like a mosquito's, was harmless enough, but multiple bites could lead to sandfly fever, which was extremely unpleasant. If the ear-splitting ack-ack gun was firing, they would try to sing over the noise, belting out verses of lewd army songs taught to them by Midge's son, Peter.

Suzanne was enjoying the company in her new surroundings. The domestic chores were divided among them, but there was still plenty of time for talk and for playing any number of word games. Sitting round the kitchen table eating large chunks of bread spread with honey, they would have lengthy discussions and arguments about the meaning and spelling of words, with the *Oxford Book of Quotations* and a *Pears' Encyclopaedia* by their side. A dictionary was also added to their list of slit-trench comforts.

Although their husbands were in the same regiment, Suzanne had not known Elisabeth Young very well before they moved in with the Labbetts, but they were becoming good friends. Suzanne was impressed by Elisabeth's independence and ability to make the best of everything. Now that the Italians had come into the war, the hectic social life Elisabeth had previously enjoyed was largely cut short – the men were out in the field and the women all living in barracks. Undeterred, Elisabeth took this as the perfect opportunity to try something new and, since she'd always wanted to be a ballet dancer when she was younger, now took up lessons. With her polo pony – called Toby – and trap, which she kept at the barracks stables, Elisabeth would disappear off to nearby St Julian's or St George's. Back at the Labbetts', she would then practise her moves. 'Elisabeth was always waving her arms about like a ballet dancer and prancing about the house on tiptoes,' says Suzanne, who thought her new companion 'great fun'.

One day, Suzanne, Midge and Elisabeth decided to plaster their faces with oatmeal – it was, they had heard, good for the complexion. But no sooner had they done so than the air raid warning droned out once more. Putting their tin hats on their heads, they rushed to the balcony. The army dentist who lived next door had also made for his balcony and looked with abject horror at the three ghost-like women next to him. They went down to the shelter giggling like schoolgirls.

Both Suzanne and Elisabeth also served as VADs at the barracks surgery – or MI room, as it was called. With the barracks now housing a sizeable population of army wives and children there were always people at the daily surgery. Suzanne and Elisabeth would help out with basic duties – putting on dressings, administering basic first aid and other simple tasks. They were also both involved with a roster for dishing out meals to the Other Ranks' families.

Suzanne was adapting quickly to this new existence. Although she didn't see her husband for three weeks – and then only for an hour or so – she was rather enjoying herself. Keeping busy, and finding her companions both lively and stimulating, she was, for the first time in her life, starting to feel truly independent, and the long shadow of her father was fading fast. Suddenly, the world seemed to be full of possibilities. The war was making her grow up.

In many ways, Suzanne's scorn for the Italian war machine was justified. After firing the opening salvoes over Malta – a warning shot and signal of future intent – Mussolini pulled back his attacks in order to concentrate the bulk of his airborne forces against the now-dying France and French-held Tunisia, which he determined should be his first objective. As France's resistance crumbled, Mussolini gambled that the now-isolated Britain would sue for peace. With Western Europe tamed and subdued, he believed he would have a golden opportunity to pursue Italian expansionism in the Mediterranean and Africa, a slice of the pie that was of little interest to Germany. But the truth was that Italy was ill-prepared for war and the slackening of the attacks over Malta demonstrated not only how limited his resources were, but also his woeful lack of judgement.

One person who had no intention of suing for peace was Admiral Cunningham, who immediately set forth from Alexandria to sweep the Central Mediterranean as far as southern Italy with his fleet: two battleships – his largest, most heavily armoured ships with massive sixteen-inch guns and a firing range of nearly fifteen miles; five cruisers, slightly less well armed and protected than his battleships, but faster; an aircraft carrier; and a force of the much smaller but highly manœuvrable destroyer, which specialized in hunting down enemy submarines. Eager to confront the enemy fleet at the earliest opportunity, he was determined to show the Italians he would not be cowed by their superiority in numbers and modernity. He also hoped to catch some Italian supply shipping heading for North Africa and, most important, to test the Italian air capabilities. They sighted neither ship nor plane. 'I expected to spend most of the daylight hours beating off heavy bombing attacks on the fleet,' ABC wrote to the First Sea Lord, Admiral Sir Dudley Pound, but 'the battle squadron never saw a 'plane.'[1]

Although encouraged by this, Cunningham was deeply concerned by the lack of British aerial reconnaissance, for although the Italians were still using the same ciphers that had been decrypted back in 1937, once they changed codes – as they surely would – the Navy would be blind. In the cat-and-mouse war that would be played out in the Mediterranean, reliable intelligence would be the critical weapon.

But on that first sweep, Cunningham's force also encountered one of the fifty-odd enemy submarines operating in the Mediterranean; off the coast of Crete an Italian U-boat torpedoed the cruiser *Calypso*. While they were away from port the Italians had also been laying mines outside Alexandria. Cunningham was able successfully to weave his way through on their return, but the absence of minesweepers was another serious concern. Undeterred, the fleet left port again and kept itself busy, bombarding Bardia on the Libyan-Egyptian border on the North African coast, and sweeping for Italian submarines. In this latter role they had some success, sinking six by the end of the month. Still, the Italians could afford to lose a few submarines, while the British could not; with just ten in the Mediterranean on 11 June, the First Flotilla had only seven left a week later.

Lack of equipment, ammunition, ships and planes was a constant concern for Cunningham during those opening weeks. His men were proving their ability and spirit, but that would not keep them going for long. He was equally concerned about Malta, which was in much the same predicament. Furthermore, his wife and two nieces were still there, and although the numbers of enemy raids had decreased, bombs were being dropped most days and it remained a far from safe place to be.

Valiantly climbing to the skies each day to meet the Italian bombers were George Burges and his companions of the Malta Fighter Flight. After the lack of success on the first day, they realized that by sitting in deckchairs waiting for a warning bell to be rung, they would never have any chance of reaching the incoming bombers in time. To try to shave off precious minutes, they decided to split themselves into different watches, and, when on duty be strapped into their cockpits ready to go. Three of the pilots would take the first and third watch of the day, while the other three would cover the second and fourth. This, in theory, would give them as much as an extra 2,000 feet by the time the enemy reached the Island. The problem was that sitting in the cockpit for hours on end, wearing heavy flying suits, boots and helmets, was stiflingly hot and uncomfortable, and they began to get piles; so instead, they decided to operate two days on, one day off, which meant watches of two pilots, not three.

It was not as if their efforts made a huge impact on the Italians anyway, as the Gladiators were still struggling to keep pace with the bombers. But they did play an important role in boosting morale, and the value of this should not be underestimated. On the first day, an Italian plane pursued by one of the Gladiators was seen to dive, with smoke trailing behind it. It did, in fact, make it back to Sicily, but for those on the ground watching the dogfights above, this was the first victory to their gallant defenders, and the three planes they saw swooping and turning in the skies over Grand Harbour. Harry Kirk, an RAF corporal based at their headquarters in Scots Street, saw the Gladiators flying in tight formation and thought they looked rather like the three silver hearts on a brooch of his mother's. Each heart had a name – Faith, Hope and Charity. 'Look, there go Faith, Hope and Charity,' he told a fellow airman.[2] The names stuck; soon everyone at HQ was calling them that. It was the beginning of a myth that endures to this day. 'People got the impression that our aircraft were shooting down enemy planes left, right and centre,' says George Burges. 'They did not, but morale was kept high.'[3]

Another bomber was damaged on the 17th, but then calamity struck the Fighter Flight on the 21st. They had acquired two more of the crated Gladiators from the Navy and had them assembled, but this still gave them little cushion for manœuvre, and so when, in the morning, one of the planes crashed while taking off, it was a major set-back; the pilot was all right, but the Gladiator was not. Worse was to come when that afternoon, a second plane struck a packing case on landing, causing the plane to flip over on its back. Again the pilot walked away, but two fifths of their planes were now out of action, until it was decided that the two crashed planes could – just about – be morphed into one. Burges was impressed and frustrated in equal measure by the amount of improvisation that went on in order to keep the planes going. Under the guidance of their engineering expert, Wing Commander Louks, wings were chopped off one and added to another, engines were souped up in an effort to increase power and speed; new fuselages were hastily constructed. By pinching parts from damaged twin-engine Blenheim bombers, their performance was so increased it was superior to those of the two Hurricanes that reached the Island later that day after flying in stages from Gibraltar and North Africa.

Dobbie had sent a message to the War Office on 12 June pleading for some modern fighters, and had been told that five heading for Egypt could be kept on the Island when they stopped to refuel. These had duly arrived on the 13th, but the message to remain where they were had not got through and so, to the distress of Air Commodore Maynard and the Fighter Flight, they had taken off again soon after, disappearing like a mirage over the horizon. The next two to appear were there to stay, although this was news to the pilots who had been expecting to fly on to Egypt. Six more arrived on the 22nd. These Ferry Pool pilots, initially relieved to have finally landed on friendly ground after a long and arduous flight, were horrified to discover they had been drafted into the Malta Fighter Flight. Only one had any fighter experience at all, and even he had been originally trained as a bomber pilot.

While the Hurricanes were arriving on the 22nd, George Burges was in the air chasing after a single enemy plane that had flown over to Malta on a photographic sortie. For once, he was several thousand feet above it. Swooping down, he closed in behind, as near as he could, and shot off the left (port) side engine. As luck would have it, this happened directly above Valletta and Sliema with plenty of witnesses on the ground. The plane caught fire and, with flames and black smoke pouring from it, slow-dived into the sea. It was a coup for public relations.

The success – or apparent success – of the Gladiators must have had some effect on the Italians too, because during Burges' next action the following day he discovered the bombers now had a fighter escort to protect them. In no time, bullets were racing past him and Burges looked round to see a Macchi 200 – the Italian equivalent of the Hurricane – on his tail and shooting like mad. But if there was one benefit of the Gladiator, it was its very tight turning circle, and so he turned the plane on its side and whizzed round and round hoping the Italian fighter might break off the attack. To his surprise, the Macchi not only persisted, but because of his superior speed kept flying past the biplane, allowing Burges to fire off a few rounds every time he went past. After this had happened four or five times, the Italian plane suddenly caught fire and dived into the sea.

Just a few hours after George Burges had shot down the first Italian plane over Malta, the French signed an armistice with Germany, in the very same *wagon-lit* in which the emissaries of a defeated Germany had been forced to surrender in 1918. A swastika now hung over the granite memorial to the events of nearly 22 years before. France, for the time being at any rate, was out of the war. Britain – and her Empire – stood alone. Just twelve days before, the whole of the Mediterranean coastline had been either Allied or neutral. Now two thirds of it – and the entire central coast – lay in enemy hands. All ports, except those in Malta, Palestine, Gibraltar and Egypt, were now closed to the British.

On 17 June, even before France had signed the armistice, the First Sea Lord, Admiral Sir Dudley Pound, had sent a message to Cunningham stating that unless the French fleet could be persuaded to hand themselves over to the British, the chances of being able to hold onto the western exit of the Mediterranean with the existing resources were slim. If Spain also came into the war on the side of the Axis, as seemed quite possible, the task would become even harder. Tough decisions needed to be made, and so Pound suggested moving the Eastern Mediterranean Fleet to Gibraltar, from where it could easily be sent into the Atlantic. Of course, there were both political and military objections to such a line of action, but at the present time, the maintenance of Britain's Atlantic convoy routes was paramount.

Cunningham replied immediately, stressing again the importance of Malta. If the Fleet moved, he warned, Malta should surely fall. He also pointed out that such a withdrawal would lead to a crushing defeat, both in terms of prestige and land: in addition to Malta, Egypt would soon become untenable, as would Palestine and Cyprus. Of course, he argued, home defence was vital, but by the end of the first week of war with the Italians, the Marina Militare – the Italian fleet – had so far shown little taste for battle, and was, as far as Cunningham was concerned, not really ready for serious fighting. If supply ships were sent without delay, ABC felt certain they could sufficiently protect them through the Mediterranean.

After Churchill's victory over Lord Halifax on 28 May, and subsequent evacuation of 340,000 British and Allied troops from Dunkirk over the ensuing days, his power and authority had become total and unquestionable. His defiant speeches proved a rallying cry that stirred not only the nation but those in Malta too. On 18 June, the *Times of Malta* printed the Prime Minister's speech of the previous night on the front page: 'We shall defend our island home and with the British Empire around us shall fight on unconquerable until the curse of Hitler is lifted from the brows of men.'[4] His intentions were clear and even Halifax had given up thoughts of either appeasement or opposing

Churchill. While there were undoubtedly others at the Admiralty and War Office who were of similar opinion to Pound, their views were given short shrift.

It has been argued, with hindsight, that the decision to remain in the Mediterranean and Middle East was foolhardy and a waste of men and resources, more to do with pride than strategic importance. But this is surely revisionism gone mad. Historical 'what ifs' are misleading, but it cannot be doubted that the inevitable Axis additions of the Middle East and North Africa to most of mainland Europe would have been catastrophic for Britain – and the rest of the free world. Hitler would have had at his disposal all the Arabian and Iraqi oilfields, and it was fuel, above all else, that enabled any country to maintain its war machine. Furthermore, by capturing the Suez Canal, the Axis would have been able to link arms with the Japanese in the East. Not only would Britain have lost her Middle Eastern territories, but in addition to the gains the Japanese were to make in the Far East, India and Australasia would almost certainly have fallen too.

But the man who talked of fighting the enemy on the beaches and who had vowed never to surrender was certainly not going to countenance any evacuation of the Mediterranean. In fact, Churchill was now thinking only in terms of counter-attack, with Malta as a vital base from which to launch offensive operations against the enemy. The Italians, while intensifying their bombing of the Island after the fall of France, had still made no moves to invade, and like Cunningham, Churchill was encouraged by the Italian unwillingness to come out and fight. Having been low on the list of priorities, Malta suddenly came to the forefront, and Churchill issued the Chiefs of Staff with directives for urgent reinforcements.

The problem was how to protect new supplies reaching the Island, and clearly Cunningham and the Eastern Fleet would have to play a major role. It was agreed that as many British non-combatants as possible – including ABC's wife and two nieces – should be evacuated to Egypt immediately, and also that some naval stores from the dockyards should also be sent to Alexandria. These convoys would be covered by the Fleet, which left Alexandria for Malta on 7 July. At around eight the following morning, Cunningham, aboard the battleship *Warspite*, was given a report that the Italian battle-fleet had been spotted by a British submarine 200 miles east of Malta and heading south. Correctly guessing that the Marina Militare was also on convoy escort duty, he instructed Malta-based seaplanes to shadow the enemy boats, while he steered towards them.

Unbeknown to Cunningham, the Italians had not only changed their codes – as he'd feared – but their intelligence had also discovered the position of the fleet. The appearance of Italian reconnaissance planes was followed soon after by high-level bombers, who then pounded the fleet for the rest of the day. Although many of the bombs were close, the Italians were dropping their loads from as high as 12,000 feet, sacrificing accuracy for their own safety. Not a single ship had been lost by the end of the day, and only one ship had even been hit.

Meanwhile one of the flying-boats occasionally detached to Malta from Gibraltar or Alexandria, had spotted the Italian fleet heading northwards back to Italy, and so Cunningham changed course in order to try to come between the Italian ships and their base. By the following morning the British fleet was 90 miles west of the Italians, and although outgunned and outnumbered, ABC continued steering towards engagement. They finally came into range just after 3 p.m. that afternoon. It was a warm, sunny day and, apart from a few high streaks of white cloud, the sky was deep blue with excellent visibility. The signal 'Enemy battle fleet in sight' was relayed from the scouting cruiser HMS *Neptune* – the first time by the British Navy in the Mediterranean since Nelson's day. It was, said Cunningham, ever mindful of the importance of history, 'a great moment for *Neptune*'.[5] Minutes later, enemy cruisers opened fire, as did *Warspite*, at the vast range of thirteen miles. The Italians then retreated behind a smoke-screen, but after turning a full circle while his other battleship *Malaya* (John Ernest Montebello's ship) caught up, Cunningham then pressed on. Many would have found such an engagement a terrifying proposition, but ABC was champing with excitement at the promise of action and relishing every second from his vantage-point on the bridge. At extreme range, *Warspite* fired again on the two Italian battleships a few minutes before four o'clock in the afternoon. It was, said ABC, another 'great moment'.[6] Much to his delight, *Warspite*'s firing was near-perfect, despite the huge distance. At 4 p.m. on the dot, he saw a great orange flash of a heavy explosion at the base of the enemy flagship's funnel, followed by a huge billow of thick black smoke.

This was too much for the Italian Admiral Riccardi, who happened to be an old friend of Cunningham's. The two had dined together on board HMS *Hood* two years before, and Riccardi had once confessed to Cunningham that he kept a *Life of Nelson* by his bunk; but now, having decided that caution was the better side of valour, the Italian admiral disappeared behind a thick pall of smoke. With a spotter plane flying above *Warspite* to keep the fleet abreast of enemy movements, it became clear that the Italians were in a state of considerable confusion, not helped when they were mistakenly bombed by their own planes. 'The observer made not a few amusing signals,' said Cunningham, considerably cheered by his success.[7]

Cunningham now sent his destroyers and cruisers in pursuit, but around the smoke-screen – it was too great a risk to sail blindly through it. Meanwhile, the Regia Aeronautica appeared once more, high in the skies above. There were hundreds of them, and over the next few hours all the British ships came under fire, with *Warspite* singled out for attack five times. Even Cunningham admitted feeling alarmed at such a bombardment. Ships were disappearing behind huge fountains of spray, only to reappear some moments later. Despite this, Cunningham forged on, and by evening was only 25 miles south of the Italian coast. With night drawing in, he at last decided to abandon the chase, and so turned towards Malta to fulfil his original role of protecting the convoys heading to Alexandria. So ended the Battle of Calabria.

The convoys had, in fact, already left and were well on their way. Cunningham took the fleet southwards only to run into more air attacks from the Italians based in Libya. At one point, *Warspite* was straddled by 24 different bombs, but again emerged from this battering unscathed. Relieved to finally make it back to Alexandria in one piece, ABC met his wife Nona, who had left Malta on 9 July, and settled her and his two nieces into a new house on the edge of the city, before pausing to take stock of the lessons learnt during the previous few days.

Of major concern was the relentless battering received from the Regia Aeronautica, who seemed to have concentrated much of their resources on attacking the British Fleet. The numbers involved were considerable and did not bode well for the future of Malta. On the other hand, the Royal Navy had taken on the Marina Militare in her own back yard and beaten them back, a confidence booster if ever there was one. Clearly, however, a heavily armoured aircraft carrier was desperately needed – one that could withstand a certain amount of bombardment and which could get within striking distance of Italy. By attacking some Italian towns, they might also draw off some of the Regia Aeronautica.

As it happened, Churchill was of much the same mind. In a note to

General Ismay on 12 July, (Secretary of the Imperial Defence and Churchill's Chief of Staff), the Prime Minister wrote: 'The contacts we have had with the Italians encourage the development of a more aggressive campaign against the Italian homeland by bombardment both from air and sea. It also seems desirable that the Fleet should be able to use Malta more freely. A plan should be prepared to reinforce the air defences of Malta in the strongest manner with AA guns of various types and with Air planes … Let a plan for the speediest anti-aircraft reinforcements of Malta be prepared forthwith.'[8]

Poor Dudley Pound, stretched beyond his resources and capabilities, must have been regretting the day he took on the mantle of First Sea Lord, and wrote to the PM urging another reappraisal of the situation. On 15 July, Churchill tersely replied, 'I do not understand what is meant by "reviewing the whole Mediterranean situation". It is now three weeks since I vetoed the proposal to evacuate the Eastern Mediterranean and bring Admiral Cunningham's fleet to Gibraltar. I hope there will be no return to that project.'[9] Instead, he stressed again the urgent need to build up Malta's anti-aircraft defences and send over several squadrons of fighters. 'We must,' he stressed again, 'take the offensive against Italy, and endeavour once again to make Malta once again a Fleet base for special occasions. ILLUSTRIOUS, with her armoured deck, would seem to be better placed in the Mediterranean.'[10]

Malta would get her reinforcements. But the question was, would they come in time? The Regia Aeronautica had been intensifying her bombing raids over the Island. By the time ABC's wife, Nona, left Malta on 9 July, there had been 72 enemy air raids over the Island in just 29 days. On 26 June, the Malta Fighter Flight had been ordered to intercept the fifth raid of the day. Although they found the five Italian bombers in question, they scored no hits; instead, the bombers hastily shed their loads and, unburdened, sped away from their pursuers. Tragically, the bombs had been jettisoned over Marsa, and one incendiary bomb hit a bus, killing 21 passengers outright and seriously injuring a further nine. Frank Rixon, stationed nearby with the Royal West Kents, heard the explosions and saw the pall of smoke, but there was little he could do about it.

Despite their proximity to this and other such tragedies, Frank and the rest of 'C' Company had come through the first few weeks largely unscathed. A few of the men had suffered minor shrapnel wounds and there had been a slight panic when the NAAFI tent had caught fire, but by and large the battalion was settling into something of a routine. Stand To was at 4.30 a.m. every day, followed by defence work on machine-gun posts or trench digging; some days the tasks could be fairly undemanding – clearing shrapnel from the tennis courts at Marsa was straightforward enough – while on others they would be sent off to help heave large blocks of sandstone and rubble from the remains of bombed-out houses. Then there were stores and ammunition to shift, and the manning of defence posts. And when the air raid warnings sounded, they would stop their work and troop into the nearest slit-trench – with noticeably less urgency than they had shown during the first raids.

Although the population of Sliema had shrunk from 20,000 to 2,000 in the days that followed 11 June, the RAF clerk John Agius and his family had stayed where they were. They were a close family and loved their home in Victoria Terrace, filled as it was with the books, pictures and pieces of furniture that John had known all his life. They were not now about to abandon it, leaving their possessions to the mercy of pilferers and thieves. Better to take their chances, and pray they would all be spared.

There were eight of them in all. Many Maltese families had six or more children; John's parents had had eight, but two had died in infancy. His father was a dispensing chemist, with a shop in Valletta. They were not well-off, and it had been a struggle having to support John's older brother Emanuel when he'd been training to become a doctor. This had involved two years in England, half of which had to be funded out of their own pocket. Another brother, Joseph, was a health inspector, while one sister, Gemma, was a teacher and the other, May, a secretary. The youngest, Anthony, was only fifteen when Italy joined the war. John had left school at sixteen. It was a shame, because he was bright and would have liked to take his studies further; but such was life – there was no money left for college or further formal education. He'd carried on studying various commercial subjects himself, hoping to sit for an exam either as a postal clerk or a customs officer. In the meantime, he'd seen in the paper an advertisement for a job as a clerk at the RAF Headquarters in Scots Street, Valletta. Carefully cutting out the advertisement (which he keeps in his wallet to this day), he made his way over to Valletta and asked the Chief Clerk there what the application process was. 'We'll give you a test in both shorthand and typing within the next few minutes,' he told him. As an unworldly sixteen-year-old, John felt somewhat flustered by this, and he began making his excuses about having to go back home and fetch a pencil and some paper. 'Don't you think we have pencils and paper here?' replied the Chief Clerk. 'All right then,' John told him, 'I'll take the test now.' The job was his. Two weeks later, on 24 October 1936, he took up his position, and was still there nearly four years later, when Italy entered the war. Nor did he stop working just because the Italians had begun to bomb the Island. Even on that first day, after he realized his services as an evacuation officer were not needed, he made his way down to the Strand, along the waterfront of Sliema Creek, and caught the steam ferry across the harbour to Valletta. A winding road then led him up from the quay, until he reached the foot of Scots Street. A long, straight, steep hill of steps took him to No. 3, at the top, where the RAF had its headquarters.

In Valletta there were a number of shelters and caves, dug many hundreds of years before into the foot of the bastions towering above. There was also the long and wide railway tunnel in which Christina Ratcliffe had found shelter on 11 June. The railway had been closed some years before, but it was ideal for its new role. Even so, there were far from enough shelters for everyone. During working hours, John was able to take cover in the cellar at Scots Street if a raid came over, but when at home he and the family simply made for the central room in the house, on the ground floor, and crouched under a table. There was an ARP Centre in Sliema, but no caves such as those in Valletta, nor slit trenches like the ones Frank Rixon could dash for at Marsa or Suzanne Parlby was using at St Andrew's Barracks.

Having openly encouraged voluntary evacuation, the Governor was now faced with the problems arising from these empty towns. Thousands of dogs and cats had been left behind in the haste to flee the bombs. With little to eat, they began to starve, and soldiers were brought in to destroy many of them. Many shops closed down as their owners had left with the fleeing masses. Valletta had become so empty that a petition was sent to the Governor with a plea to lower rents because business had ground to a standstill. The problem was not a shortage of food, but a shortage of people to sell it. It was a great relief to John Agius and his family when the Government appointed District Commissioners to look after the evacuated towns. Shops were ordered to open at least three times a week, with the owners travelling in from the country specially to do so for the remaining population. As the Agius family had foreseen, the many empty houses offered a tempting invitation to thieves, and so police patrols were stepped up in order to keep the number of burglaries in check.

The Hurricanes were soon proving a welcome addition to the Malta Fighter Flight, and George Burges was only too happy at the chance to fight in a fast, monoplane aircraft. 9 July was another hot day, the horizon shimmering with the heat, burning down from a cloudless sky. He was half-way through the morning watch – two hours already spent strapped in, the cockpit so hot it would burn his elbow if he touched it. Suddenly the horn blared from the airfield control tower and ground-crew rushed towards him with a starter battery. 'Scramble, scramble, scramble!' he was told over his R/T. This was the order to take off to meet an incoming raid. Moments later, along with one other Hurricane, he was speeding down the runway. Once airborne, more instructions came through his headset: bandits, three-plus, ten miles north, angels fifteen. In other words, there were approximately three enemy aircraft ten miles from St Paul's Bay in the north of the Island at a height of around 15,000 feet.

On this occasion, the Italians had sent out a lone bomber escorted by Fiat biplanes, the Regia Aeronautica's equivalent to the Gladiator. With the extra speed the Hurricanes possessed they found themselves for once perfectly placed for an interception. Creeping up behind, Burges opened fire and saw the bomber plummet towards the sea. His fellow pilot shot down one of the Italian biplanes. That evening, on Rome Radio, the Italians reported being attacked by two 'Spitfires', one of which had been shot down.

On the 16th, the first RAF fighter pilot was killed – Flight Lieutenant Keeble – during a vicious dogfight in which his attacker also died. Then, on the last day of the month, one of the Gladiators was finally shot down. A witness said the plane 'burnt just like a magnesium flare, an absolutely brilliant light in the sky.'[11] The pilot baled out into the sea, but was in hospital for months afterwards with terrible burns; the pilots had given up wearing flying suits, preferring the comfort of shorts and a shirt. This made their lives more comfortable while waiting to take to the skies, but there was a terrible price to pay if their planes began to burn.

By the end of July the Island's defenders had accounted for twelve enemy aircraft, and George Burges had been awarded the Island's first decoration – a Distinguished Flying Cross (DFC). Unfortunately, as July passed into August, the Fighter Flight were left with just one airworthy Hurricane and two Gladiators. Help was at hand, however. Churchill's demands that Malta be reinforced at the earliest opportunity had been taken on board, and on 31 July, the aircraft carrier HMS *Argus* entered the Mediterranean with twelve Hurricanes, which, once close enough, would fly off the flight deck and onwards to Malta. With France now in enemy hands, and with Spain a fascist neutral, this was the only practical means of getting aircraft to the Island.

All twelve safely landed at Luqa airfield on 2 August. The pilots had been drawn from Fighter Command, the part of the RAF responsible for home defence, and which was already involved in the Battle of Britain. Asked to report to RAF Uxbridge in high secrecy, they were told they would be flying some Hurricanes to an unknown destination. It was not until they were in the Mediterranean that they discovered they were headed for Malta. In what was fast becoming something of a tradition among new Hurricane pilots arriving on the Island, none of the twelve had any idea that they would be staying put. They had been led to believe that they were just ferrying the planes to the Island and would then be taken back to Gibraltar by flying boat, and on to England. Understandably, they were furious. None of them had brought anything more than overnight kit. Nor was there any spare petrol for test flights, or ammunition to practise firing. Back in England, moreover, times might have been hard, but at least the fighter pilots suffered few shortages. There were pubs to go to in the evening and periodic leave. On Malta, conditions were considerably more basic, and, when the pilots did take off, the whole procedure was something of a fiasco. Luqa had been littered with debris so as to deter any enemy landing, and buses were driven on and off the runway whenever it was needed. This had to happen not just when the pilots were scrambled into the air, but whenever they came in to land too. Sadly, these were not always driven out of the way with quite the speed required from the pilots. The drivers also tended to put personal safety first, taking cover during a raid rather than clearing the runway.

Nonetheless, with fifteen planes and eighteen pilots, Air Commodore Maynard *did* now have enough of each to make up an entire squadron. The Malta Fighter Flight was moved to Luqa to join the new arrivals, and on 16 August, they became 261 Squadron, Malta's first fighter squadron.

Fortunately, the new pilots were given the chance to acclimatize to their new surroundings and circumstances without being unduly stretched by the Italians. Although the Regia Aeronautica had intensified their attacks after France's capitulation, the number of raids dropped dramatically during the Battle of Calabria when most of their forces were concentrated on the British fleet, and then never picked up again once that episode was over. It was a curious decision by the Italian High Command, for, as the raids lessened, so Malta was slowly growing in strength; something the Italians must have noticed.

The truth was, the Italians were ill-prepared for war and, unlike their leader, had little appetite for its spoils. Despite attacking Malta from the outset, the Italians, as elsewhere, failed to press home their advantage. With Malta's defences as fragile as they were, Il Duce would soon rue the missed opportunity to invade.

CHAPTER 4

Gathering Strength

SEPTEMBER–DECEMBER 1940

URRICANES WERE NOT the only reinforcements arriving on the Island. Churchill was clearly making people jump at the Admiralty and War Office as well as the Air Ministry. The First Sea Lord had written to Cunningham towards the end of July – presumably through clenched teeth – informing him that the armour-plated aircraft carrier HMS *Illustrious* was being sent to the Eastern Mediterranean along with a battleship and two cruisers. Both *Illustrious* and the battleship *Valiant* were equipped with RDF (radar); it was the first time Cunningham would have such equipment at his disposal.

While ABC's reinforcements were steaming from Gibraltar, he was leaving Alexandria with the first three supply ships to bring reinforcements to Malta. On Pound's insistence, these – a tanker and two merchant ships – had sailed round the Cape and through the Suez Canal. The convoy was bombed south of Crete, and the SS *Cornwall* was holed below the waterline, which put her steering gear out of action. Despite this, she managed to battle on, even keeping her place in the convoy. On 2 September, all three ships safely reached Grand Harbour with a full cargo of 40,000 tonnes of much-needed guns, armour and ammunition. The warships also safely arrived from the west, entering Grand Harbour for refuelling and unloading their cargoes of more guns, gun barrels, anti-aircraft instruments, ammunition and personnel.

Back in London, Churchill was delighted with the success of the convoy operation and wrote to Cunningham on 8 September – one of the heaviest days' fighting of the Battle of Britain – urging him once again to strike quickly at the Italian fleet. 'It is of high importance to strike at the Italians this autumn because as time passes the Germans will be more likely to lay strong hands upon the Italian war machine and then the picture will be very different.'[1] ABC had, in fact, discovered the Italian fleet was only ninety miles to the north during the passage from Alexandria to Malta, but, much to his irritation, just too far away to engage. The Italians, for their part, had slunk away. But arriving on board HMS *Illustrious* was Rear-Admiral Lyster, to take charge of the Fleet Air Arm operating from the aircraft carriers. Between them, they began to hatch a plan to attack the Italian fleet – a daring plan that, if successful, would not only keep Churchill off their backs, but also swing the balance in favour of the Royal Navy in the Mediterranean.

In the meantime, other reinforcements were arriving on Malta, including a photographic reconnaissance flight – much to the delight of Cunningham, who had continually begged the First Sea Lord for such assistance. Early in the morning on 6 September – just over a year after Britain had declared war on Germany – three American-built twin-engine Glenn Martin Marylands touched down at Luqa airfield after a seven-hour flight from southern England. Their crews had decided to risk flying at night over enemy-occupied France and as a result had managed to photograph the uncharted island of Sardinia as they swept over at first light. By doing this, they had proved their worth to Cunningham before even reaching Malta.

Responsible for successfully plotting this route was a tall, fair-haired young man named Adrian Warburton. Taking into account potential enemy opposition, airfields *en route*, and weather conditions, the plan had left nothing to chance. It was just about the first thing the young pilot officer had managed to get right during his short and so far disastrous career.

In some ways, it was something of a homecoming for him. His father, Geoffrey, had been a submarine commander and had been based in Malta just after the last war. With a quirk of eccentricity his son was to inherit, Geoffrey Warburton had absolutely insisted the baby Adrian be christened on board his submarine, docked in Grand Harbour. The Warburtons had not remained in Malta long, however, and when Adrian was just two, his father had been posted to Australia. Like so many children of the services, Adrian and his older sister Alison were sent to boarding school in England, spending their holidays with their grandparents. Adrian was something of a loner as a child, and when he arrived at St Edward's School, Oxford, was immediately singled out as a misfit – he refused to play any team sports, despite an athletic build and obvious talent, and relentlessly boasted about being a voracious masturbator, presumably hoping to shock his fellow pupils. His only interest as a child – apart from masturbating – was aviation. St Edward's was to produce two of the most famous British airmen of the war – Douglas Bader and the dam-buster Guy Gibson – but few people there would have reckoned on Adrian ever forging an illustrious career for himself.

Although he'd always wanted to join the RAF, his parents were opposed to the idea, and it was not until he was twenty, in 1938, that he finally went against their wishes and joined anyway. Granted a short service commission, he finally won his coveted wings with a 'below average' rating, the lowest pass rate possible. Throughout his training he was always close to being thrown out but he was eventually sent to join 22 Squadron Coastal Command at Gosport in Hampshire – hardly the most prestigious of postings – in the summer of 1939. Whether he'd arrived there with a warning note is not clear, but certainly he was not allowed much flying and before long was packed off on a course. By January 1940, he had just over half an hour's flying time to his name since joining the squadron. Between then and May, he didn't fly again, and then he was sent on another course – the classic fate of squadron members who do not fit in. When he did return to flying, it was only in an obsolete Audax biplane, 'drogue-towing' – an exercise to give air gunners air-to-air practice. In other words, the dud job.

Clearly still as much of a misfit as he'd ever been as a child, Adrian had also managed to get himself into trouble. While at Gosport he'd become a regular visitor to a pub called The Bush, where there was an attractive and popular barmaid called Betty. Although she was some years older and had a daughter from a previous relationship, the two began seeing one another. Then, acting on a whim, they married in secret in October 1939. Nuptial bliss was not forthcoming; 22 Squadron were soon after posted to Thorney Island, and although not a million miles away, Adrian chose to spend most of his time there rather than in the small bungalow he'd rented in Gosport. Since his family were totally unaware of his marriage, he could hardly ask them for financial assistance, but his pay of ten shillings a day was not enough to cover the rent and keep a wife and step-daughter. The debts began to mount, and it wasn't long before Betty decided to sue for divorce from her absentee husband. By the following summer, Adrian was in difficulties and in danger of being kicked out of the RAF. Debt of any kind was severely frowned upon, but a junior officer writing cheques that he was unable to honour was even worse. Furthermore, from June to September he was on yet another course – this time a navigational one in Blackpool; with the Battle of Britain raging, there can have been no trained pilot who had flown less than Adrian. He was extremely fortunate that on his return from Blackpool, his Commanding Officer at 22 Squadron decided to give him another chance. The squadron had been given three Marylands and told to take them to Malta under the command of an Australian flight commander named Tich Whiteley. Planning the route, with a ticket to escape England, was the break Adrian had needed.

Although officially still a fully trained pilot, Adrian had flown to Malta as a navigator and photographic officer, and it was in this role that he continued to be used by Whiteley during their first weeks on the Island. The Marylands had a crew of three: the pilot, the navigator, and the Wireless Operator/Air Gunner (WOP/AG). These planes, originally used by the French Armée de l'Air before her capitulation, were all the RAF could spare. A twin-engine light-attack bomber, the Maryland was comparatively fast and manoeuvrable and armed with four machine-guns in the wings and two twin manually operated guns in the turret and rear ventral – which was why three crewmen were needed. But for all its advantages, there was a major stumbling block for protracted use on Malta: it was American built, unfamiliar to most RAF mechanics and electrically more complicated than most British-built planes. Admittedly, there was a shortage of spares for all planes on Malta, but this was doubly the case for the Marylands.

It was up to Whiteley and the rest of the 431 Reconnaissance Flight – as they were now called – to do the best they could. Cunningham, with his precious reconnaissance planes finally at his service, wasted no time in instructing them to photograph the Italian fleet and ports, and specifically the naval base of Taranto in the heel of Italy.

Whiteley, a skilled engineer as well as pilot, was also a natural leader, able to spot and nurture the best in people. Somehow, he had detected that in Warby – as Adrian had become known – lay a potential that had been shrouded by a lack of confidence and his eccentricities of behaviour. After arranging for part of Warby's pay to be sent home every month to pay off his debts, he then appointed his junior officer as official ship recognition expert. Once again, Warby responded well to the responsibility, assiduously learning all enemy ships and giving regular tests to each aircrew member of the Flight, Whiteley included.

It is quite possible that Warby would have remained a navigator had it not been for two of the pilots succumbing to a particularly unpleasant form of dysentery known as 'Malta Dog'. By 26 September, Warby's total flying time on twin-engine planes was a negligible 35 minutes, but with the Reconnaissance Flight in great demand already, Whiteley had little choice but to hand him one of the Marylands.

One of Warby's greatest problems was the poor quality of his take-offs and landings, something that had hindered his flying career to date. In the operational record book of 431 Flight, Warby's first flight – a supposed reconnaissance trip to Corfu – was 'abandoned owing to hydraulic failure and aircraft crashed on landing'.[2] This rather euphemistically hides the fact that he'd zig-zagged the plane so roughly across the airfield on take-off that a wheel had come off. It must have been a terrifying experience for the two other crew members, who faced enough danger as it was without the added risk of death by incompetent flying. With one of his Marylands now out of action, Whiteley must have been tempted to take Warby off flying once and for all. But a shortage of pilots and a gut feeling that his oddball junior officer would still come good, ensured another reprieve. It would be Warby's last chance to prove himself as a pilot.

While more gunners, guns and ammunition, RAF personnel and groundcrew arrived on Malta at the end of September, other reinforcements were being prepared for the Island. Cunningham now had his reconnaissance planes, but for Malta to become an effective base for offensive operations, as he and Churchill wished, another means of hitting the enemy was needed. This was to come in the form of submarines.

ABC had written to Admiral Sir Dudley Pound on 3 August, expressing his concern about the submarine situation. The undersubscribed First Flotilla had taken a pasting in the opening weeks. Four had been sunk in the first six days after 11 June and another on 1 August, halving the entire Mediterranean submarine force. 'At the moment,' he wrote, 'it is not a question of sending them where they will be useful, but where they will be safe.'[3] This unacceptable situation was due to a number of factors. Firstly, the submarines were out-of-date – like much of the Royal Navy. As Cunningham neatly put it, they were 'too large, too old, and with auxiliary machinery that was too noisy, for work in the Mediterranean.'⁴ Secondly, the Navy was still operating under pre-war rules of engagement, with restrictions against attacking merchantmen without warning them first, and obligations to ensure crew safety of those attacked. Unrestricted attacks were only permitted within thirty miles of Italy or Italian-held land – such as Libya – which was, unsurprisingly, where the most mines, Italian submarines and destroyers were operating. Clearly, the whole situation was totally unacceptable, as the enemy were following no such rules, and the Admiralty had to either forget about submarines in the Mediterranean altogether or start using the right vessels in proper numbers and under the right conditions.

The latter course did offer a very real opportunity for attacking the Italians. There was a considerable amount of enemy shipping travelling from southern Italy to North Africa, and Malta lay in between. It was the ideal place from which to operate a new submarine flotilla. The Admiralty needed to see this potential and find the necessary resources to act upon it.

Finding them during the summer of 1940, while Britain was fighting for her life in the Battle of Britain, was not an easy matter. Nonetheless, the proposal had been given the green light, and the Admiralty began looking for a new commander of the submarine base at Malta. They needed a highly experienced submariner with considerable knowledge of the Mediterranean; someone with dogged determination and plenty of common sense; someone who could inspire his men and make the best of limited resources. It was a tall order, but in Commander George Simpson, second-in-command of the Third Submarine Flotilla, currently based at Harwich in East Anglia, they felt sure they had found their man. Stocky and broad-shouldered, with a square and humorous face, he was known to all as 'Shrimp'. A naval cadet during the First World War, he'd then joined submarines in 1921. Throughout the 1920s and 1930s he served on a number of different submarines around the world, acquiring the kind of knowledge and experience the Admiralty had been looking for, and captaining the minelaying submarine *Porpoise* before joining the Third Flotilla.

On 7 September, Simpson was asked to present himself to the Admiralty in London, where he was told he would be going to Malta to take command of the submarines that, it was hoped, would be based there from the beginning of 1941. His brief was to be in Malta by Christmas. Leaving Liverpool Street railway station later that afternoon on his way back to Harwich, Simpson heard the air raid sirens wail and soon after the train came to a halt on a high embankment. A mile south of him, the docks were burning after attacks by wave after wave of German bombers. It seemed to him that the whole of the Thames was on fire. It was a depressing sight, and he was glad he would soon be far away from it all.

Meanwhile, on Malta itself, 'Pop' Giddings – part wine rep, part officer in charge of the Malta submarine base – had been busy. Despite an almost total lack of equipment, support and personnel, he had proved himself to be a man of great resourcefulness and aptitude, organizing the removal of the Malta submarines from their floating base to Manoel Island, the other side of the Valletta finger.

Just fifty acres in size, and lying in the middle of Marsamxett Harbour, this small island had housed the old Lazzaretto, a quarantine hospital since the days of the bubonic plague. This building held much in its favour as a submarine base now that the underground plans had been discarded. Built of characteristic Malta limestone blocks quarried on the site, it was about 500 feet long and 100 deep, lying on the south side of the Island looking towards Valletta. The building scored points for both practicality and comfort. The harbour was some forty feet deep there and the water lapped the front, allowing submarines to berth right alongside. Just two storeys high, Lazzaretto contained plenty of old isolation wards, which could be used as officers' cabins, and larger rooms for a mess. Along the length of the front, on both floors, were two long corridors, with various openings and windows; the lower was suitable for access to the submarines, the upper for relaxing, with wonderful views across the harbour and to Valletta. Behind lay a wall of rock into which air raid shelters could be dug. The building was spacious and strong, and only a direct hit would have caused any serious damage. A defensive boom at the entrance to Marsamxett Harbour – netting to the depth of the water – protected it from seaborne attack.

Giddings arranged for the Navy to be lent the building – but on one condition: the submariners were to preserve the names of those who had carved their names on the walls whilst incarcerated there during the previous several hundred years. On one wall Lord Byron had carved his name during his stay in 1811. It had not been a happy experience for the poet, who wrote, 'Adieu thou damnedest quarantine, That gave me fever and the spleen.' Lazzaretto's new inhabitants would find good reason to echo such sentiments during the next few years.

Elsewhere, the embryonic Malta submarine base was beginning to take shape. Several thousand miles away, a new Unity-class (U-class) submarine had just been completed. Built by the Vickers Armstrong company based at Barrow-in-Furness in the north of England, HMS/S *Upholder* had set sail for the mouth of the Clyde, where she would spend a couple of months carrying out exercises and tests in preparation for service overseas. Smaller than other British submarines and comparatively easy to build, the U-class had been intended for training surface ships in anti-submarine detection, but they did possess a particularly fast diving speed, something that made them suitable for work in the Mediterranean theatre. Furthermore, they were economical and, because they were relatively small, would be harder to detect in the clear waters in which they were due to operate. However, as they were new, and relatively untested, it was left to Admiral Cunningham to pray that these smaller, more versatile U-class boats would become, as planned, the thorn in the side of the enemy.

Although the infamous Stuka dive-bombers – with their wailing sirens and fearsome bombing accuracy – had appeared at the beginning of September, the Italians were not blasting the Island with any great intensity, and Malta soon settled down to the new wartime existence. The initial shock had given way to pragmatism. It was a relieved Acting Governor Dobbie who had reported back to London that the Maltese were bearing up well.

Isolated as she was, Malta needed to prepare for the long haul, and so in the weeks and months following 11 June, the Government introduced a number of new laws, regulations and initiatives. In communicating these changes, Dobbie had help at hand. Lord Strickland had died in August, but his daughter, the indomitable Mabel Strickland, had taken over as editor of the *Times of Malta*. While the *Malta Chronicle* was forced to shut down, the *Times* continued, albeit on a reduced scale of four pages. Although the paper reported events from Malta and around the world, it was essentially a mouthpiece for propaganda, and in Mabel Strickland, Dobbie had found, for the time being at any rate, a powerful and reliable ally.

The other principal means of communication was the Rediffusion system. This was effectively an Island radio network. Some people, like the Agius family, had sets of their own. Others, the Montebellos included, had to rely on loudspeakers installed in town and village squares. With two switches – A and B – offering English and Maltese, Rediffusion transmitted the BBC, light entertainment, news bulletins and any governmental broadcasts, which then tended to be printed in full the following day in the *Times of Malta*. At any time in the middle of an ordinary programme, on both channels, a voice might cut in announcing 'Air Raid Warning!' in English, then 'Twissija ta Hbit Mill Ghajru!' in Maltese, repeated over and over for a minute or two.

In his broadcast of 28 June, Dobbie had appealed to the people not to hoard, and to 'avoid any form of waste like the plague.' But his request for economy was largely ignored, and so the Government was forced to take measures by restricting supplies to wholesalers – and to an amount that was considerably less than the population had been used to in peacetime. As Dobbie pointed out, however, supply convoys faced enormous dangers, and so it was essential that not a single ship more than was absolutely necessary was sent to Malta.

Oil was probably the single most important commodity, as it was used in almost every part of daily life: for transport, cooking, lighting and heating in winter. But stocks were limited. Consequently, people began buying as much as they possibly could, despite pleas for thrift. The price of kerosene soon doubled.

Steps had to be taken. All private and hired cars were ordered off the road, and even bus services were curtailed. Bus became the only practical means of mechanized transport for most, and long queues built up at every stop, followed by a massed rush to get on board when one arrived. Travelling during raids could be hazardous – as had been discovered with the Marsa Bus Tragedy – so most of the glass windows were removed. Commuters' misery was heightened when taxis and motor-bicycles were also banned.

No wonder people began moving back into the towns and cities once more. The bus queues in the surrounding villages were full of dockworkers heading towards Grand Harbour, whereas before 11 June, they would have walked from their homes in the Three Cities. The Montebellos had certainly had enough of village life and, by September, Michael and his family were back in their house in Senglea. After all, the pre-war Armageddon envisaged as a result of mass-bombing had not happened. There had been no Guernica in Malta.

In any case, the Government had started building a number of air raid shelters. Private cellars were requisitioned and expanded. Under the bastions of Valletta and the Three Cities, there were a number of cellars and garages that were developed into much larger shelters. Many began digging their own as well. Maltese limestone, baked hard near the surface, is comparatively soft well below ground, friable enough to scratch a mark with a fingernail. With picks and chisels one could cut chunks of rock with comparative ease.

At St Andrew's Barracks, Suzanne Parlby was spared most of these discomforts. She was keeping busy too. Before hostilities had broken out, she'd acted in a number of shows put on by the Malta Amateur Dramatic Society, run by Kay and Ella Warren, two formidable spinster sisters. Now they decided to form a roving concert party, giving shows to the various battalions and airmen stationed across the Island, and Suzanne once again joined their troupe. On a makeshift stage made from planks and kerosene tins, and with tarpaulins serving both as a backdrop and for changing rooms, they acted out excerpts from Noël Coward plays, sang songs and performed dance routines. Suzanne, as one of the Warren sisters' principal young actresses, loved every minute: the wolf-whistles and cheers were a far cry from the life she'd known with her mother and father. And since the concert party was considered so essential to morale, they were allocated an army truck in which to travel around.

Christina Ratcliffe was also now busy entertaining the troops, although for a couple of months, with the music halls and nightclubs remaining closed, she'd been left twiddling her thumbs. All thoughts of leaving for England had been dashed, but at the same time she had to do *something*; she couldn't 'rest' for ever.

Rescue lay around the corner. Two Englishmen, Chris Sheen and the unusually named Vicki Ford, had been a music-hall comedy act working on the Island before 11 June, and, like Christina, found themselves with nothing to do. So they offered their services to the Provost Marshal, who, instead of taking them on as soldiers, asked them to form an ENSA-style concert party. Jumping at the chance, they set about forming their troupe, to which Christina was a willing recruit. With four men and seven girls, and a four-piece band, they called themselves 'The Whizz-Bangs' and began earnestly rehearsing their routine of songs, dance and comedy acts. In the absence of much alternative entertainment, their performance went down a storm, and soon, like the Warren sisters' show, the Whizz-Bangs were being dispatched all round the Island.

Many of the jokes were old chestnuts, but the audience, out to enjoy themselves, laughed raucously all the same. One such involved Vicki's entrance. A gong sounded and one of the men entered, bowing before the sultan.

'O, father, there is a woman without.'

'Without what?'

'Without food or clothing.'

'Give her food and bring her in.'

This prompted much laughter. Vicki then entered, muscles bulging, in billowing crimson trousers, bare mid-riff, with two saucepan lids for a bra, long dark wig and yashmak, and began a snake-charming dance, accompanied now by uproarious laughter. Later, they painted two red nipples onto the saucepan lids, which made the men roar even more. As Christina puts it, 'It might have been coarse and corny stuff but it made the lads laugh and that was the purpose of our mission.'[5]

One time, they took the show to the hospital at Imtarfa for the staff and some of the patients. Vicki also had an act where he pretended to be 'Madame Moya' the clairvoyant. Pulling some poor victim from the audience, he would pretend to go into a trance, then suddenly slap the man and say, 'Oh, so that's what you were thinking!' But at Imtarfa, he picked on a wounded Italian airman who, despite being a prisoner-of-war, had been allowed to see the show. Not understanding a word of what was going on, he stood on stage looking puzzled. Then, when Vicki slapped him, he burst into tears.

The Royal West Kents were still carrying out their tasks, clearing bomb damage and preparing defence posts, but with the slackening of enemy raids, there was time for other training. The company commanders held weekly conferences where they discussed any issues arising, acted upon the changing military situation and monitored the morale and standards of the men. Notes from these meetings were then written up and handed out to the officers. By September, Frank Rixon and his colleagues were being given fifteen minutes' weapons training each day, and exercises on bicycles, since these were the only means of transport. They were also being warned about German methods of attack. 'Company Commanders are to impress upon their men the great value the Germans attach to the undermining of morale,' advised one directive. 'This is carried out by "frightfulness", which, more often than not, means concentrated noise caused by such ingenious devices as whistling bombs, etc.' The men were also reminded of the great value of the steel helmet and warned that it 'should never be used as a missile'.[6] Bicycles were the cause of other adjustments. It was agreed that saluting, for example, had to be done with both hands on the handlebars and the turning of the head and eyes smartly to the required flank. Riding a bicycle with full kit and a rifle presented certain difficulties. 'It wasn't as easy as it would appear,' says Frank, 'as the roads were mainly cart tracks with lots of ruts and potholes.' There were many 'prangs', leaving the men nursing their subsequent cuts and bruises.

The troops were also encouraged to take an interest in their particular post by improving amenities. Building stone floors for their shelters and cultivating crops were seen not solely as morale-boosting exercises, but as practical too. Weapon, uniform and billet inspections were held every Sunday morning, despite a shortage of replacement clothing.

Diseases of varying kinds were always a problem, especially when living in roughly-made shelters out in the open. Sandfly fever, scabies and Malta Dog were all regular features of life in the field. In September, Frank contracted catarrhal jaundice and was so ill he spent the next couple of weeks at the military hospital at Imtarfa, where Meme Cortis was working as a VAD. Even there, military discipline was maintained and, despite a high temperature, Frank was still expected to 'lie to attention' during inspections by the matron.

Frank rejoined 'C' Company in October to discover that a new system of 24-hour leave had been introduced. The idea was that the men went to the various recognized services clubs for a night of comfort instead of being made to return to their billets, tents or shelters at 11 p.m. as had previously been the case. Frank, like most soldiers when given time off, had tended to head straight to Valletta. There, the majority would make their way to The Gut, a notorious hang-out. But it was not Frank's scene at all. 'There were prostitutes and all sorts, but that didn't suit me. I was brought up to be a good upstanding man.'

It says much about Frank that he was. Many with his background would have taken a more rebellious course. Perhaps those early years with his mother, father and sister in Padworth had instilled in him a sense of honesty and decency that, despite everything, he never lost. His father, John, had been a carter, and in summer Frank and the other kids would go down to the fields where they were cutting the corn and watch the harvesting, and then cough from the dust and chaff from the threshing machine. In winter he would ride on the back of the horses

as his father ploughed the soil. He liked helping out whenever he could
– fetching the milk from the cooling plant on Kersley Farm, or cutting
up the cow-cake and stacking the hay. On Sundays, the family went to
church and Frank went to Sunday school. Every evening, they would sit
down to supper, cooked on the stove in the fireplace. Living in the
country, they always ate well, with plenty of fresh meat, vegetables and
fruit. As a treat, his dad would sometimes take him to the local pub, the
Hare and Hounds, for a glass of lemonade while his father drank a pint
or two.

This idyllic childhood came to an abrupt end when Frank's mother
died in February 1930, three weeks after his ninth birthday. Shortly
afterwards, he was sent to St Edward's Home in Huntingdon. His father
had no choice: he had to work and could not be at home to look after
his son. From the modest comfort of a farm cottage, Frank found
himself sleeping in a large dormitory, and learning to darn his own
socks and sew his own clothes, something that would stand him in good
stead later on in the Army. The matron who looked after the boys was
strict, yet caring, but it wasn't home. Frank rarely made it back to
Padworth; he wasn't even able to go home for Christmas. 'I hope you
had a happy Christmas with daddy,' he wrote to his sister Irene, then
hastily added, 'I am very well and happy.' Life must have been hard for
him, though, especially when, the following April, his father also died.
Irene, who was older, took him away for occasional holidays, but his old
life had been snatched from him and there would be no more returns
to Padworth. At fourteen he was sent to St Augustine's Waifs and Strays
Home in Sevenoaks in Kent. It was a severe environment, but the staff
were kindly. Each boy was given different jobs, 'but they didn't mistreat
you or anything.' The experience taught him discipline, and so joining
the local regiment as a boy soldier was the obvious next step. He missed
his family terribly, but was not bitter about his fate. Instead, he learned
to take everything that life threw at him squarely on the chin, and see
the best in every situation in which he found himself.

As a small boy and then at the two homes, Frank had been taught to
trust in God and to draw comfort from the Church. This was something
he had accepted without question, and he arrived on Malta with his
faith and belief in Christian ideals intact. It was only natural, then, that
with the new 24-hour leave system, Frank should be drawn to the Toc
H Club in Sliema. Founded during the First World War, Toc H was a
Christian services club with branches all over the world. The one in

Sliema had been set up primarily for Other Ranks and was a place where servicemen could get an inexpensive meal, drink, hot shower and clean bed. Working there was a girl named Mary Whillie, and on one of Frank's first visits the two began talking. Mary's father, like Frank's, had died when she was young. She was also a devout Christian. They were immediately drawn to one another, and Frank was soon spending as much time at the Toc H Club as he possibly could. With his parents long gone, and with no home back in England, it's not surprising that his friendship with Mary soon became greatly important to him.

By the autumn, the RAF had won the Battle of Britain and staved off the threat of German invasion. Malta was surviving too and increasing her strength with every passing week. A number of twin-engine Wellington bombers arrived in October, and so George Burges and the fighter pilots of 261 Squadron were moved to Takali, further west on the Island, beneath the ancient citadel of Mdina, leaving Luqa – with its proper runways – for use by the heavier bombers.

And although curfews were still in place, it was felt no longer necessary to confine service families to barracks. A voluntary evacuation back to Britain was announced, but both Suzanne Parlby and her friend Elisabeth Young had decided to stay. Suzanne was having far too much fun and was determined not to fall back into her parents' clutches. With no desire to work as a nurse in the middle of the Island, she resigned as a VAD and moved to Valletta, taking a room at the St James Hotel. Although sorry to no longer be living with Elisabeth and Midge, her sudden independence was rather exciting. She loved the hotel too: it was a beautiful old building, built in the form of a square. Suzanne had a room on the second floor with a balcony overlooking the courtyard.

Nor was there any question of being idle. There were plenty of jobs going for young English women such as her, and she soon started work for Military Intelligence as a cipher decoder in the Auberge de Castille, the Army Headquarters and one of the largest of the old Knights' palaces. At the heart of Valletta, it was also only a five-minute walk from the St James Hotel. Working a daily eight-hour shift, she was allowed an hour off for lunch, when she would usually meet people for drinks and a bite to eat in the 'Snakepit', a long room that served as a mixed bar in the Union Club on Kingsway. Two locally grown crops were potatoes and tomatoes, and so Suzanne's regular lunchtime fare was a plate of chips and tomato ketchup. The Snakepit was also the best place to hear any new gossip. Pretty young English girls were in short supply, and despite being married, she was never short of attention. Suzanne was enjoying every minute.

On 28 October, the situation in the Mediterranean changed again when Mussolini invaded Greece. Hitler had made an unexpected visit to Il Duce specifically to try to dissuade him from doing so, only to be greeted in Florence with the news that the Italians were already on the march. Hitler was furious; he had wanted Greece to remain neutral, since then his flank in the Balkans would remain safe from British interference, and he could continue to leave his all-important Rumanian oilfields largely unprotected. Increasingly aware of Italian military unreliability, he now had to consider taking an active role in the Mediterranean to oust the British and protect his oilfields. Mussolini, with this rash drive for personal glory, was becoming more of a hindrance than a help.

Ever since 11 June, Churchill had feared Germany would be forced to come to the Italians' rescue in the Mediterranean theatre. Now he believed that the need for a decisive attack against the Italians, in their own waters, before the Germans showed up, was becoming ever more pressing.

But Cunningham and his staff had been busy with other duties. His fleet had escorted nearly 2,000 further troops to Malta at the end of September and another convoy at the beginning of October, which had used up much of his resources. On 11 October, the cruiser HMS *Ajax* had sighted three enemy destroyers, sunk two and put the third, the *Artigliere*, out of action. The following day, the cruiser HMS *York* found the stricken ship and blew her up. The plume of smoke rose several miles high. Swordfish from the aircraft carriers *Eagle* and *Illustrious* had also been bombing Leros in the Dodecanese off the coast of Turkey, but at the same time ABC's fleet had been coming under considerable night torpedo attacks, and not without damage.

As a result, he was not a little irritated to receive a signal from London suggesting he should hurry up with offensive operations. Since ABC was hardly backward in taking the fight to the enemy, it was clear that Churchill did not appreciate the limited resources at his admiral's command. His ageing ships could not do everything that was asked of them. Even so, he had been working with the staff of the Fleet Air Arm aboard HMS *Illustrious* preparing a daring attack on the Italian naval base at Taranto, using torpedo-carrying Fairey Swordfish flying off the aircraft carrier. Success would depend entirely on the closest possible co-operation with Tich Whiteley's 431 Reconnaissance Flight, newly based at Malta, which throughout October had been making regular photographic visits over the base. Plans were well under way by mid-October and ABC, again with a nod to history, had hoped to carry out the attack on 21 October, the anniversary of Nelson's great triumph at Trafalgar. Had there not been a fire in one of *Illustrious*'s hangars, he would have had his wish, but since the attack had to be at night, they now had to wait until the next suitable moon. This was to be on 11 November.

On his second flight, Adrian Warburton had not only managed to take to the air safely, but had also landed without mishap. Tich Whiteley had breathed a sigh of relief and from then on began to use him as a pilot on a more regular basis. On 9 October, though, Warby flew as Whiteley's navigator and stunned his CO by picking out all the Italian ships in Taranto, which were later confirmed by the photographs. For this work they received considerable praise. The following day, Warby flew himself, and again, managed to take some excellent pictures of the Italian fleet lying at anchor. The other members of the reconnaissance flight were beginning to take note of his exceptional eyesight and ability to pick out and accurately identify the Italian ships.

His reputation as a pilot was growing as well. His take-offs and landings were still painful to watch, but in the air he demonstrated a lightness of touch that surprised his crews. On 30 October, with just twelve days to go until the planned attack on Taranto, the weather was poor but, undeterred, Warby set off in one of the Marylands to photograph the Italian harbour once again. Because of the cloud cover, he was forced to fly in low and take oblique photographs instead of the normal high overhead shots. Unsurprisingly, they flew into considerable anti-aircraft fire. Despite this, Warby took his pictures and managed to escape. On the return trip, they ran into an Italian seaplane. Although reconnaissance planes were not fighters and were armed only for self-defence, and despite never having had any gunnery training, Warby opened fire and shot the plane into the sea.

A few days later, the weather was still poor, as gloomy and grey as anything back home in England. Nor was there any sign of it clearing between Malta and Taranto. None of the other reconnaissance crews were flying to the Italian naval base in such weather, but Warby was undaunted. 'We're going at zero feet the whole way,' he told his two crew, Sergeants Johnny Spires and Paddy Moren. 'Get yourself a sharp pencil and plenty of paper. If we can't photograph the ships you'll have to plot them on the harbour map,' he said to Spires, while instructing Moren to read out loud across the intercom the names on the sides of the ships. The two men cursed; surely it was madness to attempt such a trip.[7]

Over the sea to Taranto there was not a single break in the cloud. The air was grey and dense, the sea calm and flat. The Marylands had taken considerable punishment since their arrival eight weeks before, and theirs had been riddled by bullets and shards of flak, so that it whistled with the air going through all the holes.

As Taranto emerged, they saw that the normal barrage balloons had been lowered; the weather had clamped down so much, the Italians were not expecting visitors. Catching the enemy completely unawares, they circled twice around the harbour, calling out the names of the ships with the camera clicking. Suddenly the harbour's anti-aircraft defences woke up, and unleashed a hailstorm of tracer, flak and machine-gun fire. Warby flew the plane as low as he could and skimmed out of the fray.

Only there was an anomaly. Safely out of reach they began to compare notes and realized that their observations did not compare with the previous day's reconnaissance: they had counted out six battleships when there should have been only five. Warby's reaction was instant. 'We'll have to go in again,' he told the other two, and ordered them to count off the battleships out loud together. Turning back in, Warby took them so low the wingtips were almost skimming the surface of the sea. Although they avoided the worst of the anti-aircraft fire, there were still plenty of orange tracer flashes shooting around them and Spires wondered how they could ever escape alive. 'One, two, three, four, five,' they counted out loud as the Maryland weaved between the anchored ships. There were still only five – they had mistaken a cruiser for a battleship.[8]

Miraculously, they got away, but by this time they were being pursued by four Italian planes – three fighter biplanes and a seaplane. Moren fired off most of his ammunition, shooting down their second seaplane and damaging one of the fighters. This was enough to deter the Italians, who broke off the attack. Four hours after they had taken off, they touched back down at Luqa. It was only then that they discovered part of an aerial from one of the Italian ships was caught in their tail-wheel.

In the build-up to the attack, Warby was flying over the Italian naval base almost every day. On the 7th, he was again pursued by enemy fighters on his return to Malta. This time they were four Macchi 200s. Although they were both faster and more manœuvrable than the Maryland, Warby had discovered that lowering a wing flap – normally used when landing – slowed both the speed and turn of the aircraft to such an extent that the Macchis overshot him. In an unusually long running battle, Warby managed to claim his third enemy plane, before once again escaping unscathed. But while luck certainly played its part, mounting experience and confidence were crucial. He also had two vital advantages: outstanding eyesight and spatial awareness, attributes shared by the finest pilots.

Three days later he photographed five battleships, fourteen cruisers and 27 destroyers lying in Taranto harbour. By the following day, a sixth battleship *had* arrived, which he was able to photograph and confirm on the afternoon of the 11th, the final reconnaissance before the attack.

At six that evening, Cunningham gave the order to prepare for attack. 'Good luck, then,' he signalled to the *Illustrious*, 'to your lads and their enterprise. Their success may well have a most important bearing on the course of the war in the Mediterranean.'[9]

By 8 p.m., the *Illustrious* was in position, some 170 miles from Taranto. There would be two attacks, the plan the same for both. Aircraft would drop flares to light up the battleships in the Mar Grande – the larger, outer part of the harbour – then dive-bomb the cruisers and destroyers anchored in the smaller, inner harbour, the Mar Piccolo, while the strike force made a torpedo strike on the battleships. The first squadron began taking off at 8.35 p.m. The moon was high and clear, only a few thin clouds occasionally drifting across. Just before 11 p.m., the harbour defences heard them and the sky erupted with a cacophony of guns. The reception they received was intense, but most managed to complete their task and make good their escape. Just before midnight, the second squadron arrived, and again carried out their task as planned. Only two of the Swordfish were lost.

Although the pilots reported strikes, they had not hung around to observe their handiwork; this was left to 431 Reconnaissance Flight the following day. It was an anxious few hours for all involved, not least Cunningham, who, pacing about on HMS *Warspite*, spent the night and next morning on tenterhooks. Tich Whiteley, who flew over Taranto in the morning, was able to report considerable damage, and the photographs, once developed, confirmed what he had seen: three battle-ships sunk or damaged and a cruiser and two destroyers damaged. Half the Italian battle fleet had been put out of action. Within days, the remainder of the fleet moved out of Taranto, and further north to Naples. The strike had been a crushing blow for the Italians.

ABC was thrilled. With the Italian fleet at Naples, it would be just as easy for Warburton and his colleagues to keep tabs on their movements. With fewer battleships, the threat of Italian fleet interference with British Mediterranean convoys was lessened. It had decisively altered the balance of sea-power once more in the Mediterranean. Congratulations poured in, and ABC noted that one from the King, especially, 'gave the greatest satisfaction to the whole fleet.'[10]

Cunningham was also delighted that his cherished RAF reconnaissance team had vindicated him so emphatically; in a note to Air Commodore Maynard, the AOC Malta, he again underlined their importance, point-ing out that the Taranto attack would have been impossible without them.

Warby's contribution had been considerable. In just two months he had been transformed from a washed-up, good-for-nothing misfit into one of the most daring, reliable and indefatigable members of Whiteley's team. Something, somewhere, had clicked for Adrian Warburton. For his work over Taranto, he was awarded a Distinguished Flying Cross. His moment to shine had finally arrived.

Taranto is still celebrated by the Royal Navy every year on 11 November. Several thousand miles away to the east, the Japanese noted with interest the details of the British victory. It was to become the blueprint for their own attack on Pearl Harbor, just over a year later, in December 1941.

Later in November another convoy successfully arrived in Malta, with no losses at all. 20,000 tons of supplies were successfully unloaded. The same month, the 4th Battalion of the Royal East Kent Regiment arrived, as did more guns, spare barrels, ammunition, gun crews and RAF ground crews, which were immediately sent to reinforce the airfields of Takali and Luqa. In total, nearly three-and-a-half thousand men. It was still not enough – there was never enough fuel or ammu-nition, and fighter planes, particularly, were still in conspicuously short supply – but Malta was now teeming with troops and service personnel. At least they were now giving themselves a chance.

The only blight amidst this successful new influx was the loss of eight Hurricanes sent to reinforce 261 Squadron – a particular blow considering how few of them there were on the Island. Flying from the aircraft carrier *Argus* on 17 November, only four of the original twelve ever made it to Malta. Possibly because the *Argus* was too far away, or maybe due to pilot inexperience, the remainder ran out of fuel and ditched into the sea. It was a disaster that had to be avoided at all costs in the future.

Still, morale was high. The people of Malta, civilians and the armed services alike, were learning to work round the Italian air raids. Many had become so blasé they had stopped bothering to take cover even when the raiders arrived. Christina Ratcliffe and the Whizz-Bangs had never been more popular. And although Suzanne Parlby had given up acting since taking her job with Military Intelligence, the Warren sisters were as indefatigable as ever, coming in from the field to put on a play at a 70-seat venue in South Street, Valletta. *Lover's Leap – A Comedy in Three Acts* ran for six nights at the beginning of December. The siege had prompted a few new caveats – ticket-buyers were reassured that there was an air raid shelter on the premises and that, in the event of sudden postponement, tickets would be either transferred or refunded – but otherwise it was business as usual. The play was a roaring success.

Many of the services also held dances in the run-up to Christmas. The Vernon Club, near to the Castille, was a popular venue. There was still enough drink on the Island for everyone to have a good time. Spot dances with prizes were laid on and whilst the men paid a modest entrance fee, ladies, because of their rarity value, were 'cordially invited'.[11] Suzanne Parlby, who loved dancing, went as often as she could. Her husband was particularly light on his feet, a prowess that had done much to attract her to him in the first place.

Malta ended 1940 in good heart. The Italian attacks had been largely ineffective; the Navy and the RAF were even taking the attack to the enemy, and supplies were getting through. The *Times of Malta* was reporting with glee that Mussolini's Greek campaign, far from being the glory-march Il Duce had expected, was crumbling fast. The Greeks, with the weather and their knowledge of the terrain on their side, were now pushing the Italians back. Across the Mediterranean in North Africa, the British forces were making ground too, with General Wavell's troops clawing their way towards the Libyan border. And with the Battle of Britain won and the threat of German invasion over,

Maynard's pilots could look forward to greater fighter aircraft re-inforcements in the months to come. If this was a siege, then Malta could take it.

PART II

The Arrival of the Germans

'The entire Island rocked to the shock of battle.'

MALTA DOCKYARD WORKER E.T. HEDLEY

CHAPTER 5

The *Illustrious* Blitz

JANUARY 1941

O N TUESDAY 10 December 1940, the brand-new Unity-class
submarine, HMS/S *Upholder* inched out of Portsmouth harbour
and set course for Gibraltar. From there she would then sail on
to her ultimate destination: Malta.

Newly on board was a 23-year-old lieutenant named Michael Crawford.
A week before *Upholder* had been due to sail, the First Lieutenant
had been recommended for a Commanding Officer's course, and so
Lieutenant-Commander Wanklyn had found himself short of a second-
in-command. Crawford, with several years' experience in submarines
and operations throughout the Mediterranean, was the ideal person to
fill the breach. Glad of the opportunity to work on an active submarine
once more, Crawford nonetheless arrived with a certain degree of
apprehension. This was understandable: after all, it was not until he
joined *Upholder* that he discovered where they were headed. Nor had he
ever set foot on a Unity-class boat before (submariners refer to subs as
'boats', never ships), and was doing so by joining a crew who had
already been together for two months. Furthermore, this was his first
proper posting as a First Lieutenant.

Despite a slight frame, Michael had, ever since a young boy, been
known as 'Tubby'. He had been born a ten-pound baby, but it wasn't
until several years later, after the baby-fat had long since disappeared,
that he was given the nickname. Perhaps it had something to do with
his rounded, smiling face – at any rate, the schoolboy and services
propensity for nicknames ensured the moniker stuck.

Although Tubby had no naval background, his father had been in the Army, and when Tubby was little they had been posted to East Africa. He was sent to boarding school in England at the age of seven, then two years later his father died and Tubby's mother came back, settling on the Isle of Wight in the south of England, 'because it was the cheapest place to live at that time.' Surrounded by boats of all sizes, and the grey-green waters of the Solent, Tubby had found himself drawn to the sea. At thirteen, his widowed mother was happy to let him enter Dartmouth Naval College in Devon. 'It was quite rugged certainly,' says Tubby, but he was not put off his future career, passing out of the college at seventeen and beginning his midshipman's apprenticeship.

The path towards submarines began during this time, when he was serving on a battleship. There was plenty for a young midshipman to do, but he was always being told how and when to do it, under the command of someone else. Submarines, where each officer had a clearly defined role, seemed to offer a chance of greater responsibility. The prospect of a claustrophobic existence under water didn't worry him at all, and so having completed his sub-lieutenant's courses, he volunteered to be transferred to submarines and was sent straight to HMS *Dolphin*, the submarine training base in Gosport, near Portsmouth.

Tubby was posted from *Dolphin* to join HMS/S *Sealion* in the Mediterranean, as fourth hand – the most junior officer – with the responsibility for navigation. He was fortunate in having Commander Ben Bryant as his first skipper – an experienced submariner from whom he could learn a great deal. With the Spanish Civil War at its height, and with Italy making aggressive noises, he spent his time based at Malta working alongside the rest of the fleet in exercises preparing them for war. When this finally came in September 1939, *Sealion* initially remained where she was until it was realized she could be more use operating from home waters. During the Phoney War before Germany invaded Holland in May 1940, Tubby was taking part in regular patrols off the Dutch coast, and then *Sealion* was sent to patrol Norwegian waters. Her contribution was short-lived: in August they were rammed in the Skagerrak and her periscopes knocked off, and so had to return to England for a refit. With submarine losses already mounting and more boats being hastily built, First Lieutenants and Commanding Officers were in great demand. With *Sealion* out of action, Tubby bade farewell to his crew and hurried up to Scapa Flow in northern Scotland to train as a First Lieutenant. He had no sooner been granted his promotion than found himself being sent down the length of Britain to join *Upholder* in Portsmouth.

He had never been on a Unity-class boat before. Most current British submarines were the slightly older S- and T-class. While the T-class was the biggest and fastest in the Royal Navy, at 1,090 tons and with a surface speed of just over fifteen knots – roughly sixteen-and-a-half miles per hour – the S-class familiar to Tubby was roughly equivalent in size to the German U-boat, at just over 700 tons. But the U-class, to which *Upholder* belonged, was a mere 540 tons, with a surface speed of only eleven knots. By contrast, the German and Italian U-boats could zip along at almost twice that pace.

All submarines were cramped, and the U-class especially so. With four officers, four petty officers, four Engine Room Artificers (stokers), fifteen junior ratings and a further petty officer and three ratings when on operations, the full complement was as much as 31. To say the men were living on top of one another would be something of an understatement. The officers at least had bunks, but for the ordinary ratings, conditions were appalling. These men were confined to the forward compartment of the submarine, where the torpedoes were housed. This meant that after firing a full salvo of four torpedoes, the whole of their living quarters had to be removed to reload the torpedo tubes. Bedding came in the form of tightly packed hammocks, and in order to move, a rating had to crouch between them. There was a small washbasin, but to reach it one had to breathe in and squeeze behind the tail of a torpedo. Food and stores were also piled high, so that although there was decidedly more room towards the end of a patrol, the smell of rotting vegetables, diesel, sweat and excrement was vile. Even for the officers, who were packed into a tiny wardroom, there were no luxuries. Water was so restricted, washing could only be of the most rudimentary kind. 'Most of us didn't shave during patrol,' says Tubby, 'and it was only scraped off as we came into harbour.'

The quality of food depended on who was appointed the cook. There were no specialist cooks on board as such, so finding one of the crew who was a dab hand in the kitchen was a bonus. One of the ratings on *Upholder* had worked at the Savoy before the war, which sounded promising, but it turned out that all he'd ever done was mix sauces and peel potatoes. 'He was hopeless,' says Tubby, and so meals tended to be a combination of tinned soup, tinned meat and tinned puddings. Vegetables were brought on board, such as cabbages and potatoes, which were then either boiled or mixed up into a kind of corned beef hash. Most people got used to it. Tubby, who had survived boarding school and Dartmouth, considered he fared 'reasonably well', all things considered.

Long journeys, like the one on which *Upholder* was embarking, could be monotonous and extremely tedious. This one, at least, provided Tubby with the perfect chance to acclimatize and get to know his new crew. Once on board, the crew had little concept of night and day, although in safe waters the submarine might surface. Otherwise, she would only surface under cover of darkness to recharge her batteries. Surface speeds were faster than underwater, but the comparatively small U-class submarine suffered from any swell on the sea's surface, making conditions even more uncomfortable. The crew operated in three watches: two hours on, four hours off. Being on watch required considerable concentration. When off duty there was little to do but eat and sleep, which, because of the lack of oxygen down below, came surprisingly easily to most.

While Tubby Crawford and *Upholder* were inching their way towards Malta, Commander George Simpson, who was due to take command of the Malta submarines, had arrived in Alexandria for a meeting with Cunningham and Captain Raw, commander of the First Submarine Flotilla there. ABC, in his usual manner, gave Simpson a succinct directive. The Malta submarines were operationally under Cunningham, although in the event of an attack on Malta, he was to take orders from Wilbraham Ford, the Vice-Admiral Malta, who also, at all times, would have administrative control. The sole object of the Malta flotilla was to attack and sink Axis convoys heading towards North Africa. Northbound shipping, owing to the current shortage of torpedoes, should not be attacked unless the target was a warship, tanker or other significant merchant vessel. 'If you don't get results and don't dispose your forces to suit me I will very soon let you know,' Cunningham told him. 'Until then you have a free hand to act as you think best to achieve your object.' With that he was dismissed.[1]

On 5 January, Simpson left Alexandria, taking passage on a destroyer that arrived in Grand Harbour three days later. He was delighted with the efforts of 'Pop' Giddings, and agreed that the old Lazzaretto on Manoel Island was the ideal place to house the submarines. Giddings was to stay on to look after the maintenance of the base. Simpson also had a naval doctor and Staff Officer (Operations) on his team – the latter being an old friend of his, Lieutenant-Commander Bob Tanner.

Two days later, HMS/S *Upholder* finally reached Marsamxett Harbour, after a month's journey. They were not the only arrivals. That day, 10 January 1941, German planes made their presence felt for the first time. Just as Churchill had feared, the Luftwaffe had arrived. As Malta was to discover, this enemy was of a different calibre altogether.

Admiral Raeder, Commander-in-Chief of the German Oberkommando der Kriegsmarine (Navy High Command), had spoken to Hitler about the advantages of ousting the British from the Mediterranean on several occasions, and had found an unlikely ally in his opposite number at the Luftwaffe, Herman Göring. The two loathed each other, but both were convinced of the enormous advantages that might be brought about by German control of Suez and the Middle East. After Mussolini's intervention in Greece and the British success at Taranto, Admiral Raeder now went further, telling Hitler at the end of December, 'The naval staff regards the British fleet as the decisive factor for the outcome of the war; it is now no longer possible to drive it from the Mediterranean as we have so often proposed.' British dominance in the Mediterranean was, he warned the Führer, 'most dangerous' to the Axis powers.[2]

In fact, on 10 December, Hitler had already ordered the transfer of Fliegerkorps X – an entire air corps of some 200 planes – from their base in Norway to Sicily. By the beginning of January their Stuka dive-bombers and Junkers 88 twin-engine bombers were in place ready to attack. German intervention in the Mediterranean, however reluctantly ordered by Hitler and jealously received by Mussolini, had begun.

ABC had visited Malta before Christmas and after meetings with Governor Dobbie, and Vice-Admiral Malta Wilbraham Ford, and an official tour of the dockyards, had felt cheered that the Island seemed to be in such fine fettle. But after the Christmas lull, Cunningham was back on operations again, steaming out of Alexandria on 7 January to meet a convoy coming from Gibraltar.

To begin with, everything went according to plan, and on board *Warspite*, ABC was once more able to settle into his normal routine. A creature of habit, he rarely ventured far from the bridge and never took his clothes off except for his daily bath. His cabin and bathroom was only one ladder down, and it was here that he also had all his meals. Although the day-to-day movements of the fleet were conducted by the five commanders on his staff, Cunningham made sure he was kept informed of everything, and that he was at hand to make any decisions necessary.

Every morning, he would be on the bridge at dawn – and so he was on 10 January when, north-west of Malta, they began steering to intercept the convoy from Gibraltar. The day began promisingly enough – the fleet met with the convoy, turned and began to journey back to Malta, even though the destroyer *Gallant* was badly damaged when she hit a mine. Flying high above them were Fairey Fulmars – two-man fighter aircraft – from HMS *Illustrious*. At around 12.30 p.m., however, two Italian torpedo bombers swooped in undetected to attack. Although their efforts were unsuccessful, they did prompt the patrolling Fulmars to drop down to attack them in turn. Minutes later, a much larger formation of enemy planes appeared, which the Fulmars were now too low to do anything about. Suddenly it was action stations. Over the ship's loudspeakers came the call, 'Repel Aircraft!' Everyone rushed to their positions, the metal ladders clanging. Orders were hollered across the decks.

Then Cunningham saw them, a dark cluster high in the sky. With their tight formation and ominous gull-wing appearance, he immediately recognized these new attackers as German Stuka dive-bombers. For a moment, they seemed to hang, motionless. More Fulmars frantically flew off *Illustrious*, but there was little they could do but keep out of the way of the bombing, for it quickly became clear that the aircraft carrier was their prime target. Most, including Cunningham, had not previously experienced dive-bombing by these already infamous aircraft. Despite an intense anti-aircraft barrage put up by the fleet, the 40 Stukas peeled off, one by one, and dived, releasing their deadly load at almost point-blank range. ABC was so mesmerized by this new form of attack, he was unable to keep his eyes off them, watching as they hurtled down from around 2,000 feet, their manic sirens wailing even above the enormous din of the guns. Almost lazily, the bombs each plane carried detached themselves, prompting everyone to fall flat on the deck as the Stuka screamed past overhead – everyone, that is, except the gunners, whose ferocious barrage never let up. Colossal fountains of spray erupted into the air, soaking anyone above decks. Cunningham was keeping a watch on *Illustrious*, amazed to see the Stukas pulling out of their dives, and flying so flat along the aircraft carrier's flight deck, they were below the line of her funnel. He realized he was watching experts at work.[3]

The attack lasted just six and a half minutes, and in that time the aircraft carrier was struck six times. ABC saw it all, appalled to witness the pride of his fleet taking such a mauling. One bomb exploded just in front of the bridge; two fell through the aircraft lift, exploding in the hangar under the flight deck and setting fire to the planes there. Another obliterated one of the guns. Huge mountains of spray engulfed her, while the sky was a mass of twisting planes and exploding shells. Fierce fires broke out on and beneath the flight deck, and her crew struggled to keep them under control. Soon the deck was covered with foam from the fire extinguishers, bits of debris, including the wing of a Stuka, and empty shell cases. Thick, black smoke mushroomed high into the sky. Incredibly, she kept afloat and, despite wrecked steering gear, her engines were undamaged, and she was still able to make around seventeen knots. Having redressed the balance against the Italian fleet at Taranto, Cunningham had been shown in less than ten minutes how painfully vulnerable his fleet now was to a concerted attack from the air. Nevertheless, if they could just get *Illustrious* to Malta, where expert construction workers were available, she might have a chance.

More attacks arrived later in the afternoon, and Cunningham's heart sank; it would be a miracle if they reached the Island in time now.

Shortly after Cunningham had left Alexandria, a second convoy of two supply ships bound for Malta and a tanker sailing for Crete followed the fleet out of port. Travelling on board the escorting destroyer HMS *Diamond* was nineteen-year-old Nat Gold, on his way to join 830 Fleet Air Arm Squadron as a Swordfish Telegraphist Air Gunner (TAG). He'd already been half-way round the world since leaving Glasgow – his ship had taken him right out into the Atlantic, then down the west coast of Africa, round the Cape and back up the other side until he finally reached Port Suez. From there he took a train to Port Said, and then onto Alexandria. During the entire two-month journey, he'd had no idea where he was headed. He and three other TAGs had been serving at Lee-on-Solent in the south of England, when they'd suddenly been given an overseas posting. The only clue was the issue of tropical kit, so he knew it must be somewhere fairly warm. Only once he reached Alexandria did he finally discover his destination. Until the next convoy, Nat and his three companions had been sent to a training base at Dekheila, on the coast road west of Alexandria. Whilst there, he and one other air gunner had been drafted to join the aircrews on HMS

Illustrious in order to get a bit more experience. The same day they'd received these orders, both were on guard duty and began feeling ill – soon they were vomiting, and had diarrhoea and a high temperature, and so promptly had their postings aboard *Illustrious* withdrawn, with two others taking their place.

Having recovered, Nat was given passage on a cruiser, but again his efforts to reach Malta were foiled. No sooner had he walked up the gangway than the Officer of the Watch told him he had to turn around again as the bows were falling off. 'I thought he was joking,' says Nat. He was not: apparently two Italian torpedo bombers had attacked the ship, hitting her in the bows. These had been repaired, but on trials the day before Nat reached her, they had proved insufficiently fixed. Off he trooped, back to camp, to await instructions to join a third ship. This happened almost immediately, and the next day, 7 January, Nat boarded HMS *Diamond* and set sail for Malta, finally reaching Grand Harbour on the morning of 10 January.

Ten-year-old Michael Montebello heard the distant explosions and boom of the anti-aircraft fire and, since it was late afternoon and school had finished, he rushed up to Senglea Point Vedette, the northernmost tip of Senglea, to see what was going on. From here Michael not only had a perfect view of Grand Harbour, he could also see right out to the harbour's mouth and beyond. Fulmars from *Illustrious* were flying over, landing at Hal Far to rearm and refuel. Hurricanes of George Burges' 261 Squadron were also airborne throughout the afternoon, providing extra air cover. Around 5 p.m., as dusk was approaching, they even found themselves being fired upon by the aircraft carrier's gunners. Having been under attack, on and off, for the best part of five hours, the ship's crew were taking no chances.

Within sight of Malta's coast, *Illustrious* was again attacked, this time by Italian torpedo bombers. Earlier, the aircraft carrier's captain had been faced with the dilemma of whether to jettison her ammunition in case it was blown up, or keep hold of it for the ship's defence. He decided on the latter course, which meant *Illustrious* was able to meet any attacks with intense anti-aircraft fire. As the Italian bombers approached, her gunners peppered the sky once more. The barrage – heard by Michael Montebello in Senglea – was too much for the Italian bombers, who quickly retreated from the fray.

Down below around French Creek, Michael saw intense activity going on. Ambulances were arriving and dockyard workers were hurrying to and fro. Clearly a ship was coming into harbour, and he guessed it was one damaged in the battle raging out at sea. Tugs and two minesweepers left Grand Harbour to meet the incomer, although little did Michael realize that the ship in question was the biggest and most modern aircraft carrier in the fleet. Then, slowly, slowly, HMS *Illustrious* crept into view.

Nat Gold, who had arrived earlier at the Fleet Air Arm airfield of Hal Far, looked out and saw the ship just off the coast. Listing badly, with fires clearly visible and thick smoke following her, she struggled past the breakwaters. He couldn't help thinking he should have been on that ship and wondered what had happened to the man who'd taken his place. In fact, his replacement was already dead: he had been sitting in one of the Fulmars in the lift between the hangars and the flight deck when a bomb had scored a direct hit. Nat still owed him ten piastres.

Michael Montebello watched the aircraft carrier, straddled by tugs, creep past the harbour breakwater. He had never seen a ship in such a state before, especially not one so big, and it made him feel sad. Eventually, at around nine o'clock that night, *Illustrious* was berthed at Parlatorio Wharf, on the western side of French Creek. Against the odds, she had made it, although many onboard had not: 126 of her crew were dead and 91 wounded.

At Imtarfa Hospital, Meme Cortis and the rest of the medical staff had been on standby, waiting to receive a number of the wounded. After months of comparative calm, they were now facing their first proper emergency – 60 wounded were being sent to them. Beds had to be made ready, transfusion equipment set up. Naval medical staff had already been transferred to help out, and every surgeon, doctor, sister and nurse at the hospital was expected to be on duty.

For Meme, it was a hectic period. There was little chance for rest. Patients were continuously in and out of the operating theatre. 'It was chaotic,' she says, 'like Paddington station with everyone rushing from one person to the next.' Most suffered from severe burns, their bodies pitted black, so that Meme could not see their faces or tell what they once looked like. Many were in constant agony; she wished she could block out their screams and groans, for there was little she could do but help swab and spray their charred skin with Gentian Violet and Acraflavine. With the smell of burnt flesh and antiseptic filling the wards, the brief moments when she could go outside to breathe fresh air were to be savoured.

At Takali airfield on the morning of the 11th, George Burges and the rest of the fighter pilots were waiting for the Germans to arrive. News about the newly arrived Luftwaffe and the intensity with which they attacked had spread fast. Clearly, it was only a matter of time before *Illustrious* was attacked again. Yet to their amazement, only a few Italian bombers appeared all day. It was a much-needed respite, allowing the merchant vessel *Essex*, which Cunningham and his fleet had originally been protecting, to reach Malta safely. With more guns and ammunition, as well as twelve crated Hurricanes, it was imperative that her cargo was unloaded as quickly as possible; every gun and shell available would be needed in the attack that would surely come. Frustratingly, the stevedores first had to unload 3,000 tons of potatoes under which the guns were buried.

Malta's dockworkers were also struggling round the clock to repair *Illustrious* as quickly as possible and ensure she safely made her escape back to Alexandria. Once the fires were finally extinguished, her decks were cleared of rubble and hastily painted yellow in an effort to camouflage her against the docks and buildings of French Creek. Most of her dead were also put aboard a minesweeper and taken out of the harbour and along the south coast to be given the traditional naval burial at sea. For many, however, this was to be an ignominious end. The burial was conducted with too much haste, and many of the bodies were not suitably weighted and later resurfaced, to be found grimly bobbing beneath the southern cliffs.

But safeguarding the living was now the primary concern. With only sixteen serviceable Hurricanes and a couple of Gladiators, the brunt of the defence was to be borne by the anti-aircraft gunners around the harbour. These were all trained to create the maximum intensity barrage possible – a box of destructive metal – through which any dive-bomber would have to fly. It was agreed that the fighters would only attack before the enemy planes came into range of the gunners, and afterwards, when the Stukas were coming out of their dive and at their most vulnerable. In a pre-emptive move, Luqa-based Wellington bombers also made a night-time strike on the Axis airfield of Catania, in Sicily.

The defenders of Malta held their breath, and waited.

Nothing happened on the 12th. A few Stukas appeared on the 13th – the *Illustrious* their obvious target – but were way off their mark, as were the Hurricanes, scrambled too late to intercept them. And apart from an occasional reconnaissance plane, no bombers appeared on the next two days either. All was strangely quiet. No sirens, no explosions; only the clanging and banging of the workers on *Illustrious* ringing out across Grand Harbour.

Michael Montebello and his friends had spent a lot of time watching the activity going on around French Creek since the aircraft carrier's arrival. They too had heard talk about the Germans reaching Sicily, and knew all about the Stuka dive-bombers and the Messerschmitt 109 fighters. There were pictures of them in magazines and Michael had seen footage of the Stukas on the newsreels they showed at the cinema. For a young boy, the prospect of seeing these infamous machines for real seemed more exciting than frightening.

Thursday 16 January was bright and sunny, even quite warm for the time of year. Just before two o'clock in the afternoon, Michael was making his way back to school after his lunch break, when the siren suddenly rang out. It had been drummed into all the children that in the event of a raid they were to make for the nearest shelter straight away, and so, clutching his gas mask, he hurried into the one next to his school along with many of the others.

In what seemed like no time at all, they heard the first explosions crash above them, and then the barrage opened up, a continual staccato boom reverberating through the rock.

'Oh my God, my God, those bombs,' recalls Michael. Despite being deep underground, the whole Island appeared to shake and tremble. The intensity and ferocity of the attack was unlike anything that had come before. Most began crying and screaming; some shouted prayers. Thick, choking dust filled the air. More whistles and muffled crumps from above, then suddenly a louder, more defined explosion, followed by a strong wave of blast. Michael sat there, terrified, a ten-year-old boy hugging his knees tightly into his chest, with the smell of cordite filling his nose and lungs, and wondering whether the shelter would collapse. It sounded as though the whole of Senglea was being pounded into dust. He didn't want to be on his own – he wanted to be with his mother and father and his younger brother Freddie, and began panicking about where they were. The worst possible thoughts kept going through his mind. What if they hadn't got to a shelter in time? What if they'd still been in the house and a bomb had landed on top of them?

The raid continued. Even below ground, the noise of the bombs and the rumbling crash of falling masonry were deafening.

Suddenly it was over, the noise stopped, so that all that could be heard were the cries and wails of the people in the shelter with him. They were supposed to wait for the All Clear, but he just wanted to get home and see that everything was still all right, and so he ran up the steps and out into the street. Huge clouds of smoke and dust still enveloped the whole of Senglea and French Creek; he could not see the *Illustrious*. High piles of stone and rubble littered the road. Reaching Victory Street, which ran the length of Senglea, he saw nothing but carnage and destroyed buildings. Terrified for the safety of his family, he clambered as quickly as he could from Our Lady of Victories Church to his own church of St Philip's. As far as he could tell not a single building had been left untouched.

Then he saw his house – still standing. Moments later his mother appeared and he ran to her. The relief was overwhelming for both of them, for she had been every bit as concerned about him as he had about her. Both she and Freddie had been in a different shelter, while his father had stayed above ground and was already helping with the rescue work. However, the Senglea that Michael had known just a half-hour before – the town where he had been born and brought up and where he'd spent nearly all his life – now lay in ruins.

Frank Rixon was helping to man a defence post on the edge of Luqa airfield when the sirens had rung out. Lying on a plateau a couple of miles south of Grand Harbour, Luqa afforded a clear view of Valletta and the harbour, and Frank found himself with a grandstand view of the attack that was about to happen. The distant drone of aircraft gradually became clearer and closer and he looked up to see the sky thick with Stuka dive-bombers and other German aircraft. He had never seen so many nor the attackers this low – the Italian bombers were often so high it was impossible to see them.

Then one by one they peeled off and dived, just as the anti-aircraft barrage opened fire. The guns recently installed at Marsa and Luqa had been trained to join the harbour barrage and now began firing furiously. Frank clutched his helmet tightly onto his head: it wasn't just the enemy one needed to worry about, but the shrapnel falling back down to the ground from the exploding shells. The noise was absolutely deafening and, from where he was, Frank could hear nothing but the roar of the barrage. The reverberations made the ground tremble. As though in a silent film, the dive-bombers plummeted over the harbour – it looked as if they were going to crash straight into houses, or into the harbour itself, but then a bomb would fall and the plane would level out. The sky was filled with swirling aircraft and dotted thick with black puffs of smoke from exploding shells. Huge fountains of water spurted high above Grand Harbour. Soon smoke from the bomb damage began drifting into the sky as well. Occasionally, a Stuka could be seen trailing smoke, or even exploding in mid-air with a bright and sudden orange flash. One plane even landed in the sea just in front of Senglea Point Vedette, where Michael Montebello had watched *Illustrious* arrive the previous weekend.

Christina Ratcliffe had been in a bad way all week, ever since hearing the news about her friends Jacques and René. She'd known them some months, ever since a performance by the Whizz-Bangs at Hal Far. The two had been Free French airmen who had crash-landed on Malta and been drafted into 431 Reconnaissance Flight. She was particularly fond of Jacques Mehouas, who, she knew, had fallen in love with her and with whom she had started an affair. But on 10 January, Jacques had visited her in a state of great agitation. He had some new top secret information, he told her, and urged her from now on to take immediate cover as soon as an air raid siren rang out. 'Promise, chérie,' he asked her. Christina promised. The next day, Jacques was shot down over Sicily. His 'top secret' information had been the arrival of the Germans, discovered during reconnaissance trips over Italy.[4]

Now, on the afternoon of the 16th, Christina sensed something more sinister in the wailing of the warning siren, and her promise to Jacques came back to her. Hurrying from her flat in Floriana, she made for the concrete shelter underneath the nearby Engine Room Artificers' Club. She was only just in time. The attack that followed was 'an aerial Armageddon that beggars description'.[5] She and a friend crouched in the shelter, terrified and clutching one another every time another bomb fell nearby.

After the raid, she cautiously went back up to the streets, fully expecting to find the whole of Floriana flattened. But as had happened six months before, the town gradually emerged once more through the dust. Then she became aware of the streets filling with people, all surging towards the ramparts overlooking the harbour. Christina followed them.

Illustrious was still there, but the Three Cities lay in ruins. She felt numb, thinking of the dead lying there among the rubble.

At Scots Street, in Valletta, John Agius had been working as usual at the RAF Headquarters when the sirens sounded. Few bombs had yet landed on the city and in recent weeks the raids had trickled to almost nothing, so even though he knew the *Illustrious* was in harbour, he did not bother heading for the shelter. Instead, once the barrage opened, he got down on his knees and crouched under his desk, a large metal trestle table, six foot by three foot, and hoped for the best. The noise was unlike anything he had ever heard before. 'With all the stuff coming down and all the stuff going up, it was the most terrific din, absolutely terrific,' says John. After the second wave had passed, he went outside to see what was going on. Looking down the hill, he saw a large block of flats on Old Mint Street now lay in ruins. Realizing it must have received a direct hit, he made his way down there. All that remained were piles of rubble some twelve feet high. He couldn't imagine how anyone could possibly have survived under it all, and shuddered at the thought; while he was not afraid of death itself, the prospect of being entombed under a pile of rubble and slowly suffocating terrified him. But John had been right about those trapped underneath the collapsed block of flats. Seven died there that afternoon, buried under hundreds of tons of sandstone and masonry. Later that evening, John returned home. All his family were safe, but Emanuel had experienced a curious coincidence. The raiders had finally passed at a quarter to four in the afternoon, and he had stepped out of the hospital for some fresh air. He had with him a book of Hilaire Belloc's poems and by chance opened it on the following lines:

It is now a quarter to four
We have had quite enough of this horrible stuff
And we don't want to hear any more.[6]

No wonder the battle had been so fierce: the Germans had sent over a hundred planes during that first raid on *Illustrious*. Commander George Simpson had been in Valletta, on an appointment to see Wilbraham Ford, the Vice-Admiral Malta, when the bombers had arrived. 'Looking up, the bombers were in flights of five like arrowheads in a straight line, at precise intervals of about 800 yards as far as the eye could see. Silver flashes around and above them indicated their fighter escorts glinting in the sun.'[7] Unable to bear watching the inevitable destruction of *Illustrious*, Simpson had taken shelter with a heavy heart.

But *Illustrious* survived. The narrow French Creek, surrounded by Corradino Heights on one side and Senglea on the other, offered considerable protection. Despite the experience of the bomber pilots, scoring a direct hit was a tall order, even when dropping a bomb at less than 500 feet. With the huge clouds of dust and smoke caused by damage to buildings either side of the ship, this task was made even harder. The Stuka pilots, diving through a curtain of molten steel, simply could not see their target after the first few bombs had exploded. Even so, the ship was hit by one bomb, although it caused little damage. The merchant vessel *Essex* was also struck, killing fifteen of her crew and seven stevedores. By this time, all the potatoes and guns had been unloaded, but not all the ammunition. Crew and fire-fighters rushed frantically to extinguish the fires caused by the blast before the whole ship blew. Part of the ancient bastions around Senglea had also collapsed, crashing into the rocks beneath them.

As soon as the raids had passed, the Montebellos wasted no time in gathering themselves together and once more fleeing their home. With his parents, grandparents, brother and several aunts and uncles, Michael made his way down to the harbour. There they loaded themselves and basic belongings onto a *dghajsa* – a Maltese gondola – and set off out towards the far end of Grand Harbour. From there they trudged wearily back to the house in Hamrun where they had stayed after the first attacks back in June. Nor were they the only ones – by the following morning, Senglea was once again a ghost town, although this time it lay in ruins. Michael was not to know it then, but he had just left Senglea for the last time.

The following day, Christina Ratcliffe and a friend took the ferry across Grand Harbour to see the damage to Senglea for themselves. Boulders and blocks of stone barred their way. They moved cautiously beneath overhanging balconies and walls, which looked as though they were about to tumble any moment. They scrambled over piles of rock. One street had been entirely razed to the ground. A line of washing flapped against the only remaining wall of a three-storey house. Goats, normally driven from doorstep to doorstep delivering milk, lay dead, strewn in every street. Around certain houses, rescue workers were digging for corpses. A number of onlookers, mostly relatives of the missing, were standing about, distraught and singing a kind of Maltese dirge, oblivious of requests to keep quiet to enable the rescuers to listen for a cry or noise from beneath the debris. Christina and her friend returned to Floriana with heavy hearts.

The Luftwaffe returned in strength on Saturday 18 January, this time making for the airfields of Luqa and Hal Far in an attempt to cripple the RAF fighters before returning to finish off the *Illustrious*. As it was the weekend, John Agius was at home in Sliema, and so he and his brother Joseph climbed onto the flat roof of the house and watched the airfields being attacked three miles to the south of them. 'My God, they're just like a horde of ants,' said his brother. Watching the tiny, vicious specks peeling off one after the other, John had to agree.

Most of the fighters were now based at Takali, and George Burges found himself scrambled four times that day. Their efforts to intercept the bombers on the 16th had been largely unsuccessful, but this time they were more fortunate, and Burges managed to shoot down one Stuka and damage two others. The greatest difficulty was avoiding their own anti-aircraft fire – when pursuing a plane it was very easy to keep on going then find oneself flying straight into the curtain of fire.

The raiders continued with their attacks on *Illustrious* the following day, the first wave arriving just after eight-thirty in the morning. By ten o'clock, George Burges had added another couple of Stukas to his name. He, like many of his colleagues, could not help but rather admire the German pilots, who fearlessly dived into the storm of concentrated fire without ever deviating from their task. The contrast with the Italians could not have been greater. Furthermore, despite their terrifying siren and deadly bombing ability, Stukas were comparatively easy meat even for the Hurricanes, which had considerably greater agility, speed and fire-power – as many pilots had discovered in England during the early stages of the Battle of Britain.

Because of the shortage of men, the fighter pilots were still working in four-hour shifts. This meant sitting strapped into their cockpits while they waited for enemy raids in order to save a few precious minutes in getting airborne. The planes were tired, past their shelf-life and often patched up with bits and pieces cobbled together from other aircraft. George Burges, in 'A' Flight, was on the eight till noon shift, and having a frantic morning – one which was even putting the early days of the Gladiators into the shade. By eleven he had just returned from his second flight of the day, when there was another alarm. His plane had not yet been refuelled and rearmed, so he jumped straight into another, already prepared for take-off. This time the Germans were attacking with Junkers 88s – twin-engine bombers – their target once again the *Illustrious*. Over Grand Harbour Burges saw the sky was dotted with black puffs – the now familiar sight of anti-aircraft shells exploding. Spotting a formation of German bombers, he dived in after them, and latched onto the tail of one. Although he was firing long bursts from his guns, so was the rear-gunner of the Junkers. Suddenly a bullet burst through the cockpit and miraculously hit the buckle of his parachute harness, leaving him with nothing worse than a bruised shoulder. It had happened in a trice, but had been a heart-stopping moment nonetheless. Undeterred, Burges pressed on, his finger jammed down on the firing button until, with his fifteen seconds' ammunition almost spent, he saw the Junkers' port engine catch fire.

John Agius had once again been watching the raids, amazed by the huge clouds of smoke and dust that drifted into the air, covering Grand Harbour and then wafting out to sea. These clouds once again saved the *Illustrious*, making the German bombers virtually blind as they released their loads. Several bombs landed in the water nearby, exploding with much the same effect as a mine, but the aircraft carrier suffered no serious damage. Instead it was the dockyards and the surrounding Three Cities, and especially Senglea once again, that suffered most damage. By the last raid on Sunday 19, Senglea had lost nearly a hundred lives and 330 buildings. The damage was too great for the local services to deal with and so the Royal West Kents were asked to help clear up. After months of being static, Frank Rixon was suddenly very busy. 'We just did whatever needed to be done. Half the time we didn't know where we were headed until we got there,' he says. Sometimes this meant moving the whole company, at other times just a platoon. One day they were at Marsa, the next Luqa. Now, they were off to Senglea to shift lumps of sandstone and heave away the mounting piles of rubble. Having set up an HQ at the Senglea police station, men of the Royal West Kents assisted in the rescue work, toiling round the clock for the next ten days. Any minute the Germans were expected to attack again, and so with desperate urgency they cleared away the debris. Troops, civilians, ARP services, police, dockworkers, stevedores all worked together; around Grand Harbour and the Three Cities they never stopped.

But the Germans, for the time being at any rate, had had enough. On the night of 23 January, after Herculean efforts on the part of the dockyard workers, HMS *Illustrious* was considered fit enough to sail. Slipping out of Grand Harbour, she steamed towards Alexandria, arriving safely at noon on the 25th. Cunningham, in *Warspite*, was there to cheer her in. Her survival was little short of a miracle.

The '*Illustrious* Blitz', as it came to be known, signalled the beginning of the siege proper. Civilians had witnessed destruction on a scale they had not previously imagined, while the gunners and pilots had been tested harder than at any stage during the war. Malta might have been reinforced since the days following 11 June, but whether this would be enough to see off the kind of sustained attack the Germans had produced on 16, 18 and 19 January was extremely doubtful.

CHAPTER 6

The Tightening of the Screw
JANUARY–FEBRUARY 1941

UBBY CRAWFORD HAD known Malta was likely to be a tough posting, but his first two weeks had exceeded all expectations. After the long voyage from Portsmouth, a number of adjustments and repairs needed to be carried out on *Upholder* before there was any question of her heading off for her first combat patrol. However, because the maintenance depot at Manoel Island was not yet up and running, Tubby and the rest of the crew had taken her into Grand Harbour, where they had later watched the stricken *Illustrious* pull into the neighbouring berth in French Creek. *Upholder* had still been there when the German bombers had begun their blitz on 16 January. With the rest of the crew sheltering safely on shore, Tubby and two junior ratings had remained on board. Manning the twin Lewis machine-guns, they had valiantly fired at the dive-bombing Stukas, although with little to show for their efforts save a good soaking from the enormous fountains of spray bursting all around them. 'It was quite shattering to see so many German bombers,' admits Tubby, who was beginning to think he would be safer on patrol at sea than hanging about Malta.

As for their new submarine base, it was far from fully functioning. The building itself was pleasant enough – the rooms were spacious and the first-floor gallery overlooking Valletta a bonus – but the more essential facilities were still pretty basic.

Despite all this, morale on *Upholder* was high. The crew was gelling well, they had at least made it to Malta, and, despite a few near misses, their boat would soon be ready for action. Tubby was also considerably cheered to have 'Shrimp' Simpson running the base. The two had first met in Malta at the outbreak of war, and Tubby had then served under him at Harwich with the Third Flotilla. When Ben Bryant, the commander of *Sealion*, had been ill, Simpson had even taken command of the submarine for one patrol off the Dutch coast. 'It was good to know that at Malta the man in charge was someone I respected greatly and liked very much,' says Tubby. If anyone could make a success of the new base, Tubby was sure that man was 'Shrimp' Simpson.

Simpson was 39 – an age older than his Commanding Officers – when he arrived on Malta to take over as Commander of Submarines, HMS *Talbot*, as the new base was officially called. His fighting days on board a submarine were over; now he had to carry the responsibility for all his crews and their COs, a burden that would take its toll in the months to come. Like many men of action, Simpson would far rather have been at sea than ordering others out on patrol, often to their deaths. It was a source of frustration that would never go away.

For the moment, however, he had little time for regrets. His first objective was to create a suitable base from which his men could operate. There was much to be done and those days in January were certainly a frantic time for the new Commander. When Cunningham had told Simpson he was giving him a 'free hand', he was effectively telling him to run not just the day-to-day operations of his submarines, but rather the logistics, mechanics and complete organization of every aspect of their existence – a formidable task. But this was wartime, and Simpson's command was on a tiny island where more was expected of men in such positions. The responsibility was something of a mixed blessing, for while it ensured there was little interference from above, it also meant he would have minimal back-up and support. As the RAF engineers had discovered, if they needed spare parts, there wasn't some-one they could simply ring up to place an order; they would have to go out and find or make it themselves. Resourcefulness and ingenuity were to be their new bywords.

With this in mind, Simpson was determined to have the best technical team he possibly could, and was fortunate to be sent a small number of equally determined engineers, old friends whom he knew he could depend on. They wasted no time in scouring the Island for machinery and suitable tools for his embryonic workshops, even 'borrowing' equipment from the dockyards in Grand Harbour.

While Simpson hardly needed reminding that conditions on Malta were likely to be tough, the *Illustrious* Blitz, coming so soon after his arrival, must have shaken him considerably, and underlined the deficiencies of his base. If they were to operate with any kind of efficiency it was imperative the base as a whole offered sufficient protection to all parties. There was neither the time nor money to resurrect the earlier pre-war plans to build protective pens for the submarines, but digging out shelters for the crews and maintenance workshops into the rock behind the Lazzaretto building was a top priority, and Simpson made sure work started on them right away. Again, their construction was entirely his responsibility, and he soon not only had Maltese labourers at work, chipping, drilling and hacking away at the soft limestone, but made some of the submariners lend a hand too.

Years serving in all waters had taught Simpson the importance of unwinding after a patrol. Spending between ten days and a fortnight on board a submarine – in often fetid, stale, cramped conditions – took its toll, and it was essential the men had drink, plenty of food and opportunities for relaxation once back on dry land. Yet Malta would be a far tougher posting than any of his men had ever experienced before. It was a given that patrols would be extremely hazardous, but with the severe conditions on Malta itself, Simpson was very worried that his crews would be unable to get either the essential rest or recreation needed between missions.

It was a conundrum. Lazzaretto, though, did have plenty of space and outbuildings, and it occurred to him that pig-keeping might at least solve the food shortage. He couldn't admit his fear of starvation to the men, so instead suggested that having their own pigs might both offer amusement and bolster their diet. The men agreed, and so while 'Pop' Giddings was sent off to prepare the sties, Simpson went to a country market and bought two magnificent Middle White sows.

A submariner is trained in many skills, but few on Malta could ever have imagined pig-keeping would be one of them.

Finally, under the command of her captain, Lieutenant-Commander David Wanklyn, *Upholder* set off for her first combat patrol on 24 January. Tubby Crawford was relieved to be away from the Island, although there were a few nerves jangling inside him. Submarines all operated on the same principles: the main hull of the submarine was encased by what were known as ballast tanks. On the surface, these were full of nothing but air, giving the submarine added buoyancy. In order to dive, the air was allowed to escape through vents at the top of the tanks and was gradually replaced by water. As the far heavier water replaced the air, so the submarine lost its buoyancy and began to sink – or rather, dive. For the rise back up again, the process was reversed, with compressed air released into the ballast tanks.

Movement underwater was determined by the rudder for turning, and by hydroplanes for going up and down. Hydroplanes were effectively horizontal rudders for'ard and aft of the submarine, fins that could be tilted by someone operating them from the control room.

Although the principles remained the same, submarines came in different sizes and forms, and each type – indeed, each submarine within that type – had its own quirks and foibles, and the long journey out to Malta had taught Tubby and the rest of the crew much about the U-class boat. For a start, they discovered that it suffered from extremely sensitive trim – or, balance – so that in anything other than perfectly calm waters, it was extremely difficult to keep her steady. The submarine needed to be at periscope depth for an attack – that is, twelve feet below water – which was not very deep, but firing could also disturb the trim, forcing her to the surface with all its accompanying dangers. Other factors – anything from sudden changes of depth to the salinity in the Mediterranean – could also play havoc with her trim. Keeping her steady clearly required considerable skill and patience.

Another headache was the two generators. The U-class submarine was driven forward by two propellers, which were turned by two motors. These received their power in two ways: from two diesel generators when on the surface, and from the main battery – i.e., electrically – when underwater. This was because the diesel engines needed air to operate and so couldn't function underwater. As a result, the submarine had to be on the surface in order to recharge the batteries. If travelling very slowly (at about two knots, or half walking pace), these might last up to 60 hours, but if travelling at the maximum underwater speed of eight knots – just under nine miles per hour – it would be considerably less. This was coupled with the problem of speed – or rather, the U's lack of it. Submarines were, generally speaking, considerably slower than most surface vessels, but the U-class was especially slow. Most merchant vessels travelled at between eight and fifteen knots. Naval vessels tended to be faster – *Illustrious* had sped back to Alexandria at 24 knots. In other words, *Upholder* would rarely be able to *catch* a ship. The only chance of getting into a decent firing position was to anticipate where a ship was likely to be passing and position herself as close as possible. And this was no easy task.

With decent intelligence, *Upholder* might be given advance warning of an enemy convoy. All being well, she could then lie in wait and pounce. The problem was that in January 1941, the Government Code and Cipher School (GC&CS) at Bletchley Park in England, had not yet broken the new Italian codes, and so air reconnaissance was still the only reliable means of anticipating enemy shipping movements.

When within a few miles' range, an enemy could be tracked down with the use of 'asdic'. This came into being in the First World War as an anti-submarine detection device pioneered by the Allied Submarine Detection Investigation Committee – hence the acronym – and was essentially used as a hydrophone. This means that it sent out waves of ultrasonic sound in a cone-shaped beam which reflected back echoes from a ship or any other dense object in its path. Then the time elapsed since the transmission of the pulse and reception of the echo was converted into range.

Once closing in for an attack, a number of considerations came into play. For a torpedo to successfully hit a target, a calculation had to be made taking into account the speed, range and course of the enemy ship, the submarine and the torpedo. The Captain – in this case Wanklyn – would look through the periscope, and, with the help of a graduated ring around the lens, make a number of visual calculations. Range was calculated by reading the angle between the waterline of the target and its bridge or masthead. This was tricky because an estimate had to be made having already assumed the size and class of the ship, not an easy task when simply peering through a periscope. Although an estimate of speed was made visually, asdic helped with this calculation by deducing the number of revolutions per minute of the target's propeller.

The Captain would call out his estimates, which would then be passed to the Navigating Officer, so that he could start to plot a course for a suitable interception. The crucial factor was working out the Director Angle (DA), or, in plain terms, the 'aim-off' needed in order to hit a moving target. The torpedo, effectively a mini-submarine itself, was most effective when hitting a target at somewhere close to ninety degrees. As the Captain continually refined his estimates, so the different information would be programmed into a primitive kind of computer known as a 'fruit machine', which would then produce the DA. As soon as the Captain was happy, he would give the order to fire.

All this needed to happen very quickly, and there is no doubt that the best way to assess range, course and speed was through snap assessments made by the naked eye. Although there was no substitute for experience and confidence, the best captains still needed a calm, calculating mind, yet had to be daring and decisive; unfortunately, these two character-istics rarely went together. Even so, regardless of talent and experience, hitting a target, unless at almost point-blank range, was very difficult indeed, and made only more so by the U's delicate trim. A large number of COs never really mastered it. One either had the 'knack' or not. This was why eighty per cent of all successes were achieved by just twenty per cent of the commanding officers.

A final consideration for all the Malta COs was the shortage of torpedoes. Each U-class submarine could carry a maximum of eight on any patrol. With four firing tubes, this meant two rounds of four per trip, although they were not encouraged to fire unless the opportunity for success was highly favourable. When successful attacks were all about speed and decisiveness, this extra consideration was one the inexperienced COs could have done without.

At one-thirty in the morning on 26 January, *Upholder* was patrolling north-west of Tripoli in North Africa when a convoy of three supply ships, escorted by a destroyer, was sighted. They manœuvred to attack, but could get no closer than 2,500 yards. Obviously, the further away the target, the harder it was to hit. Because of the shortage of torpedoes, Simpson had told his COs not to fire from distances of more than 2,000 yards. But what was Wanklyn to do? Should he not attack a three-ship convoy just because he was 500 yards long on range? He decided to ignore the instruction and attack anyway, but over-estimated the speed at which the convoy was travelling, so both torpedoes missed. They hadn't been detected, however, and Wanklyn ordered two more torpedoes to be fired – this time at 3,000 yards – but again, both went wide of their mark, although the margin was less on this second attempt. By the time they had loaded the remaining four torpedoes, the convoy had slipped well away.

Two nights later, they spied another merchant ship and this time managed to get within 900 yards. They fired two further torpedoes, after which there were some anxious moments while they waited to see if they had been successful. Then came the boom of an explosion, although what damage they had caused, it was impossible to know.

After a hit, the first priority was to dive and manœuvre quickly away.

Enemy traffic in the area was considerable, and on the 30th *Upholder* moved in to attack two large merchant ships. This time Wanklyn gave the order to fire from a range of 4,000 yards – a considerable distance – and, miraculously, one hit. Again, they did not hang around to see the result of their efforts, especially since the escorting destroyers quickly came after them, attacking with a number of depth charges. Trusting to their asdic, they quietly manœuvred themselves out of the fray and headed back to Malta, their first patrol complete. Although they had used all eight torpedoes, they had scored two hits and successfully escaped a noisy depth charge attack. All in all, not a bad start. They reached Malta on 1 February – in the middle of another air raid. The Germans had not been idle while they were away.

The air raids were fast becoming a feature of daily life. Sometimes, the sirens seemed to be wailing almost all day and night. Suzanne Parlby was now spending most of her nights in the shelter carved deep into the rock beneath the hotel. There were about forty staff and guests, and each soon established their own patch where they would put down their bedding. Suzanne used to troop down the steps with her deck-chair, rug, cushion and a basket. In this she kept a wide-necked thermos of water, her gas mask, biscuits, sweets, jewellery, a torch and, most importantly, her insect repellent. The mosquitoes and sand-flies never seemed to be far away. Suzanne took her gas mask with her everywhere, less for protection against enemy gas attacks than the choking dust and possible gas leaks caused by bomb blasts.

The shelter was a large, circular cave. Most of the Maltese were down away to the left of the entrance. Suzanne's patch was over to the right, near the wife of a naval officer and her young baby, and next to an alternative exit up onto St Lucy Street. Down there, in winter, it was not cold but warm – or rather, warm *and* damp. One could feel the moisture on walls. Any bedding left in the cave would soon be covered in mildew. Candles placed on little ledges cut into the rock would flicker gently, suffusing the shelter with a dingy orange glow. There were no facilities, just what they took down with them. While Suzanne considered herself perfectly capable of hanging on all night if she needed to go to the toilet, she was slightly horrified to find the Maltese simply did whatever they needed to into a bucket. Fortunately the cave was so big that she did not feel cramped in any way, and despite the humidity and all the noise – bombs crashing overhead, babies crying, people praying – Suzanne still managed to sleep. 'You had to,' she says. 'You simply had to – that was your only chance in twenty-four hours.'

Although she hated the damp and the choking dust that came with a bombing raid, Suzanne did at least feel safe, and not just during the night, but for much of the day too now that Military Intelligence had moved out of the Auberge de Castille. After the *Illustrious* Blitz, this was no longer considered safe enough, and so Suzanne and everyone else were moved into the underground complex of Lascaris where the RAF Fighter Control was already stationed. Lascaris was built into the bastions at the Floriana end of Valletta, and was a labyrinthine complex of tunnels and rooms. Because she was now spending most of her time underground, she began to relish her lunch-hour even more; it was when she could head off to the Snakepit at the Union Club.

Across Grand Harbour from Valletta, the Three Cities once again lay empty, although this time it was a compulsory evacuation. Such was the damage, the only people there were troops and rescue services clearing away the debris. For the Montebellos there was no chance of a return, but nor could they stay where they were, living all together with another family in one small house in Hamrun. Having taken a desk job for a while, Michael's father was now back at sea, and so it was left to his mother to find them a new home. She had heard there was a shelter in Valletta next door to the Wills cigarette factory on the harbour front, and so with their belongings packed into just a few battered suitcases, they began walking down from Hamrun into Valletta. They'd not gone far when another large raid developed. Taking cover, they held each other tight and waited for it to pass. For Michael, now that he was with most of his family, the ordeal did not seem quite so bad.

Eventually they made it safely to the quayside in Valletta. 'The shelter supervisor was very nice to us,' says Michael. 'He didn't know where to put us at first because we were a large family and there were lots of people ahead of us, but he told us to stay put while he went to see what he could do.' After an anxious hour standing on the quayside, the supervisor returned – he had found them a room, but it wouldn't fit them all. Some of the family would have to go elsewhere. They agreed to split up. His uncle and his wife and three children volunteered to go back to Hamrun, while Michael and his mother and brother Freddie moved into their new living quarters: a hundred feet below ground, a room of about eight feet by four cut into the rock off the main passage of the shelter. The 'room' had roughly constructed bunks and even electric lights, but nothing more; no doors, no toilet, no water and no natural light. This hell-hole was now home, as it was for 780 other people in the shelter.

A couple of miles to the south, Adrian Warburton had still not mastered the art of taking off and landing in the Maryland. On one occasion, he had set off before first light on a reconnaissance mission to Taranto and Corfu. Zig-zagging down the runway in his usual haphazard manner, he mowed down a number of the flares lit to show the way, leaving a trail of burning paraffin cascading behind him. Some even caught on the rudder, flaming wildly.

Once in the air, however, he was a different person altogether. No matter how bad the visibility, how severe the flak, or how many enemy planes came after him, Warby always managed to get his pictures. Far from being the unit liability, he was fast becoming Tich Whiteley's most trusted pilot. On Christmas Eve he had shot down a three-engine Italian bomber, adding another plane to his mounting total. In early January, he and the rest of the Flight had been busy photographing the Sicilian airfields, keeping a check on the rising numbers of Luftwaffe planes there. Recognition of his contribution was not long in coming: Warby was promoted from Pilot Officer to Flying Officer as well as receiving his DFC.

Meanwhile, 431 Flight was also given full squadron status, and renamed 69 Squadron. More planes and personnel were arriving, including George Burges. Throughout his time as a fighter pilot, he had, incredibly, continued his role as aide-de-camp to Air Commodore Maynard, only turning up at the airfield for his shift. But after the *Illustrious* Blitz he decided to give up the ADC job and revert to reconnaissance, the line of flying for which he'd originally been trained. Tich Whiteley was an old friend of his – they'd been on a course together back in England – and invited him to come and join the newly formed 69 Squadron. With new, trained pilots arriving, Burges was no longer needed in his role as a stop-gap fighter pilot.

At the beginning of February, Whiteley received an unusual request for some pictures. Back in England, the Commandos had been formed and the first ever British airborne raid planned. Under the grandiose title of 'Operation Colossus' 36 volunteers were going to parachute into southern Italy and blow up an aqueduct, and in so doing cut off the water supplies to some two million Italians. The idea was that by bringing the war to ordinary Italians in their own backyard, they would inflict a severe blow to Italian morale. It was also designed as a test for inter-service co-operation and the RAF's dropping accuracy.

Whiteley immediately entrusted Warby with the task of taking reconnaissance pictures of the aqueduct. On 9 February, he set off and 'very successfully' took the necessary pictures.[1] Three days later, with the operation completed and the commandos now struggling through the Italian winter towards the coast, Warby was assigned to fly over Calitri again and assess the damage. As his photographs showed, the main pipe was blown apart, but the supports, made of ferro-concrete and much stronger than anticipated, remained intact. The Italians were able to repair the damage without too much inconvenience.

Commander George Simpson had also been called in to play his part in this extraordinary operation. Expected to house the commandos once they had arrived on Malta prior to the drop-off, he was also asked to help with the rescue operation. With the raid successfully carried out, the parachutists were then to make their way to an agreed point on the west Italian coast, where one of Simpson's submarines would be waiting to pick them up. Worried that one of his precious boats would be a sitting duck were there to be any security leaks, Simpson reluctantly agreed.

In the end, the operation turned out to be something of a fiasco. One of the planes dropping off the commandos suffered engine failure and signalled to say it was crash-landing near the rendezvous point. Knowing this message would be intercepted by the Italians, Simpson immediately gained permission to recall the submarine to Malta. Nor were the commandos left stranded on the coast: not a single one made the rendezvous. All were captured and one even executed.

The Engineer Artificers' Club, known simply as the 'ERA', was fast becoming one of the most sociable places on the Island. A highly exclusive pre-war naval club, it had been forced to seriously relax its membership criteria since the Navy had left at the beginning of the war; which was very convenient for Christina Ratcliffe as it was just round the corner from her flat in Floriana. With its restaurant, bar, regular dances and tombola nights, it was always busy, and particularly on the night after the *Illustrious* had escaped Grand Harbour, with service men eager to unwind after the tensions of the previous week.

Christina had been having a quiet drink with a friend, when a group of drunken naval officers burst in, singing and yelling. One of them, though, was in RAF uniform, and breaking away from his friends, walked over to her table.

'I'm so terribly sorry, Christina, about poor old Jacques and René,' he said to her. 'They were wonderful fellows.'

Christina, rather taken aback, asked him how he knew who she was.

'Because Jacques was always talking about Christina of the Whizz-Bangs. And I've seen you in a show or two myself, you know.'[2]

The penny dropped. Jacques and René had often mentioned their friend, the brilliant pilot, the man who took incredible risks to get his pictures. She glanced up at him, noticing the new purple-and-white striped ribbon of his DFC. His eyes were very blue, and his hair fair and rather long. He smiled at her and his left cheek developed a deep crease. She thought he looked like a Greek god, and found herself instantly smitten.[3] They talked most of the evening, Warby as drawn to her as she was to him.

Romance was also in the air for Frank Rixon. He'd seen less of Mary since the Germans had arrived on the scene, as he and the rest of 'C' Company had been busy rushing from one place to another, clearing bomb damage and latterly filling bomb craters at Luqa airfield. Even so, whenever he had the chance, he would head over to the Toc H in Sliema and see his sweetheart. Then one day, Mary took him to meet her mother. Frank, on his best behaviour, immediately made the right impression. 'We got on straight away,' he says. From then on, there was no question of Frank staying in the Toc H – if he needed somewhere to get away from it all, he would stay with Mary's mother, bedding down in the front room. He would even get his khaki drill washed too. It was good to be welcomed into her home so openly, especially since he was so enamoured of her daughter.

But the air raids were increasing, and since 'C' Company was invariably at one of the airfields or within the vicinity of Grand Harbour, Frank was never very far away from the bombs. There had been over fifty air raid alerts in January, and twice that many in the first two weeks of February. He began to think his chances of survival were slim. 'You see all these cluster bombs coming down and you're only protected by a sandbag or a little slit trench – you don't feel all that safe.'

He was, he readily admits, scared. One time the bombers came over and he dived underneath the first thing available – it was a Wellington. Well, he'd already seen what happened to one of those when it burned. In moments there was very little left. He might just as well have stood out in the open.

But he was determined to make the most of what life God had left in store for him – and that life involved Mary. In February, having just turned twenty, he asked her to marry him, and she accepted. Because of his youth, Frank had to ask the permission of his company commander. Captain Buckle had frowned upon the idea, warning him that, in his opinion, such wartime marriages never worked out. But Frank was adamant. Reluctantly, the Captain agreed.

The advertisement had run, 'The Thrill of the Air Plus the Grand Life of the Sea', accompanied by a picture of a Fairey Swordfish flying above the aircraft carrier *Ark Royal*. Nat Gold had been working at the General Electric Company in North Wembley just before war broke out and the poster had made quite an impression. Of medium height and with dark hair and eyes and a wide, thoughtful face, Nat was a quiet, practical young man, but with an understated adventurous spirit. As a teenager, he'd been on a school trip to Denmark and Norway and then, with a couple of friends, toured Belgium. At that time, this was quite unusual for a working-class lad from North London. He'd been intending to go to the South of France, too, before the prospect of war put paid to such plans.

The Fleet Air Arm looked pretty exciting, however, and although he knew little about life on the sea and nothing about flying, he decided that when the time came, that was the service he would join. Two of his friends from work had volunteered right away, but Nat had not been in such a hurry – his draft would arrive in due course. And it did, not long after, on 26 September 1939.

Basic training included learning about gunnery, signals and Morse Code, and applying this knowledge during flying exercises. After eight months he was sent on a course to become a Telegraphist Air Gunner (TAG). The Fleet Air Arm's principal planes were the monoplane Fairey Fulmar and the biplane Fairey Swordfish. Both were two- or three-man machines – the pilot, TAG and sometimes an observer. Nat's role was to operate the radio and fire the single rear-mounted machine-gun. By the end of July 1940, he was fully trained and posted to HMS *Daedalus*, a

1. ABC. This is a good picture of Admiral Cunningham – determined, bullish,
but with a hint of the humour that was never far away.

2. *Top left* Meme Cortis flanked by two other VAD nurses outside the 90th General Hospital at Imtarfa. Like most Maltese, she had much to worry about, but even during the darkest days tried her best to remain cheerful. Not for nothing did the patients nickname her 'Smiler'.

3. *Top right* George Burges leaning against one of the many dry-stone walls that made crash-landing on the Island so hazardous.

4. *Above left* Frank Rixon in boxing mode. The Army offered this orphan opportunities he would not find elsewhere. This was taken before he was posted to Malta.

5. *Above middle* Suzanne Parlby. Young English women were few and far between on Malta, and despite being bombed, shot at and suffering all the accompanying hardships, she blossomed during the siege, free at last from the influence of her bullying father.

6. *Above right* John Agius outside the RAF Headquarters at Scots Street, Valletta, where he worked as a civilian clerk.

7. George Burges strapped into one of the Gloster Gladiator biplanes, ready to go at a moment's notice. In the foreground is a starter trolley and battery. Gladiators usually only had twin propellers, but this has three – one of the many modifications they underwent in a desperate attempt to gain extra speed.

8. The Whizz-Bangs, the travelling cabaret show that brought much welcome relief to the troops around the Island. Christina Ratcliffe is second from the left in the front row.

9. General Sir William Dobbie, Acting Governor, then later Governor of Malta. This much-maligned member of the Plymouth Brethren took on the post in impossible circumstances, yet led the Islanders' resistance during the worst days of the siege.

10. Warby. Cigarette in hand, battered cap perched on his head, grey slacks and the favoured battle-blouse. This picture was actually taken in late 1943, but clearly shows something of Warby's informal and devil-may-care character.

11. Final moments. An Italian Savoia-Marchetti S.M. 79 bomber plunges towards Grand Harbour on 10 July 1940. This was one of the first victories by the Island's newly arrived Hurricanes.

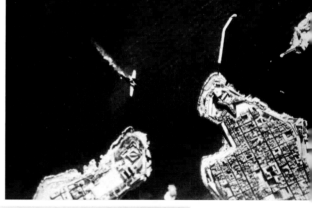

12. Warby's battle-scarred Glenn Martin Maryland at Luqa. It is a wonder it managed to make it into the air at all, and says much about the conditions facing both ground- and aircrew on Malta. Patches and holes are clearly visible, making it easy to understand why it 'whistled'.

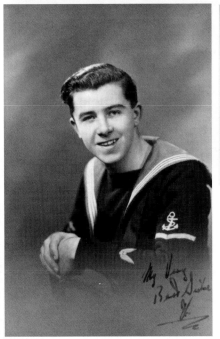

13. Bombs falling on Grand Harbour and the Three Cities in January 1941. HMS *Illustrious* is behind the fountain of spray rising several hundred feet into the air just to the right of centre. Senglea, home to Michael Montebello, is to the left. This photograph was taken from Castille Square in Valletta.

14. Nat Gold. He looks cheerful enough here, but he discovered there was little to smile about during his year on Malta serving with 830 Fleet Air Arm Squadron.

15. A Fairey Swordfish at Hal Far. The 'Stringbag' is loaded with a torpedo. No wonder Nat Gold felt vulnerable taking off with one of these strapped underneath – its end lies suspended just inches from the ground.

16. The remains of a Swordfish at Hal Far. With a metal frame but covered in Irish linen, it didn't take much to completely destroy these fragile-looking biplanes.

17. Shrimp Simpson, the indefatigable and inspirational commander of the Tenth Submarine Flotilla. This photo was taken outside their base, the Lazzaretto on Manoel Island, a former quarantine hospital where Lord Byron had once languished.

18. The crew of HMS/S *Upholder*, the most successful Allied submarine of the war. David Wanklyn is unmistakable with his beard in the front row. Tubby Crawford is on his right.

19. Tommy Thompson, who volunteered to join the fledgling Malta Night Fighter Unit. With new improved digs and plenty to drink, Tommy knew he'd made the right decision to transfer from 249 Squadron.

20. Tom Neil of 249 Squadron. Having emerged from the Battle of Britain as a fighter ace, he was one of the more experienced pilots on Malta in 1941. For Tom, the sub-standard Hurricanes and difficult conditions were to prove an even greater enemy than the Germans and Italians they were flying against.

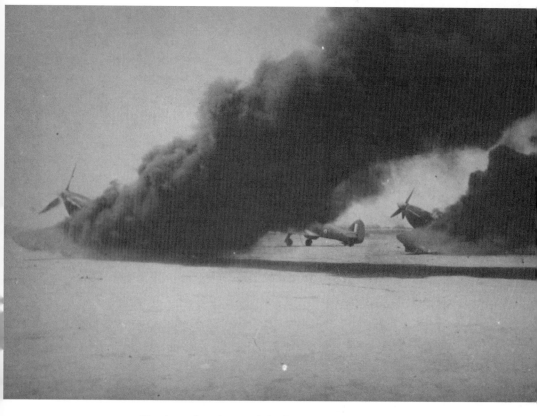

21. Hurricanes burning at Takali after Müncheberg's attack on 25 May.

naval coastal station at Lee-on-Solent on the south coast of England. With the Battle of Britain just beginning, the majority of German attacks were still coastal or directed onto Channel shipping, and within an hour of arriving at this first posting, the base was bombed by twelve Stuka dive-bombers. Nat thought it utterly terrifying. The destruction was considerable, and a dozen men were killed, including one of the TAGs. One of his first tasks was to help carry the remains to the morgue. A couple of days later, he was acting as a pallbearer at the TAG's funeral. He had begun to wonder whether the Fleet Air Arm was for him after all.

Nat was still wondering this after his arrival on Malta, having reached the Island just in time for the *Illustrious* Blitz. Hal Far had not escaped the attacks and he'd begun to think the bombers were following him around. Still, he'd been lucky too – as he'd found out from the surviving Fulmar crews who were now temporarily based at Hal Far alongside 830 Squadron. These men had been through hell and were feeling pretty bitter about the state of their ship and, more particularly, the number of comrades they'd lost. One pilot – Lieutenant William Barnes – decided to do something about it. Driven by a furious need for revenge, he took off alone in his Fulmar, without an observer or TAG, and climbed high over Grand Harbour. Circling, he waited for the German bombers to dive, then followed after, straight through the box barrage of flak bursting from below. As the Stuka released his bomb and began to pull out of his dive, Barnes picked him off.

Shortly after, he returned to Hal Far to rearm. While the armourers were busily preparing his Fulmar again, Barnes paced up and down, drawing deeply on a cigarette. As soon as his plane was ready, he sprang back into the cockpit and took off again. Once more, Nat watched him circle above the harbour then dive through the hail of shrapnel after a Stuka, and again pick off the plane. It was one of the bravest things he'd ever seen. 'How he got away with it, God only knows,' says Nat.

A week later, the *Illustrious* Blitz over, Lieutenant Barnes was travelling in a car and was challenged by a sentry. It seems the chauffeur never saw him, and so the sentry took aim and fired. He missed but, in one of those cruel twists of fate that so often happen in wartime, the bullet hit a rock, ricocheted and hit the lieutenant in the back, killing him instantly. It was an apalling waste of life and, like everyone else at Hal Far, Nat was stunned.[4]

A further tragedy lay just around the corner. 830 Fleet Air Arm

Squadron on Malta were flying Fairey Swordfish. Despite their open cockpits and slow speed, and despite being built from little more than wire and Irish linen, these had been the Island's principal attack planes since they had arrived in July the previous year. And although the twin-engine Wellingtons had taken over a large part of the bombing duties, the Swordfish were still used for a number of offensive operations. Essentially, their role was threefold: as torpedo attackers, as dive-bombers, and as minelayers. All three duties involved strapping a highly explosive weapon underneath the fragile frame of the Swordfish, a considerable danger in itself. Nat had only been with the squadron a few weeks when the Chief Coxswain was demonstrating the arming of a magnetic mine to a group of armourers. Something went wrong and it exploded, blowing all eight to pieces. It could have been far worse – the demonstration had been taking place near to the NAAFI, but in a stone pen, and the walls caused the blast to burst upwards rather than out.

Nat also had a close call of his own while practising torpedo bombing on the tiny rocky outcrop of Filfla, just south of Malta. This required considerable skill, as the pilot had to fly down to around 100 feet, then at the critical moment release the torpedo. With its forward momentum, it would then drop into the water and arc upwards, hopefully hitting the target just below the surface. The trick was to get the right angle of descent, because if this were too steep, the plane simply wouldn't come out of the dive in time; and 100 feet above the surface is a tiny distance when flying a plane, with very little margin for error. In this case they were only using a dummy torpedo, but as they approached Filfla, the pilot dropped too low. With the sea hurtling towards them, Nat thought they were going to crash straight into the water. Barely daring to look, he felt the plane creak and groan, but in the nick of time the pilot released the torpedo, and the loss of its weight gave them just enough extra lift. With the wheels of the undercarriage skimming the water, they were literally inches away from death.

Nat Gold had not known what to expect when he arrived on Malta. Of course, combat operations could be extremely hazardous, but even before his first mission he had been bombed, nearly killed during a practice flight, and seen his colleagues strewn across the airfield by an exploding mine. This Island seemed to be fraught with danger. It was unnerving, to say the least.

★

Things had not been going well for the submariners either. By the middle of February, *Upholder* was the only U-class submarine to have scored a single hit. On her second patrol, beginning on 12 February, the only boat she came close to sinking was one of their own. Tubby Crawford had been the Officer of the Watch (OOW) at the time; it was night and, with a favourable moon, a submarine had been clearly silhouetted ahead. Only 25 miles south of Malta, hopes ran high that it might be an enemy U-boat. Wanklyn wasn't so sure – to him it looked more like a T-class from Malta. Even so, they made ready to fire and gave the warning challenge four times. This went unanswered. Wanklyn asked Tubby's opinion; it was a difficult call, but it would be a disaster to sink one of their own submarines. Tubby agreed – best to err on the side of caution. Wanklyn had another look. Although no friendly submarines were reported in the area, and despite the lack of response to their challenge, he was now convinced the submarine was a T-class and refused to give the order to attack. He had been right: HMS/S *Truant* was returning home early with radio failure.

The Mediterranean was particularly calm during this patrol, and they realized with frightening clarity that the upper bows of the submarine could be seen through the periscope even though the top of the conning tower was twelve feet below the surface. A number of aircraft had flown over them, and they had the distinct impression they had been spotted. On their return, Wanklyn suggested painting the upper half of their submarines pale blue as a means of camouflage, a plan that was immediately adopted.

Still comparatively new to the U-class submarines, and lacking experience of operating in the Mediterranean in war conditions, the commanders had yet to find their feet. The lack of torpedoes exacerbated the situation, encouraging two-torpedo salvoes rather than four; but until they had had more practice, they really needed the full four shots to give them the best possible chance of a strike. Compounding their difficulties were the ludicrous attack restrictions that were still in place. This meant they were unable to fire on a merchant vessel thirty miles beyond the enemy coastline which, of course, put them at a considerable disadvantage since they faced a far higher chance of being either mined or attacked in turn by aircraft and motor torpedo boats. On top of all that, the submariners were expected to weave through the densely mined waters all round Malta. Laid down by the Italians, the minefields even included acoustic mines that lay submerged and detonated when a vessel passed over. The submariners were now advised to fire machine-gun bullets into the water a hundred yards ahead as they passed though the minefield.

The thirty-mile restriction was finally lifted on 22 February. Why this took so long is unclear, but it was a major hindrance to the submariners at a time when they needed every bit of help they could get, rather than further obstacles thrown in their way. It was also too late to stop the German arrival in North Africa, which was unfortunate since by 10 February the British had captured the whole of Cyrenaica from the Italians – including Tobruk, Gazala, Derna and Benghazi – and the North Africa campaign had been there for the winning. But by the end of the month, the situation had changed. Almost a hundred per cent of German troops and supplies sent across the Mediterranean had reached Tripoli.[5] Most had arrived by sea, having been precisely the targets the submariners were supposed to hit. That they failed to do so was a missed opportunity of massive proportions. Blame lay not with the commanders or even Simpson; it was hardly their fault they lacked experience, or that needless restrictions had taken so long to be lifted; nor was the shortage of torpedoes something they had any control over.

But their lack of success was not the only matter worrying Simpson. German air raids had been continuing without respite, and when on shore, his crews had been forced to spend most of their time huddled in insufficient half-finished rock shelters. It was not the kind of relaxation and recreation he'd had in mind. Furthermore, it only needed a direct hit on, say, the Engineer Artificers' Mess, to put the whole base out of action. The only answer was to encourage his men to take apartments or houses off the base, in the largely empty towns of Sliema and Msida, where rents were now at rock bottom prices. At least that way he might have the crews left to fight another day.

On 14 February, a week before the thirty-mile restriction was finally lifted, Major-General Erwin Rommel arrived in North Africa. During the next eighteen months he would beat the British back to within sixty miles of Alexandria, rise to the rank of Field Marshal and carve a reputation as one of Germany's greatest generals.

Now it was Britain's turn to rue the missed opportunity.

CHAPTER 7

Success and Failure

MARCH–APRIL 1941

IT WAS NOT until the beginning of March that the Germans first used Messerschmitt 109 fighters over Malta, but they quickly made their presence felt, as Suzanne Parlby was to discover. One morning she found herself covered in spots and soon realized she had contracted chicken-pox. Fortunately, there were few on her face, and she did not feel especially unwell, so she kept quiet at the hotel and only told her boss at the cipher office in Lascaris, who immediately sent her home again. But mindful that the naval wife and her baby were living next to her in the hotel, she thought it only fair to keep out of their way as much as possible. Johnny White, the Irish army padre to the Devons, came to her rescue. A man who never took life too seriously, Johnny could always make her laugh and had become a good friend, and so she was delighted when he turned up at the hotel on his day off and suggested they take their bikes out to the country for a picnic. It was a perfectly clear, sunny, early spring day and they paused to watch the bombers come over to attack the harbour and the airfields. High above them were condensation trails from the various dogfights going on overhead. Being in open countryside, and nowhere near any village or obvious target, they felt quite safe despite the sound of distant machine-gun fire and the blast of bombs exploding. Then suddenly they heard the whine of an engine far too close for comfort. Johnny yelled at her, and they both flung down their bikes and jumped into a stone drain that ran under the road. A second later, a 109 raced past, strafing the road with machine-gun bullets. The German pilot had been deliberately aiming for them, and although they soon dusted themselves down and tried to laugh it off, it was clear that nowhere on the Island was safe any more.

Not long after, Suzanne was down in the cave beneath the St James Hotel when the bombing began once again. For her, the noise of the raids was part of the terror: first the booming of the anti-aircraft guns, next the screaming siren sound made by the bombers as they dived; and then the whistle of the bombs falling through the air, followed by the crump of explosions starting in the distance but growing ever louder and more ear-piercing the closer they fell. The ground shook, clouds of dust and grit filled the air and then there would be the noise of falling rubble. Then a pause, before yet more crashes as the debris settled. 'It was terrifying,' recalls Suzanne. 'You had to use your will-power to quell the fear, which would be trying to burst out from within.' She often noticed her hands shaking and clenched them tight to stop them. 'Showing your fear was unthinkable, but sometimes it was very hard not to.'

The Germans had used a variety of different bombs by this time, including incendiaries, which had caused all manner of destruction in Britain. But in Malta they were less effective. Most Maltese buildings were made in the same way: thick limestone blocks, insulating the heat in the winter and cool in the summer. Very little wood was used, partly because there was no need and partly because it was very expensive as it had to be imported. Ordinary bombs caused limited destruction: they would knock down buildings if there was a direct hit, but the blast effect was usually comparatively small. Now, however, the Germans had begun using parachute mines, which had far greater blast power, and were consequently considerably more destructive.

It was one of these devices that struck the St James Hotel. In the cave underneath, Suzanne and the rest of the guests heard the most hideous explosion and the crash of tumbling stone and masonry. Reverberations ran through the rock. In moments, the cavern filled with a thick impenetrable fog. Breathing became very difficult because of all the dust and grit that blew down with the blast. Suzanne immediately put on her gas mask, but incredibly, despite the intensity of the recent bombing, no one else had thought to bring either their gas mask or a flask of water. Although it was hard to see what one was doing, she managed to take her Thermos from her basket and hand it round so that everyone could soak their handkerchiefs in order to cover their faces with a makeshift dust-mask. The naval wife also had some of her baby's nappies with her, which were hastily used for the same purpose.

As the dust began to settle, they all saw to their horror that large blocks of stone, once the hotel walls, now completely blocked both entrances to the shelter. They were entombed. Suzanne could also hear a hissing sound and guessed there must be a gas leak somewhere nearby. Although frightened, she did not think they would die, as she was sure they would be rescued. She was also calm enough to realize that since she couldn't smell the gas, the threat could not be that serious. Meanwhile, the raid continued overhead, with more bombs exploding nearby. All of them were covered in dust. Suzanne's hair was thick with grit, her throat dry. There was little any of them could do but wait, and hope.

The raid passed and they were left sitting down there in an eerie silence. Not a sound could be heard from above. Several hours went by – an eternity. Then, suddenly, muffled voices. At last, rescue was at hand.

'Anyone down there?' a man shouted. They all yelled back.

Then another voice said, 'Are we near the entrance? Give us a shout so we can hear where you are.'

Was anyone hurt? they asked. No, they shouted back once more. 'OK. We'll soon get you out. Hold on a jiffy, we won't be long.'

Suzanne had never felt so relieved in all her life. Soon they heard the scraping and grinding of stones being moved until Suzanne was able to look up and see faces peering down at them. Although there were nearly forty of them down there, the mother of the Maltese hotel owner had had enough and now rushed to the newly formed gap in the rubble. But the hole was not yet big enough for her ample girth and she found herself stuck fast. Panicking, she only managed to wedge herself more tightly. The rescuers pulled her from above, while those trapped pushed from below. Eventually, after much huffing and puffing at both ends, the old lady was uncorked. There were not many who saw the funny side.

With encouragement from the soldiers and rescuers who had cleared the way, they all clambered out into fresh air once more. Suzanne breathed in deeply. Someone gave her a mug of tea. Looking up at the remains of the hotel, she saw three of the four walls had collapsed. But incredibly, hanging at the top of the remaining wall, she could see her room, with her bottle of scent and a vase of flowers on her dressing-table completely untouched.

Having assessed the damage, her friend Johnny White told her it might be possible to rescue her belongings, and so a few days later he turned up with a lorry and a group of soldiers. While Suzanne sat on the boulders below, some men clambered up to the remains of the second floor. A crowd began to gather, watching this bizarre rescue mission. Much to her embarrassment, they began clearing out her underwear draw. Silk knickers, petticoats and bras, fluttered down accompanied by cheers and wolf-whistles.

Nearly all her clothes and belongings were saved, including her lipsticks and bottle of Guerlain scent. Although there was no serious shortage of food yet, luxury items had been scarce for a while. There might have been a war on, but Suzanne still wanted to look her best; to have lost them would have been nothing short of disaster.

Meanwhile, Adrian Warburton had been seeing a good deal of Christina Ratcliffe. When not on duty, he would often slip away from Luqa and the two of them would meet up at the ERA Club, or at Captain Caruana's, another favoured bar in Valletta. He also frequently spent the night with her at her flat in Floriana, rather than returning to his digs at the airfield. Betty, to whom he was still legally married, was never mentioned; she belonged to a part of his life he was glad to have left behind him.

But Warby was no party animal. Despite a penchant for brandy and ginger ale ('Horse's Neck'), he drank little and was hopeless at dancing. Rather, it was his love of adventure and devil-may-care attitude that drew Christina to him; by now she had fallen madly in love. One evening at the beginning of March, Warby told her he was due to be flying the following morning, but if she later heard he was missing, she was not to worry. Although it was in no way part of his brief, he intended to develop 'engine trouble' and land in Greece in order to pick up some booze for the lads in the squadron, then return the next day. He then made her swear not to breathe a word.[1]

The following morning, 7 March, Warby set off around 11.30 a.m. in one of the Marylands. The weather was fine and clear and he carried out his mission to photograph Taranto at the comparatively safe height of 25,000 feet, then pressed on towards Greece. In the squadron Operations Record Book, Warby has written, '4 Macchi 200s were sighted on the starboard bow. Aircraft turned away and was chased across Italy into the Adriatic, where enemy fighters were shaken off. On return was intercepted by two more M.200s off Cap St Maria Leoutia and chased south for 100 miles, shots being exchanged. Fighters eventually gave up attack

& aircraft being short of petrol made a landfall at Strovathi and landed at Menidi.'[2]

All very plausible, but, with the exception of the landing, entirely untrue. Even so, that evening at the ERA Club there were a few long faces. By now he had been reported missing. No one could believe it – poor old Warby. Really, it was too bad. Christina was made a great fuss of, and played her part to perfection until one of the RAF crew arrived saying Warby had been shot down in flames. That was not part of the script. Immediately she believed the worst; he had tempted fate and now the unthinkable had happened. She was inconsolable.

But sure enough, the following afternoon, he reappeared at the flat, grinning from ear to ear and armed with several bottles of brandy, some Greek records and an ashtray pinched from the hotel where they'd stayed. He had also brought her a brooch. But these offerings were nothing compared to the large quantities of liquor crammed into the Maryland for the general consumption of the squadron. Warby had promised to bring back a bottle for each day of the year. He wasn't far off the mark.

A full moon was due on the night of 17–18 March, the ideal conditions for the Swordfish of 830 Fleet Air Squadron to launch an attack. Down at the airfield, in the early afternoon of the 17th, Nat Gold was watching the armourers preparing the aircraft. This was the first indication the crews had as to what they would be doing that night. In this case, five were being loaded up with magnetic mines, which because of their long narrow shape were always known as 'cucumbers'. Underneath the fragile-looking airframe of the Swordfish, they looked huge. No one liked taking off with those things strapped underneath, especially after what had happened at the beginning of February. Four other planes were being fixed up with a number of 250-pound bombs and marker flares.

There was still a long time to sit around and wait; they wouldn't get their briefing until eight o'clock at the earliest. Too much time to dwell on things, making it hard not to feel apprehensive. Nat knew that if he went back to his billet for some rest, he'd miss out on tea. That bar of chocolate was a life-saver. If he was going on a mission that night, there was no way he was going to pass on that.

Ten days earlier, after yet another air raid, they had finally been moved out of their bomb-damaged digs at the aerodrome and billeted instead in a house in the village of Zurrieq, a couple of miles to the west. The block house at Hal Far had been rudimentary – blown-out windows, draughty as hell – but at least it had been near the NAAFI. This new place, though, really was basic. It had four walls, windows and a door, but other than that it was positively medieval. Rats and mice scurried about the place, and in no time all of them had been bitten to pieces by fleas. There was no toilet as such. Nor were there any beds; they were expected to fashion their own form of camp-bed from whatever they could – bits of sacking, an old stretcher – with little more than a rough blanket to cover them. It was very difficult to keep clean. There was only one tap, providing small amounts of cold water. The closest they came to having a shower was sluicing themselves down with the contents of a bucket. Shaving was also carried out with cold water and blunt razors. When he'd first seen that Fleet Air Arm advertisement back home in Wembley, he'd never imagined he would end up living like this.

At eight o'clock that evening, Nat was sitting in the briefing room at Hal Far along with the other crew – nineteen in all – who would be taking part that night. The room was noisy with nervous chatter, but as soon as the CO walked in, everyone went deathly quiet. Walking to the end of the room, he stood by the board. The target, he told them, was to be Tripoli harbour. 'A' and 'B' planes would carry observers and would lead the formation in, dropping flares to mark the point at which the mines should be dropped, which was to be as close to the harbour entrance as possible. They would then drop their bombs on any anti-aircraft emplacements around the harbour moles or on ships lying in the harbour. After the mines had been dropped, the remaining two planes would immediately follow and release their bombs too. Nat, as TAG to the most junior pilot, would be on the last plane in. Both of them were still nineteen.

They trundled out of the briefing room. Departure was planned for half an hour before midnight; in other words, they would have to wait another two-and-a-half hours. Nat wished they could leave right away, get it over and done with.

Just before 11.30 p.m. he was sitting in the back of the Swordfish, waiting to take off. The moon was high and visibility fairly good. The runway could not be lit up because of the risk of enemy bombers, but a few guiding lights were briefly flashed on and off. Incredibly, it was then up to the pilot to memorize what lay ahead and to use the light of the moon. On the signal, the pilot released the brakes, opened the throttle and sped off into the darkness, hoping for the best.

Talk to any Hurricane or Spitfire pilot and they all say there is no way they would ever go off to battle in something quite so slow, flimsy and old-fashioned as the Fairey Swordfish. The plane had first come into operation in 1934, which in terms of aircraft development was an age ago. Really, by the outbreak of war, the biplane had had its day, having long since been developed to its maximum potential. It was as though a twenty-year-old saloon was trying to keep pace with a state-of-the-art sports car. To look at, one could be forgiven for thinking it belonged to the First rather than the Second World War: all-fabric Irish linen covering a metal substructure, wires and struts all over the place, and an open double-cockpit; it even had a manually operated machine-gun, rather like the Sopwith Camels and Bristol Fighters of the 1914–18 War. And it was horribly slow, with a maximum speed of 138 miles per hour. Not for nothing was it known as the 'Stringbag'.

Yet for all this, the Swordfish had certain advantages. A naval aircraft, it was ideal for using on the (generally speaking) equally out-of-date aircraft carriers, with their short flight decks. As one wartime Swordfish pilot wrote, 'You could pull a Swordfish off the deck and put her in a climbing turn at 55 knots. [i.e., very slow]. She would manoeuvre in a vertical plane as easily as she would straight and level, and even when diving from 10,000 feet her indicated air speed never rose much above 200 knots ... The approach to the carrier deck could be made at a staggeringly low speed, yet response to the controls remained firm and insistent. Consider what such qualities meant on a dark night when the carrier deck was pitching the height of a house.'[3]

The nine Swordfish of 830 Squadron had an uneventful passage across the sea that night, and Tripoli came into view just before 1.30 a.m. There had been small patches of cloud the closer they got, but by and large, visibility, with the help of the moon, lay at around fifteen miles. The flares were dropped and, in no time at all, they were all dropping down towards their targets. Having spent much of the three-hour journey in a state of nervous frenzy, his thoughts running riot, Nat Gold had finally reached the critical moment.

Ahead of them, the minelayers went in, although their planned approach was blocked by ships outside the harbour. Then, at last, it was their turn. Although there were no barrage balloons, it didn't take long for the anti-aircraft fire to start booming all around them. Nat could see the flashes of the guns, as well as tiny orange arrows of tracer. The long journey across the Mediterranean had given them ample time to adjust their eyes to the light, but the sudden glare from the guns and the explosions was dazzling, and impaired their vision considerably.

Even so, his pilot spotted a large ship lying in the harbour and told Nat he was going to aim for that, rather than the gun emplacements. At 4,000 feet they began their dive. At 800, they dropped their bombs, straddling the ship with a hit across the fo'c'sle. But at that dangerously low height, there was no question of hanging around to see the damage – they had to get out of there as quickly as possible. The pilot flung the plane all over the place, trying to dodge the searchlights and flak. Occasionally a shell burst uncomfortably close, the force of it causing the lightweight Swordfish to lurch and drop. Despite his harness, Nat was yanked back and forth, this way and that, as if on the worst kind of fairground ride, although with shells bursting all round them, the din of the guns ringing in their ears, and lines of tracer darting past, this was no pleasure ride. He felt very vulnerable indeed.

It had been considered unlikely that all the dive-bombers would make it back, and tonight was no exception. 'Q' plane was shot down in the attack. Both men managed to bale out, but faced the prospect of a brutal Italian prisoner-of-war camp in the desert. The TAG (Telegraphist Air Gunner) had been a friend of Nat's, one of the original four who had left Lee-on-Solent the previous year. He thought about the TAG who'd been blown up on *Illustrious*; that was two down now.

Although breathing a huge sigh of relief to be safely out of the fray, there was still the landing back at Hal Far to worry about. Taking off was bad enough, but touching down again could be even more lethal, when there was absolutely no lighting on offer along the runway. Even with a full moon, making a perfect landing at night on all three wheels was incredibly difficult. Added to this was the problem of craters and pot-holes along the runway. The moon was just as full over Sicily as it was over Malta and Tripoli, and so Axis night raiders often paid night visits at the same time as the Swordfish were carrying out their own operations. It was all too easy to land and hit a newly made hole in the runway. Blinking madly in an attempt to gain maximum night-vision, and listening to his radio head-set for the movements of the other planes, Nat readied himself for the landing. The ground seemed to loom towards them and they hit the deck only to bounce back up into the air. Another crunch as the plane bounced once more, then another, and then they were down, and drawing off the runway, mercifully unscathed and with the mission complete. It was now 4.20 in the morning.

In Alexandria, Admiral Cunningham was not happy. With *Illustrious* out of action he once again had no armoured aircraft carrier, which considerably restricted his fleet movements. And although 69 Squadron were doing sterling reconnaissance work from the Island, the situation in the Mediterranean was hotting up considerably, and not even their superhuman efforts were enough. What was needed were aircraft, and lots of them, not just to help with reconnaissance work, but also with defence, anti-submarine duties and convoy protection.

This was largely prompted by the demands facing him as a result of the situation developing in the Aegean. Although Rommel and his Afrika Korps had arrived in North Africa, German intervention in Greece was expected at any moment, and it had been decided to transfer large numbers of troops from North Africa to help bolster the Greeks. This meant shipping them across the Mediterranean. In turn, escorting this kind of force meant stretching the fleet to its absolute limits and leaving other areas – Malta and Suez, for instance – woefully vulnerable. Further-more, as Cunningham pointed out in a message to the First Sea Lord, the movement of such a force from North Africa still constituted a consider-able risk, especially if the Germans decided to concentrate their air attacks on these convoys. A number of destroyers and minesweepers had already been lost or damaged off the coast of North Africa in recent weeks. 'I hope it will turn out that our policy of helping Greece is the right one,' he wrote in a letter to Pound. 'To me it is absolutely right, but I much doubt if our resources, particularly naval and air, are equal to the strain.'[4] He had reason for worry: just a few weeks before, Rommel had been facing a considerable, battle-hardened army. By 11 March, there were only sixteen heavy anti-aircraft guns left between Benghazi and Alexandria, and all were at Tobruk; and while the Luftwaffe had amassed over 200 planes in Libya by this stage, the RAF had just 30.

The situation in Malta was also critical, and another major concern for the Admiral. The Hurricanes had just about been holding their own against the bombers, but since the Messerschmitt 109 fighters had arrived, they were barely allowed to take to the air. Nor were the 109s flown by any old pilots. They were, in fact, a crack unit – 7 Staffel of Jagdgeschwader 26 – one of the most experienced German fighter squadrons, and led by former Battle of Britain ace Joachim Müncheberg.

If pilot skill was of crucial importance in any aerial battle, so too was the quality of the aircraft, and the Hurricane Mk Is were no match for the 109Fs they were now coming up against. Even a brand-new Hurricane, considerably slower than the 109F, would have struggled, but the planes the Malta fighter pilots were expected to fly were patched, repaired and bastardized well beyond their expected shelf-life, and their performance was greatly lowered as a result. Nor were there many left anyway. A small number of replacements arrived: five from North Africa at the beginning of March, and another six on the 18th, but in the case of the latter they did little more than plug a hole; moments before their arrival, five Hurricanes had been shot down during a dogfight with the 109s. As one Hurricane pilot noted, 'This was the one day when we thought we had the edge. It was the first time we had managed to get eight aircraft into the air in one formation in the two months I had been on the Island. Of the eight pilots, only three returned.' He went off to search for survivors but found only marks of crashed aircraft.[5] If scrambling eight aircraft against a potential enemy strength of several hundred was considered good, it's no wonder Cunningham was fretting. Odds of survival were now worse than for those who'd fought in the Battle of Britain a few months before. As one flight lieutenant recorded in his diary, 'The risk of death is so much more increased, I've been doing a bit of philosophising. My attitude is that if I get bumped off, I have experienced much more than the average bloke.' Like many of his colleagues, he was barely twenty years old.[6]

'I am really seriously concerned about Malta,' ABC continued in his letter to Pound. 'I am running a convoy there in about ten days' time; but with their defences in the present state I am quite expecting some of the ships to be damaged. The Grand Harbour and the creeks are also being mined whenever the enemy cares to come. This is a gloomy picture; but someone is misinforming the Chiefs of Staff about the real state of affairs out here. We must have large numbers of fighters rushed out to us if we are to make any headway, and, indeed, they are needed to save what may be a serious set-back.'[7]

But instead of receiving a swift and positive reply, ABC was warned by Anthony Eden, the Secretary of State, that plans to fly out more Hurricanes had been shelved owing to a shortage of aircraft carriers. Cunningham sent another frantic message to Pound, who curtly replied that no such decision had been made, but that the earliest any Hurricane reinforcements could be brought into the Mediterranean was 28 March, i.e. after the convoy was to have been run to Malta and after a large part of the reinforcements to Greece had been transported.

But the First Sea Lord was in London, and to him – as had been the case the previous summer and throughout the autumn – the greatest threat to Britain came from the Atlantic, where the U-boats were wreaking havoc with the Allied convoys. If these ultimately failed, Britain would collapse anyway; therefore, he still saw the Mediterranean as of secondary importance. If Cunningham thought the use of aircraft carriers to ferry out fighters was to be a regular occurrence, he could think again. 'Although glad to use carriers as air transports in grave emergency,' he replied to ABC, 'I feel this is wrong when it can be avoided by looking ahead sufficiently.'[8]

As it happened, the convoy reached Malta safely, and although the three merchant ships were bombed once in harbour, nearly 24,000 tons of supplies were safely unloaded. This at least brought some relief to the Islanders and to Cunningham as well, although he was soon distracted by the prospect of the one big opportunity he had been hoping for ever since 11 June: taking on the Italian fleet in a full-scale naval battle.

Trying to draw the Italian fleet out to do battle had proved a difficult task, but at last, during the latter half of March, there were signs that the enemy fleet was planning a big operation. Axis reconnaissance planes had been buzzing all around the Aegean, but also making regular visits to Alexandria. It was Cunningham's job, as C-in-C Mediterranean Fleet, to try to second-guess his counterpart. 'No deductions,' he would bark at his staff. 'Give me the facts. I will make the deductions.'[9] In this instance, there were a number of possibilities: the Italian Admiral Iachino might be planning a cover for a convoy of reinforcements of their own; or a diversion while a landing was made in Greece or North Africa; or even an all-out attack on Malta. Or maybe the Italians were planning an attack on the lightly armed British convoys of troops and supplies heading to Greece. Of all the options, ABC felt this was the most likely, and he was soon proved right from Ultra[10] signals sent over from Bletchley Park in England. Although they had still not cracked the Italian book ciphers since they had changed the previous July, they had for some years known about their naval machine ciphers, although these were never more than a couple a day and rarely of great significance. That was not the case in March 1941, when these intercepted codes were to prove of crucial importance to Cunningham.

For the successful interception of the Italian fleet, ABC needed his battle-fleet to be to the west of Crete. The problem was how to get it there without being spotted. ABC ordered his second-in-command, Vice-Admiral Pridham-Wippell to sail his four battle-cruisers and a small number of destroyers out of Piraeus in Greece on the evening of 27 March and rendezvous with him and the battle-fleet, and another force of destroyers, the following morning. Meanwhile, ABC was putting together his plan to slip away from Alexandria under the cover of darkness. It had been known for some time that the Japanese consul in Alexandria – protected by Japan's current neutrality and diplomatic immunity – had been passing on information to the Axis. The time had come to call his bluff. On the afternoon of the 27th, Cunningham walked off *Warspite* with his case and golf clubs. Echoing Sir Francis Drake's famous game of bowls nearly four hundred years before, ABC spent the rest of the afternoon on the links, where, as he suspected, he was able to wave at the Japanese consul teeing up across the fairway. Eighteen holes later, he discreetly nipped back on board and set sail to meet the rest of his fleet, while the one troop convoy at sea was ordered to quietly about-turn. The Japanese consul never suspected a thing.

Even so, ABC hardly dared to believe they would ever catch up with the Italians and bet one of his staff officers ten shillings that they would not even sight the enemy. But the following morning, as they were steaming towards their rendezvous, Pridham-Wippell reported three enemy cruisers and a force of destroyers just to the north of him. Rubbing his hands together with glee, Cunningham had never been so glad to lose a bet and promptly handed over the ten shillings wagered the previous evening.

Pridham-Wippell was now uncomfortably close to the Italian cruiser squadron, and, fully aware that the enemy were faster and with greater firing range, decided to turn away and try to draw them towards Cunningham and the battle-fleet. Although they came under fire, the shelling was initially inaccurate and, more importantly, the ploy appeared to be working. Then, just after eleven in the morning, *Warspite* began to intercept a number of urgent and frenetic signals from Pridham-Wippell to the rest of his force. On board *Warspite*, the commanders were pricking up their ears, wondering what was going on. 'Don't be so damned silly,' ABC barked at them. 'He's sighted the enemy battle-fleet, and if you'd ever done any reasonable time in destroyers, you'd know it without waiting for the amplifying report.'[11] ABC now went into his 'caged tiger' mode,[12] pacing the side of the bridge closest to the enemy. Desperate for a chance to get among the Italian fleet and blast them out of the water, he was also acutely aware that his second-in-command's force was in serious peril. Not only were superior battle-cruisers closing, they were now up against the mightiest battleship ever to grace the Mediterranean. With nine fifteen-inch guns capable of a massive range of sixteen miles, and with a top speed of 30 knots (six knots faster than the fastest British ship), the *Vittorio Veneto* had the potential to make short work of Pridham-Wippell's ships.

Shells were raining down on the British cruiser force. The second-in-command's flagship, the *Orion*, suffered one very near miss and a number of close calls. A smoke-screen had been put up to shield them, but they were now in very serious danger of annihilation. They needed back-up, and fast.

It had been Cunningham's intention to send off the torpedo-bombers from the carrier *Formidable* only when the battle-fleet was close enough to join in the attack, but he now sent orders for the aircraft to strike the enemy battleship right away. They arrived in the nick of time; the Italian battleship had already fired 94 shells, so it's little wonder Pridham-Wippell's signals sounded urgent. But while the subsequent air attack distracted the enemy and took the pressure off the cruiser force, it also prompted the Italian battleship to fall back, as ABC had feared. The only way the British battle-fleet could catch up now was if the torpedo-bombers from the carriers made more attacks and sufficiently slowed down the Italians' retreat. Even then, the earliest interception would be after dusk.

Another strike force of torpedo-bombers flew off from *Formidable* at three o'clock. Although there were a number of near misses, one torpedo hit the battleship, shearing off one of the propellers and halving her speed. Twin-engine RAF Blenheim bombers from Greece and Alexandria also joined in the attack, as did Swordfish from Crete, but their reports on landing were all conflicting: the battleship had been hit three times; it had stopped; it was travelling at eight knots; it was 65 miles away; only 40 miles away. Misleading and contradictory information was one of the major difficulties facing ABC when making decisions. How could he be sure of the Italians' position? He decided to send off *Warspite's* own observer plane, whose pilot was highly experienced and had ABC's trust. The reports came back soon after, at around six-thirty: the Italian battleship was 45 miles west, doing fifteen knots and flanked by six battle-cruisers and eleven destroyers. A second cruiser force was somewhere further north-west.

Having rejoined the battle-fleet earlier in the afternoon, the second-in-command was now ordered back to give chase to the Italian fleet, and establish visual contact. A rapid strike force of eight destroyers was also sent forward to try to make contact with the stricken *Vittorio Veneto*. In the meantime, *Formidable's* torpedo-bombers were sent off for a third time to harry the Italian fleet once more.

By the morning the Italians would be within easy range of their own air forces and the chance for battle would have been missed. If the British were to attack, a night action was now the only option. Night engagements posed considerable risks, as they tended to be more confusing than a daylight attack. The chances of crashing into other ships, and firing on one's own side, were high. Furthermore, the fleet had not carried out a night-attack exercise for some while and were very short of practice. ABC asked the opinion of his staff officers. None of them liked it much. They were also wary of charging after a superior force, running the risk of major damage to their battle-fleet and finding themselves dangerously exposed by the morning. 'You're a pack of yellow-livered skunks,' he told them. 'I'll go and have my supper now and see after supper if my morale isn't higher than yours.' But he had already made up his mind; the steely blue look in his eyes told them that. The battle was on.[13]

As dusk fell, the distant sky was filled with the rumbling and quivering orange glow of the Italian anti-aircraft barrage as the final air strike attacked the enemy fleet. The eight destroyers of Pridham-Wippell's force were ordered to close and attack the Italian battleship, but this was a risky proposition even by Cunningham's brazen standards, and the chance of them succeeding against such a superior force were slight.

Luck, much needed by the greatest of leaders, played into ABC's hands. Unbeknown to him, the Italian cruiser *Pola* had been torpedoed during the final air attack and had now stopped in the water. Admiral Iachino, instead of sparing only a couple of destroyers to help, instructed two of his heavy cruisers, *Fiume* and *Zara*, and a smaller cruiser and their accompanying destroyers to support the listing ship – in other words, three of his best fighting vessels. Clearly, he had not anticipated ABC's determination to fight at night. *Pola* was then picked up by Pridham-Wippell's radar, although he was unaware that much of the Italian fleet had now turned back and continued on the same course after the *Vittorio Veneto*.

Cunningham, peering through his night-glasses on the bridge of *Warspite*, was astounded to see the enemy cruisers steaming on an opposite course and now just two miles away. Once more the PA systems clicked on and the bugle for 'Action Stations' rang out across the British battle-fleet. Crews rushed to their posts, unsure in the dark of the situation or what lay in store for them. Nerves had been running high all day – ABC's desire for battle was known to all, but so was the superior strength of the Italians. The thought of suffering a direct hit – of raging fires and torrents of gushing water – preyed heavily on the minds of all the men.

Then there was silence, silence that could almost be felt – a sensation ABC would never forget. The only noise was the succinct orders from the gun control personnel and the clicking as the guns were brought into position. Looking forward, Cunningham watched the turrets swing and steady as the fifteen-inch guns were pointed towards the enemy cruisers. Then he heard the calm voice from the director tower, 'Director layer sees target' – indicating the moment when the guns were primed and ready. The enemy lay less than 4,000 yards away – almost point-blank range. 'Never in the whole of my life,' wrote Cunningham, 'have I experienced a more thrilling moment.'[14]

It was the Chief Gunnery Officer, rather than Cunningham, who actually gave the order to fire. First came the 'ting-ting-ting' of the firing gongs, then a great orange flash and a violent shudder, felt throughout the ship, as the six big guns fired simultaneously. At the same time, Cunningham had ordered the searchlight of one of the destroyers to be directed onto one of the enemy cruisers. The six shells could actually be seen caught in the light as they whistled across the sky. The silvery-blue outline of the cruiser *Fiume* briefly shone like a spectre in the night until five of the six shells struck with an eruption of brilliant flame. 'Good Lord! We've hit her!' *Warspite's* Captain said with surprise to ABC.[15] They could hardly have missed.

It was soon apparent that the Italians had not been aware of the British battle-fleet, and certainly had had no idea they were walking into the lion's den. Even Cunningham was appalled by the devastation caused by their attack: whole turrets and masses of debris whirled through the air and cascaded into the sea. In no time at all, they were nothing but burning torches of fire. The second cruiser, the *Zara*, was hit by at least 25 separate fifteen-inch shells. Some four hours later, her burning hulk was found drifting a short distance further south. The destroyer *Jervis* finished her off with a single torpedo.

A number of enemy destroyers appeared and began firing torpedoes. *Warspite* hit the leading ship, but then ABC ordered the battle-fleet to retire to the north to avoid the counter-attack, while launching his own destroyers, in pairs, into the fray. Shortly afterwards, he saw star-shell, tracer and heavy gunfire to the south-west – but there were no British ships in that area. The Italians had begun firing on themselves.

Meanwhile, *Pola*, the cruiser hit by the torpedo-bombers earlier in the evening, was still afloat, but dead in the water. When she was mistaken by one of ABC's destroyers for the *Vittorio Veneto*, Pridham-Wippell's destroyer force immediately turned back towards her. When the leading destroyer, the *Jervis*, reached her, they found a scene of utter mayhem. The decks were littered with bottles and personal belongings. Many of the Italian sailors were drunk. In panic, a large number were jumping over the side. *Jervis*'s CO, Captain Mack, ordered the rest of the crew to be taken off and then, at four in the morning, sank her. It was the final action of the battle.

The following morning ABC brought the fleet back to the battle site. He was fairly certain *Warspite* had sunk a destroyer, and it was with a certain degree of trepidation that he counted out his ships. They were all there. In fact, the only loss during the whole battle was one two-man aircraft.

The sea was calm, but the debris betrayed the carnage of the previous night. The water was covered with a film of oil and littered with bits of wreckage. Floating corpses bobbed gently in the still morning air. ABC ordered his destroyers to pick up any survivors – some 900 including those from *Pola*. The arrival of a few German planes then brought the mopping-up to an end, although ABC ensured the Italians were signalled the position; their hospital ship later picked up a further 160 Italian sailors.

On Sunday 30 March, ABC returned in triumph to Alexandria. The *Vittorio Veneto* had escaped, but it had been an emphatic victory none-theless. Britain's Navy once again reigned supreme in the Mediterranean.

The victory of the Night Battle of Cape Matapan was greeted with unanimous joy on Malta. John Agius heard the news on the BBC, broadcast over the Rediffusion system. To him, listening to how the searchlights had been shone on to the Italian ships, followed by the night-time broadside from the British battle-fleet, it sounded like a *Boy's Own* story. But it was nothing less than he expected. He had grown up seeing the Royal Navy on show in port – looking huge and deadly and magnificent – and had always assumed they must be invincible. Cunningham was also well-known and hugely popular in Malta; to Maltese like John Agius, it was as though one of their own had led this victory.

Matapan, then, was a much-needed fillip amid the otherwise gloomy situation. The RAF might just as well have had no fighter aircraft at all for all the good they were able to do. The Axis bombers were still coming over several times a day – there were 107 air raid alerts in February and 105 in March – and now the Messerschmitt 109s were adding to the misery by spraying anything that moved with machine-gun bullets.

Rationing of food had also begun. In February, the Government had established a new department, the Food Distribution Office, to ensure the even distribution of food and to discourage hoarding. In effect this was rationing on a national basis. The Island had a certain quantity of food reserves, but it was essential these supplies were very carefully monitored. Individual rationing began on 7 April, with sugar, matches, soap and coffee the first commodities to be on the list. Lack of kerosene was also another major headache, and from 2 April no individual was allowed to buy more than half a gallon at any one time. By the beginning of May, it was also on the ration list, with a family of three receiving only half a gallon per week. This did not go very far, although the Montebellos in their underground shelter had limited means with which to cook hot food anyway. It was larger families living in outlying areas who felt the pinch more. The Agius family, with seven mouths to feed and a comparatively large house to light, had to alter their lifestyle considerably in the wake of these new restrictions.

General conscription had been introduced on 3 March. All men between sixteen and 56 were now liable for National Service, although it was the 20- and 21-year-olds who were first to be called up. John Agius, as a civilian working for the RAF, was exempt from military service; it was rightly considered he was already doing his bit. In fact, a large number of Maltese had already answered the call to arms. The Royal Malta Artillery now manned many of the gun positions around the harbour, while the King's Own Malta Regiment was also swelling in numbers. Many more were at sea.

★

Meme Cortis was also still doing her bit for the war effort up at the 90th General Hospital at Imtarfa. She heard the air raid sirens just like everyone else, but rarely spent any time in a shelter. After all, if all the nurses took cover every time a plane came over, who would look after the patients? Shelters were being built at the hospital, however, as were ramps in order to wheel the worst cases quickly to safety. Even so, despite their proximity to Takali, the Germans appeared to have no interest in attacking the hospital; it was the military targets they were after. Meme could see them sometimes from the VAD Mess: bombs exploding over Hal Far in the south-east, then Luqa, then Takali. It was almost a straight line, and then they turned north, bypassing Imtarfa, straight over St Paul's Bay and back to Sicily.

But Meme and her colleagues were soon to discover they, too, were not immune from the bombing. Although the Barrack Hospital at the centre of Imtarfa had been slightly hit in February, on 13 April, as many as 28 bombs fell on Imtarfa, including a direct hit on the Isolation wing. Although no one was killed, the damage was considerable – windows and doors blown in, many of the electrical fittings and equipment ruined, glass and debris everywhere – and highly disruptive.

Meme felt more angry than frightened. Ever since the *Illustrious* had arrived in Grand Harbour, she had been very busy. New cases were coming in all the time, and although she enjoyed her work, at the end of the day she would be exhausted. If the Germans were now bombing the hospital, that was too bad; but she was not going to be cowed. Instead, she decided, she would simply take each day as it came, living with no regrets.

By and large, it was the harbours, airfields and surrounding areas that had suffered most. The Three Cities, particularly, were full of rubble and destroyed buildings. Initial feelings of shock and horror had been replaced by a sense of determined defiance, however. Between air raids, most people tried to continue their everyday lives as best they could. 'We were blasted well out, but we have blasted well started again,' ran one advertisement for a military tailor, assuring their customers they had plenty of stocks of khaki drill and other material.[16]

While the Island as a whole was generally bearing up well, it was often peripheral events that did most damage to morale – and the sinking of the harbour vessel, *Moor*, on 8 April, was just such an event. It was carrying out maintenance work on the boom defence nets at the entrance of Grand Harbour when it struck a mine. Michael Montebello saw it all. Then a Boy Scout, he was encouraged to keep a watch out for anything unusual and then to report it straight away. It was late afternoon, around five o'clock, and Michael had been outside their shelter on the harbour's edge watching the comings and goings on the water. Suddenly, he heard a massive explosion, and looked round to see the *Moor* disappear in just a few seconds. 'There was an incredible "whoosh", like a kind of sucking noise, and then it vanished. Just like that,' says Michael. There was only one survivor from the 29-strong Maltese crew. Later that evening, some of the dead men's relatives came down to the harbour front, in considerable distress and asking for any information. Michael told them what he could; but it had all happened so quickly. A few days later some of the bodies floated up. 'You could see the white hair and blue faces,' says Michael. He and his friends rushed off to tell the police; as Scouts, that was their job.

Although the submariners were trying to maintain good spirits, it was becoming harder with their continued lack of success at sea. *Upholder* had now been on five patrols but recorded hits on just one. And, if anything, they seemed to be getting worse. Captain Raw, commander of the First Submarine Flotilla in Alexandria, wrote to Simpson after their fifth patrol from 3–14 April. 'Eight torpedoes were fired without scoring a single hit, a result which can only be considered extremely disappointing.'[17]

'There is no doubt Simpson was getting worried,' says Tubby Crawford. David Wanklyn had been Shrimp Simpson's First Lieutenant when he had commanded *Porpoise*, and Simpson had considerable faith in him; but even so, the results were not good. Tubby was obviously disappointed, but, like Simpson, had great confidence in his CO, and felt sure their turn would come. 'I am sure Simpson must have had a heart to heart with Wanklyn, though,' adds Tubby. In fact, Simpson was already wondering whether his former protégé should be relieved of his command. Wanklyn and the crew of *Upholder* had just one more chance to prove themselves.

CHAPTER 8

Valour at Sea

MAY 1941

ABC SOMETIMES FELT he was fighting on two fronts: against the Axis forces in the Mediterranean, and the decision-makers back in London, who were constantly harrying him for improved results against Axis shipping. Their agitation was understandable, though: having been in a position of comparative strength a couple of months before, the British were now in dire straits. The Germans had, as expected, invaded Greece at the beginning of April, and the Greek Army and the three divisions of the British Expeditionary Force were not strong enough to mount any serious opposition. They were fighting valiantly but, with almost no air power, stood little chance. Meanwhile, Axis supplies continued the run across the Mediterranean to North Africa virtually unopposed. Rommel, too, had quickly made his mark. By 11 April Tobruk was surrounded. Two days later, the Germans had bypassed the town and hammered back the depleted British as far as Sollum on the Egyptian border.

ABC believed the most effective way to attack Axis shipping was from Malta. The submarines there were already out on continuous patrol, but small destroyer fleets operating from Grand Harbour could potentially cause considerable damage, as Churchill had suggested the previous year. The problem, as ever, was that without sufficient air cover – and at present there was virtually none – such forces would have to operate at night and then at their absolute maximum speed, which meant a greater consumption of fuel from Malta's dwindling stocks. But although ABC repeatedly signalled the Admiralty and Government alerting them to this quandary, instead of encouragement he only received more demands upon his fleet. His frustration mounted; how could anyone sitting behind a desk in London possibly appreciate how stretched his resources were? Without the right tools, those back in London were expecting the impossible.

Even so, Cunningham tried sending a force of four destroyers to Malta under Captain Mack of the *Jervis*. They soon demonstrated their potential by sinking five Axis merchant ships and three Italian destroyers in just one action on 16 April, although one of the British destroyers was sunk in the process. The attack illustrated ABC's dilemma: yes, his ships could be highly effective, but to make any noticeable impression on the enemy, he needed about half a dozen of these small destroyer forces with the necessary supplies of fuel and ammunition to sustain them.

Churchill and the Admiralty then proposed another plan: the bombardment and blockade of Tripoli. They told ABC that the battleship *Barham* and one cruiser should be used for the purpose, even though it would inevitably mean the loss of both ships. Two thousand miles away, this must have looked good on paper: Tripoli being the principal port in Libya, this would seriously disrupt Axis supplies, and so the loss of the ships was a price worth paying. But ABC was furious – to him it was a scheme so impracticable it could only have been devised by people who knew nothing of the navigational difficulties of reaching such a position outside the harbour. Chances of success, he reckoned, were ten to one against, and that was being optimistic.

He told this to Pound who tersely replied, 'HM Government has given instructions that every possible step must be taken by the Navy to prevent supplies reaching Libya from Italy … Failure by the Navy to concentrate on prevention of such movements to the exclusion of everything not absolutely vital will be considered as having let the side down.'[1] In other words, stop whingeing and get on with it.

ABC felt as though he were banging his head against a wall. Was no one in London listening to what he was saying? And what did they think he was doing all day? He'd been as busy as ever in recent weeks, bombarding German supply columns along the North African coast as well as trying to bring in supplies to the now besieged Tobruk. 'No less than four operations are in train for the next 24 hours including two landings,' he signalled to Pound. 'We are not idle in Libya and nobody out here will say the Navy has let them down.'[2]

Finally, the Admiralty backed down, agreeing to a bombardment of Tripoli from further out at sea and using the entire fleet rather than two ships right outside the harbour entrance. ABC would not be expected to use any of his ships to literally block the mouth of the harbour. A plan was hastily devised: after escorting the tanker *Breconshire* to Malta with much-needed fuel, the fleet would steam towards Tripoli on the 20th, so as to be in position to attack at dawn, and gain maximum chance of surprise. Before them, Wellingtons from Egypt and Swordfish from Malta would also bomb the harbour. The submarine, *Truant*, from Malta, was to act as a navigational marker outside the harbour.

All went according to plan, and, in the event, the operation was carried out without loss. Despite the port being pounded with over five hundred tons of explosives, however, Tripoli was fully operational again just a day later. By then, the Admiralty's obsession with Tripoli had – for the time being at any rate – passed, overtaken by the course of events in Greece. That was where Cunningham was needed next, to evacuate the army he had spent much of the previous month ferrying from North Africa.

But the problem of how to damage Axis supply routes remained. Bombardment of Axis ports was of limited effect, and a Malta-based destroyer force impracticable. ABC would have to look elsewhere for his offensive assault on the enemy convoys – to a force that could operate without aerial protection and without a complex harbour system; a force that was not reliant on vast quantities of fuel and a force that could, when necessary, become invisible.

What he needed was the Malta submarines to make good their potential.

Shortly after noon on 24 April, a ship had been sighted. Although it had neither flag nor markings, it was clearly laden and its position, between the tiny island of Lampedusa and the east coast of Tunisia, suggested it could only be headed for Italy. Lieutenant-Commander David Wanklyn had no hesitation in assessing it as enemy.

Although the sea was choppy, he ordered *Upholder* to close at full speed. Tubby Crawford glanced across at his CO. Tall, hawkish, with intense eyes and a patriarchal beard, 'Wanks', as his crew knew him, peered into the periscope, a model of calm concentration. Having given the order, 'Start the attack,' he began calling out range and bearings. The crew were all at their stations, poised for action. In the centre of the

Control Room was Wanklyn, standing at the periscope. To one side, near the ladder to the bridge, was Tubby. As Number One, he was in for a testing time; commanding the control of the submarine and maintaining perfect trim in these conditions required total concentration and a clear view of the two hydroplane operators and their instrument dials. Standing by the upright torpedo calculator was the Torpedo Officer, while the Navigation Officer was ready by the 'fruit machine'. From floor to ceiling, the Control Room was covered with dials, instruments, valve wheels and cables and lined with insulating cork. Not an inch was spared, and although they could stand upright, the space was, to say the least, cramped.

The tension was palpable: everyone on board knew just how much they needed to hit this ship.

Tubby had nothing but praise for his CO. Wanklyn was highly popular with the crew and although he must have been greatly troubled by their recent disappointments, he never once showed any outward sign of concern. In the Control Room, the skipper was even more under scrutiny, for it was easy to spot the slightest expression of nerves or anxiety at such close quarters. Despite the high stakes, however, Wanklyn remained as calm and confident as ever. Tubby still had total faith in him.

They were as close as 700 yards when Wanklyn gave the order to fire the first two torpedoes. As they shot out of the prow, Tubby felt the pressure on his ears and steadied himself as the boat lurched backwards. Everyone held their breath. Seconds passed. Were the torpedoes on the right course? Would they hit this time, or was it another missed opportunity? Twenty seconds, twenty-five … then at last an explosion as the torpedoes hit. Being so close, *Upholder* rocked violently from the blast. The lights flickered and forward some bulbs even smashed. Tubby was busy trying to steady the submarine, but noticed his CO smile with satisfaction and order them to move north-east. Watching the crippled ship from a safe distance, Wanklyn saw she was sinking, albeit slowly, and with her decks already awash, there was no need to go in again and finish her off.

Despite this, there was little time for them to enjoy their success. New orders arrived. They were to head north to the Kerkenah Bank off Tunisia and finish off a destroyer and supply ship that had been attacked and run aground. This was potentially an extremely dangerous situation. The waters there were uncomfortably shallow; if they were attacked, there would be no chance of diving. 'It was the kind of situation no submariner relishes,' says Tubby, especially since they would be so close to the coast and within easy range of enemy aircraft.

Approaching the targets early the following afternoon, Wanklyn decided to dive where the sea was still deep enough and then approach once it had become dark. They had hoped to be able to torpedo the ships, but they soon discovered the water was too shallow even for that. Their only hope was to surface and run alongside the supply ship and set her on fire. Both ships looked to be deserted, but it was a nerve-wracking exercise inching towards their quarry. There was always the possibility that a gun crew had been left behind until a rescue could be hatched, and they might easily run aground themselves – and then they really would be in trouble.

But as they gingerly inched alongside, no enemy guns opened fire. A boarding party clambered onto her deck and, after searching the ship and taking a number of papers, laid demolition charges. The men then returned, gleefully clutching German tin helmets and other souvenirs, and they set course for deeper water. A short while after, they heard the explosives detonate. Standing on the bridge, with the dark waters of the Mediterranean lapping over *Upholder*'s prows, Tubby watched the remains of the ship burning late into the night.

The destroyer, in even shallower waters, was spared, but a few days later, and now further south once more, they ran into a convoy of five ships with four escorting destroyers. The weather was terrible and Tubby was having great difficulty in keeping *Upholder* steady. Trying to make periscope observations was even trickier, but, with his confidence now mounting, Wanklyn ordered a full salvo of four torpedoes to be fired. Just under a minute later, they heard three explosions. Two had struck a German ship of over 7,000 tons, and she sank immediately. A third hit a second, smaller vessel. Although the destroyers launched a counter-attack, *Upholder* escaped, returning an hour later to finish off the maimed ship.

The submariners based at Malta had revived a tradition started in the First World War. This was the raising of a Jolly Roger – the skull and crossbones of pirate legend – if they had been successful on patrol. The flags had been embroidered for them by Maltese nuns, although it was up to the crew to stitch on a white bar if an enemy ship was destroyed. It must, then, have been a great relief to Shrimp Simpson to see *Upholder* triumphantly enter Marsamxett Harbour, her Jolly Roger fluttering in the breeze above a German ensign, and with no fewer than four bars already stitched on. Clambering for position on the bridge were a number of her crew, wearing their looted German tin helmets.

Nat Gold and the rest of 830 Fleet Air Arm Squadron were getting to know Tripoli pretty well. Although ABC's bombardment of the port had only achieved modest results, it was felt that continual attacks on the primary Axis harbour in North Africa were essential, and 830 Squadron were to play a large role in this continued offensive.

On 5 May, Nat was sent on another minelaying exercise along with three other aircraft. He particularly loathed taking off with these enormous long cylinders strapped underneath, especially since the gap between the ground and the 'cucumber' was less than one foot; he was fully aware that on the rough bomb-damaged airfield of Hal Far, it was all too easy to take off and hit an object that might cause the mine to explode. Nor had any of them forgotten what had happened back in February when eight men had been killed after one had accidentally detonated.

These 'cucumbers' were magnetic mines – lethal weapons, which would sit below the surface of the water and were set to detonate after they had been passed over a number of different times, from once up to eleven. Each mine had a different setting, so the enemy would never know if the minefield had been cleared or not.

On this occasion, they set off much earlier than usual, at around 6.45 p.m. Although the weather was clear over Malta, that soon changed and they were fortunate to be able to spot the Libyan coast through a gap in the clouds some two hours later. This soon closed again and it was only when they saw the thin beam of the searchlights and anti-aircraft fire bursting through that they realized they were approaching Tripoli, and began their descent.

Sparks from the exhaust could be a problem because they showed up their position beautifully. Because of this, and because the exhaust on the Swordfish was on the starboard (right-hand) side, they used to try to descend with the coast to port. Slowly they dropped until, at about 4,000 feet, the pilot cut his engine. Then they glided towards the target in silence, in the hope that the searchlights would take longer to spot them. As they drifted down towards the harbour, Nat felt a wave of nerves sweep over him.

It is easy to appreciate how terrifying this must have been: strapped into the Swordfish, Nat felt desperately vulnerable; with little other than treated cloth between him and the sky, he was descending into a heavily defended enemy port with *no engine running* and, consequently, severely restricted manoeuvrability. It was also incredibly dark, with clouds covering the moon; in fact, they were only able to see their target because of the light from the searchlights reflecting off the cloud. With the wind whistling through the wings, the harbour loomed towards them. Although the open cockpit may have been draughty, at least he could see all around him. He craned his neck, strained his eyes expecting the heavy ack-ack to start pounding around them at any moment. Then, at just 100 feet above sea-level – lower than a five-storey building – and just 400 yards from the target, the cucumber was dropped. Nat crossed his fingers, praying the engine would start again.

With a splutter and a roar, it did. 'The old Pegasus engine never let us down,' says Nat, 'although we always maintained that even if it did, the wings would start to flap.' But with the engines restarted, the light ack-ack gunners soon found their targets. Rapid darts of tracer curved towards them, not just from the harbour moles, but also, Nat saw, from a destroyer lying in harbour. He noticed a number of merchant vessels too – it was a pity they hadn't brought some dive-bombers with them.

For once, they all made it safely out of the fray and despite the cloud, managed to reform over another marker flare and head back to Malta together.

A persistent problem was that with only a radio headset and no radar it was all too easy to get lost, especially at night time, and particularly when there was plenty of cloud. On finishing an attack, the flight leader would drop a flare and then fly around in circles until everyone had congregated, and then, having flashed his navigation lights, would lead them all back to Malta.

By and large, this seemingly haphazard method of mustering worked quite well, although one time Nat Gold and his pilot did find themselves hopelessly lost. Crews in 830 Squadron were always mixed up, although for some reason, Nat was invariably given the youngest pilot with the least experience, as he was on this occasion.

An Italian cruiser had sailed from Trapani Harbour on the west coast of Sicily and was being shadowed by an RAF Wellington bomber. 830 Squadron had been briefed to attack her with torpedoes. Once again, Nat was flying with a new and inexperienced pilot, and they reached the target area to 'a hot reception' – more searchlights than Nat had ever seen before, and with tracer flying in all directions. Again, Nat's plane was the last to attack. Standing up in his cockpit, his hands at the ready with the Lewis gun, he strained to see the cruiser, whilst also keeping a steady eye on the searchlights. One came swinging underneath them, so that they seemed to be right on the edge of the beam. Nat's pilot immediately shot upwards out of the way. Then he yelled into the intercom, 'Is that a ship down there?' Nat peered down, and thought it probably was, as he was sure he could see a slight bow wave. They lost height, levelled out at sea-level and approaching the bow of the ship, dropped the torpedo, before banking sharply to the left. They didn't see any explosion. 'I think we dropped it too soon,' says Nat.

They made their way out to sea, and in the distance could see a flame float – their 'rendezvous' – but as they neared, the flame went out. Another light appeared in a different position, so they made for that instead, but as they drew nearer, that, too, vanished. 'We were on our own,' says Nat. 'This was the pilot's first operational flight and I didn't know quite what to do.' On a previous trip, however, he had noticed a couple of lighthouses along the coast, and they had proved good markers, as they'd then turned right and eventually found themselves on course for Malta. Nat suggested they try to find them again now. The pilot agreed to chance it, and sure enough, in the distance they spotted a lighthouse, then another one. Then they saw one more. And another. This wasn't right. They began to worry – they were alone, fuel was running low and they hadn't the faintest idea where they were. Nat tried sending a coded message on his radio, hoping to pick up Malta and be given a course to steer, but he couldn't get through. The RAF boys were obviously still out and taking up the air space. Fast running out of options, Nat decided to send out an SOS. Nothing happened, so he sent out another. Suddenly, a perfectly loud and clear signal came over his headphones – from Bombay, telling the RAF to keep radio silence and to listen out for Nat's SOS signal. 'When that came through I very nearly fell off my seat it was so loud,' says Nat. Shortly afterwards, he picked up a very faint signal giving him a course to steer; in fact, they had been only two degrees off Malta.

There were no further hiccups, and soon they were safely on the ground. The pilot clambered out and hugged Nat tightly, thanking him profusely. 'I thought he was going to kiss me, he was so overjoyed,' says Nat. 'He said, "I'm going to ask the CO if you'll fly with me again."' Nat smiled ruefully. Not if I can help it, he thought to himself.

★

At last, ABC's requests for more fighter planes for Malta were being answered, which was just as well since 261 Squadron – or what remained of it – was on its knees. Their fighter airfield at Takali was being pasted daily by the bombers and strafed by the Messerschmitt 109s; and the pilots might as well have stayed safely on the ground for all the good they could do in the air. On 27 April, however, 23 new Hurricanes arrived, whilst an even bigger batch was planned for May.

Among the pilots earmarked for Malta was Pilot Officer Tommy Thompson, a six-foot three-inch 20-year-old with seven months' experience in a fighter squadron under his belt. Tommy had finished his training the previous September, and then been posted to 85 Squadron up at Church Fenton in Lincolnshire. 85 had been in the front line of the Battle of Britain, but by the time Tommy arrived, they had been moved north for a well-earned breather. Although officially operational, there was little enemy activity up there and it gave Tommy the perfect chance to bring his flying skills up to scratch.

After a couple of weeks he was ordered to join 249 Squadron at North Weald, in Essex.[3] Before he left to join them, the CO of 85 Squadron, Squadron Leader Peter Townsend (who later almost married Princess Margaret), grabbed him and said, 'Right, you and I will go and practise some dog-fighting before you go.' The idea was to start flying head-to-head towards one another and then see who could get on the other's tail first. The first three times, Tommy soon found Townsend behind him, but on the last, he managed to bring the CO into his sights. 'With hindsight, I'm sure he let me do that in order to boost my confidence,' says Tommy. Which it did: later that day he headed down to North Weald believing that if he could get on the tail of someone with Townsend's experience and skill, he would have a good chance against the Germans.

He had wanted to fly from an early age and was far more interested in aircraft than his school-work. Having failed his school certificate twice, he asked his father if he could join the RAF. Only if he went to the RAF College at Cranwell, he was told. The exams, however, were quite beyond him, and so he took a job in Ipswich, near where he lived and persuaded his father to let him join the RAF Volunteer Reserves instead. He was still flying at weekends and training to be an engineering assistant for a tea company when war broke out. Called up immediately, he reported to his call centre in Ipswich. There he was paid and told to go on three weeks' leave. He was pretty happy being given three pounds ten shillings a week for doing nothing, but before too long was sent to an initial training unit near Hastings on the south coast. Billeted in a block of luxury flats overlooking the sea, he and his fellow recruits were taught drill, given plenty of physical training and instructed about the theory of flight. In the evening they went to the pub to spend their wages and chatted up the local girls. 'They started feeding us bromide in our tea because so many of the local girls were getting up the spout. So we stopped drinking the tea.'

Flying training followed, while the war still seemed very distant. Everyone on his course wanted to fly fighters, but the majority were sidelined for bombers and twin-engine planes. But Tommy was discovering flying was one thing he was good at and scored above average on both elementary and advanced flying, and so was sent to fighter training.

Although it was over a year between joining up in Ipswich and arriving at North Weald to join 249 Squadron, Tommy still had a lot to learn when he took off for his first combat sortie as Number Two to another tall young airman, Pilot Officer Tom Neil. Tom had joined the squadron in May, and, with eight-and-a-half kills and a DFC to his name, was an 'ace', despite being only twenty years old.[4] What mattered, however, was experience, not age, and having survived the summer, Tom had that in spades. 'Stick with me,' he'd told Tommy. 'Don't lose me, just stay with me and you'll be all right.' They took off and flew into a swarm of twenty 109s. Tommy watched Tom shoot down one of them then all of a sudden the sky was empty. 'I never even fired my guns,' says Tommy, 'but I learnt more in those two minutes than in all my training.'

Six months later both men were still alive and still with 249. The Battle of Britain had been won, and now, instead of waiting for the Germans to come over, the squadron were flying over to France on fighter sweeps, looking to attack enemy aircraft instead. It wasn't a bad way to fight a war – Tommy still enjoyed flying, he was being well fed and there was always plenty to drink and people around to have a laugh with. There were showers, baths and a decent bed, and during days off or when on leave, he could go back home or make trips to London. And, of course, the girls liked the fighter pilots. It was still an extremely dangerous occupation, but compared with what many others had to put up with, life could have been a whole lot worse.

Then came the news. Both Tommy and Tom Neil were in their

dispersal hut one morning in late April when they were told the whole squadron was being posted overseas, although it was not specified where.

Tommy was pretty sure he knew why this bolt from the blue had occurred. A short while before, the North Weald squadrons – 249 and 46 – had mistakenly attacked Douglas Bader's Duxford Wing of three squadrons and shot one of their number down. Fortunately, the man baled out safely, but the next day Bader turned up at 249's dispersal hut and started angrily peppering them with questions. Tommy and the rest of the squadron clammed up – they wouldn't say a word. Fuming, Bader got into his car and screeched off to see 46 Squadron. Someone at 249 quickly got on the phone to warn them that Bader was on the warpath, and so they barricaded the door to their dispersal hut and wouldn't let him in. 'It was a strange thing that not long after both 249 and 46 Squadrons were sent overseas.' As Tommy points out, Bader had considerable influence at the Air Ministry.

Whether it was Bader who was the influencing factor in getting the squadron posted overseas, or Victor Beamish, the North Weald Station Commander – as Tom Neil believes – there was no denying there had been a lull in the air fighting over Britain and with Cunningham – not to mention Governor Dobbie – screaming out for more planes, a few squadrons could certainly be spared from Fighter Command. Tom, Tommy and the rest of 249 were still in the dark about where they were being posted, although the arrival at North Weald of a Mark I Hurricane with a tropicalized air filter a few days before their departure had given them a big clue. Clearly it was going to be somewhere hot and the Middle East seemed the most likely.

Tom Neil was shocked by the sight of the aircraft carrier HMS *Furious*, moored up and waiting for them at Liverpool. Brought up in Liverpool, he'd seen plenty of ships in his time and had always believed in the superiority of the Royal Navy, and had assumed all her ships were pristine, shiny and magnificent. But the war had taken its toll, and arriving at the quayside he looked up to see a tired, rusting hulk. He couldn't believe they were really going to war in such a vessel. The crew treated them with utter indifference and the pilots were appalled to learn they would be sleeping in hammocks the whole way. First port of call, they were told, would be Gibraltar.

After a long detour into the heart of the Atlantic in order to minimize the chance of running into U-boats and enemy attack from the air, they reached Gibraltar. There, they transferred on to HMS *Ark Royal* and steamed off back out into the Atlantic to join a much larger fleet. Only on turning back towards the Mediterranean did they discover the plan was to fly off 450 miles from Malta. They would stop there to refuel and rearm, and then take off again for Egypt. Tom Neil was not looking forward to it one bit. Firstly, none of them had ever taken off from an aircraft carrier before and although the Hurricane did not require a long runway, the flight deck of the *Ark Royal* looked horribly short. Secondly, their flights would take them over largely hostile waters with little land in case anything went wrong. Although the planes were fitted with extra fuel tanks, it was quite possible that the change-over mechanism might not work. It was quite possible any *number* of things could go wrong. As a Flight Commander, it would be up to him to lead half the squadron on this trip. Right now, he wasn't so sure he wanted such a responsibility and began thinking about North Weald – the cosy fire in the Mess and quiet games of snooker after dinner. He liked this whole trip less and less.

249 Squadron were to fly off *Ark Royal* in two groups, each guided by a Royal Navy Fulmar. Tommy Thompson was in the first group, led by the CO, Squadron Leader 'Butch' Barton. Although apprehensive about taking off from the carrier, in the event he found it a lot less traumatic than he'd imagined. There was a slight hiccup when their Fulmar split an oil tank and had to turn back, but another soon took its place and they flew to Malta without further incident.

Not so for Tom Neil, whose feelings of foreboding had been justified. Each man was only allowed thirty pounds in weight of kit, as there was virtually no storage space in the Hurricane. Clothes and other small items were placed in the ammunition boxes in the wings, while their bulky and ridiculous-looking tropical pith helmets were wedged into the radio compartment behind the cockpit. He prayed they wouldn't meet any enemy – with the gun ports now full of kit, they were defenceless.

Like Tommy before him, he took off from the flight deck with little fuss, but no sooner was he airborne than he heard a loud bang and his aircraft began to slew badly to one side. With his stomach lurching, he grabbed the throttle only to be blinded by bits of paper and maps on which he had his course written. The sudden movement of the plane had caused them to be sucked from where he had wedged them and, after briefly flapping around his head, out of his still-open cockpit.

Cursing, he frantically looked at his wing, hoping he hadn't already lost a fuel tank. It was still there, but the damage was almost as bad: one of the gun panels on his port wing had partially come undone, and was now sticking up into the air and acting as an effective yet unwanted air-brake.

He could still fly the Hurricane, but only by keeping one foot hard down on the rudder. Even after a couple of minutes his foot was aching badly, and he wondered how on earth he was going to keep going for another couple of hours. But the only alternative was to land back on the carrier, an option fraught with even more danger. He decided to carry on, but after half an hour his leg began to spasm, then went numb. The minutes seemed like hours.

Worse was to come, however. Having been slightly cheered to discover his extra fuel tanks worked, to his horror, he suddenly realized the Fulmar guiding them had vanished. For a few moments panic gripped him and, feeling incapable of decision, he began flying around in a circle, the other ten Hurricanes following obediently behind. With no maps and no guide they had little chance of finding Malta; but if they returned to the aircraft carrier, now steaming back to Gibraltar, they would surely run out of fuel. Beside himself with worry and on the point of tears, he helplessly continued circling, and wondering what on earth he should do.

Breaking the strict radio silence he asked if anyone else was capable of leading them to Malta. No one was. Tom began some mental arithmetic and decided that leading his flight back to Gibraltar was the only option. After flying for an hour or so, by pure chance he spotted the wake of the Fleet, and so realized that if they flew over the *Ark Royal* and collected another Fulmar they might – just – have enough fuel left to reach Malta.

After some confusion as to whether they were friendly or enemy aircraft, the carrier appeared to understand what had happened and sent off a fourth Fulmar. By this time, they had already been airborne for over two hours, and there was now around six hundred – rather than four-hundred-and-fifty – miles between them and Malta. They continued west, Tom's acute discomfort and anxiety about the fuel situation troubling him greatly. By the time he reached his final thirty gallons there was still nothing to be seen but wide open sea. Nor could he see anything with just fifteen minutes' flying time left.

Then, suddenly, there it was – like a large dusty brown leaf floating on the sea. He spotted Luqa, but was horrified to discover the airfield was under attack – they had arrived in the middle of another raid. Minutes later the enemy bombers had gone, and he finally touched down at Luqa amid clouds of dust. He sat in hot, still silence for a few moments, and then a khaki-clad man appeared and jumped onto his wing, pointing to where he should taxi the plane. Overwhelming relief at landing was spoiled when a spark of tobacco from the man's pipe caught in the slipstream and went straight into Tom's eye. In excruciating pain, he taxied off the runway using his good eye, and at last switched off the engine.

Having finally clambered out of the Hurricane, his leg still stiff and his eye stinging, he was directed to the safety of a shelter, where he discovered the day's drama was not yet over. Continuing the long tradition of fighter pilots arriving on Malta, he and the rest of the squadron were told they would not, as planned, be going to Egypt. It was felt 261 Squadron had long since had enough and so would be going to Egypt in their place – *and* taking the newly arrived Hurricanes with them. 249 were to use what was left of 261's aircraft. Back in North Weald, they had been flying brand-new Hurricane Mark IIs. They had flown out with older Mark Is, which had caused a few grumbles. Now they were expected to fly against crack Axis units in planes that would have long ago been taken out of service back in England. After the All Clear had sounded, both Tom and Tommy went back to their planes and unloaded their belongings. The rest of their kit – along with the squadron groundcrew – was still steaming the long way round the Cape towards Egypt. They would not see either again.

Soon they were being driven in an ancient bus along dusty, pot-holed lanes to Takali. It was hot and they were all hungry. Half a mile from the airfield was the Officers' Mess, although since 261 had yet to depart, there was a problem of overcrowding. Tom Neil spent his first night on a camp bed in a stone corridor, listening to a regular procession of people troop past him to the only lavatory in the place. Most were suffering from Malta Dog, and the noise and smell accompanying each visit made him yearn for North Weald even more. But he could have put up with the racket coming from the toilet had it not been for the mosquitoes, who bit and whined around him all night. Although exhausted, he barely slept a wink. He had never felt so low in all his life.

★

Two days before 249 Squadron's arrival, General Dobbie was appointed official Governor of the Island, so shedding his 'Acting-Governor' title. It must have been a welcome confidence boost for him after a testing period, especially since a few question marks over his mettle had begun to arise. Chief among the doubters was Mabel Strickland, proprietor and editor of the *Times of Malta*, who back in January, after the *Illustrious* Blitz, had written a stinging editorial criticizing the Government's handling of the clean-up operation. By April, she had begun to feel convinced he would surrender the Island, a view shared by Lord Louis Mountbatten, who had discussed the situation at length during a meal at the palace while his ship, HMS *Kelly*, had been briefly in port. Mabel Strickland was so concerned she even used her contacts back in London to get a letter outlining her fears to Churchill.

Dobbie was certainly an unusual character. Throughout the early months of 1941, he remained at the Governor's Palace in Valletta, and would regularly invite lunch or dinner guests up onto the roof to watch the air raids over Grand Harbour, apparently oblivious to the fact that most people would far prefer to safely take cover in a shelter than expose themselves so needlessly. His devout adherence to the Plymouth Brethren was also a cause for mistrust, although it seems very unlikely that he was contemplating surrender at that time, and on 8 May he wrote to Churchill saying, 'I am not anxious about the security of Malta. It can and will hold on, whatever happens elsewhere.'[5] He was concerned, however, about how effective the Island could be in an offensive role without sufficient supplies of up-to-date equipment, especially aircraft – but in this he was only echoing the same sentiments as ABC. Dobbie also felt a very real responsibility for both the Maltese and service personnel under his charge. Unlike most theatres of operation, on Malta there was little chance for people ever to get away from the strain of continual attack and bombardment. The services, particularly, could not be taken out of the firing line or sent on leave. 'Consequently, the strain on certain units, especially air units which are constantly in action, is very great.'[6] This could have a massive bearing on morale and performance; and as Governor, maintaining morale was very much part of his brief.

In fact, the Germans *had* seriously considered invading Malta. That spring, Section L of the Oberkommando der Wehrmacht (OKW) had been asked to prepare an appreciation of whether it would be better to invade Malta or Crete.[7] All officers in the section – from the Army,

Navy and Air Force – unanimously agreed it should be Malta, as this seemed to be the only way to secure the sea-route to North Africa permanently. But despite this, Hitler overruled them, insisting it should be Crete because he still feared British air-strikes on the Rumanian oilfields and mistakenly believed the Island could have far-reaching possibilities for the Luftwaffe.

So Crete it was, the airborne invasion starting at dawn on 20 May. The Germans suffered high casualties, but the British forces were once again outgunned and out-manned. Although he had desperately tried to resupply the Island, by 27 May ABC was preparing his second evacuation in as many months. While his victory at Matapan ensured there was at least no sight of the Italian navy, he and his fleet came under continual German air attack. It was a disastrous few days for the Admiral. Three cruisers and six destroyers were sunk; seven further ships, including *Warspite*, were sufficiently damaged to be out of action for several months, and over 1,800 of his men were now dead. Although at the end of it all, the majority – around 16,500 men – had been safely lifted from the island, Cunningham felt very heavy-hearted. 'Once again it had borne in upon us that the Navy and the Army could not make up for the lack of air forces. In my opinion three squadrons of long-range fighters and a few heavy bombing squadrons would have saved Crete.'[8] He was also concerned about the state of his men, who had endured their most hectic two months since the beginning of the war. They were now utterly exhausted. ABC felt pretty drained himself, his enormous confidence sapped by the trauma of the Cretan evacuation. For the first time in his life, he began to worry his men might have lost their faith in him.

While ABC was busy at Crete, *Upholder* was out to prove her new-found success was not just a flash in the pan. Sailing on 15 May, they were ordered to patrol along the toe of Italy. Trouble began soon after leaving when one of the torpedoes developed a leak and had to be swapped, causing a major upheaval in the crew space. Three days later, the asdic broke down, a far more serious problem, since without it they had no listening device – either for targets or when targeted themselves. Despite this blow, they continued on their patrol rather than heading back to base and, on the 19th, were signalled that a convoy was expected from the western Italian ports. The following evening they spotted the ships and, although quite a way off, tried their best to intercept. At 7,000 yards, Wanklyn believed he could get no closer and, still bristling with confidence, gave the order to fire three torpedoes. Despite this massive range of over six miles, one of them hit a tanker. Three days later, they spotted what looked to be French ships. It was a dilemma – were they Vichy or Free French? Wanklyn had about thirty seconds to decide whether to attack or not, and concluding they must be under Italian charter, pressed home the attack. Once more he hit his target.

On the 24th, they were preparing to head back to Malta and looking forward to being safely tucked up in port and having their asdic repaired. Tubby Crawford was on watch in the Control Room, peering through the periscope just as the light was fading, when he suddenly noticed something on the horizon. At first he could make out nothing but a dark shape, but slowly he realized he was looking at an enormous troopship headed to North Africa and surrounded by a screen of five destroyers. In fact, there was not one, but four troopships, zig-zagging to the west of *Upholder*, and silhouetted against the last of the sun's glow. Even so, initially Tubby didn't think an attack possible. There was quite a swell, which not only made periscope observation very difficult, but also affected trim. Furthermore, they only had two torpedoes left, and their asdic was still out of order. The odds of success were stacked against them.

Despite such major handicaps, Wanklyn decided to press home the attack. It was getting dark, he reasoned, which would make it harder for the destroyers to spot them. If they could just get close enough, then they could fire at almost point-blank range. But it was still a high-risk strategy, and escaping from the fray would be, to put it mildly, extremely dangerous.

With *Upholder* bobbing up and down and the sea sluicing against the periscope, they manœuvred into position. They were now so close, they were at risk from being rammed by one of the escorting destroyers, something that very nearly happened. With Tubby frantically trying to keep the submarine steady, Wanklyn was preparing to fire on the largest troopship, when suddenly one of the destroyers loomed in front of the periscope view. Rapidly diving, they avoided collision by a hair's breadth. They were now *inside* the destroyer screen and prepared to attack again. They needed to be quick, very quick. Being surrounded by enemy destroyers was not a good position to be in. In fact, circling a submarine was how many of the German U-boats were eventually destroyed in the Atlantic – once trapped, their chances of escape were considered to be virtually nil.

Moments later, they fired, but the track of torpedoes was immediately spotted and a warning flare fired. It was too late to save the largest of the troopships, which was struck with a massive explosion and began sinking almost immediately.

The problem now was how to safely escape the wrath of the enemy escort. They immediately dived once more, but avoiding the depth charges of five determined destroyers steaming after them at ten times their own speed required nerves of steel and considerable skill. Tubby watched their skipper anxiously. There was little anyone else could do to help Wanklyn, apart from those with responsibility for controlling the course and depth of the submarine. Getting them out of there was almost entirely the skipper's responsibility and his alone. In the Control Room, there was complete silence apart from a few orders from the CO. Even then, Tubby remembers, he exuded calm, gently stroking his beard and changing the course, speed and depth constantly. Tubby tried to console himself by thinking how hard it was for a depth charge to hit – it needed to be accurate on three planes: forward, sideways and vertically. 'We always thought it was difficult for them to get us. That was the only reason we were able to keep going, really,' he says. But as they heard the swish of a destroyer's propellers increasing in intensity as it passed overhead, Tubby found himself gripping tightly onto the chair of the hydroplane operator and involuntarily crouching, waiting for the cascade of depth charges which he knew would come any second. It was almost a relief when they began exploding, with a series of deafening thumps. The submarine shuddered violently. Needles on the depth gauges jumped wildly, a few lights went out and they were sprinkled with a shower of cork granules from the deckhead – ceiling – above.

Attack followed attack. No sooner had they recovered from one series of explosions, than another began, with the whirring of the enemy propeller starting faintly and gradually growing in volume until it passed overhead once more. Then they all held their breath again and waited for the explosions. How close these were, they had no real idea – the only gauge was damage done and the rolling of the boat; noise was unreliable as it varied according to depth of water and conditions. What was certain was that *Upholder* would be forced up noticeably if a charge exploded underneath and rolled sideways if the blast was to one side of them. Some of the men kept a tally of the charges, others tried desperately to focus on their own tasks.

No fewer than 37 depth charges were counted between 8.45 and 9.05 p.m., leaving the men with hearts pounding and severely bitten finger-nails. One crewman couldn't stop his legs shaking, although he made sure nobody saw.[9] For another, the experience was too much: he lost his nerve and suddenly dashed to the conning tower and began trying to unclip the hatch, until he was grabbed and forcibly held down.[10] The last four charges seemed to be particularly close, yet it looked as though Wanklyn, despite groping blindly with little more than his instinct and wits to guide him, had steered them to safety. Then a curious noise began, an awful creaking, like the scraping of wire along the hull. All eyes immediately turned to Wanklyn. It was the sound of the troopship breaking up, he reassured them. At such moments, Tubby believed Wanklyn showed his brilliant qualities of leadership; no matter what doubts he himself may have had, their captain always exuded confidence and authority, and this had a direct effect on every member of the crew.

They eventually surfaced at around 11 p.m. All was dark, but there was an oily smell drifting across the sea around them. Of the rest of the convoy and the destroyers, there was no sign. Wanklyn smiled with satisfaction, then asked for a cup of tea. None of them knew it, but they had sunk the 18,000-ton troopship, the *Conte Rosso*. 1,300 Axis soldiers were lost that day. The Germans were at last learning what it was like to be on the receiving end of a brilliantly executed submarine attack.

PART III

Respite

'We felt as though we had emerged from a long dark tunnel into the summer sunshine.'

SYBIL DOBBIE

CHAPTER 9

Summer Calm
JUNE–AUGUST 1941

THROUGHOUT MAY, ADRIAN Warburton and the rest of 69 Squadron had been reporting the departure of the Luftwaffe. With Hitler preparing to launch Barbarossa – the invasion of the Soviet Union – Fliegerkorps X were needed in Poland. It turned out that the news for Malta was doubly good: not only had Hitler overruled all advice to invade, he was now handing back all responsibility for the continued offensive against the Island to the Italians. In other words, Malta was being given a respite.

Last to leave was Müncheberg's crack fighter unit, and on 25 May, the day Tom Neil, Tommy Thompson and the rest of 249 took over from 261 Squadron, the German ace and his cronies flew over Takali to give them a welcome and farewell visit rolled into one.

The day before, the squadron had been divided into two flights, 'A' and 'B'. Tommy was in 'A' under Squadron Leader Butch Barton, while Tom was to command 'B'. It was agreed the two flights would operate in half-day shifts, basing themselves at the dispersal at Takali when on duty. On any airfield, the pilots had a dispersal-point near the aircraft, usually a hut or building of some description, where they could base themselves while waiting to fly. At Takali, however, facilities were basic to say the least. All the pilots were given were a few chairs and a couple of bell-tents, with a number of telephones wired up inside, linked to fighter control at Lascaris. As soon as the radar high on Dingli Cliffs picked up a plot of enemy planes approaching, the RAF controller would ring down to Takali and order the pilots to scramble to intercept.

It was primitive compared with what they had been used to at North Weald.

25 May was a Sunday, and stiflingly hot. The first shift belonged to 'A' Flight, who had a quiet morning and the kinder weather conditions. By lunchtime, when 'B' Flight took over, the whole place was wilting in still, humid heat. Tom Neil was sweating profusely, watching the lizards scurrying over the stones. All was quiet; not a bird could be heard. Behind him, the bastions of Mdina shimmered in the sun. An old cart, pulled by a straw-hatted horse, creaked slowly across one end of the airfield.

Tom rang through to fighter control and was told there were no reports of any enemy. Despite such assurances, soon afterwards they all heard a distant air raid siren drone out. Tom ordered everyone to get into their planes right away on standby to take off, and then hurriedly rang control again. What the hell was going on? he asked them. Nothing, they told him, but they would let him know. Frustrated, Tom went back to his Hurricane and strapped himself back in. When another, closer, siren rang out, he flung off his straps and ran towards the dispersal tent once again, ordering the airman to ring through to control immediately. He couldn't believe what was going on; the whole set-up on Malta was a complete farce.

He hadn't even reached the tent when three 109s screamed past, their machine-guns crackling across the airfield. Tom threw himself on the ground and looked up to see a 109, only fifty feet off the ground, aiming straight at him. With his hands clasped to his head, he cringed, waiting for the bullets to hit him and wondering whether they would go right through his body or only partly so. But he was spared. The Germans had had their sport and moments later, with a final explosion of noise, they were gone, followed vainly by the tonk-tonk-tonk from the Bofors guns.

Two of the Hurricanes were burning badly, narrow columns of black smoke pitching high into the still air. One of the pilots, Pat Wells, had been hit above the ankle, although such was his shock he only realized once he clambered out of his aircraft and saw the blood. Another broke a leg jumping over a wall to escape the maelstrom. The two burning Hurricanes collapsed with a crash, and then, as their ammunition caught fire, pings of bullets could be heard as they started whipping across the airfield, making the recovering pilots jump in shock. A further two planes were badly – possibly irretrievably – damaged.

Fortunately for 249 Squadron, it was the one and only time they saw Müncheberg's 109s. On 1 June they were posted to North Africa. During their two months over Malta, they had claimed at least 42 Hurricanes in the air, of which Müncheberg himself had shot down 20. Even more had been destroyed on the ground. There can hardly be a better illustration of German fighter supremacy and the woeful inadequacy of the battered old Hurricanes. During that time Müncheberg did not suffer a single operational loss.[1]

The German fighter pilots were not the only ones leaving the battle. At the end of May, Air Commodore Maynard was replaced as AOC Malta by Air Commodore Hugh Pughe Lloyd. Almost immediately promoted to Air Vice-Marshal, 'Hugh Pughe', as he was known by all on the Island, had been briefed to continue the offensive operations against Axis supply lines. A former Bomber Command officer, he was well qualified for this task. He also fully understood the importance of photographic reconnaissance and in the months ahead would become well acquainted with one of his star performers, Adrian Warburton.

One of his first tasks, however, was to check on the state of his pilots. More and more reinforcements were now arriving – including 249's partners at North Weald, 46 Squadron – which meant that some of the longest serving could now be sent home. One of those was George Burges, who, Lloyd believed, had been on the Island quite long enough. A couple of days before he was due to fly out, Burges was asked to go along to Captain Caruana's bar in Valletta for a farewell drink. He duly turned up to find the bar heaving with Maltese people, all wanting to wish him well. They even gave him a silver cigarette case with his initials on, and inside an inscription, 'A small token of appreciation from a handful of Maltese.'[2] He didn't know who any of the people were, nor did he ever find out.

Christina Ratcliffe was travelling with the rest of the Whizz-Bangs to give a performance to the Manchester Regiment at their camp at Ghajn Tuffieha on the far side of the Island. They were being driven along the rough roads in their special bus, when the driver suddenly brought them to a screeching halt, and shouting 'Air raid!' jumped out and began running off down the road. The others clambered out and looked up to see a lone aircraft swirling about the sky. The aircraft came closer and closer, seemingly directly for them. Christina suddenly twigged. 'Don't worry,' she told the others, 'It's only Warby.' He'd told her the previous evening that he would fly over their bus.

But when the plane was almost overhead, it went into a vertical dive. 'Look out, he's crashing,' someone shouted, and several of them flung themselves flat on the ground. 'With an ear-splitting roar,' wrote Christina, 'the plane skimmed over the bus by what seemed inches. Poor Warby. Sick at heart I closed my eyes and waited for the crash. It never came. When I had recovered my senses, the Beaufighter [sic] was climbing away to the sky, the roar of its engines coming back to us like a loud mocking laugh.'[3]

Diving over buses wasn't the only dangerous antic Warby was getting up to. He and his usual crewman, Paddy Moren, had begun carrying a few 25-pound incendiary bombs, scrounged easily enough from the armoury. Once over an enemy port or airfield, they simply opened the lower hatch and kicked them out. This was a slightly haphazard way to bomb, however, and once, when in a steep dive, one of the incendiaries fell back inside, ignited and blazed away at the back of the fuselage until they managed to shove it out again.

Warby was also very nearly killed while attacking another Italian seaplane over the Gulf of Patras. Opening fire, he closed to about fifty yards, although he appeared to have missed. He had just turned for a second run when the rear gunner in the seaplane hit the Perspex canopy over the cockpit, shattering it completely.

'I've been hit,' Warby told his two crewmen, Paddy Moren and Johnny Spires.

'Where?' yelled Moren.

'In the heart,' shouted back Warby.

His air-gunner pointed out that if that were the case he'd be dead. Well, almost in the heart, Warby yelled back. In fact, a bullet had gone through the instrument panel, through the webbing of his parachute strap and entered his chest to a depth of a quarter of an inch. One of the engines on the Maryland had also caught fire and the flames were beginning to increase. Moren asked him if he was OK. Warby told him he thought so, then put the plane into a steep dive to extinguish the flames. Straightening out, he then turned back for home.

'Are you OK, skipper?' asked Moren.

'I'm all right now,' Warby replied.

'But what are you doing?'

'I'm extracting a bullet from my chest!'[4]

Moren managed to signal Luqa and warn them, and when they landed, Tich Whiteley ran over to their plane himself, clutching a first-aid kit. Jumping onto the wing, he reached Warby and ripped open his shirt. Despite the blood, the wound didn't look to be too serious. Meanwhile, Warby was fumbling in his pocket. 'Here it is,' he told Whiteley, holding up the bullet.[5]

Perhaps for his own safety as much as anything, Warby was sent to Gibraltar at the end of May to pick up another Maryland. It was also a chance for a breather, since he had not taken any leave at all since his arrival the previous September. He and Paddy Moren took passage on a flying boat, and reached Gibraltar on 26 May. Once there, they collected the Maryland and decided to fly to neutral Tangiers. Borrowing some civilian clothing, they set off to spend several days relaxing on the coast and sampling the Tangiers night-life. One evening they went to a club and were sitting chatting when a waiter appeared with some drinks. When they asked who had sent them, the waiter told them they had been bought with the good wishes of the Luftwaffe. Warby and Paddy looked round and saw a group of German pilots, also in civvies and also on leave, raising their glasses to them. They went over to join them for an amusing evening's détente with their enemies.

Meanwhile, the Whizz-Bangs had been forced to cut back the number of shows to three performances a week. Increased petrol rationing meant not even a morale booster such as they could afford to keep on travelling around the Island. Finding herself now with more time on her hands, Christina Ratcliffe decided to apply to be trained for RAF plotting duties. Fighter Control at Lascaris needed twenty women for such a job, although unlike the WAAFs back in England, they were to remain civilians. Christina was chosen from among the 59 applicants. Knowing a couple of men who already worked there no doubt helped her cause. She began work on 15 June.

Lascaris was a large complex of passageways and tunnels built deep into the bastions overlooking Grand Harbour. Walking down a long flight of steps from nearby the Castille, one arrived at a courtyard under a huge arch. At one end was the entrance to 'The Hole', where authorized personnel showed their pass to the guard and then walked down a dimly lit stone corridor, gradually descending deeper into the rock. From this, a number of doors led off to a series of sizeable chambers. Here all the services had a number of rooms filled with charts, galleries, cubicles for wireless operators, bunks, offices and stores. This was the nerve-centre for Malta's war effort. Most of those serving on the Island never went there – instead, it remained a mysterious underground labyrinth, the lair of those trying to run their war. The RAF Operations Room had a large map of Sicily, Malta and the surrounding Mediterranean laid out on a large board. This was the plotting table, some eighteen by twelve feet wide. The entire table was marked off into lettered squares, each then further subdivided into numbered grids. News of approaching enemy aircraft came in from the radar stations and observers along the coast, and was fed to the Filter Room. This information was then passed to the plotters, who, listening to direction through their headphones, would then chart the progress of the enemy 'plot' on the board. Overlooking these developments from the gallery above would be the controller and his team, who would be in radio contact with the pilots and would direct – or 'vector' – them to the best possible position from which to engage the enemy. On the opposite wall was a chart indicating the number and progress of planes being scrambled to intercept. Hugh Pughe Lloyd, the new AOC, now had considerably more planes on the Island than his predecessor, which was why the increase in Operation Room personnel was needed. Having worked for Bomber Command back in Britain, however, he also had more experience than Maynard in running such an outfit. The disaster at Takali on 25 May had occurred because the seven 109s had flown low enough to escape detection by the radar. Observers must have spotted them approaching, however, and raised the alarm; so the fact that Control knew nothing about it showed a major breakdown of communication. Under Hugh Pughe, Tom Neil would not receive such a feeble response to an air raid in future.

In a separate part of Lascaris, Suzanne Parlby was still working for Military Intelligence, encoding and decoding messages. When she first started, this had been done manually. The key was changed daily, and she would look up each number in a coding book according to what the current key was. But by June, she was working on a Typex machine, which was rather like a typewriter. The key was still changed daily, but this could be altered on the machine itself. Once it had been set, Suzanne typed the message, which would then appear printed in the current key. These machines made a loud metallic clatter, which resounded around the stone walls of their underground office. In recent weeks, the amount of signals and codes coming through had increased.

Italian naval ciphers were now being regularly intercepted, and in May a German Enigma decoding machine had been captured from a U-boat in the Atlantic.

After the bombing of the St James Hotel, Suzanne had been temporarily homeless, but had been invited to go and stay with General Dobbie and his family at St Anton Palace, the Governor's country residence. The Governor had known her parents, but they also offered a temporary home to a number of wounded and recovering servicemen. While the Dobbies were both kind and hospitable, all guests were expected to join them for morning and evening prayers.

At the time, there had been much to pray for, but throughout June the lessening of the air raids had become more and more noticeable. Suzanne was now living in Guardamangia, an upmarket residential area on the hill overlooking Marsamxett Harbour. Full of large elegant old houses, it was the favoured location for high-ranking officers and officials. ABC and his wife had lived here before the war, as had Lord and Lady Mountbatten, but now the house had been divided into flats, one of which Suzanne now rented. To begin with, she had shared the basement and ground floor with another army wife, but they had little in common and soon decided to live separately, with Suzanne taking the basement. Although dark and smaller than the spacious ground-floor flat above, her new home did have the enormous advantage of opening onto a walled garden filled with orange and grapefruit trees.

Citrus trees abounded on the Island, and in the summer bore plenty of brightly coloured fruit. There were also a number of fig, almond and plum trees in quiet courtyard gardens of the town houses, and in groves between the craggy, stone-walled fields of the interior. There were vineyards too. Walking or cycling in the countryside, Suzanne would see Maltese farmers working harder than ever, picking fruit, or tilling their small fields with a tired-looking horse pulling a simple plough. The soil was a deep orange brown, the colour of a strong mug of tea. Women worked alongside the men, bending over to pick the variety of crops crammed into every field – onions and wheat, and bushes of capers and pomegranates.

The Island was also rich in wild flowers – jonquils and anemones lined the roadsides, while bougainvillaea, plum-coloured or rust, sprang up everywhere, climbing over walls and buildings adding splashes of bright colour amid grey-cream stonework. High on Dingli Cliffs, a popular place for walking, Suzanne could see the Mediterranean shimmering beneath her and, further out, the tiny outcrop of Filfla. The cliffs, offering a sheer drop in places, were terraced where the slope was more gradual, and the Maltese farmers would walk down steep, narrow paths to reach tiny fields perched on narrow ledges. And along the top, among the rough grass, were an abundance of dwarf irises, no more than a couple of inches high.

It was such a relief to be able to enjoy these sights once more, to be able to go for a ride with little risk of being shot at by a 109. The bombers mostly came at night now, but there were still dances every Saturday night. Suzanne loved dancing and most Saturdays would head off to the Sliema Club on her bicycle, with her ball gown packed in a cardboard box along with her basic shelter kit in her basket on the handlebars. On arrival, she would sneak into the wash-room to change into her dress – no war was going to stop her looking her best on a Saturday night – and then step out on to the dance floor. Her husband John would try to take his day off on Saturday whenever possible so they could spend the night dancing. 'Those evenings at the Sliema Club were great fun – such a release,' she says. Even so, the place was closed down at eleven, after which the worst raids tended to occur, and Suzanne would change into her old clothes again and cycle back. The road ran along the edge of the sea and regardless of the size of the moon, there was always enough reflected light from the water to be able to see where she was going. There were also a number of Z-shaped shelters running underneath the road, and on more than one occasion she had to fling her bike down and dive for cover.

A number of the submariners were living in Sliema and would go to the dances as well. Suzanne soon got to know them, including Shrimp Simpson and his second-in-command, Hubert Marsham. Both were bachelors and Marsham, in particular, would often escort her to the club in her husband's place, collecting her on his motorbike. And if Simpson knew that Suzanne was alone in her flat and a raid was approaching, he would sometimes send Marsham off to go and pick her up and bring her to their own shelters, now completed and entirely bomb-proof, on Manoel Island.

It was on one such occasion, while taking cover in the submariners' air raid shelter, that she happened to mention the large number of grapefruit trees growing in her garden. She would, she told them, have liked to make the most of the fruit, but with sugar now strictly rationed, it was out of the question. The problem was promptly solved when they gave her a sack of naval-issue sugar, and a week later sent a Jeep to collect 30 pounds of home-made Malta grapefruit marmalade for the submariners.

Shrimp Simpson had reason to feel pleased. The base was running well, the crews were having some notable successes, and he was getting to grips with the job assigned to him. It was important for him to be able to prioritize the signals coming in from the 'C-in-C', and to recognize which were from ABC himself, which were from one of the C-in-C's staff, and which from a more junior staff officer. Typically, a highly detailed signal soaked in overstatement would be from the latter, and Simpson needed to do little to comply. A signal from ABC's staff might warn him of enemy movement and would ask him to make every endeavour to intercept, which Simpson would do his best to achieve. Then there were messages direct from the Admiral. Usually unexpected, always direct and to the point:

'From C-in-C. To Submarines Malta.
Kesselring has established HQ at Miramar Hotel Taormina. Eliminate him.'[6]

This was pure ABC – and a genuine signal that Simpson had received back in April, when it was discovered where Kesselring was staying on Sicily. Wanklyn, who had stayed at Taormina during his honeymoon before the war, had been detailed to take some commandos to carry out the order, although the German field marshal moved before they had a chance to follow through the plan.

However well things were going, Simpson was never complacent about his men. He'd once been told to treat his COs as 'Derby winners',[7] and so when Wanklyn expressed concern about the health of his crew, he took note. The attack on the *Conte Rosso* on 24 May had been during their seventh combat patrol. In between, they had suffered continual air raids and had very little chance to relax. Although Simpson had ensured his COs found lodgings off the base, the rest of the officers and all the crew remained billeted on Manoel Island. Conditions on board the submarines became even worse during summer months. Because the hours of daylight were longer, they had less time to spend on the surface, and so the air on board became increasingly stale and hot. The last few hours before surfacing were always particularly unpleasant, with most of the crew sweating profusely and struggling for every breath. Owing to the lack of water, hygiene was poor and, unsurprisingly, their health suffered. Many, especially the ratings, struggled with skin conditions such as scabies, lice and a number of other ailments. Because of the sweating, the hammocks and corking around the decking were usually damp. Simpson had done his best to establish some rest camps around the northern area of the Island, away from the fray, and so on return from patrol at the beginning of June, Wanklyn wrote in his report, 'It is noticeable that all hands are keen to get away to Ghajn Tuffieha [a small bay on the north-west of the Island] and enjoy a complete rest. It is thought that this rest is most necessary, before the really hot weather starts, in order to build up the general health of the crew and to heal a few raw nerves.'[8]

Simpson readily agreed to this, although he believed that no one needed a rest more than Wanklyn himself; consequently, he was given several weeks off and even missed *Upholder's* next patrol. Many of the senior submariners had been to Malta before and had friends on the Island; Wanklyn was no exception and spent most of the time between patrols staying with people away from the base, only appearing at Lazzaretto for brief periods.

Tubby Crawford didn't mind his CO's absence. He had a number of friends at the base, and got on very well with the other officers on *Upholder.* 'In between patrols one used to go ashore and have a pretty riotous time,' he says. They soon developed a routine on their return from patrol. They'd head off to Valletta to a place called Marich's, where they'd drink egg-nogs. Then they went on to another bar that had a good supply of Pimm's. The idea was to drink every type of Pimm's there was – Pimm's No. 1, No.3, and so on, and finish with a Pimm's No. 1 'Special', which had a tot of some other spirit in it. After that, they would troop down to the Union Club on Kingsway. They also used to have horse and cart races, careering round Valletta in gharries as fast as they could. 'It could get a bit raucous,' admits Tubby. This was hardly surprising. Most were still under 25 and after the stress of life on board the submarine, they were given the latitude to let off a bit of steam.

Wanklyn would sometimes go out with the other officers, however, and it was on one such occasion that he introduced Tubby to Margaret Lewis at the Union Club. Margaret's father was in the Navy and had been Engineer Officer Malta (EOM) before the war, although he had by now been given the additional job of Director of Transport and Controller of Fuel on the Island. She and her mother had been on leave in England when war was declared and had then hurried back to Malta, taking the train from Paris all the way down to Syracuse and then catching the old *Knight of Malta* ferry across the final stretch. They had arrived just before Christmas in 1939 and stayed ever since; like Suzanne Parlby, Margaret passed over the chance to be evacuated. In fact, their paths through the first year of war were markedly similar: after a stint at St George's Barracks at the outbreak of war, Margaret moved into the Great Britain Hotel, before finally taking a flat in Scots Street in Valletta. She was also working in Lascaris in the RAF cipher office, but had come to know several of the submariners, including Dick Cayley, the CO of *Utmost*, and David Wanklyn. Tubby and Margaret soon became good friends, and when Tubby was back from patrol, they would frequently bump into one another at dances or in the Union Club.

Frank Rixon was grateful for the respite. After a frantic few months of being sent from one place to the other, it was good to get back to steadier, more regular duties. Despite rationing he was still being given enough to eat and, having spent many days stripped to the waist heaving blocks of stone from one place to the other, he was in good physical shape.

But despite the slackening of the air attacks, he was still given only four days off for his wedding and honeymoon. He and Mary had rented a small flat at Tigne, near the sea at the far end of Sliema, and on Saturday 5 July, they were married at St Gaetano Church in Hamrun. They specially hired a two white-horse carriage to take them to and from the church, and after the service had their photograph taken in a nearby studio. Then it was back to their flat for a small reception – just family and a couple of Frank's friends from the Regiment.

They stayed in their flat for their honeymoon – time was so short and transport so hard to come by, it was pointless to do otherwise. It was a happy time, nonetheless: they swam in the sea and took a trip across the harbour to Valletta; and spent a few precious nights together, living in their own flat as a newly married couple.

All too soon it was over, and Frank was back at Marsa, continuing life with 'C' Company as though he'd never been married at all. If he was lucky, he would spend one night a week with his new bride. Mostly his visits were even less frequent than that.

★

While life may have been quieter on the Island, there was no let-up in the offensive battle. Intelligence reports brought word of a fast German troop convoy heading for Tripoli, and orders came through to stop it at all costs. Tubby Crawford was called on patrol immediately, and on 24 June, *Upholder*, along with *Unbeaten*, set sail from Malta to try to intercept the enemy ships before nightfall on the 25th. Meanwhile, 830 Squadron were also detailed to attack the convoy that evening, followed by some RAF Blenheim low-level torpedo-bombers. These had suffered badly in recent weeks, and so 69 Squadron was asked to help out and cause a distraction by dive-bombing the convoy.

Only too happy to have his role as part-time bomber properly sanctioned, Warby and the three other Marylands involved spent the morning of the 25th practising over Filfla. He soon discovered, however, that these planes were not designed for dive-bombing. As he came out of a practice dive, a hatch cover tore off, damaging the turret and tail section, and although he managed to regain control, the aircraft needed urgent attention.

Thirteen Swordfish were due to take part in the attack. Nat Gold was in the second striking force – as usual, he would be the last man over the target. One of these days he worried his luck would run out, but at least it was an early flight – rather than in the middle of the night. This gave him less time to brood about the forthcoming action. Setting off at 6 p.m., they were directed towards the convoy just under an hour later by another of the Marylands, which was shadowing the troopships. The first strike force of Swordfish sighted the convoy and her escort just after 7.15 p.m. and immediately closed in for the attack. But much to Nat Gold's frustration, he still had a little while to wait. The leader of his section was struggling with a loss of power in his engine, so they were unable to attack until some twenty minutes after the first Swordfish, by which time the anti-aircraft gunners were primed ready and waiting. The barrage that faced them was intense, and Nat's aircraft was flung all over the place, partly by the pilot and partly by the flak bursting all around them. They swooped down and dropped their torpedo, but missed. He was just glad to get away in one piece – one crew was not so fortunate that night.

At Luqa, the Marylands were due to take off with the Blenheims for a night-time attack after the Swordfish. Warby's Maryland had not been sufficiently repaired by the evening, but the only alternative was a notoriously slow machine with suspect engines. Undeterred, he decided to take it anyway. Very quickly, he and his crew fell behind the rest of the aircraft. Flying alone across the sea they spotted a number of twin-engine aircraft and joined the formation, only to discover they had run into a flight of German Junkers 88s. Presumably believing the Maryland was one of them, the Germans made no attempt to attack. Warby pulled back the throttle and let them fly on ahead. By the time they reached the convoy, there were no other aircraft in the vicinity.

Tubby Crawford and the crew of *Upholder* were nearby, but not close enough to attack. After nine o'clock, they surfaced and saw some ferocious anti-aircraft fire on the horizon. This was the main body of Blenheims and Marylands attacking. Half an hour later, the guns opened up again, bright flashes of light and starshells exploding like fireworks in the darkening sky. Warby had finally caught up with the convoy, and although now entirely on his own, had begun his dive from 12,000 feet. Since the main point of the Marylands' involvement was to draw the anti-aircraft fire away from the low-level attack by the Blenheims, they were all instructed to pull out of their dives and drop their bombs at 6,000 feet, a height that it was considered would not overly stress the aircraft.

Warby ignored this and kept diving; he wanted to hit those ships. 'It was my guess as to whether us or the bombs would hit first,' said one of his crewmen.[9] The first bomb landed right across the deck, the other nearby. With the engines screaming, he pulled the aircraft out of the dive and safely flew back to Malta.

Eight miles away, *Upholder* had given up any hopes of reaching an attack position. Her knack of finding herself in the line of enemy shipping had, for this patrol at least, deserted her. That night she was recalled, arriving back in Malta on the 27th.

Before the war, co-operation between the Services was poor, but as the months passed on Malta, so they were learning to work more and more closely together. Two of the troopships were hit that night in a joint operation that involved completely different squadrons of the RAF, the Fleet Air Arm and the Malta-based submarines.[10]

Whatever thoughts of despair and anxiety he may have had, ABC was careful never to let on to his men. In his daily Staff Meetings he was just the same as always – briskly demanding reports, always referring to his team by their position (SOO or FEO, for example) or surname, and never their Christian name. If they used certain words or phrases he didn't like, he would fine them a piastre and the money went into his 'Comeuppance Box'. No one was sure what he did with the money, but it was suspected he spent it on the boiled sweets he always kept in a tin on his desk. Whenever he took one of his staff to task about something, he would return a few minutes later with his tin of sweets as a peace offering. Between the stormy scenes and 'pungent' language,[11] there was plenty of laughter, and ABC loved to hear new jokes, his eyes gleaming and hands rubbing his jacket. He need never have doubted either his abilities or the loyalty of the men under his command. They all adored him and trusted his judgement unequivocally.

But the Admiral did have cause for deep concern. Many of his ships had been sunk or were being repaired – including *Warspite* – and it would now be even harder to stop the Axis convoys reaching North Africa. He felt as though the situation was slipping out of his control. Re-supplying Malta was another major worry. With half his fleet out of action, he was unable to provide the necessary escort needed to make such an operation possible, especially since his surviving ships were needed either along the North African coast or in the Middle East where the Germans had just launched an attack in Syria. In an action against some Vichy French ships off the Syrian coast, another ship, the destroyer *Janus*, was seriously damaged. Twelve were killed and twenty injured, including Michael Montebello's father. But if Malta was to continue any kind of defensive, let alone offensive, operations at all, she particularly needed fuel, especially of the aviation variety.

At least the Malta-based submarines were doing well. And then it dawned on ABC that the older and larger submarines also had a very useful part to play. From now on, they could become secret supply vessels, delivering crucial cargoes to the Island. On 12 June, the mine-layer submarine *Rorqual* arrived safely in Malta from Alexandria, laden to the hilt with two tons of medical stores, 62 tons of 100-octane aviation fuel, 45 tons of kerosene, 24 passengers and 147 bags of mail. She came back again with a similar load ten days later.[12] This 'Magic Carpet Service', as it became known, saved Malta at a critical time. Although each of the several submarines used could only ferry around three days' worth of aviation fuel at one time, it did mean the RAF and Fleet Air Arm were never forced to cease operations.

Which was just as well, because at last large numbers of fighters were reaching the Island. In June, no fewer than 143 Hurricanes arrived on

Malta, and very soon they had achieved air superiority for the first time since 11 June the previous year. ABC was delighted, and with the news that Germany had attacked Russia on 22 June, he was in considerably better spirits when the month ended than when it had begun.

Michael Montebello's mother had managed to supplement their tiny stone dug-out with a room in the old Fish Market. Perched along the water's edge, this building was a stone's throw from the mouth of the shelter. The fish had been sold along a central atrium, but running off that were a number of storerooms. Now, with the war on, the market was empty, and so the Montebellos used one of the old stores during the day; it gave them a bit of privacy. 'It stunk a bit,' says Michael, 'but we got used to it.'

Michael was worried about his father. He closely followed the actions of the fleet, hearing about their exploits in the newsreels at the cinema and in the newspaper. They were, of course, heavily biased, but his father also wrote them coded letters. The Battle of Crete had been an anxious time – *Janus* had been there, but had been one of the destroyers that slipped away unscathed.

Then one day, Michael was walking along the waterfront when a *dghajsa* man stopped him and said, 'Your father has just arrived,' and offered to take him to see him. They drew alongside a newly arrived destroyer and sure enough, there was his father, being supported on the ship's rail. Michael couldn't help crying, he was so relieved and happy to see him. With a nasty wound in his leg, John Ernest Montebello was sent straight to Imtarfa, but at least he was safely back on Malta.

Tom Neil and Tommy Thompson were slowly acclimatizing to their new surroundings. They were now housed in a proper Mess, a large building between the airfield and Mosta, called the Torri Cumbo. Cool and dark inside, it had a twin spiral staircase on the outside and a number of rooms off an inner courtyard. Facilities were basic, but at least they were each given a bed. Tom shared a room and a batman – or rather bat-boy, since he was only twelve – who would try his best to kill off the mosquitoes by filling the place with 'Flit', a slow-burning insect repellent. It had little effect, and Tom still spent much of the night hearing the mosquitoes buzzing in his ear and scratching himself all over.

On one of his first scrambles, Tom climbed into the air with eight other Hurricanes from his flight to intercept a raid of fifty enemy aircraft. Suddenly he noticed his oil pressure gauge was dangerously low; as he looked at it, the needle dropped off the dial altogether. Any second now the engine would seize. Fortunately, news arrived that the enemy formation had turned back, but even so, he doubted he could make it back to the airfield in time. But much to his relief it did, although no sooner had his wheels touched the ground than the propeller stopped and blue smoke began pouring from the engine.

Walking back over to the dispersal tents, he found a fitter and asked to see the Form 700. Although it was wartime, there was still a strict RAF procedure for checking an aeroplane. Every day, the plane's groundcrew – its fitter and rigger – performed a daily inspection, or 'DI', in which the engine and all the main features of the aircraft were thoroughly examined, and the results of which were written up on its service record, the Form 700. An obvious precaution, and one that saved many lives. And throughout the Battle of Britain, Tom had taken to the skies safe in the knowledge that his fitter and rigger would never let him – or his Hurricane – down.

Now it seemed the fitter knew nothing about a Form 700. Horrified, Tom said to the fitter, 'But you must have signed the 700 after the DI. Before you declared it serviceable. You *did* sign for it, I take it?'[13] But he hadn't. No one had. Wearily, Tom trudged off with him to have a look at the oil tank. It was empty. It might have been a leak, the fitter suggested; then again, it might not. He couldn't remember filling it up with oil, but perhaps someone else had. Such incompetence and lack of organization was beginning to get Tom down. How was he supposed to look after himself, let alone his flight, when he couldn't trust the aircraft they were supposed to be flying, nor even some of the crews preparing them?

A few days later, Tom and a few others finally escaped the dust, heat and aged Hurricanes, and headed off to Ghajn Tuffieha, the quiet cove on the north-west of the Island favoured by the submariners. No sooner had they changed into their swimming trunks than they noticed a few people huddling over what looked like a seal. As they drew closer, they saw it was, in fact, a man – bloated, pale and very dead. Now he couldn't even have a quiet swim without something going wrong. Not for the first time, Tom wished he'd never set eyes on Malta.

★

Almost every day, both Tom and Tommy were scrambled to intercept an approaching enemy formation, but rarely did they ever see anything. 'The Italians tended to turn back before they ever reached the Island,' says Tommy. He's not sure why, although with more and more Hurricanes arriving throughout June, it may be the Italians simply did not fancy their chances against a strengthened opposition. In addition to a number of patrols and air tests of previously damaged aircraft, Tommy was scrambled on fifteen different occasions in June, although not once did he get close enough to the enemy to fire his guns. In July, it was a similar story: scrambled thirteen times, but the Italians were either nowhere to be seen or too far away for him to do anything about it.

Instead Malta-based Blenheim and Wellington bombers were regularly flying over to Sicily to give the Italians a piece of their own medicine. Hurricanes too were fitted with racks that could accommodate between four and eight small twenty-five-pound bombs, and sent over to attack the Regia Aeronautica's airfields. Adrian Warburton also decided to join in the action. On 14 July, he was carrying out a reconnaissance of Catania, in Sicily. There was quite a lot of cloud cover, so he dropped down low to take oblique, rather than high-altitude, photographs. As he approached, he realized he'd been given the green light signal to land by the airfield controller. Clearly, he had been mistaken for an Italian. Instead of turning away, he put down his wheels and approached the runway.

Johnny Spires, one of his crewmen, yelled at him, 'What the hell do you think you're doing? This is Catania not Luqa!'

'I know,' said Warby calmly, then began shooting at all the planes he could see lined up on the ground.[14]

With most of the Italian bombing raids now at night, the Malta Night Fighter Unit was formed at the end of July. One of the first volunteers was Tommy Thompson's great friend in 249, Edward Cassidy. Both had joined the squadron on the same day the previous October, although Cassidy had come from a night-fighter unit, and so was glad to return to his original role. He urged Tommy to join too, which he did with little persuasion. A great incentive was the new digs they were given. No one could pretend the Torri Cumbo had much in its favour, but the Xara Palace in Mdina, owned by the Baron Chapelle but requisitioned by the RAF, was something else. Built high into the bastions of the ancient city of Mdina, it was an elegant old building of long corridors and open courtyards. Best of all was the roof balcony from where they could see almost all the Island, even as far as Valletta on a clear day. And the new CO, Squadron Leader George Powell-Sheddon, wanted a team of pilots who would all get on well, who liked their drink and knew how to have a good time when off duty. Well, Tommy was all for that. A third pilot from 249 joined them, as did a number from the other fighter squadrons now on the Island, 185 and 126. One of those was a diminutive young Scot, called Alex Mackie.

With eight planes – soon painted all-black – and ten pilots, the MNFU began life as a purely defensive force. Camp beds were set up in the dispersal tents at Takali, and then when warning arrived of an enemy raid, they would be scrambled to intercept. As with the Swordfish of 830 Squadron, the runway was briefly illuminated and they took off into the dark. The idea was to work in conjunction with the searchlights: these would illuminate a bomber and Tommy or one of the other night fighters would then close in for the kill. At least, that was the theory, but to begin with it was the fighters rather than the enemy bombers who were finding themselves lit up like beacons in the sky. Both pilots and searchlight batteries needed a bit of practice before the partnership would prove its worth. In the meantime, the Unit was gelling well, and Tommy, for one, now ensconced in the Xara Palace, was glad he'd made the switch.

Despite the improved situation in the air, the situation on Malta was still causing ABC great anxiety. Although the Magic Carpet Service had proved invaluable, no proper convoy had reached Malta since March and supplies were once again desperately short. As Cunningham pointed out to the First Sea Lord, it was essential a large convoy came through before the end of the month. He suggested the fleet steam from Alexandria out into the Mediterranean as a decoy, while a convoy and escort set sail from Gibraltar.

The ruse worked. While ABC's ships came under attack from the air, six merchant vessels and a number of troop-carrying cruisers and destroyers successfully reached Malta on 24 July.

More guns and gunners had been arriving ever since the outbreak of hostilities, so that by the end of July 1941, the numbers had swelled to a far more respectable 94 heavy anti-aircraft and around 96 light anti-aircraft guns around the Island.[15]

Amongst the new arrivals was Ken Griffiths, a lance-bombardier with the 32nd Light Ack-Ack Regiment. Nineteen years old, with a slight frame and a narrow, gentle face, Ken was a quiet and introverted young man. He'd never been abroad before, and the sweltering heat was already quite a shock to the system and certainly very different from anything he had known as a boy growing up in Wales. With his kit strapped to his back, he was already sweating badly as they disembarked by the Customs House, beneath the Upper Barracca Gardens in Valletta. The waters of Grand Harbour were brilliantly blue, a deep turquoise that twinkled in the sunlight. Stretching up above him on the quayside were the great limestone bastions of the city. Lots of Maltese children were calling out for coins. Ken, like others, flicked coppers into the sea and the children dived for them. 'We can't see the coppers,' they shouted, 'only silver coins.' He might not have seen much of the world, but he wasn't falling for that trick. On the journey out, they'd been warned about the heat, and to watch out for the fruit and water, but even so Ken knew little about the Island and was unsure of what to expect. Watching the boys jumping into the deep blue water, he felt a tingle of apprehension about what lay in wait for them all.

Transport was already lined up along the quayside, and so the men walked straight off the ship and on to the trucks, ushered by the sergeants and officers. From there, they were taken to Tigné Barracks on the far side of Marsamxett Harbour. With the Mediterranean on one side of the peninsula, and the harbour on the other, the men lined up on the enormous parade ground. Ken was only newly promoted, and it was the first parade he'd ever taken – as well as the hottest. The whole Island seemed to shimmer in the heat, and although they were now wearing tropical kit, (KD) – sand-coloured shirts, shorts and pith helmets – most of the men had already developed dark patches of sweat across their backs and front.

After a couple of days acclimatization at Tigné Barracks, the three batteries of the 32nd Light Ack-Ack Regiment were to be split up and posted around the Island, but they were still there on the night of 26 July, when they were given an unexpected welcome call.

Sometimes Suzanne Parlby would worry about how long she could survive the raids and mounting rationing. These fears mainly came to her at night when she was lying alone in bed, and so she would often turn to the radio for distraction. On one such night, 26 July, she heard the sound of Italian voices and guns coming over the airwaves, quickly followed by the guns around Valletta booming in the dark. Some kind of attack was going on, but other than that she had no idea what was happening.

Michael Montebello, from his bunk under the rock, also heard the sound of machine-guns and explosions. To begin with he wondered whether they were being invaded, as did Ken Griffiths, woken with a start in his billet at Tigné. The same was true of the pilots at Torri Cumbo. Tom Neil awoke to the distant sound of gun-fire, and with just a towel wrapped around him for protection, went out into the court-yard where several of the others were gathered, listening intently. Was it an invasion? They couldn't be sure – but maybe. Tom had been given a revolver, but wasn't even sure where it was. He'd never fired it and had had no weapons training whatsoever. 'If we'd been invaded, we wouldn't have stood a chance,' says Tom.

It wasn't an invasion. What they were all hearing was the doomed attack by rapid Italian light motor launches – known as E-boats – directed against Grand Harbour and Marsamxett in an attempt to destroy the newly arrived convoy which was still being unloaded. Michael Montebello and a number of others in the shelter had come out on to the quayside to try to find out what was going on. Many Maltese had become blasé about Italian attacks and preferred to watch the action than stay in their shelters, and Michael was no exception. From his position down by the water, he could not see the mouth of the harbour, but above them, on the Lower Barraccas, a number of people had gathered and they were shouting down, giving a running commentary. The sky was alight with tracer, explosions and searchlights, the Italian attack lit up like a *son et lumière* performance.

The Italians had very successfully used E-boats to cripple the cruiser HMS *York* while it was anchored at Suda Bay in Crete back in March. On this occasion, however, the operation was a complete fiasco. How the Italians must have cursed the failed opportunities of the previous year: from a group of packing cases, the Island's defences had grown consider-ably, and that night's attacking forces had been detected by a flight of Hurricane night fighters. As the force approached Fort St Elmo, the bastion overlooking the entrance to Grand Harbour, searchlights had been focused on the Italian boats, followed by a criss-cross barrage of anti-aircraft guns, six-pound artillery shells and machine guns from the harbour defence. Although one span of the breakwater viaduct at the mouth of Grand Harbour was blown up and collapsed, it only took six

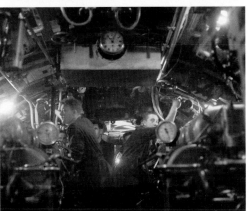

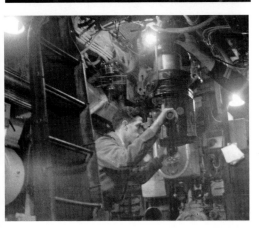

22. Lazzaretto and Manoel Island, home to the Malta-based submarines. Moored in front of the building are two U-class submarines, one of which may even be *Upholder*, since it was one of the few made that shared a high bow like the two in the photograph.

23. & 24. The control room of a U-class submarine such as *Upholder*. Almost every inch is covered in pipes, dials and other bits of equipment. These photographs give some indication of the lack of space and claustrophobia of living and working on such vessels.

25. 'Pop' Giddings with Mary and Annie, two of the submariners' pigs.

26. Soldiers cycling across the Maltese countryside. Accidents were fairly frequent, as Frank Rixon discovered.

27. Takali some time in 1941. There are no blast pens yet, the Hurricanes lined up on the far side are an easy target for any would-be attackers. In the centre background is the rotunda church of Mosta. In the foreground is a Bristol Blenheim and behind it a steamroller for flattening repaired bomb craters.

28. Ken Griffiths on the motorcycle he was taught to ride on the Island. It was whilst riding his motorbike in February 1942 that he was caught in the middle of a raid and wounded in the thigh.

29. A six-man Bofors gun crew, like the one to which Ken Griffiths belonged. The two at the back on the left are holding the four-round clip, while the firer and trainer are in the seated positions. These men are stripped to the waist, but gunners could be in serious trouble if they let themselves become sunburnt.

30. The dispersal hut at Takali, built by Maltese labourers in 1941. Pilots snatch a brief sleep on canvas stretchers. There were few home comforts here.

31. Ghajn Tuffieha, a bay on the north-west of the Island and a favoured rest camp for the submariners.

32. Digging shelters. Machinery of any kind was few and far between, and so most were dug with picks and chisels, like the men in this picture are doing. Fortunately, the Malta limestone was extremely soft.

33. The Control Room at Lascaris, where Christina Ratcliffe worked as a civilian plotter for the RAF. This underground network of rooms and corridors was the nerve-centre of Malta's war effort.

34. Peter Rothwell who, at just twenty-one, took over command of the Special Duties Flight making night-time searching missions and bombing raids in their customized Wellington bombers.

35. Bombs explode on Malta, while the anti-aircraft barrage bursts above.

36. Ken Griffiths and his company of the 32nd Light Anti-Aircraft Regiment. Ken is standing in the back row, on the far left.

37. Raoul Daddo-Langlois, the young Spitfire pilot who, in England, had craved action and excitement and found it in spades during his time on Malta. This studio portrait not only shows his youth, but also clearly reveals a rather sensitive and shy character.

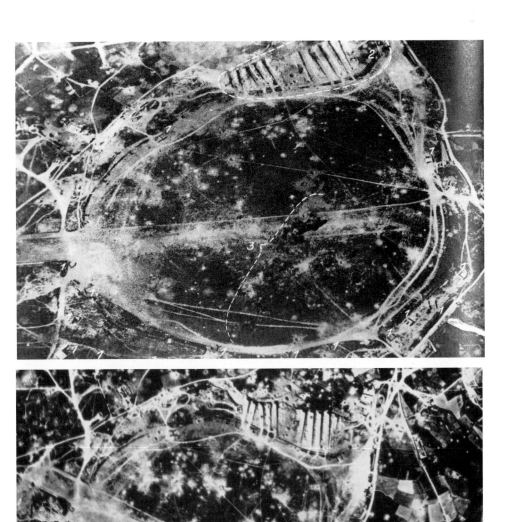

38. A German reconnaissance photograph of Takali airfield. This was taken before the massed bombing raids of 20–21 March, and shows some of the faulty German intelligence. 1. correctly indicates aircraft pens; 2 incorrectly identifies 'aircraft hangars'; 3. marks out bomb damage to the main airstrip and hardstanding. Takali was used as a civil airstrip for aircraft flying between Malta and Italy before the war. Because it lay on a dried-up lake, the Italians christened it 'Ta Venezia'. What the Germans highlighted as hangars were, in fact, no such thing. Had the German attacks not especially targeted this area on 20–21 March, the consequences of the attacks may well have been far worse for the Island's defenders.

39. Takali airfield again, after the bombing raids. The white dots and patches are bomb craters. With the attacks of 20–21 March 1942, it became the most heavily bombed Allied airfield in the world.

40. HMS *Talabot* burning. This picture is taken from Castille Square looking across Grand Harbour towards the Corradino Heights. The smoke could be seen by just about anyone on the Island. Precious newly arrived supplies were literally burning before their eyes.

41. The remains of the Royal Opera House after the raids of 7 April 1942. It remains a ruin to this day.

minutes for the entire Italian force to be wiped out. Most of the gunners positioned around the harbour had been Maltese from the Royal Malta Artillery; it was their finest moment. In contrast, it was one of the Italians' most ignoble. In Rome, the national radio called the annihilation a 'monstrous atrocity'. Mussolini's military humiliations were mounting.

CHAPTER 10

Hurting Hitler

SEPTEMBER–DECEMBER 1941

SOME OF THE Italians wounded in the E-boat attack of 26 July were sent to Imtarfa Hospital. Meme Cortis nursed one with a broken leg, and remembers that, when he saw his guards, he had muttered, 'As if I can run away.' At least she could understand him – despite growing up speaking English, she often found herself struggling to follow the Scots, Geordie, Welsh and other regional accents of her patients. But she was enjoying her work as a nurse, and made sure she was as cheery as possible when on the wards. 'I used to sing away when coming round with the food trolley,' she said. ' "It's a Lovely Day Tomorrow" was my favourite.' The patients started calling her 'Smiler'.

Death was never far away, however. One evening a young soldier was brought in for an emergency operation, but it was too late. Meme held his hand while the army Catholic priest delivered the last rites. She couldn't help wondering about his loved ones, his mother or girlfriend back home, and how they would take the news; there had been so many like him already.

Today, Meme admits, she cries at the slightest thing, but she never shed any tears back then. 'I don't know whether this was because I'd lost my mother or because there was a war on and we simply had to get on with it,' she says. Nor was she squeamish in any way. Since being at Imtarfa, she'd seen all manner of horrific wounds – amputations, people's intestines, burns so bad they covered nearly every inch of the body – but never batted an eye. Nor did she ever have difficulty sleeping at night, no matter what was going on outside. Even during periods of comparative calm, it was a long day. She would wake up at 6.30 a.m., ready for duty at 8. To begin with, there had been an old First World War ambulance that would come and collect them from the VAD Mess and take them the short distance to the main hospital. Soon after hostilities began, that was stopped and a gharry would sometimes collect them. Now they all had to walk each way. Her shift would end at 8 p.m., unless there was an emergency on, in which case she would be on duty until told otherwise. When she made it back to her room in the evening she would have a bath or a wash then be asleep as soon as her head hit the pillow.

Two months of day shifts would be followed by a month of nights. There was some light relief, however. On Monday nights, they used to hold social evenings in the large NAAFI hall, where the walking wounded would come along with some of the airmen from Takali. There were also cinema shows, and the Whizz-Bangs would sometimes give concert parties there, while at Christmas there was always a pantomime. Efforts were made to keep the morale of the hospital staff as high as possible because most of them spent 24 hours, seven days a week, in or around Imtarfa. Days off were limited to just two or three a month, when Meme would make every effort to visit her father and sister. But making it back to the family home in Sliema, where they, like the Agius family, were still living, was sometimes difficult. Buses were now very irregular and so usually she had to rely on lifts from army personnel heading that way, or on borrowing a bicycle. It was worth the hassle, though, and she looked forward to seeing her father, who was always overjoyed when she appeared. 'Oh, thank God you are safe!' he would say. 'I have been so worried.' On one occasion she had been given a few days off after recovering from a fever. Her father repeatedly asked her whether she was now all right. Yes, she told him, she was fine; she had not been especially ill. It puzzled her for a long time and then the penny dropped – he had feared she was pregnant!

He need never have worried. Although Meme became friendly with a number of young men, if she was ever asked on a date, she refused. She wasn't going to fall in love with someone, only for him to be killed; she did not want her heart broken.

Six miles east of Imtarfa, Ken Griffiths was now with the regimental headquarters at Spinola, near St George's Bay on the northern coast of the Island. He was living with a number of his company in a requisitioned house. The officers were on the ground floor, while the other ranks were upstairs. It was a shell of a place with no facilities; his bed was just two blankets on the stone floor. With little chance of a shower, most of the men would wash in the sea, just a hundred yards down the road, with special salt-water soap.

Keeping clean and presentable was an important part of their daily life during those first months. Raids had dropped to the lowest number since 11 June – often just one a day – and so regular parades and kit inspections were held to keep the men on their toes. The guns still had to be manned in regular shifts, but in between, Ken spent much of his time cleaning and buffing his belts and buttons. It was difficult, as polish was scarce and there were few means of keeping clothes cleaned and ironed, until one of Ken's friends found a solution. Archie Jones was a dispatch rider and used to travel round all the various batteries stationed over the Island on a motorbike delivering missives. He soon got to know some of the locals, including a Maltese lady who agreed to do some of their washing for them in return for cigarettes and army rations. 'They came back cleaned and ironed, which saved us an awful lot of bother,' says Ken.

Kit inspections caused great anxiety and took a great deal of time and effort. On a couple of occasions, Ken never bothered going to bed for fear of disturbing all his things, which were neatly laid out on his blanket.

While they were manning the guns, personal presentation was less of an issue, but they had to be very careful not to get sunburnt. This was a major offence, and so during the day Ken would keep his shirt on and the sleeves rolled down, despite the intense heat. For years afterwards he had a dark patch of skin between the bottom of his shorts and his socks where the tan refused to fade.

The regiment was largely made up of Scots, and so coming from Wales, Ken was inevitably nicknamed 'Taffy'. Like Frank Rixon, his had been a tough upbringing. His father was a civil engineer in the market town of Llandrindod Wells. They were not particularly well-off, but his childhood was happy enough until he was ten, when his mother contracted cancer. His uncle ran a school in London and so Ken was sent to stay with him. But there was no preferential treatment. 'He soon gave me the cane,' says Ken. The following year, his mother died and he was brought home. His father soon remarried, but Ken didn't take to his new stepmother and so was sent away again, this time to a boarding school in North Devon. He left as soon as he could, a quiet introverted fifteen-year-old, and joined a company of surveyors in Llandrindod Wells as an articled clerk, as well as volunteering for the local Territorial Army (TA). Called up at the beginning of the war, he was too young to be sent overseas and so missed out on the Battle of France and Dunkirk. Instead, he and the other juniors were sent to Scotland until posted to Malta in July 1941. The journey out there had been something of an eye-opener: the convoy had been harassed much of the way by aerial attacks, and what with the constant threat of mines, he had felt hugely relieved on finally reaching the Island.

Now here he was, relentlessly bitten by mosquitoes, baking in the heat and trying his best to make his boots and buckles shiny.

While Ken was struggling to acclimatize to his new surroundings, Tommy Thompson was feeling much more his usual self. Ten days stuck in Imtarfa with Malta Dog had taken its toll, but now, at the beginning of September, he was eating again, and more importantly, back on the grog. As he had been assured, most of the men in the MNFU liked 'a drink or four', and so they had set up a little bar on their balcony at the top of the Xara Palace. Drinking was the major pastime when they weren't flying: beer at lunchtime and whisky at night. They would hold parties up there as often as they could, since it was the perfect way to meet what few English girls there were on the Island. On one occasion they had invited along a few girls and couldn't understand why they kept disappearing to the lavatory and then coming back out giggling. Then they remembered the message written above the toilet paper: 'Two Sheets Per Shit – Any More And You Are One.' They'd forgotten to take it down.

Being tall, charming *and* a fighter pilot with impressive digs gave Tommy certain advantages over the vast majority of sex-starved servicemen, and he wasted no time. Soon he was going out with Betty Bishop, a young English girl who worked alongside Christina Ratcliffe as an RAF plotter at Lascaris. On days off he would meet her in Valletta, at Captain Caruana's or Maxim's. She also had a flat in Valletta, and whenever he could, he would stay the night with her.

During an early trip to the capital – only a few weeks after his arrival on Malta – he had even managed to get himself arrested. Tommy, his friend Cassidy and a few other pilots had made straight for the Great Britain Hotel, and no sooner had they bought their first drink than a number of policemen burst in and rounded them up on the charge of 'causing riotous behaviour'. Despite protesting their innocence, they were all frog-marched up Kingsway and spent the night in the cells. Although they were released the following morning, they soon discovered a group of drunken sailors had been in the bar before them and it was they, rather than the pilots, who were supposed to have been arrested. Tommy, though, has another theory. One of their number was Squadron Leader 'Bull' Halahan, a veteran of the Battle of France, but now working at RAF HQ in Lascaris. It was widely known that Hugh Pughe Lloyd loathed him and was looking for an excuse to push him out. Tommy believes the whole charade was a put-up job by Lloyd. Within 24 hours, Halahan left Malta for good. 'Halahan had a bit of a reputation,' says Tommy, 'and there was a saying about him that he would have been better off plotting the fuckers than fucking the Plotters.'[1]

This wasn't the only time Tommy found himself in trouble. Restless and easily bored, he was always on the look-out for new sources of amusement. At Takali there was a Miles Magister two-seater training aircraft and one day he and Cassidy stole it and went flying round the airfield. They had also found a box of light bulbs, and swooping down over the newly-completed dispersal hut, threw them out one by one on to the pilots below. 'Pure light entertainment,' he wrote in his logbook. 'We were just larking about, pretending to dive-bomb the others,' says Tommy now. Another time he flew so low over the town of Attard, he made the people below dive for cover. Unfortunately for him, he was reported and severely reprimanded. Not that it bothered him much. He wasn't particularly set on promotion and if there was fun to be had, he was going to take every opportunity going.

Far greater were the responsibilities of Tom Neil, who, as a Flight Commander, had less opportunity for 'larking' about. Few of the squadron were getting themselves shot down, but there were other hazards, which were proving more lethal than any Italian fighter pilot.

Chief among these was the condition of the aircraft. By the end of August, Tom had suffered no fewer than five engine failures. The Squadron Leader, 'Butch' Barton, had been forced to crash-land when his engine had seized at several hundred feet – ploughing into a stone wall, he had been lucky to get away with just a few burns; Tom had used the aircraft the day before. Part of the problem was the vast amounts of

dust and grit kicked up by the slipstream of the aircraft, which then fed
into the engine and sandpapered it to death. Even with special 'Vokes'
filters, the problem was only lessened, not halted. On top of that was the
continual headache of the lack of spare parts. New propellers were now
being fashioned by naval workers in the dockyards, and parts and planes
that would have long ago been scrapped in England were being mended,
patched up and used once again.

These anxieties were compounded by his concern about the obsoles-
cence of the Hurricane. The Mark Is, of which there were still some
survivors despite the reinforcements, were now totally ineffectual and a
danger to anyone who flew them. The Mark IIs were not much better
– on a par with the Italian Macchi 200s, but not the newer 202s – and
would certainly be no good whatsoever were the 109s to reappear.

Whenever he had the chance, Tom appealed to Lloyd for new aircraft.
Why couldn't he get them some Spitfires? Even some American
Tomahawks would have been an improvement. But Lloyd never gave
him either a direct answer or a reasoned response. Instead, he talked to
Tom about being more offensive-minded and taking the fight to the
enemy. 'He was a bullshitter of the first order,' says Tom. 'He adopted a
Cromwellian attitude and it really irritated me.' Also, as a man from a
Bomber Command background, Lloyd had little concept of the needs
of the fighter pilots. Later, Tom had a chance to appeal directly to the
Air Officer Commanding the Middle East, Air Marshal Arthur Tedder,
who visited Malta in the autumn. Tedder had not been wearing his
AM's stripes and so Tom had strolled with him between the lined-up
aircraft, ignorant of who his guest was. Serviceability rates were still
appallingly low and recently their ammunition belts had begun sponta-
neously firing. What they needed, Tom told him, were Spitfires, and
plenty of them. Only later did he discover he'd been talking to the
commander of the RAF in the Middle East. Perhaps, he thought
hopefully, something might now be done.

Spirits were far higher among the submariners, however, and by the
beginning of September, George Simpson had good cause to feel pleased
with the way his submarines were doing. A great morale boost came on
the 1st, when the base was given official flotilla status: henceforth it
would be called the 'Tenth Submarine Flotilla', with Simpson promoted
to Captain. The *London Gazette* also announced a number of awards for
the submariners, including eleven to the crew of *Upholder*. Wanklyn

received a Distinguished Service Order (DSO), while Tubby Crawford was awarded a Distinguished Service Cross (DSC).

Work on Lazzaretto still continued, with further shelters dug into the rock behind. There were now large workshops with vaulted ceilings and there was even room for their own cinema. By keeping in touch with the Gibraltar film distributor for the Royal Navy Cinema Service,[2] the submariners were able to sneak in the latest American films, although only on the strict understanding that they were not to be taken off the base. Walt Disney's new cartoon, *Dumbo*, despite being a children's movie, was a particular favourite that autumn. Rabbits were also now kept at Lazzaretto and the men were encouraged to grow a few vegetables and fruit, while the piggery had proved a highly successful venture. There were other comforts rarely available elsewhere on the Island: a large domestic boiler had been installed, which ensured hot water for baths was nearly always available; there was plenty of food and drink and a number of radio sets for the men to use – Lord Haw-Haw's broadcasts from Berlin were considered particularly good entertainment.[3]

If life on the base was bolstering their morale, so was success at sea. A number of the submarines were now doing exactly as Churchill, Pound and ABC had so desperately yearned for in the spring: wreaking havoc on Axis supplies to North Africa. Pick of the crop was still *Upholder*. Her skipper, David Wanklyn, with his intense appearance and reserved nature, was becoming increasingly revered. As Suzanne Parlby admits, 'Everyone worshipped Wanks,' while Simpson held a special fondness for his old First Lieutenant and protégé, and admitted he was 'loved and respected by all'.

They would soon have reason to think even more highly of him. In the middle of September, Simpson received information via an Ultra decrypt of a fast convoy of troop carriers heading from Italy to Tripoli. He had to act fast – the information would be useless unless a string of his submarines could be lying in wait for the approaching convoy, and so called in his COs and asked for volunteers. Wanklyn agreed to take out *Upholder*, even though his men were supposed to be having a holiday, and along with three others – *Upright*, *Ursula* and *Unbeaten* – was sent to try to intercept it. By midnight on the 17th, all the submarines had reached their appointed positions. In the case of *Upholder* this was something of an achievement: her gyro compass had broken, meaning navigation depended on the magnetic compass which was nothing like as reliable. The crew's mounting confidence and experience were paying dividends. In the early hours of the 18th, the convoy was sighted. The deadly game of cat and mouse had begun once more. *Unbeaten* was the first to sight it and soon realized the enemy ships were heading straight towards *Upholder's* patch. But *Upholder* was suffering from yet more electronic defects; this time her Subsonic Transmission (SST) – her means of rapid communication with other submarines – wasn't working, and it took *Unbeaten* nearly half an hour of precious time to relay a radio message to her via Malta. Ten minutes after receiving the signal, Tubby Crawford, as Officer of the Watch, also spotted the convoy – three large funnel liners and an escort of half a dozen destroyers. The sea was choppy, and *Upholder* was bucking and bobbing in the swell. Out on the bridge, Tubby was soaked from the spray. It was still dark, but the ships were silhouetted against the rising moon. *Upholder* remained surfaced and Wanklyn gave the order to 'Start the attack' immediately, despite the horrendous conditions. The submarine was lurching from side to side, her helmsman desperately trying to maintain course with the flickering needle of the magnetic compass. Nor were the enemy ships anywhere near as close as they would have liked them to be. This was going to be a long shot, whichever way they looked at it.

Tubby was still on the bridge, watching the convoy intently as the spray continued to whip across his face. He looked round and saw Wanklyn had joined him. If they were to have any chance at all of pulling this off, they needed to be quick and decisive; there was neither time nor the appropriate equipment to start working out the angle of attack with the help of the fruit machine. Human judgement was the only way these ships were going to be hit.

Suddenly, they saw their opportunity. Two of the liners appeared to overlap, providing a much larger target. With the submarine yawing from side to side, Wanklyn immediately ordered one torpedo to be fired just as the submarine was facing the bow of the first ship and another as she swung back and pointed towards the stern of the second; then two more towards the middle. The two men waited in silence. The ships were, they guessed, nearly 5,000 yards away – a distance of over four miles. But then, after what seemed like hours, they heard an explosion – and then another. Wanklyn's timing, achieved purely by eyesight with nothing but the moon to aid him, had been near-perfect.

A slight smile of satisfaction, then Tubby turned to hurry down the conning tower into the Control Room. Wanklyn looked at him and asked him where he was going. Weren't they about to dive? Tubby replied. With a large number of destroyers, they could expect a savage counter-attack. Wanklyn hesitated for a moment, then agreed. For once, he had wanted to see the outcome of his handiwork.

But no depth charges came. No swish of the propeller above, no sudden shuddering and flickering lights. Breathlessly they waited, hardly daring to believe their good fortune. Half an hour later, dawn was beginning to break, and having reloaded, they cautiously raised the periscope. One of the ships had stopped in the water, with two destroyers nearby picking up survivors. Another was sailing away, escorted by another destroyer. The third was nowhere to be seen; it had already hit the bottom of the Mediterranean.

Remaining under the surface, *Upholder* crept forward to finish off the stricken ship. Arriving with the sun behind her, Wanklyn was about to give the order to fire when they were nearly rammed by one of the circling destroyers. So close were they to the liner, they had little choice but to dive underneath it, turn and fire from the other side. Unbeknown to them, *Unbeaten* had also approached the liner and was getting ready to fire. 'A bit naughty of them really,' says Tubby; submarines were not supposed to cross over patrol areas in case of collision, but *Upholder* beat her to it anyway. As *Unbeaten* was about to fire, the torpedoes exploded. The second ship went down in eight minutes; Tubby and the rest of the crew heard a number of creaking groans and popping noises as the liner began to break up on her journey to the bottom.

A great many men, mostly German soldiers, lost their lives in the attack. Tubby knew this – all the crew did – but it was something he had to put to one side. 'Our job was to stop reinforcements reaching North Africa and by sinking these ships, this was achieved. But, of course, afterwards, one always had a thought about the appalling loss of life – but war is awful,' says Tubby. And with every enemy ship sunk, he tried to think of the Allied lives that might be saved as a result.

Upholder sank the liners *Neptunia* and *Oceania* that morning, each of 19,500 tons, and just about the largest ships they were ever likely to catch. Captain Raw of the First Submarine Flotilla later wrote to ABC saying, 'Lieutenant Wanklyn's devastating accuracy at 5,000 yards' range in poor light and with his ship yawing badly was almost unbelievable and shows the highest skill, not altogether unexpected from this most able officer.'[4]

★

In October, ABC had two pieces of good news from home. The first was that at last he was to be given the equivalent of the RAF Coastal Command for the Mediterranean, although it was to be called 201 (Naval Co-operation) Group, and included twin-engine light medium bombers and reconnaissance planes. Based in Alexandria, this would help ABC's attempts to re-supply Tobruk and the Allied North African coast no end. The second development was the birth of Force K, a fast surface force of two cruisers – *Aurora* and *Penelope*, and two destroyers – *Lance* and *Lively*, which would operate from Malta. ABC was delighted with the way the submariners and aircraft at Malta were performing, but with the Germans still preoccupied with their march into Russia, and with the Italian raids dropping to just one a day, it was the perfect opportunity to establish the kind of surface force they had dabbled with in the spring. The problem, as ever, was fuel, but it was believed such a force could safely operate for two months before another fuel convoy became essential.

Force K was soon to prove its worth. On 8 November, an Ultra decrypt, supported by reconnaissance work, reported an enemy convoy off the toe of Italy. The four ships immediately set sail from Malta, and in the early hours of the 9th intercepted the convoy of ten merchant ships and six destroyers. 'The result,' ABC noted, 'was a holocaust for the Italians.'[5] After a brief, but violent action, nine of the ten merchant ships were sunk, and the tenth, a tanker, left ablaze. Three destroyers were also sent to the bottom of the sea. This 'Saturday Night Club' run, as it became known, was repeated later in the month, when one German ammunition ship and one tanker were also summarily sunk. In Rome, Count Ciano, the Minister for Foreign Affairs, had to admit that this action would have 'profound repercussions in Italy, Germany and above all, in Libya'.[6]

Aware that most of the attacks on Axis shipping were originating from Malta, the Italians gradually increased their efforts to attack the harbour installations. 14 October was Tommy Thompson's twenty-first birthday, and it began very early with a dawn scramble to intercept an incoming attack. On this occasion, they flew together in groups of four, Cassidy leading and with Dennis Barnwell as Tommy's Number 2. In the mêlée, Barnwell shot down one of the superior Macchi 202s. Tommy heard him excitedly shouting, 'Got one!' then moments later, 'Baling out, engine cut; am coming down in the sea.'[7] Aircraft from 249 and 185 Squadrons were also scrambled to join in, although one of them began shooting at Tommy over Grand Harbour. 'Fortunately all the rounds went underneath – it was lousy shooting,' says Tommy, 'although I seem to remember the pilot, Graham Leggett, did later apologize and bought me a few beers.' Later, along with some of the other pilots, he took off again to try to find his friend, who had baled out into the sea. They failed. Barnwell was never found, probably plunging into the sea with his Hurricane and drowning. A terrible fate, shared by many pilots fighting above this tiny Island. Tommy's birthday had been a day to forget.

Despite the lull in the fighting, the bombing never ceased, and the strain of living on the Island, with no chance of escape, began to take its toll. Nat Gold, for one, was beginning to feel he'd had enough. Back in July he'd had a lucky escape when they'd been ordered to attack another convoy at dusk. Yet again, he'd been with a junior pilot and was the last plane into the attack. 'Our turn came,' says Nat, 'and we went in and dropped our torpedo and actually hit it. It was really frightening – it just disintegrated, blew up in front of us. We must have hit a magazine or something. It made you sick to watch it.' They were over the ship just as this happened and the blast of the fireball blew the light Swordfish high into the air. 'We were totally out of control, being pushed upwards.' Somehow the pilot managed to regain control, but not before both of them had had the fright of their life.

In August he'd been given a bit of time off and sent up to the rest camp at Ghajn Tuffieha, but what he really needed was extended leave. The following month he caught catarrhal jaundice, the same illness that Frank Rixon had suffered from the previous year. Rather like hepatitis, this was a virus that caused bile pigments in the blood and which made the sufferer feel drowsy, irritable and depressed, as well as sick. By the time Nat reached Imtarfa, there were already 250 other cases – it had become something of an epidemic. Extra beds had been brought in and there was hardly any room left in the corridors. The nurses, including Meme Cortis, were suddenly so stretched they had to show the patients how to carry out a number of routine tests on themselves as well as where to empty their bed pans. Nat was firmly told not to worry the nurses unless he had a specific problem. Row after row of suffering servicemen lay there feeling miserable and run down. After a month,

Nat was eventually discharged, but he was still so weak, the Squadron Medical Officer told him to take a further five days off.

They were now back in digs at Hal Far, but the conditions were little better than they had been in Zurrieq. There was no glass in the windows and there were holes in the walls from shrapnel blasts, and with winter drawing in there was often a chill wind whistling through the place. Nat decided to make himself an electric fire – this was where his training at the General Electric Company in North Wembley came in useful. Made from the side of a 100-octane petrol tank, some asbestos and an aerial wire as a filament, it worked rather well. 'It was the worst mistake I ever made,' admits Nat. Having positioned it by his camp-bed, he was never given a moment's peace. 'I could hardly get onto my bed because all the other lads were sitting on it, warming themselves or toasting little pieces of bread.'

Since Tich Whiteley had left 69 Squadron in June, Warby had become even more his own man. He rarely spent time with his fellow officers, preferring to talk to the groundcrews, and spent most of his nights, not in the mess, but with Christina in Floriana. He was also fascinated by photography and would regularly oversee the development of his pictures in the squadron dark rooms. On one occasion, a camera mechanic was asking Warby whether he'd ever seen a camel train during his trips over North Africa. The next time he flew there, he spotted the very thing and took a picture, which the mechanic found himself developing a day later.[8]

Most of the time, Warby looked a mess. Whiteley had been a stickler for the right dress code, but, since his departure, attitudes to such matters had relaxed considerably. Warby began favouring a pair of grey flannel slacks, suede desert boots and an old army battledress-blouse; his cap was battered and oil-stained. Not that anyone seemed to mind; as long as the pictures came in, that was all that mattered.

And they did. Back in June, 69 Squadron had been asked to photograph the entire North African coastal road from Benghazi to Tripoli, a 250-mile stretch that was expected to take a dozen trips spread over a week. Despite being chased out to sea four times, Warby photographed the entire length in just one trip – and without a single gap. On another occasion, he had been sent to photograph Taranto, but one of his cameras failed to work. Worried the other camera might not produce sufficient pictures, he flew over the harbour three times to make sure he had captured all the detail needed. And he was still shooting down more planes – another seaplane in July and one more in September. On 29 September he added another Macchi 200 to his total. Warby, with eight planes to his credit, was now officially an 'ace'. It was more than many fighter pilots could claim.

No one could explain how he managed to keep going. Despite being addicted to aspirin – he swallowed a phenomenal twenty or thirty tablets *every day* – he still looked healthy and in good shape. By the end of September, he had stacked up 155 operational flights and been twice awarded the DFC. But most of the original band of 431 Flight had already gone, and now it was his turn. Although he could ill afford to lose him, Lloyd decided not even Warby could keep going without a rest. Reluctantly, Warby prepared to return to England.

Tom Neil's largely frustrating time on the Island was also drawing to a close. Now used as fighter-bombers, 249 had been making several forays over to Sicily. His hope that Tedder might have arranged for them to be sent some Spitfires had proved unfounded. It was certainly not the pilots who were letting the side down. Since hostilities had begun, they had shot down just under two hundred enemy aircraft – quite an achievement considering the conditions, and machinery and equipment available, and a testimony to the dogged determination and guts of the fighter pilots posted to Malta. But tired, out-dated aircraft were letting everyone down: Tommy Thompson's friend Don Stones of the MNFU had been forced to bale out – having borrowed Tommy's parachute – when his engine seized. Their squadron leader had also suffered an engine failure on take-off. Neil appealed one last time to Lloyd, who dismissed him out of hand, telling him 'it wasn't the aircraft, it was the man.'[9] For a moment, Tom thought he was going to hit him.

So why did they have to put up with out-of-date Hurricanes? Why weren't they sent Spitfires? As Tom says, 'There were Spitfires coming out of people's ears back in Britain, and he is absolutely right. Between the beginning of November 1940 (the official end of the Battle of Britain is 31 October 1940) and the end of December 1941, 8,442 Hurricanes were built. In the same period, the output of Spitfires was 11,797. The old argument that Spitfires were harder to build quickly was no longer valid [Appendix II]. So where did they all go? This is hard to fathom because Britain's air forces were essentially involved in just two theatres throughout 1941: at home, and in the Mediterranean and

Middle East. In Britain, Fighter Command had 26 Spitfire and 31 Hurricane squadrons in June 1941. Nor was it the case that Spitfire production suddenly grew as the year progressed – rather, the greatest output came at the beginning of 1941, and so there seems to be no real reason why Tom and the rest of 249 could not have arrived with new Spitfires and then kept them on their arrival in Malta. He believes there is a simple answer: the Commanders at home were closest to the highest authorities and have a greater influence over what decisions are made than those thousands of miles away. 'Their Airships back in London didn't give a bugger about Malta,' he says. Nor did Lloyd demonstrate sufficient understanding of fighter warfare. His bomber background seems to have left him blinkered. In the latter half of 1941, nearly all his requests were for bombers – about which types he was very specific – and only occasionally for fighters, about which he was not. ABC and General Dobbie, too, in all their joint pleas for more aircraft, only ever specified 'fighters' rather than Spitfires.

This vagueness from Lloyd, particularly, cannot have helped Malta's cause, but there were a number of other factors involved.

The real reason was most likely a combination of factors, of which the 'out of sound, out of mind' principle was one. At the beginning of 1941, the home situation, even with the Battle of Britain won, probably still seemed extremely critical – certainly Britain was losing the convoy Battle of the Atlantic at that point, and it is likely those in the Air Ministry were still remembering Air Marshal Hugh Dowding's line about not allowing any Spitfires to leave England. By the middle of that year, with the Germans gone, the situation in Malta cannot have seemed so pressing – and it was the ideal place to off-load the increasingly obsolete Hurricanes. Furthermore, there was a perception that Spitfires, with a comparatively narrow undercarriage, were too spindly to safely take off from and land on rough, dusty airfields. This was nonsense. The Messerschmitt 109 had an even narrower undercarriage, and although this had caused problems for a number of those who flew it, it had operated successfully from Sicily and North Africa. In Britain, pilots had been taking off from muddy grass airfields ever since the Spitfire came into service. Another Air Ministry concern was the shortage of parts and men to service them on Malta. But again, this was a false argument as these problems were the same for any aircraft.

The truth is that most of those making such decisions would not have seen any wartime overseas service – they were middle-aged men quickly having to come to terms with rapidly developing machines and tactics – with little appreciation of what was really happening in the Mediterranean. But, as Tom Neil says, 'If you have had a bomb dropped on your head or been chased around the sky by an enemy aircraft 100 miles per hour faster than your own, you tended to take a more realistic views of things.' Certainly it is easy to see why Tom Neil and the other fighter pilots felt they were banging their heads against the wall. Their complaints were wholly justified; it was never a case of bad workmen blaming their tools. The Hurricanes on Malta were being totally out-classed by 1941. Essentially, it was a 1930s fighter at the end of its development by 1940, whilst the Spitfire was at the beginning. The Hurricane never went beyond the Mark II; the Spitfire continued in production until 1947 and was developed into 24 different varieties. If Malta's fighter pilots were going to have any chance at all, they needed Spitfires, and lots of them. It was as simple as that.

Another leaving the Island was Tubby Crawford, who was being sent home to train as a future commanding officer himself. It had been quite a year for him and in many ways he was sorry to be leaving; the crew had become a close team. He would be saying farewell to many friends both on the base and off, including Margaret Lewis, with whom he had become increasingly close. 'I am very sorry to lose him,' wrote Wanklyn in a letter to his wife. 'He has done marvellous work and is a great friend.'[10] Having been given a riotous farewell dinner, Tubby left Malta on 7 November, wondering whether he would ever see the Island and the crew of *Upholder* again.

A few weeks later, it was announced on the BBC that Wanklyn had been awarded the Victoria Cross, the highest British award for gallantry, for his attack on the *Conte Rosso* back in May. Tubby had been given an inkling of this on his arrival back in England during an interview with Admiral Horton, but he had kept quiet. Wanklyn was on patrol once again when the news arrived, but on his return no one said a thing. That night, Simpson arranged for his tunic to be removed and the VC ribbon sewn on the breast. The following day, Wanklyn got dressed without noticing anything unusual. It wasn't until lunchtime that he saw it and then came into the mess demanding who had had the bad taste to play such a joke. Simpson came forward and finally confirmed the award. A great celebration followed – his VC was the first awarded to a sub-mariner in the war. He had his photograph taken with the rest of his officers and was then interviewed by the *Times of Malta*. The submariners had been largely protected from the glare of publicity up to that point. After their autumn successes Pound had suggested to ABC that more be made of them in the press, but both he and Simpson had discouraged the idea. With the VC, Wanklyn was immediately thrust into the spotlight. 'Lieutenant-Commander Wanklyn is a man of resolute character, quiet speech and has penetrating brown eyes,' wrote the *Times of Malta* on Christmas Eve. 'He is over six feet in height and like most submariners in wartime, sports a beard. He married his wife, Elspeth Kinloch, in Malta and has a two-year-old son, Ian, now staying at Ellangowan, Meigle. He is a Scot by birth, but best known in Cheltenham.' For most readers, this was the first they had ever heard of him. 'Asked what quality was most needed in submarine warfare for success, Britain's submarine ace replied: "That's a nasty one, so I will use a long word: 'Imperturbability.'"'[11]

What he might also have added was a large dose of luck. *Upholder* had survived her first year, but others had not been so fortunate. Five of Simpson's U-class submarines were lost in 1941. 'If three submarines were ever sailing at one time,' says Tubby Crawford, 'we knew pretty certainly that one of those wouldn't be coming back, although you'd never think it was going to be you.' Boats were sent out on patrol at different times, and those left at the base would keep tabs on who was due back when. A crew would start off being 24 hours overdue, then two days, until eventually fatalism would set in and it would be conceded that she was lost. Usually there were no survivors. If depth charged, the boat would generally sink rather than rise to the surface; the same was the case if mined. It was an appalling death, largely because crews would know what was coming. Rarely was it instantaneous. Instead, the submarine would gradually flood and the men drown, or the engines would fail and they would suffocate. Trapped in an iron coffin, they had time to think about their fate. The sense of desperation – of panic – hardly bears considering.

But the Tenth Flotilla had done well that year. In tandem with the Fleet Air Arm, the RAF and the newly arrived Force K, they were beginning to hurt the Axis supply lines between Italy and North Africa very badly indeed. In November, 77 per cent of all Rommel's supplies had been sunk, and when the British launched Operation Crusader on 18 November, they were immediately able to push the Axis forces back. Starved of fuel, food, arms and ammunition, Rommel retreated 500 miles in just six weeks.

Retribution was not long in coming. Hitler took control personally, moving Luftflotte II – one of the three Luftwaffe Air Armies facing Moscow on the Eastern Front – back to Sicily and giving command of all Germany's Mediterranean forces to Air Field Marshal Kesselring. Even Count Ciano, who resented Mussolini's humiliation in having German commanders operating from Italy, realized they were hardly in a position to grumble. Admittedly, there was a winter lull in the fighting in Russia, but it was significant that Hitler chose to move Luftflotte II to Sicily, not North Africa.

Rather more crucially, Hitler had also ordered half of his Atlantic submarine U-boat fleet to the Mediterranean, where they soon made their presence felt by sinking the British aircraft carrier, *Ark Royal*, on 13–14 November. In spite of this success, Admiral Dönitz, whose work with the U-boats had so effectively strangled the Atlantic convoys to the point where Britain was almost on her knees, was furious. But Hitler was adamant: Malta needed to be neutralized, and quickly. Not only would she be bombed into submission, she would now be starved as well. And then invaded.

Tom Neil had heard something of these rumours about the German return. But during a night in Valletta in early December, he still found cause for some optimism. With a few drinks inside him, he found his sense of bravado rising and argued with his companions that Britain could never be beaten, not after the Battle of Britain. And since the shock attack on Pearl Harbor on 7 December, America would enter the war on their side, and that *had* to be a good thing. Not all those round the table agreed with him. The Japanese had also sunk two British battleships off the coast of Malaya. Now Britain would have to take on a war in the East as well. And it was all very well for Tom – he was going home and wouldn't have to face the 109s priming their engines in Sicily.

Although Tom was now off operations, he was still at Takali to witness the German return. In three days before Christmas, 249 Squadron lost over half its number to the newly returned Messerschmitt 109s. He finally left on Boxing Day, 1941, relieved, yet with sympathy for those who remained. As his boat sailed out of Grand Harbour and headed to Egypt, he prayed he might never fly a Hurricane again.

★

Christmas Day, 1941. At Hal Far, the officers were serving the men their dinner, a tradition that Nat Gold, for one, greatly appreciated. Then a rumour began to go round that they would be going out on an operation that night. On Christmas Day! They had to be joking. Nat and the other ratings hastily filled their glasses. There was one way to prevent it – by getting themselves drunk.

A few miles away, Tommy Thompson and the rest of the MNFU had been stood down for the day, but they were still at Takali when they heard the roar of an aeroplane. Suddenly an Italian biplane appeared, zooming over at hedge height, and dropped out a bag with streamers attached, right in the middle of the airfield. An armament officer was sent out to look at it, but after a brief inspection decided it wasn't a booby trap. Inside was a hand-drawn Christmas card of an Italian sitting astride his plane with the inscription 'Happy Christmas to the Gentlemen of the Royal Air Force at Takali from the Gentlemen of the Regia Aeronautica, Sicily.'

There would be no more such gestures in the months to come. A few miles away, John Agius and his family were sitting down to their Christmas meal. There was still food and drink on the Island, and their house remained unscathed. They, like most Maltese, had survived the first eighteen months of the siege with comparative ease. But the number of raids was on the increase again and it was already widely known that the Luftwaffe was back.

John and the rest of the civilian population had reason to be apprehensive. From now on, Malta would face a brutal, incessant onslaught from men hardened by the horrors of the war raging in Russia. Kesselring, the new Commander-in-Chief South of the Axis forces, understood the situation perfectly. 'Every day showed more plainly the naval and air supremacy of the British in these waters,' he later wrote in his memoirs. 'Meanwhile Malta had assumed decisive importance as a strategic key-point, and my primary objective at the beginning was to safeguard our supply lines by smoking out that hornet's nest.' [12]

This couldn't be done overnight: it took time to organize his forces in Sicily, but by the beginning of the New Year everything was in place.

PART IV

A Siege of Annihilation

'One after another all the other great sieges were eclipsed — England and Odessa, Sebastopol and Tobruk. Malta became the most bombed place on earth.'

ALAN MOOREHEAD, *THE DESERT WAR*

Kesselring Unleashes Hell
JANUARY—FEBRUARY 1942

A S THE CLOCK crept past midnight, a lone bomber swept towards Malta to deliver the first New Year greeting from the Luftwaffe. It was a clear night and the Island glowed in the bright moonlight as the plane turned towards the airfield at Takali. Pounding up and down the airstrip half a dozen times, the German aircraft unleashed a hail of bullets and cannon-fire, resounding sharply in the still air and pinging around the Hurricanes lined up along the perimeter. It was the 1,175th air raid since hostilities began eighteen months before, and the beginning of the most critical phase for Malta in the entire war.

Kesselring, with his new seniority over all other German forces in the Mediterranean as well as command of the Regia Aeronautica, wasted no time in issuing categorical orders to his new charges. He'd faced British fighters before, in the summer of 1940. Back then, there'd been Göring to contend with too, hampering his decisions at every turn. Now that he was in sole charge, he wasn't going to let the enemy off the hook again. This time he was going to pulverize them into dust, cut them off from the rest of the world; and then, as they'd failed to do in 1940, invade — the plans for which were already in active preparation.

Naturally, Tommy Thompson knew nothing of such plans, but like every pilot on the Island, was only too aware the Luftwaffe were back. From the Xara Palace he'd watched the 109s raking the airfield and during his nightime patrols there'd been considerably more enemy planes to contend with in recent weeks. Still, he and the other night fighters had been performing well, particularly when they were working in tandem with the new radio-controlled searchlights, and the MNFU, now renamed 1435 Flight, had achieved a number of successes. Among those, Alex Mackie had shot down an Italian bomber, while Tommy Thompson had shared in the destruction of another. Then, three days into the New Year, Tommy had flown head on towards a Junkers 88 and, firing a short burst, had watched pieces of the aircraft fly off into the air, although whether the plane had eventually crashed, he wasn't sure. In the dark it was impossible to see unless they blew up right in front of you.

Then the weather turned for the worse and the battle stopped for both sides. December had brought rain, but in January the weather was appalling, restricting both offensive and defensive flying severely. As if bombs weren't bad enough, lashing winds and torrential rain were now battering the Island. The fighter airfields of Luqa and Takali became so waterlogged the planes had to be transferred to the bomber airfield at Luqa, and with the move came not just congestion, but disorganization and an increased target for the enemy. Tommy and the rest of the night fighters found themselves grounded for days on end.

They finally made it back into the air on the 22nd, testing new long-range fuel tanks that would enable them to fly over to Sicily and patrol above the enemy airfields. Since so many of the raids were at night, it made sense for the night fighters, under the cover of darkness, to try to catch the enemy bombers as they took off from their airfields in Sicily – in other words, before they'd had a chance to drop their bomb loads. It is odd, however, that it took nearly six months after the Night Fighter Unit was formed for Lloyd to authorize such a plan, and seems to demonstrate the limitation of the AOC's experience. His background was with Bomber Command and before arriving on the Island he had no operational or command experience with modern fighters. The appointment of Lloyd made sense when the primary objective of the RAF on Malta was to take the attack to the enemy; but with the return of the Luftwaffe, defending the Island became the prime concern, and as in the Battle of Britain, it was the fighters who would play the decisive role. Lloyd was about to face his toughest test.

The first night fighter sortie over Sicily was on the night of 25 January, and proved highly successful, although sadly, that day had been the worst for the Island's fighter pilots in recent months. With two supply ships having just left Grand Harbour, 22 Hurricanes from the four fighter squadrons on the Island had been sent up to provide air support. While they were still labouring to gain sufficient height, a dozen 109s had swooped down upon them and, with the advantages of height, sun and speed, made short work of the opposition. In this brief encounter, seven Hurricanes had been shot down and three forced to return early with engine failure. Of the pilots, four had managed to bale out, two crash-landed and one had been killed. Effectively, the score was ten-nil. For good measure, the 109s had then roared over Hal Far and shot up another Hurricane and damaged a further aircraft so badly it never flew again; instead it was chopped up and used for spares. That made it twelve-nil.

Later in the afternoon, in preparation for their first foray to Sicily, Alex Mackie, of the Malta Night Fighters, had taken off on a final air test only to be shot down and killed as more 109s raced in undetected at low level. Thirteen planes had been destroyed and two pilots killed with no loss to the enemy.

The rest of 1435 Flight were understandably upset about losing Mackie. Over the previous six months they had become a close-knit unit. Tommy Thompson remembers Mackie as a 'bright, fresh-faced young man' who had been popular with the unit. 'It was always hard when someone died,' says Tommy. 'Suddenly there was an empty place. But on the other hand, there was little time to grieve. You didn't become callous exactly, but if you took death too heavily, you wouldn't have been able to carry on.'

Carry on is exactly what the night fighters did. That evening they set off as planned, and destroyed an enemy bomber at Comiso airfield in Sicily. A few days later, Tommy and the rest of the flight were over Sicily again, and shot up anything they saw move. During their first trip they had encountered heavy flak, but this time they arrived almost un-opposed. Tommy spotted two army lorries and opened fire. He saw them run off the road and explode. Next he found a staff car and destroyed that as well. As he turned for home, he thought he might as well finish off his ammunition and so fired his remaining rounds into the coastguard station at Cape Passero.

Did he ever worry about killing other people? He tried not to think about it. This was easy to do when he was attacking another aircraft. 'You were fighting a machine, not a man,' he explains. Shooting up ground targets was a slightly different matter, though. One time, when still at North Weald, he and another pilot from the squadron had been flying over France when they'd spotted a platoon of German soldiers exercising on the beach. 'We shot them up and I've no idea how many we killed but I felt very bad about that; but on the other hand, it was war. They did it to us too.' It was nothing personal, though – Tommy felt very little animosity towards the enemy. Of the two, he regarded the Italians as the softer option, although he respected their flying abilities and regarded them as a chivalrous opponent. For many of the Germans, he had great respect. On one occasion he and the other night fighters had been sitting on their roof-top balcony at the Xara Palace, when they had seen a Junkers 88 being shot down. 'The plane was badly on fire, but the pilot kept the aircraft going until all his crew had safely baled out, then at only 800 feet had jumped out himself,' recalls Tommy. They all agreed the German pilot had showed extraordinary bravery and found themselves hoping he would survive his injuries. The hospital at Imtarfa was only a stone's throw away, so several of them – including Tommy – went over to see him. 'He spoke good English and seemed a nice chap. He wasn't an out-and-out Nazi, just an ordinary bloke like us. We took him cigarettes and things like that. He'd done a bloody good job and we admired him for that.'

Life for the pilots was certainly far tougher now the Germans were back. Tom Neil was well out of it all. In January, no fewer than 50 Hurricanes had been destroyed or severely damaged on the ground and eight shot out of the sky. By the end of the month only 28 Hurricanes – out of the 340 that had been sent to Malta – remained fit to fly. It was a desperate situation and, despite his public bravado, Lloyd was already beginning to worry about how long his fighters would hold out.

Unbeknown to Tom Neil, the AOC had been repeatedly sending signals to his immediate superior, Air Marshal Tedder, the AOC-in-C Middle East, and to the Air Ministry back in London asking for major reinforcements, hoping such pleas would then be discussed and approved by the Chiefs of Staff; but his pleas seem to have fallen on deaf ears, something that he could hardly admit to a young Flight Lieutenant. Not that Lloyd should have seen this lack of reinforcements as a reflection on him. Both ABC's and Dobbie's requests appeared to have been brushed to one side too. Even Wilbraham Ford, the Vice Admiral Malta, had joined in the chorus for fighter reinforcements. In a letter to ABC on 3 January, he wrote, 'Malta must be made stiff with *modern* fighters – Mosquitoes ... and Spitfires.'[1]

It was Tedder, ABC's opposite number in the RAF, who eventually made the first move to redress Malta's woeful lack of Spitfires. Perhaps Tom Neil's complaints to the AOC-in-C the previous autumn had not gone entirely unheeded. At any rate, towards the end of January, the Air Marshal sent his Senior Air Staff Officer, Group Captain Basil Embry, to Malta to make a first-hand report of the air situation on the Island. A man of great experience, who had commanded a bomber squadron in the Battle for France and then been a Sector Commander during the Battle of Britain, Embry understood the role of both pilots and aircraft in a modern war, and was not worried about ruffling feathers. He arrived on Malta determined to give as frank an appreciation of the situation as he could.

Embry visited not only RAF headquarters in Valletta, but also the three airfields, talking to pilots and groundcrew. Over and over he heard the same thing: the Hurricanes were useless; Spitfires were their only hope. 'I am informed that the German fighter pilots often fly in front of our Hurricanes in order to show off the superiority of the 109Fs,' Embry wrote in his report. 'This is bound to have an increasingly adverse effect on the morale of the pilots. I therefore consider that every possible step should be taken to make Spitfire Vs and Kittyhawks available with the least delay.'[2] He also pointed out that while a Spitfire Mark V could climb to the required 25,000 feet in the fifteen minutes it took the enemy to reach Malta from Sicily, the Hurricanes could only manage 15,000 feet. This made them ineffective against incoming bombers and easy prey for the 109s. Embry was also shocked by the conditions in which the pilots were living, the same concern Governor Dobbie had frequently aired, and recommended fighter pilots should not serve on the Island for more than six months. Finally, he suggested the appointment of an operations controller of considerable skill and experience was of paramount importance.

Embry was Tedder's own personal envoy, but whether 'their Airships' – as Tom Neil called them – in London would listen was another matter. Lloyd and the rest of the pilots could only pray they would, because time was running out. Fast.

How much fortunes had changed in just a few weeks. The Island's triumphs of the previous autumn now seemed far behind them. Increasingly the terrible weather and Hitler's Mediterranean reinforcements were proving formidable obstacles to Malta's offensive capability. The successful career of Force K had come to an abrupt end just before

Christmas when they'd run into a minefield off the Libyan coast near Tripoli. The cruiser *Neptune* – having only recently joined the force – hit four mines and sank with the loss of all but one of her crew. Three other ships were badly damaged and forced to limp back to Malta for urgent repair work. With just one cruiser left, Force K – for the time being at any rate – was finished. ABC took the news with a heavy heart, but he was not altogether surprised. Such a catastrophe was precisely what he'd been fearing the previous summer when ordered to bombard Tripoli. They'd been lucky then, but he'd known they couldn't always expect fortune to smile on them so favourably. Unsurprisingly, the vast majority of Axis supplies, so crucial to Rommel's efforts in North Africa, were once again getting through.

Ill-fortune had dogged ABC in recent weeks. The E-boat attack on Malta may have failed back in July, but on 18–19 December – the same night that Force K ran into trouble – Italians had stolen into the harbour at Alexandria with a number of human-directed torpedoes and blown holes in his two remaining battleships, *Valiant* and *Queen Elizabeth*, putting them out of action for a considerable period. ABC had been on the *Queen Elizabeth* at the time and had been flung five feet into the air by the explosion. With no let-up in the fleet's commitments, Cunningham began the year with no battle-fleet whatsoever, a situation that was 'depressing in the extreme'.[3] Fighting against the odds was one thing, and ABC would back his men any day, but skill, confidence and experience were worthless without ships.

Force K had been storming towards another Axis convoy when they hit the minefield, but Swordfish from 830 Squadron had also been sent out to attack the enemy ships. Nat Gold had been flying with the leader and so, for a change, was first rather than last at the scene, with the task of dropping marker flares. No sooner had they done so than the destroyer escort released a number of smoke canisters to screen them from view. But the effect was ruined when the merchant vessels gave away their precise location by spraying their anti-aircraft fire into the sky above them. During recent missions, the squadron had taken to unorthodox means of harassing the enemy. 'We used to take up empty beer bottles,' says Nat, 'and tie a heavy stone around its neck and throw it over.' As it was dropping, the wind going into the neck would make a lot of noise – rather like a screaming bomb. Designed to frighten the enemy sailors, this was an unsophisticated, but effective ruse, even though instead of an explosion, there'd only be the tinkling of crashing glass. Now, as the Swordfish drifted in with their torpedoes, Nat flew above, chucking beer bottles over the edge and watching for any hits among the merchantmen below.

Although this attack was before Christmas, it was to be Nat's last operational trip. In January, Hal Far, like Takali, was waterlogged and with the marked increase of enemy raids, they were struggling to get enough Swordfish airborne. Nat was beginning to feel he'd had enough. The relentless bombing, especially, was really getting to him. On one occasion he watched a formation of over one hundred enemy planes come over. He and several others ran off the edge of the airfield and were standing sheltering in a little goat-shed when they watched a Stuka come right over them and drop a bomb just twenty feet away. Nat dived flat on to the ground, but the blast lifted him up and dropped him on top of an RAF man lying next to him. 'We've been hit, we've been hit!' screamed the startled man, but in fact they were unharmed. Dusting themselves down, they scrambled to their feet and looked outside, only to see a 109 roaring towards them. A split second later bullets started raking the ground all around them and they jumped back inside the hut.

'I was becoming a bit bomb-happy,' Nat admits. If somebody slammed a door, he'd jump. His nerves were fraying at the ends, and with so many bombs being dropped at night, sleep deprivation was becoming a problem. Added to which were severely primitive conditions and an increasing shortage of food and drink. Bars were now closing, so there weren't many ways to fill in the time. A number of his friends had been shot down and were now prisoners of war; others had been killed. In fact, he'd had more than enough.

830 Squadron were given a new CO in January and soon after his arrival he called in Nat and one of the other TAGs and told them they would shortly be going home. At least he was given some recognition for his long months on the Island: on 20 January, he was mentioned in despatches in the *London Gazette*. However, just as Nat had struggled to reach Malta in the first place, so he had difficulty in leaving. Initially earmarked for a place on board a merchant ship headed for Gibraltar, he was then told that it was full and there was no room for him. Next he was offered a passage on board a submarine, but as it was due to be on patrol for a month *en route* back to Gibraltar, he turned the place down. It wasn't until 25 January that he left on board a merchantman

headed for Alexandria. 'The Germans gave us a rousing send-off,' says Nat. Screaming bombs rained down around them, and Nat watched with mounting horror as a number of explosions erupted around the stern of the escorting destroyer next to them, lifting it right out of the water – the propellers racing – before crashing back again. Despite more attacks, they somehow escaped unscathed. Nat had finally left Malta and he was still in one piece.

So long as there were bombers on the Island and submarines in Marsamxett Harbour, Malta's offensive battle would continue – even if they lacked the efficacy of the previous autumn. On 4 January, for instance, ten Blenheim twin-engine bombers attacked the Castel Vetrano airfield in Sicily, catching the enemy unawares. The submariners were also still on constant patrol. *Upholder*, now without Tubby Crawford, had not scored a single hit during December, but then sank a merchant vessel and an Italian U-boat at the beginning of January. A number of other Tenth Flotilla submarines had left Malta for a rest and refit. Simpson had been told that most of his crews should not remain on active service for more than a year, such were the stresses and strains of operating from there; but *Upholder*, his talisman, was not spared. Wanklyn and his crew would, for the moment, continue a while longer.

Despite the appalling weather conditions, the Malta-based torpedo-bombers were still being sent out to attack shipping as well, and on 23 January sank the *Victoria*, the pride of the Italian merchant fleet. A large part of this and the previous autumn's successes had been due to improved intelligence. Ultra decrypts were now able to warn of enemy convoys leaving harbour, although safeguarding this information meant 69 Aerial Reconnaissance Squadron were kept busy, flying very obviously over any Axis shipping activity so as not to arouse suspicion that the German Enigma and Italian naval codes had been broken.

One reconnaissance pilot flying almost every day was Adrian Warburton. Warby had not gone back to England the previous September. Instead, there had been a last-minute change of plan and he had been sent to Egypt as an instructor at an Operational Training Unit (OTU), where pilots received the final part of their training before joining a squadron. Due some leave, he'd arranged to borrow a plane and had gone to see his father, who had been recalled to the Navy and was now serving at Haifa in Palestine.

On his return to Egypt, Warby soon decided he didn't like instructing and discovered that nearby at Heliopolis, just outside Cairo, there was No. 2 Photo Reconnaissance Unit (PRU). He offered his services, a transfer was soon arranged, and he began working as a reconnaissance pilot once more.

2 PRU had been due to use Marylands, just like 69 Squadron on Malta, but the ship carrying their planes was sunk *en route*, and so they began flying Hurricanes stripped of their guns instead. By the time Warby joined them, they also had a couple of stripped-down Beaufighters – twin-engine long-range strike fighters – painted dark blue for high-altitude flying, which although similar in size, were both faster and more manoeuvrable than a Maryland.

With the British successes in North Africa, Middle East Command had begun looking to the future and a possible invasion of Sicily, and 2 PRU was asked to photograph the Sicily beaches. Malta was the obvious base from which to do it, and Warby an obvious choice of pilot. Along with another Beaufighter crew, Warby was posted back to Malta on 29 December 1941. On learning the weather over Malta was bad, Warby's fellow pilot – and superior – decided to wait until conditions were more favourable before setting off across the Mediterranean. But Warby, eager to see Christina once more, took off straight away, landing safely despite low cloud and torrential rain.

By the time his 2 PRU colleague arrived nine days later, Warby had already flown a dozen missions and photographed all the Sicilian and southern Italian airfields – the Sicilian beaches went unphotographed. Using his old 69 Squadron groundcrew to service his Beaufighter, he couldn't have cared less whether he was a part of the Malta-based squadron or 2 PRU – he was still his own man, as he always had been. Nor was Hugh Pughe Lloyd going to quibble – he was just pleased to have his ace reconnaissance pilot back.

Despite the weather, Warby continued to get his pictures, and Lloyd was soon sending him back over Tripoli. On one occasion, he approached the harbour amid intense anti-aircraft fire. Swirling the plane from side to side in an effort to dodge the flak, he then reached his camera run and straightened out. Suddenly a near miss bucketed the Beaufighter furiously. His crewman that day was photo-mechanic Ron Hadden. He thought they'd had it. The armour-plate door between him and Warby flew open. 'Then I saw him,' Hadden later recounted. 'He had his hat on top of his helmet, cigarette hanging from his lips; one elbow resting on the side of the cockpit, driving the plane with the other hand. His complete lack of fear and nonchalant attitude to the noise and from the flak was fantastic. Warby at his best. Fighters were chasing us, the port engine had failed but he pressed home his recce and safely returned.'[4]

While the valiant work of Warby and the other reconnaissance crews was invaluable for alerting the Allies to enemy shipping movements, it was still easy to lose sight of a convoy once it was out at sea, and especially at night when many of the attacks took place. Intrinsic to both the operations of Force K and the Malta-based Fleet Air Arm was the work of the Special Duties Flight. This had been formed the previous September and was made up of three twin-engine Wellington bombers specially adapted for night-time detection work. The key piece of equipment was the still-secret Air to Surface Vessel radar (ASV). Rather like the submariners' asdic, the radar operated by transmitting a number of signals or pulses in a steady stream. If these pulses hit an object, they would rebound; the nearer the object it hit, the quicker the return. By timing the rebound, distance could be established, and the object was shown up on a screen as a fluorescent 'blip'.

With three large antennae – looking rather like television aerials – stuck along the fuselage and another two under each wing, these Wellingtons looked like curious hybrids of their former selves, but on Malta, they had soon proved invaluable, and had worked especially well in conjunction with the Royal Navy's Force K. Intelligence of a convoy about to leave an Italian port would reach Malta; then, in the early evening, a Special Duties Flight Wellington would take off, and, with its ASV casting a wide net, would track the convoy's movement. Force K would then set off, directed towards their quarry by the Wellington, which would also relay, via a simple code, details of the size and escort capability of the convoy. As the British ships approached, the Wellington would then drop a whole number of marker flares around the target, and, if necessary, a few bombs as well. Their contributions had been a prime example of the increased co-operation between the services developing on the Island.

Force K was finished by January, but the Wellingtons had suffered too. Because of their size, these planes were particularly hard to hide on the ground, and frequently came under attack. By January, the Special Duties Flight had only one aircraft left, and so the CO was given permission to commandeer more crews and planes to make up the numbers. One of those was Peter Rothwell, a young Pilot Officer who had been based firstly in Cornwall, working with ASV on anti-submarine patrols in the Bay of Biscay, and then Iceland, covering the Arctic convoys. Peter had joined the RAF Volunteer Reserve in October 1938 – the 'Weekend Fliers' – as it promised some excitement and light relief away from his daily office job. Brought up mostly in Hampshire, Peter was the son of a country vicar who had served at Gallipoli in the First World War. When his father died, Peter continued at boarding school, but by the time he was seventeen, his mother could no longer afford the fees, and so he left and took a job with Imperial Tobacco in the secretaries department.

He was mobilized on 1 September 1939, two days before the outbreak of war. After his initial training, he was transferred to twin-engine bombers. He also grew a long luxurious moustache the colour of his sandy, light-brown hair (which, although a bit greyer, he maintains to this day).

After a year flying over the Arctic and North Atlantic, Peter welcomed the prospect of being posted somewhere warm, but he was going to have to wait a while before he gained a tan on Malta. As with most arrivals on the Island, the journey had been somewhat fraught. Just getting off the runway at Gibraltar, notoriously short at only 950 yards, was a task in itself. A number of Wellingtons had never made it, crashing straight into the sea. Setting off full-throttle down the runway, fully laden and carrying extra fuel tanks as well, Peter had made it into the air with precious little to spare. That had been a considerable relief, but landing on Malta some seven hours later was to prove just as risky. As he touched down at Luqa, he saw everyone scurrying out of sight as fast as they could. He had arrived in the middle of yet another raid.

Tony Spooner, his CO and former colleague from 221 Squadron back in England, looked a wreck. Clearly over-worked and run down, he was suffering from dermatitis as well as his fair share of Malta Dog. The Medical Officer at Luqa had also given him gentian violet for his boils and carbuncles, so he had blotches of purple all over his face. But it didn't take long for Peter to understand why a stint on Malta would take its toll. A biting wind swept over the Island and wrecks of shot-up aircraft littered the airfield. A number of buildings had already been knocked down and those still standing were pitted with holes and shrapnel marks. To begin with Peter was shown a billet near the airfield. Before the war it had been a leper asylum. 'It was freezing,' he says. 'The boys were all drinking gin with hot water and eating tiny pickled onions to help them forget the cold.' Within a fortnight, the building had been hit by bombs and blown to smithereens, and so the whole of the Special Duties Flight was moved to the sea-plane base at Kalafrana, and told to bunk down there. Comfortable living quarters were, however, short-lived, and by the end of March they were sleeping in caves cut from the rock, and plagued by bugs and sandflies. They did have use of the pre-war Mess, which was 'a lovely old building', shared by the naval seaplane crews who were still flying into Kalafrana. The bombing was almost constant – an average of nine raids a day. Peter had not seen or heard anything like it before.

Conditions on the ground were fairly dismal, but they weren't much better in the air. With the weather so severe, the aerials on the Wellingtons were often icing up, resulting in confusing signals on the ASV screen. Despite being thrown in at the deep end, however, Peter managed to acquit himself well. On 7 February, only his second operational sortie, he helped lead the Fleet Air Arm squadrons on to a convoy of one merchant ship and one tanker, and both were sunk. A week later, a further three merchantmen were sent to the bottom of the sea. But these few successes were nothing compared with the damage inflicted just a few months before. Although Ultra decrypts about Axis shipping were still reaching Malta, enemy bombing of the Island was relentless; many aircraft had been destroyed on the ground, and there were insufficient numbers to carry out the necessary reconnaissance work. This, together with the poor weather, ensured most enemy convoys sneaked through to Tripoli unmolested. Throughout December and January, Rommel was able to completely recharge his batteries with troops, ammunition, fuel and other essential provisions.

Increasingly, the fate of the Allied armies in North Africa – and hence the Middle East – was tied to that of Malta. As Rommel drew strength, so the Allies' was sapped both in North Africa and Malta. On 21 January, the Afrika Korps counter-attacked, catching the British Eighth Army off-guard and forcing them back across Cyrenaica. This was a disaster for Malta, because the success of any convoy relied on the British holding forward airfields in Libya from which air cover could be provided, and came at a time when the problem of resupplying Malta was becoming ever more pressing. ABC signalled the Admiralty in January warning them that unless major reinforcements of aircraft and naval vessels were provided, running a convoy would be almost impossible – and were this the case, he did not see how Malta could be maintained. Despite the weather, there were four-hundred-and-thirty-two enemy raids over the Island in December and January; ABC further warned that such was the magnitude of Axis bombing, even an invasion could not be ruled out. At the beginning of February he wrote again to the First Sea Lord outlining the situation in Malta: there was just about enough aviation spirit to last until 1 August, but most other supplies would have run out by 1 June. A further convoy was now urgently needed. This was finally sanctioned, although it was up to ABC to organize – no easy task. Finding the right number of merchant ships of the right speed at the right time could be difficult, especially after the many losses in the Atlantic. ABC managed it, however, and three merchantmen set sail on 12 February. Despite a heavy escort, however, all three merchantmen were so badly bombed and harried by Axis aircraft from Libya that the entire convoy was forced to turn back to Alexandria. This was a major disaster.

The Magic Carpet Service was still tirelessly bringing in what key supplies it could, as were two fast naval supply ships – the *Breconshire* and the *Glengyle* – but it wasn't enough, and on 19 February, just a few days after the news of the failed convoy reached the Island, new cuts were made. 'Supplies of MT petrol and other commodities which were expected have not arrived in Malta and so long as the situation remains as it is in North Africa, the supply situation is bound to remain difficult,' said the Press Notice from the Lieutenant-Governor's office. Sugar rations were cut again, as was fodder for livestock. This latter decision was a particular blow because, with the lack of motorized transport more people were dependent on horses; goats too, were used widely for their milk. Suzanne Parlby, for one, had loved seeing and listening to the herds of goats that were driven around the streets to be milked on people's doorsteps. These wore cotton brassieres to prevent their udders dragging in the dust, and the animals were milked into jugs and bowls, while the rest of the herd milled about scrounging for discarded fruit peel, empty cigarette cartons and other waste that added grist to their diet. But with the new restrictions, this everyday sight would become increasingly rare. Bus services were also cut; the new timetables provided fewer weekday routes and none at weekends. 'In Malta the conserving of stocks, in order to make them last longer, is one of the most important aspects of the war effort,' the Lieutenant-Governor reminded the people.[5]

The Island and its people had begun to look tired. Threadbare uniforms remained worn. Most shops were boarded up – or were now craters in the ground. Many of the bars had run dry. The Gut, once a teeming blur of drunken servicemen, was almost dead. Apart from essential service personnel, Valletta was becoming a ghost town.

John Agius was still travelling to work every day and was at his desk by 7.30 a.m. The ferry service rarely operated these days – the lack of fuel and the risk of hitting a mine put paid to that – but with foresight John had bought himself a brand-new Phillips bicycle with chromium-plated handlebars, for three pounds and five shillings. This was expensive, but nothing like as costly as they would become. Before the war, he could have leant his bicycle against a wall and known it would be safe, but by February 1942, bikes were prized possessions and a prime target for theft. John always carefully brought his into the courtyard at Scots Street. It would be nothing short of disaster if he lost it now.

He was still extremely busy. It was up to him to make a note of any new personnel in the RAF and ensure they were correctly paid and accounted for. Promotions also meant an increase in daily pay and this too had to be amended. Similarly, if someone died, their accounts had to be finalized and sent to the correct next of kin. Largely left to his own devices at the beginning of the war, he now had two other people to help. There'd been a problem with one of them a few months before – he'd resented John telling him how to do things. 'I'm not here as your servant,' he told him one day. 'No, you're a servant of the King, but you've got to learn the job,' John replied. Eventually, he went to his superior and explained why the new clerk was getting on his nerves. 'It's either him or me,' John told him. The other clerk left the office that afternoon.

Air raids were a constant disruption. A new warning device had been devised. If a raid was headed for the harbour areas, a red flag would be raised above Fort St Angelo on the tip of Vittoriosa and above the Castille in Valletta. This meant people there could ignore sirens sounded for attacks elsewhere on the Island. It was intended to be less disruptive, but since many of the attacks *were* on Grand Harbour and the red flags were not always easy to see, John still found himself regularly trooping off to the shelters during the middle of his working day. He was also caught out on several occasions when cycling to and from work. One time he was with a friend when the siren droned once more. They both stopped and were briefly unsure whether they should find a shelter or carry on cycling. By the time they had finished debating this quandary, the bombs had already begun falling. A colleague at Scots Street was killed during an attack one lunchtime. He'd been in Floriana when the sirens began wailing and was unable to get to a shelter in time. It was simply bad luck, but being caught in the open when the bombs began to fall was a constant anxiety. For people like John, it was sometimes unavoidable – he had to get to work, after all. One just had to hope for the best.

At least there was now a shelter in Victoria Terrace, about fifty yards from the front of the Agius family home. Despite the lack of machinery, shelters had been dug in every town and every village, enough to keep the entire population safely underground. Most had been carved by hand with picks and chisels. Because the majority of raids were at night, many people spent their sleeping hours in these underground caverns. For the most part, people took to these conditions well, adjusting to the lack of privacy and difficulties with hygiene.

But while they accepted these privations, they did not have to like them. Still living in her flat in Guardamangia, Suzanne Parlby would go to the public shelter down the hill, mostly used by Maltese. It was like most others – dark, damp and dismal. Suzanne would go down some steps, then pass a shrine to the Virgin Mary, permanently lit by a small lamp. Next to the shrine, a dark corner was used as a toilet. Throughout the night a large number of Maltese would pray and chant aloud. Babies cried. And although it was cold above ground, underneath it was still hot and humid, and smelled of sweat, cigarettes, urine and garlic. 'The stink down there was truly awful,' says Suzanne. 'Life in the shelter really was very unpleasant. You had to take your bedding down every day – if you left it overnight it would soon become damp and mouldy.' Almost the worst aspect, however, was the maddening inactivity of sitting or lying in deck-chairs, and just listening to the raids above – estimating where each whistling bomb was going to land. On her house? On the shelter? She had begun to fear being trapped underground again and that she might not be so lucky a second time.

Instead of going to parties and bars, Suzanne now met most of her friends either at her or someone else's flat. She would dress up as much as the lack of make-up and clothing would allow and spend the evening simply talking. Still friends with Hubert Marsham and Shrimp Simpson, she had also come to know a number of the other submariners. One who had taken a particular shine to her was Boris Karnicki, the captain of a Polish crew who had joined the Tenth Flotilla the previous autumn. 'Boris was devastatingly sexy and attractive, and with a delicious accent,' says Suzanne. Calling her his 'Little English Rose', he tried every ploy he could to get her into bed. Very reluctantly, she resisted. Simpson, too, had immediately taken to the Polish skipper. On his arrival Karnicki assured Simpson that his boat and crew were at his disposal. During the voyage out, he had announced to his crew that he, Boris Karnicki, had declared personal war on Benito Mussolini. The rest of the crew, he told Simpson, were quite happy with this proclamation. Boris and his officers soon found a flat in Sliema and bought an upright piano, around which they would sing Polish marches. Evenings spent in their flat were always entertaining. 'They were a wild, utterly charming bunch,' recalls Suzanne.

Life was becoming harder by the day. The shelters might have been warm and clammy, but homes above ground were icy cold. Heating the house became impossible, and cooking extremely difficult owing to the lack of kerosene. Although Michael Montebello rarely went hungry, he and his mother would regularly travel into one of the villages to buy extra bits of food to supplement their rations. His clothes were filthy most of the time and decidedly frayed, but they were learning to make the best of what they could get. The *Times of Malta*, once read, came in very useful as toilet paper. So did propaganda leaflets dropped over the Island by the Italians.

Living on the edge of Grand Harbour, Michael was often in the firing line. One day he was standing outside the shelter with a couple of his friends when they saw a Stuka begin its dive from above Fort St Angelo. Suddenly it looked as though the bomb was coming straight for them and they all rushed towards the shelter. Michael saw a man run for cover in the public toilets just a hundred yards away. The bomb exploded before they'd made it to safety and they were blown over like a pack of cards on to the ground. When they picked themselves up again, they saw the toilet was nothing but rubble. 'We never saw that man again,' says Michael.

Another time, Michael was sneaking off to the Regent Cinema in Valletta. His mother had forbidden him to roam far from the shelter, but he still went into the centre of the city to scavenge or to watch a film. On this occasion, the Regent was showing *The North-West Mounted Police* starring Gary Cooper, a movie Michael was anxious to see. On his way there, his uncle spotted him, and frog-marched him back to the shelter where he received a severe scolding and a smacked backside from his mother. He soon had reason to thank his uncle. Half-way through the screening, a bomb hit the cinema. Although a small auditorium, the Regent was packed that afternoon, mostly with servicemen taking a day's leave. The ceiling completely collapsed, showering the audience with masonry. Forty-one people were killed.

While Ken Griffiths was glad there were no longer so many kit inspections and parades, he would have preferred it if they hadn't been quite so busy on the guns. It was exhausting work: up at first light, a quick wash and shave, then, when it was his shift, he'd be on duty for 24 hours. Because of the number of raids this meant they had to be at readiness at all times, i.e. within the vicinity of the gun and ready to begin firing at a moment's notice. Unlike the heavy anti-aircraft gun emplacements, the light ack-ack teams were more manœuvrable. The Swedish 40mm Bofors could be transported on wheels, but once in position staked down with semi-permanent struts. At Spinola, the Bofors guns were set down and surrounded by a wall of protective sandbags. Ammunition came in clips of four 40mm shells, of which one would usually be tracer, so as to light up the passage of their fire. Capable of firing up to 160 rounds per minute, each gun needed a crew of at least six men, four of whom would do nothing but pass and load ammunition, while the other two would train the gun on to a target and fire. With an effective range of nearly four miles, it had been the preferred light anti-aircraft gun of the British since the outbreak of war.

Ken, like the rest of the gun crew, was fully trained in all aspects of manning the Bofors, and they would take turns at each job. The firer and trainer each had a metal seat, so these tasks were less arduous than lugging clips of ammunition. At the end of a 24-hour shift they would be absolutely exhausted. Sometimes the sky would be thick with enemy planes, at other times it would be a lone bomber or reconnaissance raid, but whatever the scale of attack, they still had to be there manning the gun and firing their rounds into the sky. The noise, of course, was deafening. They were issued with ear-plugs, but then they couldn't hear each other, so most – Ken included – tended not to bother with them. He has suffered the consequences ever since.

Even when off-duty, there was little respite. At night, Ken would lie on the hard stone floor, wrapped in his blankets, listening to the crash of bombs and the nearby anti-aircraft guns: the tonk-tonk-tonk-tonk of the Bofors and boom of the heavy 3.7-inch guns at Spinola Battery. Sleep was hard to come by and Ken spent most of the time feeling on edge. The screaming bombs got to him most. 'Oh God, it would frighten you,' he says. 'Oh dear me, they were terrible.' The house was also infested with fleas and other bugs, and all of them scratched themselves raw. Malta Dog was rife. Even the HQ cook suffered. One day, Ken was asked to find him, but he wasn't in the usual place where he heated up the tins of Maconachie's pies and bully beef. Ken looked everywhere and eventually found the cook sitting on the toilet next to the Officers' Mess, with his trousers down and the primus stove in front of him, doing the cooking. 'He had diarrhoea in a bad way,' says Ken.

When they had first arrived on the Island, they would regularly walk into Valletta on their days off, a trip of several miles. But with many of the bars and cinemas now closed, there was less enthusiasm for such outings. Ken would often accompany his friend Archie Jones on his errands, riding pillion – just for a change of scenery and for something to do. Archie also taught him how to ride a motorbike.

As they were based at Regimental HQ, there were always odd jobs and bits of administration to be done, and Ken would occasionally volunteer for a bit of dispatch riding himself. One day he was on an errand to the battery on Manoel Island when the sirens began and aircraft appeared overhead. Ken looked up anxiously and gunned the throttle; there were so many raids, they couldn't just stop everything every time the bombers came over. This time, though, he was unlucky – a shard of shrapnel struck him in the thigh. The wound was not particularly severe, but bad enough for him to be taken straight to St Patrick's Hospital at Pembroke Barracks. His room overlooked the sea, but his bed faced away from the window and because he was flat on his back with his entire leg in the air in a splint, he couldn't see a thing. Towards the end of February, the hospital was bombed, and Ken was taken on a stretcher to the shelter. At the time, workers were extending and expanding this, and Ken was put down next to a line of rails used for carts, which took the excavated rock away. It was dark and humid down there, and the rubble carts vibrated and made a terrible din. 'The nurses were incredible,' says Ken. 'No one panicked. They just got on with their jobs. One nurse calmly carried on with her job even though she had been hit in the leg. She must have been in agony, but she never showed any sign of pain.'

★

Stray bombs were a hazard for everyone, but the airfields were being specifically pounded several times a day. Junkers 88 bombers would drop their cluster of bombs, and then the 109s would often follow up by roaring across at 300 m.p.h., just fifty feet above the ground, shooting at anything they could see. Around Takali, the buildings were being pulverized into the ground one by one. Eighteen-year-old Pete Watson was an RAF electrician who had arrived the previous September. He was nominally attached to 249 Squadron, but in practice everyone pitched in together, so he would work on any of the aircraft at Takali. To begin with, he'd been billeted in blockhouses at one end of the airfield. Long, rectangular stone buildings, with washrooms and a toilet, they housed twenty or so groundcrew – 'erks' as they were known throughout the RAF. When that was bombed, they were moved to the 'Mad House', a gothic Victorian monstrosity of marble staircases and pointed towers. That, too, was hit, as was the nearby pottery, and so they were moved again, this time to billets in Rabat, to which they had to walk up a steep hill, as it was perched on the same promontory as Mdina. Throughout the early months of 1942, both the pottery and the Mad House were hit or suffered bomb damage on a number of occasions. Fewer walls were left standing every week, as though they were being gradually hacked away by a giant chisel.

As an electrician, Pete's job was to sort out any wiring and battery problems in the Hurricanes. A stray bullet might have severed a cable somewhere and this would have to be mended, either on the spot, or in their 'workshop' – a large trench, some 25 yards wide by 75 yards long, dug out of the rock away at one end of the airfield. There was always a severe lack of equipment and parts; and no sooner did he start work on a plane than another raid would appear and they would have to run for cover. His working day was a long one. Because the pilots had to be at readiness at first light, he and the other erks needed to be at the airfield even earlier, before dawn. This was bad enough when he was billeted at the Mad House, but from Rabat it took the best part of three-quarters of an hour to walk down. He rarely finished work before dark.

Damage to aircraft on the ground was considerable, so it was decided that protective pens should be built around the edge of the airfield, into which the planes would be wheeled. These, it was hoped, would protect them from the blast of exploding bombs and even marauding 109s spraying the airfields with bullets. Such an undertaking could not be achieved overnight, but everyone pitched in to help: RAF groundcrew, pilots, Maltese workmen, and particularly soldiers from the various regiments on the Island.

Frank Rixon was now spending most of his time at one or other of the airfields. Usually it was Luqa, but sometimes he might be sent to Takali. It was back-breaking work. Any available material was used to build the pens: sandbags, limestone blocks, even the square four-gallon fuel cans, filled with sand. A pen for one of Peter Rothwell's Wellingtons needed as many of 60,000 individually filled fuel cans. And when Frank wasn't building pens, he was filling in bomb craters. Up before dawn, he would clamber on to his bike and head down to the airfield, where the first task was to fill in craters from the previous night's bombing. This was done almost entirely with picks and shovels, although there were still a few steamrollers working to flatten down the in-fill. Then he would carry on building blast pens. Invariably there would be an attack at some point during the morning. They would jump into the nearest slit-trench, and Frank would pray that they wouldn't get caught by a direct hit. The ground would shake, and huge columns of dust and grit would tower into the air. Every so often he would feel a ping on the top of his steel helmet from a piece of shrapnel or stone. Then, as the blast subsided, they would be showered by dirt, sand and grit.

In the aftermath, if there were dead and wounded lying nearby, it would be up to Frank and whoever was nearest to help them and pick up the pieces. 'You'd see people trapped in burning planes and there was nothing you could do about it. All this was very traumatic, but it was what happened. Sometimes you felt so frustrated, you cursed because you couldn't get back at them.' At least he could occasionally let off a few rounds as the planes flew over. Anyone near a gun post when the sirens rang was expected to make for it and start shooting. One time, he ran towards a pair of twin Lewis guns, but tripped over and cut his leg. 'I was so angry, I got on those guns and as the Stukas were coming over I started firing. Someone was helping me, so I kept on firing until they'd all gone.'

Once the raiders had passed, the first job was filling in the craters once again, before resuming the main task of building pens. At lunch-time, a tired-looking horse and cart would come round with some food – more bully beef, and maybe some bread. A drink of chlorinated water, then back to work again. Pen-building, taking cover, crater filling, pen-building. So it went on. Day after day.

He also found himself worrying a great deal about Mary. They only had their flat in Tigné for a few weeks before it was bombed. Luckily, Mary had been in a shelter and so was unhurt herself. They moved into another rented home – Villa Almira in Tigné Street – but that too was bombed. Eventually, Mary went back to live with her mother. By now, she was pregnant; they were expecting their first child in July. Every time he saw the bombers over Grand Harbour, all he could think was, 'Oh God, please let them be all right.'

Nor was Tommy Thompson impressed by what was happening. During one flight over Comiso, his engine had cut no less than *five times*. It was a heart-stopping experience. Flying over enemy territory, at night, in an aircraft that continually cut out, was not his idea of fun. In his cramped cockpit, so narrow his shoulders almost touched the sides, he would have felt particularly vulnerable. A fighter pilot had much to worry about without the added stress of flying an unreliable aircraft, and with almost no vision it was all too easy to start doubting one's instruments. With his heart pounding, he had managed to start her up again each time, but as he noted in his logbook at the time, the experience took '10 years off my life!'

In the middle of February, 1435 Flight was taken off night-fighter duties and reverted to day-time operations once again. Tommy had seen quite enough 109s back in England, but now here they were, swarming all over Malta once more. On one occasion he and some of the other pilots had been up on the roof at the Xara Palace when a Messerschmitt had flown towards them at the height of the Mdina bastions. The CO had jumped up and, grabbing the twin Lewis guns, shot the 109 down. It crashed in a ball of flames a few hundred yards away.

But such triumphs were rare. On his first day back as a day fighter, Tommy was flying with two other Hurricanes, which together made up the only three serviceable fighters on the entire Island that day. Warned of an approaching enemy raid, they made their way towards it, only to discover they were heading straight into the path of fifty 109s. Instead of turning away, which would have been fatal, the three of them flew headlong into the enemy formation, blasting their guns for their full fifteen-second capacity before diving out of the fray as quickly as they could. Tommy had no idea whether they hit anything or not, but their action had the desired effect of breaking up the formation. In the middle of most engagements, the rush of adrenalin and the speed of events tended to leave little time for feeling scared – but not so on this occasion. 'It was very frightening. Sheer terror, even though none of us were hit.'

A few days later, Tommy was posted to Egypt. He was only too happy to be leaving, especially as the whisky was running short – the final nail in Malta's coffin as far as he was concerned. 'Above average on the bar and on the job,' wrote the CO as a final assessment of Tommy's perform- ance during his nine months on the Island. On Saturday 21 February, Tommy took his seat on board a Wellington departing for Egypt. The pilot had only just finished his training and Tommy had to persuade him to fly at under 300 feet to avoid the Germans. The pilot had looked alarmed and Tommy had wondered why they were sending greenhorns to Malta. Taking off from Luqa, he looked down at the Island rapidly shrinking beneath him. He took out his logbook and made a final entry for his time there: 'Last view of Malta was the best!'

CHAPTER 12

Malta Sinking

MARCH 1942

T HE NEWS FROM abroad was bleak. In the Far East, Britain was suffering one humiliation after another. Hong Kong had fallen to the Japanese on Christmas Day 1941. By the end of January, Malaya had been overrun, and on 15 February, General Percival surrendered Singapore. It was the biggest capitulation in British history, as well as the most ignoble. 80,000 men were taken prisoner by a Japanese force of just 35,000, a catastrophic blow.

On New Year's Eve 1941, an editorial in the *Times of Malta* had spoken with confidence about the entry of the United States into the war. 'The resources and inventive genius of the people of America alone ensure aircraft production which is fifteen times anything which Japan can hope to produce, while American industrial production is greater than the whole of Europe, including the German Reich,' it argued. Most importantly, Britain was no longer alone, but now 'one branch of a mighty federation, which will not only smash Hitlerism but build a new and better world in the future.'[1]

By March 1942, this could have been viewed as hopelessly optimistic. The United States were still reeling from the devastating attack on Pearl Harbor on 7 December, and struggling to maintain their own interests in the Far East. Having been sent especially to hold the American Philippines, General MacArthur was forced back to the Bataan Peninsula, then to the island of Corregidor, and finally to leave altogether. US surrender in the Far East looked inevitable.

In Russia, the Germans were within twenty miles of Moscow. Nearly all of Europe was under fascist control. Britain, with her Empire under threat in the Far East, was still losing critical amounts of shipping in the Atlantic – the U-boats had sunk a staggering two million tons by 1942. And in North Africa, Rommel had consolidated his gains in Cyrenaica and looked ever more likely to march into Egypt.

But at least Malta – isolated and increasingly defenceless – was, at long last, going to get some Spitfires and replacement pilots. Basil Embry's report had shaken the Air Ministry back in London, and plans were finally afoot to send both replacement pilots *and* Spitfires to Malta. It might have been one of the smaller islands of Britain's beleaguered dominions, but, they conceded, it *was* a crucial one.

On a quiet airfield in southern England, there was one fighter pilot who knew nothing of these plans. Since the previous July, Raoul Daddo-Langlois – pronounced 'Rowel Daddo-Longlay' – had been with 66 Squadron, based at Portreath in Cornwall. Part of 10 Group, Fighter Command, the squadron was in a 'quiet' sector. Operations were fairly humdrum – shipping patrols and occasional escort duties for the bombers over to Brittany. They rarely saw many enemy planes, and even more rarely any action. Raoul was bored.

Like many nineteen-year-olds, he had a low boredom threshold. Impetuous, intelligent and with a natural inquisitiveness, Raoul soon became restless when he felt life was standing still. And like most boys his age, he was too callow to think of his own mortality – all he wanted was excitement and adventure.

Coming from a services background, Raoul had lived a very ordinary middle-class life. His father was a Group Captain in the RAF, a pioneer flying-boat pilot. Although the Daddo-Langlois family originally hailed from Guernsey in the Channel Islands, Raoul's childhood had been spent at various RAF stations around the country and at boarding school. At Chard School, in Somerset, he had done well, both academically and on the sports field, winning colours for both cricket and rugby. In the summer of 1939, he had even captained the cricket eleven, leading them during a record-breaking season. He was a House Captain too, considered dependable, efficient and determined, and known for his 'multitude of interests'. His ambition was to become a journalist. 'By the way,' he wrote to his mother while still at Chard, 'if you get the chance do read a Penguin special called "The Press" by William Steed; it is a very enlightening account of how and why freedom of the Press is necessary to preserve democracy ... I suppose Pop hasn't said anything about my career has he?'

He hadn't because his mother had yet to mention it; and when Raoul eventually plucked up the courage to ask his father, the idea was instantly quashed. Instead, he left school and became a junior master at a prep school in Horley, Sussex. 'I used to think I was bored at Chard, but I *know* I'm bored here,' he said in a letter to his sister, Angela. 'Life is so boring here I think I'll volunteer to serve in Finland, or go on a tramp steamer or something manly and exciting … By golly, I feel the urge for action with a capital A.'

He didn't have to wait long. Having finished the summer term at Horley he joined the RAF. Sent to an Initial Training Wing at Cambridge, he soon met P.B. 'Laddie' Lucas, who was six years older and a sports writer for the *Sunday Express* – the job of Raoul's dreams. They quickly became friends.

There was plenty of excitement in those first weeks of training. He was given rooms in St John's College, where the food was 'excellent', and he was playing cricket every weekend, so had to ask his mother to send his whites and cricket boots. After Cambridge, both he and his new friend Laddie Lucas were not sent to an Elementary Flying Training School in the UK, but to one in Ontario, Canada.

He soon showed a natural aptitude for flying and passed his wings with an above-average mark. Then it was back across the Atlantic for his Operational Training Unit, his flying 'finishing school'. Desperate to be posted to fighters, he had an anxious few days back in England waiting to hear where he would be sent, although it gave him the opportunity to see his family and to hand out the cigarettes and nylon stockings he had brought back with him for his mother and two sisters.

As he'd hoped, he had been singled out for fighters, and after eight weeks at Debden in Essex, both he and Laddie Lucas were posted to 66 Squadron in Cornwall to fly Spitfires. Raoul was then still only nineteen. Brown eyes and a deep brow, together with a slight frame, suggested an air of winsome innocence that made him look even younger. Bright and well-read he may have been, but Raoul was nonetheless an unworldly teenager being flung into an adult war. Like many before him, he needed some time to grow up, and so it was as well for him that his first operational posting was away from the front line.

Not that Raoul saw it that way. The initial thrill of joining an operational squadron soon wore off. The neighbouring countryside was quiet and there was little opportunity for letting off steam. Each pilot had his own Spitfire, though, and they soon developed a craze for decorating them with their own individual 'emblem'. Laddie Lucas painted a dragon's head on his, while Raoul designed a Cornish 'ghoulie backed by a red swastika', of which he was quite proud.

By the end of the year, Raoul was once again champing at the bit. With the shortening days, there was even less flying to be done, and his patience finally snapped. Sent on a brief half-hour practice flight, he took it upon himself to fly over to Brittany, below radar cover, and shoot up any military target he could see. Back at Portreath, they were beginning to worry seriously about what had happened to him until, an hour and a half later, he eventually appeared, coming into land with a large hole in his wing. He could have been court-martialled, but the CO, only 21 himself and a veteran of the Battle of Britain, chose to hush the matter up, believing a major rollicking would be punishment enough.

Despite this recklessness and desire for adventure, Raoul was essentially a shy person, and when, at the beginning of December, he had been asked to command a flight, he had turned it down, feeling he lacked experience and the confidence to lead his fellow pilots. However, this did not stop him being very single-minded when he chose to be. As 1941 gave way to 1942 – and there was still no sign of any action – he determined to be posted elsewhere. He had begun thinking about a transfer to 11 Group in the south-east of England, whose squadrons supplied most of the fighters for operations over France. But then another opportunity arose. Fighter Command Headquarters put through a request for two pilots to go to Burma – and so the squadron adjutant asked whether anyone wanted to volunteer. Raoul offered his services immediately, as did Laddie Lucas; after all, they'd stuck together so far. Their names were put forward that afternoon.

A week later, with his embarkation leave nearly over, Raoul was told he would no longer be going to Burma, but to Malta. 'God knows what it will be like,' he wrote to his father, 'fairly busy I should think. I don't know how long [it will be] for ... Well, I shall see you again soon, and let's hope the war is over then.' While in Plymouth waiting for his departure by Sunderland flying boat, he scribbled to his sister, Angela, to whom he was particularly close. 'Have nothing much to fill this letter with, except to say that I shan't be seeing you for a time.' Always conscientious, he also sent her written instructions to draw any funds left in his bank account in case 'anything should happen to me'. Then he assured her, 'By doing so immediately you hear, you can get it free of tax and duties etc, before the Bank realize I've pulled a fast one.'

There were fifteen of them in all, including a number of Canadians, a Rhodesian, a New Zealander, an Australian and an American. After a nerve-wracking journey in the Sunderland through electrical storms and uncomfortably close to enemy fighters, they approached Malta before dawn on 16 February. It was still dark, and ahead of them they could see searchlights flickering. For two hours they circled from a safe distance while the raids continued. At first light, with the enemy bombers departed, they landed at Kalafrana.

Raoul had been somewhat taken aback by the lack of facilities when he'd arrived at 66 Squadron in Cornwall – after his OTU at Debden it had seemed positively primitive – but nothing had prepared him for life as a fighter pilot on Malta. Like Tom Neil before him, Raoul's life pre-Malta had been cosseted in comparison. At the Mess at Portreath, he had a comfortable bed, baths and showers, plenty of food and drink and a warm fire to come back to at the end of the day. The local pubs may have been quiet and a little dingy, but there was plenty of beer and the opportunity to get off base at regular intervals.

Raoul and the other pilots had only been allowed to take 36 pounds in weight of kit with them to Malta – 'just about a pair of socks and a toothbrush', he'd told his mother – and so they'd clambered off the Sunderland clutching little more than a knapsack. There was no car or truck there to meet them, only a dilapidated bus. The glass had long since gone from the windows and they jolted along the track, still muddy and full of puddles from the recent rain, occasionally stopping for the driver to check the engine. Eventually, they reached the bottom of a hill on top of which stood an ancient walled city. With the bus rammed into bottom gear, they spluttered up to Mdina. By the time they reached the city gates, steam was pouring from the engine.

Raoul and Laddie Lucas were both assigned to 185 Squadron, based at Takali, and joined the rest of the squadron now billeted at Tommy Thompson's old Mess, the Xara Palace. The magnitude of what he'd let himself in for quickly became clear. There were no Spitfires, only Hurricanes, which were few in number and very obviously on their last legs. Although Takali was still operational, it resembled a quagmire owing to the recent rain. There was slush everywhere, and both pilots and anyone else to hand were expected to help if a plane was stuck in the mud. Raoul had thought the food at Portreath 'lousy', but compared to the staple McConachie's stew and corned beef, it must have seemed like *haute cuisine.*

Nor had Raoul ever been bombed before, although he'd once seen bomb damage in London. Listening to sirens, anti-aircraft guns, droning aircraft, and bombs blasting throughout the night and much of the day was a new and startling experience. Of the large sheds of supplies and spares he was used to, there was no sign. Malta had become a barren hell-hole where little, if anything, operated at full capacity, and 'making do' was the code by which everyone was expected to live. But there was no turning back. Raoul was stuck here now, on this tiny Island, a thousand miles from the nearest friendly neighbour.

Basil Embry had suggested a 'first-class' controller was urgently required, and undoubtedly, in Group Captain A.B. Woodhall, Hugh Pughe Lloyd found his man. A fighter pilot during the First World War, he had developed a thorough knowledge of modern aircraft and their perform-ances while a controller at Duxford in Cambridgeshire during the Battle of Britain, and then later with the Tangmere Wing led by Douglas Bader. 'He seemed to know instinctively how to take the utmost advan-tage from even the weakest position,' wrote one Malta fighter pilot.[2] 'Woody', as everyone knew him, quickly gained the complete trust of the pilots in his care, and the sound of his calm, assured voice through the pilots' headphones was often a great comfort when everything else seemed stacked against them.

Woodhall had made some important changes as soon as he arrived, first of which was the establishment of a pool of serviceable aircraft that would be rotated between the squadrons. This meant that instead of a particular squadron only being able to send up a couple of planes, they would – in theory – always have enough for several full sections of four.

Raoul, who had never flown a Hurricane before, managed to crash-land on only his second flight – a humiliating start, and doubly embarrassing with Hurricanes at a premium. That was a week after his arrival, yet despite the need for replacement pilots, he didn't fly again until 9 March; there simply weren't enough planes to go round. On 3 March, not a single Hurricane had been in a fit state to fly.

By that time, however, he had been moved from 185 to 249 Squadron, and was back in the aircraft he knew best – the Spitfire.

★

Rumours of the imminent arrival of Spitfires had abounded on the Island for several weeks. Sixteen pilots and Mark V Spitfires had been ready to fly off the aircraft carrier HMS *Eagle* on 27 February, but at the last minute a defect in the aircrafts' auxiliary fuel tanks was spotted, and so they turned round and steamed back to Gibraltar to have the problem remedied. A week later, they were finally ready and all but one took off as planned. Mid-morning on Saturday 7 March, the first Spitfire fighters to see service outside Britain touched down at Takali. 249 Squadron, which had become so depleted it had been forced temporarily to disband, was reformed, made up of the new replacements, most of whom had experience of flying Spitfires rather than Hurricanes. But the Spitfires were not sent into action immediately, as some urgent modifications were needed first. Although they had always been destined for Malta, they had been painted in brown and sand desert camouflage, entirely wrong for the current conditions on Malta and for fighting over water. Paint was found and mixed up into grey-blue, which was daubed across the lighter patches. From then on this became the preferred mixture for Spitfires over Malta, while the undersides were also repainted a darker blue. The guns on any fighter needed to be trained so the bullets converged to a single point at a certain distance for maximum fire-power, but this had not been carried out on any of the new aircraft, and so each had to be harmonized before being sent into action. All these adjustments and alterations proved a time-consuming exercise.

Raoul was given a brief practice flight on the 9th, and then, at last, he and the Spitfires were scrambled for the first time. Using the same tactics as had been adopted in the Battle of Britain, Hurricanes were sent out to tackle the incoming bombers, while Raoul and the other Spitfires were to fly above and fend off any 109s that appeared. They were at 19,000 feet above the Island when they saw the Junkers 88s and the escorting 109s below them. Attacking from above, with the sun behind, was the classic fighter attack – or 'bounce' as it was called – and with his heart thumping heavily, Raoul and the other six Spitfires swooped down on the unsuspecting 109s. It was the first time Malta fighters had ever had the advantage over their German counterparts, and soon one of the 109s was trailing smoke and plummeting into the sea. Raoul pounced on another and drawing close behind it, switched off the gun safety catch and pressed down with his thumb. The drum of machine-gun and cannon-fire poured from his wings and the Spitfire trembled with the recoil. The 109 in his sights immediately began taking evasive action, but not before Raoul had seen pieces of its tail structure flying off into the air.

'Spitfires Over Malta – Their First Kill,' ran the gleeful leader in the *Times of Malta*. ' "Spitfires engaging!" These dramatic two words that have chilled the hearts of many German pilots again made history today. They came through the earphones of the RAF fighter controller in the operations room of Malta at 11.03 this morning. For the first time since the war began, Spitfires were in battle over this tiny island fortress and the Central Mediterranean. And they met with success in their first engagement. A Flight Lieutenant had the honour of the first "kill".'[3] It was, it declared, a 'great tonic', although for how long, was not clear. Fifteen Spitfires were not going to win the air battle.

By February, the Germans had finally discovered the submarine base at Manoel Island and were pounding it daily. On Friday, 13 February – an inauspicious day at the best of times – Lazzaretto had its windows blown in by a near miss from an attacking Stuka, and then, a short while later, parachute mines were dropped, hitting the western end of the base and demolishing it. Three men were killed and the barracks destroyed. All that was left of that end of the building were bare walls stretching thirty feet into the sky. At the end of the month, they were bombed again, the eastern end being struck this time, and the officers' quarters ruined. Four Greek officers assigned to the Tenth Flotilla were killed. It took three hours just to recover the bodies, pulverized by the weight of falling stone.

Eighty yards from Lazzaretto was an underground oil tank, now empty, and with floor space of around 100 feet long and 40 feet wide. Simpson realized there was no longer any question of his men sleeping in the base, and so ordered the ratings to spend their nights on tiered bunks in the deep underground shelter, and the officers to move into the empty sub-rock oil tank. The stench of oil pervaded everything and pools of the stuff still lay congealing on the uneven floor. Beds, tables, chests of drawers and a few chairs were taken down the 30 steps that led down to the cavern, and duck boards laid down over the worst of the oil. Simpson and his secretary were forced to relocate their offices down there and to work around the comings and goings of the officers, who now smelled of oil and sweat on the base as well as during patrol. The officers and ratings resorted to messing together – an unheard-of breach of protocol – in the roofless Lazzaretto, under the glare of the sun and the twinkling of the stars.

On 5 March, three submarines moored next to the base were badly damaged and Simpson's flagship, the stationary fuel barge, HMS *Talbot*, was sunk. Another submarine was damaged a few days later. The farm was also hit, killing one sow and her litter, a hundred rabbits and one turkey. It was the end for the submariners' attempt at animal husbandry, although Simpson signalled to one of his COs, 'Casualties from shock are mincing down satisfactorily.'[4] This final supply of extra food was to keep his engineers going while they valiantly repaired the damaged boats through the following days and nights. 109s were also sweeping over Marsamxett Harbour, strafing ships and submarines alike. One young officer ran into the shelter and angrily told Simpson, 'A fighter pilot just waved at me and the bastard had painted finger nails!'[5]

On 9 March, Simpson gathered all his COs together. Already it had become necessary to dive the submarines to the bottom of the harbour during daylight hours, but he hoped all his captains would still consider leaving Malta unthinkable. Their role remained an offensive one, and to achieve success at sea, they needed to keep at least five submarines out on patrol at any one time. With several of the boats undergoing repairs, Simpson believed it had become necessary to use two complete crews for each submarine, something he had never asked of his men before. Both David Wanklyn and Boris Karnicki agreed to the scheme. So did all the others. But after the meeting, Simpson was approached by Lieutenant Tompkinson, the CO of *Urge* – second only to *Upholder* in terms of ships sunk. He could not, he told Simpson, under any circumstances, share his boat. He was sorry, but if Simpson insisted, he would resign his command. Then he broke down and wept. Simpson was shaken. He regarded Tompkinson very highly, as one of his most valued COs, and immediately assured him that nobody but he and his crew would take *Urge* to sea.

Simpson thought hard about what Tompkinson had said. Although his COs had agreed with him, he now realized none of them had liked the idea. He was trying to make decisions for the best, but, if this meant undermining morale, was such a precaution the right thing to do? All his men were tired and stretched beyond what could reasonably be expected of them, yet the loyalty a crew felt for their boat was of crucial importance. He remembered how ABC had originally told him he would be given a free hand to do as he thought fit. Sometimes, he wished he didn't have to deal with such a responsibility. In many respects, this was one of the toughest decisions he had had to make since taking command in Malta. But his men *had* to come first. Tompkinson was right. For the time being, there would be no sharing of submarines.

Suzanne Parlby had been seeing less of her submariner friends. Boris Karnicki's flat in Sliema had been bombed out, and they were all spending more and more time underground on the base. Also Suzanne, now expecting her first child, had her own problems. One day in early March, she cycled home for lunch and was about to sit down for a small salad when the sirens sounded once more. Nina, her maid, became very agitated and pleaded with her to go down to the shelter, but she refused. 'Don't be silly, Nina,' Suzanne told her, 'it's only the usual midday raid.' A few minutes later she heard a stick of bombs begin to whistle down. By now, she had become quite adept at judging the line in which the bombs would fall and the distance between explosions. She heard three crash down, each one closer, and suddenly she knew Nina had been right: the sixth was going to fall right on top of her.

A moment later, a massive explosion sent her flying across the room, glass and debris showering all around her. The bomb had landed right outside the front door, breaking all the windows and cracking the walls. Had she not been in the basement flat, she would almost certainly have been killed.

Apart from a few cuts and bruises, however, she was apparently unharmed, although the accumulative strain was taking its toll. She was exhausted, both emotionally and physically, and shortly afterwards suffered a miscarriage. Increasingly forced to take time off from work, she had twice even been admitted to Imtarfa. Then her husband John arrived at the flat one day, and told her he had secured a place for her on one of the remaining Wellingtons which were flying out of the Island. With just one suitcase, he took her to Luqa. Elisabeth Young, her old friend from St Andrew's Barracks, was also there; she, too, was ready to leave Malta. As the Wellington set off down the runway and rose into the air, Suzanne heard guns frantically firing behind her. Then gradually the noise petered out and they were flying low over a calm sea with the moon shining peacefully above them. Suzanne was one of the lucky ones.

Adrian Warburton was also about to leave Malta for the second time. His return to the Island had only ever been temporary and now he was ordered back to his official unit, 2 PRU, in Egypt. During his last two months he had completed no fewer than 43 operational trips, a large amount even by his standards. Christina Ratcliffe was sorry he was to be leaving her again, but also relieved. Working in the control room at Lascaris, she had often been given vivid demonstrations of how dangerous his missions were.

On 4 March, she'd been at the plotting table as he'd returned from a sortie over Palermo. Through her headphones, she was warned of a number of 109s fast approaching him, which she repeated to Woodhall, sitting above in the gallery.

'Look out Stallion Two Seven,' Woody told Warby, 'Messerschmitts on your tail.' With her long croupier stick, Christina pushed Warby's plot closer to Malta. She also moved the 109s forward too – and the gap between the two was closing. A hush descended over the Operations Room. Everyone was watching the table. Then Christina pushed the two plots together.

Standing there, she waited for the next instruction from the radar station. 'Plot on Stallion Two Seven faded,' came the voice. Her heart thudded. Slowly, she repeated the words to the controller. Woodhall looked grim. 'I had the utmost difficulty in carrying on,' said Christina, 'but I had to. Personal feelings didn't count.'[6] But she and everyone there knew what had happened – Warby had been shot down.

No one spoke for a while, then through her headphones came the words, 'Stallion Two Seven landed safely.' The relief around the room was palpable. He had flown down through cloud cover and so low the radar station had been unable to detect him. When Christina later told Warby of the scare he'd given her, he just laughed. 'I didn't always appreciate his sense of humour,' she said.[7]

Not long after, she had returned from a night's work and was determined to get some sleep – and in her bed, rather than the ERA shelter as normal. But she was soon woken by gunfire and bombs crashing nearby. Then came an enormous explosion and her bedroom door burst open. The whole building rocked and she thought it was about to collapse. Wearing only her silk nightgown – made from an old parachute Warby had given her – she ran out on to the street, dazed, and with grit and bits of shrapnel falling all around her. For a moment she stood rooted to the spot, in shock and unsure whether to try to dash for the ERA shelter. A soldier called to her – he was sheltering in the hallway of the next-door flat – and so she ran over. Seeing her shivering in her see-through gown, the soldier offered her his greatcoat and a cigarette, which she gratefully accepted and then waited until the All Clear was sounded. The two of them then surveyed the damage. Two doors away, the corner flat was now a pile of rubble.

Warby rushed to see her as soon as he could – he'd been told her flat had received a direct hit. Still in shock, Christina sobbed out her story. Seeing her tears, he tried to make her laugh instead. Why had she not just jumped out of her window? he asked her – after all, hadn't she been wearing her parachute?

By the time Warby left for the second time on 19 March, he had become something of a legend on Malta. Awarded a Distinguished Service Order (DSO) in addition to his DFC and Bar, he had also been promoted to Flight Lieutenant. Not that he ever commanded a flight – Warby just commanded himself. Officially still attached to 2 PRU, but working alongside 69 Squadron, he had become even more a law unto himself, uncontrollable and unpredictable. But he *always* got his pictures, and his skill, bravery and hard work were incomparable. Hugh Pughe Lloyd recognized this and made no effort to rein him in. 'Warburton was the absolute king of photographic reconnaissance,' said Lloyd after the war. 'If I wanted pictures of Naples, Tripoli or any of the other Axis ports he would say, "Yes, sir" and go out and get them at no matter what cost.'[8] Warby took his orders not from his immediate superiors, but directly from Lloyd. Because of this, he was frequently seen both at Lascaris and Scots Street. 'He used to regularly come into the office,' says John Agius. 'He was mad as a hatter. He would be wearing anything that was comfortable. He couldn't care what anyone thought, and the authorities let him because they knew he was doing his job.' Tommy Thompson also knew Warby while they were both on Malta. 'He was a remarkable man,' he says. 'I think he was almost without fear.' Tommy remembers seeing him once at Luqa. Warby and one of his crewmen were sitting on the ground throwing stones at each other. The first to flinch lost the game. 'He had blood pouring down the side of his face,' says Tommy, 'but he wouldn't move.' Peter Rothwell, flying out of Luqa and working closely with 69 Squadron, remembers him too. 'I knew him, but no one could get to know Warby very well. He was wild, and used to rugger tackle people in the Mess, things like that.' Like John Agius, Peter thought Warby had a screw loose somewhere. 'He was crazy, all right,' he says.

Only on Malta could an individual such as Warby have thrived. He and Christina had become the most glamorous couple on the Island, a status he seemed to enjoy. But such blatant individualism was not popular with everyone, especially some of his fellow officers, who saw him as a disruptive and self-centred egoist. Not that he cared; Warby had always been an eccentric – a misfit who refused to tow the line. The difference was that instead of being pushed to one side, he was now being given a free hand to do what he did best, in the way that suited him. He may have ruffled a few feathers, but no one doubted either his ability or his achievements. Lloyd was going to miss his reconnaissance ace.

Since the failed convoy in February, ABC had been giving much thought to how he could get another through to Malta. At least the seriousness of the situation was now appreciated by the Chiefs of Staff back in London, who signalled to ABC, 'Our view is that Malta is of such importance both as an air staging post and as an impediment to enemy reinforcement routes that the most drastic steps are justifiable to sustain it.'[9] Obviously, these were the Admiral's sentiments exactly. But they needed to act quickly. Not only were food and aviation fuel in critically short supply, so too was ammunition. Ken Griffiths and the other gunners had already been told to fire only at the bombers, in an effort to cut back on the amount of shells used.

Bringing the ships from Alexandria was the only feasible route – from Gibraltar was simply *too* risky – but even so, if they were to have any chance of success, the full co-operation and attention of all three services were required. The plan was for the Army to make a feint advance in North Africa to threaten enemy airfields and so distract hostile aircraft from attacking the convoy. The RAF was to send all available bombers to attack airfields in Crete and Cyrenaica, and fighters from North Africa to escort the convoy as far as possible, and then more fighters from Malta as the convoy approached. The largest naval force available under Pridham-Wippell's replacement, Rear-Admiral Vian, would escort the four merchant ships assembled: the *Clan Campbell*, now repaired after being attacked during the previous attempt; the *Pampas*; the *Talabot*; and the naval supply ship HMS *Breconshire*, which had already made several rapid dashes across the Mediterranean to supply Malta. At dawn on 20 March, the convoy and her escort set sail. It *had* to succeed; the stakes could not have been higher.

★

At the same time, Raoul Daddo-Langlois was at readiness down at Takali. With him were Laddie Lucas, the Rhodesian Dougie Leggo, and Robert 'Buck' McNair, a tough 22-year-old Canadian from Nova Scotia, who had flown out with Raoul in February.

They were all a bit concerned about Dougie, who had been in Valletta the previous night with a girl and had only just come back, short on sleep and still a bit drunk. Someone had offered to swap shifts with him, but Dougie had refused. They were soon scrambled and were still climbing when Raoul spotted a number of 109s behind and above them. They immediately turned into the enemy fighters and Buck McNair opened fire, shooting bits off one, and following it down right over the roofs of Valletta until it crashed into the sea. It was his first 'kill' since arriving on the Island.

Raoul had also turned into the 109s and had fired all his ammunition in one long, twelve-second burst, but missed completely. He was climbing up out of the fray, thinking about what a lousy shot he must be, when he heard Dougie asking him where he was.

'Twelve thousand feet,' Raoul told him.

'Well, I'm at eight. I'll come up and join you,' Dougie replied.

But Raoul could see him below, with the German fighters not far behind and warned him to dive, the quickest means of escape. But Dougie seemed to be ignoring him. Raoul couldn't understand it – what the hell was he playing at? By now the 109s were almost upon him. 'Break now!' Raoul yelled, but with his wits dulled by the lack of sleep and alcohol, Dougie was too slow. Helplessly, Raoul watched a 109 creep up close behind him and open fire at almost point-blank range. Then a dark burst of smoke appeared and the Spitfire began to spin. As the plane plummeted down over Valletta, Raoul's relief at seeing Dougie bale out turned to horror as he realized that the parachute had collapsed. The Rhodesian was killed instantly as he hit the ground.

Baling out from a plane was not without risks at the best of times, especially since the first time most pilots ever experienced it was in the middle of an air battle. The procedure was drummed into them: undo the radio and oxygen leads, and the Sutton safety harness, pull back the canopy, flip the plane over on its back, then drop out. After fifteen seconds or so, pull the rip-cord and float down to safety. In practice, the plane was invariably in a very bad way, with smoke billowing into the cockpit, and flames licking at the pilot's arms and legs. It was all too easy to panic and either forget to do something, or, with shaking and fumbling fingers simply be unable to release the harness and leads. Frequently, a pilot would have been wounded too. It was reckoned that if the plane was on fire, there were about ten seconds in which to get out. There was then the chance that a pilot might be shot on his way down – considered extremely unsporting but perfectly legitimate. And on Malta, there was a much higher than usual chance that the parachute wouldn't open properly – many were damaged by bomb blasts, something that could not always be detected when they were packed tightly in their cases.

It was a horrific way to die, and afterwards Raoul and the other pilots all felt terrible, especially since Dougie should never have been flying; they should have made greater efforts to stop him. They became even more bitter when Raoul's friend, Laddie Lucas, who had also been flying on that sortie, claimed to have seen a German 109 deliberately shoot at Dougie's parachute then fly overhead so that it collapsed in the wake of the aircraft's slipstream.

Raoul was stood down during the afternoon and evening. It had been a busy few days, but he'd wanted action and now he was getting it. That evening, he was at the Xara Palace when the sirens began wailing once more. It was dusk, but soon the sky was thick with enemy aircraft. He'd never seen anything like it – row after row of black shapes as far as the eye could see. And they all seemed to be heading for Takali.

Pete Watson had been working at the airfield along with the other erks since before dawn and was still there when the siren sounded. It had been an intense few weeks. He'd been as excited as the rest of the groundcrew when the Spitfires had arrived, but they were trickier to work on than the Hurricanes. For a start, the batteries were awkward to get out: the whole bucket seat had to be removed to reach it, which could be quite a lengthy exercise. And he never seemed to have enough time to do everything – especially since they were constantly interrupted by raids. The last few days had been particularly bad. On the 18th, there had been so many bomb craters, the airfield had been made temporarily unusable. Two more Hurricanes had been destroyed on the ground and two Spitfires damaged. One of the precious petrol bowsers had been set on fire – a double blow, as it had held 800 gallons of fuel. When the smoke and dust from the bombs finally settled, the bowser and the burnt-out Hurricanes had still been billowing thick, dark smoke high into the sky. The following day, with the bowser still smouldering, there had been another attack. A new term had crept into the jargon of the RAF boys: 'spitchered', from the Maltese 'spicca', meaning 'no further use'. After this raid, a Beaufighter, two further Hurricanes and a Spitfire were 'spitchered', and badly so.

The 20th was pay-day for the erks, but Pete hadn't had much chance to spend any of his hard-earned cash – around two shillings a day – and now there was yet another raid. Putting on his tin hat, he once more ran for the nearest slit-trench. His heart nearly stopped when he saw how many planes were heading for the airfield.

What Pete was witnessing from his slit-trench, and Raoul from the balcony of the Xara Palace, were 63 Junkers 88s and their fighter escorts. Kesselring had been concerned that he was losing too many aircraft through small raids, and so had decided to switch tactics by sending over large concentrated forces instead. By 20 March, the German commander knew that Takali housed most of the Island's fighters, including the newly arrived Spitfires, and so was determined to bomb the place into dust.

The airfield was totally shrouded in smoke in a matter of minutes. Debris poured down on Pete as the ground trembled and shook. Bombs were whistling and screaming, and buildings crumbling as huge eruptions burst all around him. Hangars were ruined, blast pens smashed, billets blown apart and more planes and another bowser set on fire. Pete thought the end had surely come – but as the aircraft finally left, he was still in one piece. His ears were ringing so badly he was almost totally deaf. The air was thick with choking smoke, dust and the acrid smell of cordite. The Luftwaffe had just dropped 114 tons of bombs – on an airfield the size of a small village. Fortunately, a large part of the attack had been concentrated on one edge of the airfield where they mistakenly believed there was an underground hangar. Even so, the damage was considerable and Takali was once again rendered unusable.

Work had begun straight away on clearing up the wreckage, but early the following morning another heavy raid appeared – this time over 200 aircraft, dropping a massive 182 tons of bombs, including a number of delayed-action explosives. This was the first example of carpet bombing and, taken together with the previous night's attack, was the single biggest attack on an Allied airfield ever. Takali looked like the surface of the moon – pock-marked and cratered beyond recognition. Over a thousand bombs had fallen on this tiny airfield in the two attacks. The city of Coventry, in the English Midlands, was destroyed by 260 tons of bombs, less than Takali had received in a little over twelve hours.

The surrounding areas had not been spared either. Raoul Daddo-Langlois in Mdina was safe, but Buck McNair had not been so fortunate. Some of the 249 pilots were billeted not at the Xara Palace, but at the Hotel Point de Vue, a short walk away just outside the Mdina city walls in Rabat. Buck had just entered the hotel that morning when a stray bomb landed above the entrance. When he came to he did not know where he was; he didn't think he was dead, but then he didn't feel whole either. His eyes were open, but it was dark and he felt nothing, no pain at all. Slowly light began to filter through, and so he groped for his tin hat and then touched his face and chest – they were all there and he began to feel a bit better. The room began to grow lighter as showers of dust caused by the blast cleared. As he gradually became more conscious he realized he was lying upstairs – which was impossible, as he'd been entering downstairs by the front door. Then he realised he must have been blown upstairs: thrown up some twenty or thirty feet.

Buck shook himself down and staggered down the remains of the main staircase. In the hallway were bodies. The raid was still on, but a strange quiet had descended over the place. He couldn't see any blood, for all the bodies were covered in heavy dust. He looked at them, studying them in turn. One was headless, with the head cut very cleanly from the shoulders. Hearing a moan, he put his hand gently on each figure in turn to see which of them was alive. One had a hole, more than a foot wide, through the abdomen. Another's head was split wide open into two halves. The face looked twice the size and Buck wondered how the man could still be alive. He thought about shooting him there and then.

Stumbling, he put his hand on the wall to steady himself but found that it slithered off. The wall had appeared dry and plastered in dust, but when he looked at his hand, found it was covered in blood and studded with flesh. When a friend of his from the squadron appeared, Buck looked down at himself and saw his clothes were torn and ripped. They both staggered outside and tried to talk about what happened, but could hardly find the words – instead they stole several bottles of White Horse whisky and, mad with rage, made themselves very drunk indeed.

At Imtarfa, Meme Cortis had heard the two raids. Although she continued work throughout the day, she and the other VADs had begun sleeping in the shelter below their Mess. Clutching a hot-water bottle and a blanket, she would try to make herself as comfortable as possible.

Then she would say her prayers and thank God for getting through another day. She and the other girls told stories and jokes to keep their spirits up, then they would try to get as much sleep as they could.

Takali had still been smouldering when she had awoken on the morning of the 21st. She was desperately worried about her father and eldest sister. They had finally been forced to abandon the family home in Sliema after all the doors and windows has been blown in, but were now living with friends in Balzan, dangerously close to Takali. With such large raids now coming over, the surrounding areas were bound to suffer, and she began to wonder which was worse – Balzan or Sliema. Both Mosta and Attard – also close to Balzan – had been hit, Mosta particularly badly.

Bombs had also been dropped on the hospital, both in the morning and afternoon. Two people were killed and three seriously wounded. The Imtarfa Club and children's school were badly damaged, as were two sections of the hospital – 'A' and 'H' Block – and the football field and tennis courts. As always, Meme carried on working: there was even more for her to do after a big raid.

Meanwhile, the convoy from Alexandria was slowly making its way towards Malta. Once again, the weather was poor, and the ships were pitching in the rising swell. Thanks to the attacks on the Axis airfields in North Africa, they had crept through the danger zone between Crete and Cyrenaica without a single attack, but then on the evening of the 21st, German transport planes were spotted flying over them. Inevitably, they would report the position of the convoy steaming below. Early the following morning, a Malta submarine reported a number of Italian naval ships leaving Taranto. ABC, pacing his office in Alexandria, knew the convoy could expect aerial attacks any minute and that enemy ships were likely to appear a few hours later.

He was not wrong. The first enemy aircraft attacked the convoy at around 9.30 a.m. on the 22nd, and the attacks continued with increasing intensity until dusk. Two Italian cruisers approached in the early after-noon, and Rear-Admiral Vian led his force out to meet them, having ordered the convoy and close escort to turn away southwards. Having laid a smoke-screen, he then opened fire on the Italians, although at very long range. After a brief exchange, the enemy cruisers withdrew. 'Enemy driven off', Vian signalled ABC, but both men suspected they would soon be back.

While Vian had been firing at the Italians, a large number of Junkers 88s had attacked the rest of the convoy, although with little success, largely thanks to an intense anti-aircraft barrage thrown up by the merchant ships and the destroyer escort. The main worry was the shortage of ammunition – they had already used sixty per cent and the closer they came to Malta the more persistent the enemy air attack would be.

Vian now discovered the Italians – with three cruisers, a battleship and eight destroyers – were heading to cut off the convoy as they approached Malta. It put him in a very difficult position. If he left the convoy to engage the enemy – which considerably outgunned and out-powered his force – he would leave the supply ships dangerously exposed. Yet to stay with them and run into the Italians was also a high-risk strategy. Opting for the lesser of two evils, he ordered the convoy and close escort to turn south once more, laid a smoke-screen between him and the merchantmen, and headed off to try to hold the Italian force at bay.

In Alexandria, ABC was in his caged-tiger mode. Following exactly what was happening, he could only stay where he was and wait for the signals to come in. 'Never have I felt so keenly the mortifying bitterness of sitting behind the scenes with a heavy load of responsibility while others were in action with a vastly superior force of the enemy,' he wrote later.[10] He could imagine clearly what was happening – the smoke-screen wafting across the sea, the Junkers dropping their bombs, huge fountains of spray all around the convoy, Vian and his force dodging the fifteen-inch shells from the Italian battleship, and the rising swell that made life so hard for the destroyers. He had cursed the gregale before, and he cursed it again now.

Eventually, the Italians, unable to break through either the smoke-screen or Vian's constantly weaving force, withdrew. It was now dusk, and although he had ordered the convoy to disperse and try to make their way to Malta under their own steam by morning, he had to return with his force to Alexandria in an effort to try to make it through the most dangerous stretches before dawn. Had he continued, he would have been caught short with a lack of fuel and ammunition.

Talabot and *Pampas* passed into Grand Harbour just after 9 a.m. on the 23rd, each accompanied by a destroyer. Both had had narrow escapes – two bombs had even hit *Pampas*, but had failed to explode. Shortly after, *Breconshire*, only eight miles away and having survived a large number of attacks, was hit in the engine-room and stopped dead. Two destroyers tried to tow her in, but because of the bad weather and heavy swell, all attempts were unsuccessful. As she drifted towards the shore she dropped anchor, protected vainly by three destroyers and their smoke-screens. The fourth ship, the *Clan Campbell* was attacked again when still fifty miles away. This time a bomb struck her engine-room and she sank soon afterwards – with all her cargo, a quarter of the convoy's supplies.

Nine more Spitfires had arrived on Malta on the 21st – at Luqa. But again, their guns had been neither tested nor aligned, and tropical air filters had not been attached, and so it took a couple of days of prepara-tion before they could be flown operationally. Nor were there enough spares; ludicrously, one of the original Spitfires had to be cannibalized to provide parts for the others. There were still nowhere near enough planes to go round, and so 249 were to share the new arrivals with the largely American 126 Squadron, rotating pilots and aircraft according to who was on readiness.

As far as Lloyd was concerned, Takali now resembled a First World War battlefield and he had expected it to be out of action for a week. In the event, it was possible to fly the surviving planes over to Luqa by the afternoon of the 22nd, thanks to the superhuman efforts of the RAF and Army – one of whom was Frank Rixon – working round the clock clearing away the rubble and filling in the bomb craters. Raoul Daddo-Langlois then flew a convoy patrol, but saw little. By the following day, as the first merchantmen arrived at Grand Harbour, the collective damage to all three airfields meant only five fighters were in sufficient working order to take to the skies; five fighters to take on over two hundred Junkers 88s, newly arrived Stukas, 109s and Messerschmitt 110s all out to blast the convoy before they had a chance to unload their precious cargo.

Vice-Admiral Wilbraham Ford had written to ABC in January warning him that such was the state of the docks, he worried they would not be able to unload a convoy even if it did arrive.[11] Two months on, the situation was only worse. The wharves and quaysides were in a terrible state, as were the storehouses, and so the unloading process was hampered from the start, with *Pampas* and *Talabot* moored in the middle of Grand Harbour rather than docked alongside the Corradino Heights in French Creek, as the *Illustrious* had been fourteen months before.

42. A dilapidated bus, very much like the one that greeted Raoul Daddo-Langlois and Denis Barnham on their arrival on the Island.

43. A Spitfire Mark V on Malta. Because the squadron lettering has been clearly painted over, this photograph must have been taken in March or early April 1942, when the few Spitfires available were shared between squadrons. The large 'Vokes' tropical filter protrudes underneath the engine cowling.

44. An aerial photograph of a raid on Grand Harbour taken from a German Junkers 88. This photograph featured in the German propaganda magazine *Signal* in July 1942.

45. Carnage in Grand Harbour. This picture shows the Senglea side of Dockyard Creek, and shows very clearly why it was so difficult mooring and unloading any supply ships that arrived.

46. Pete Watson (far right) and colleagues outside their billet in Rabat. As an RAF electrician working at Takali, Pete regularly found himself on the receiving end of some of the worst bombing raids, and with little protection other than a slit-trench and a tin hat.

47. The tough twenty-two-year-old Canadian Buck McNair, who was deeply affected by the bombing of the Pointe du Vue when several of his colleagues were blown up in front of him.

48. HMS *Penelope*. No wonder she was nicknamed HMS *'Pepperpot'*.

49. Takali under attack and completely covered by dust and smoke. Taken from Luqa, this is much the same sight that would have greeted Denis Barnham on his arrival on Malta.

50. A Bofors gun crew.

51. Cartoon from the *Times of Malta*,
7 May 1942.

52. The future? What? Denis
Barnham's self-portrait of 16 May
1942.

The future? What?
16/5/42.

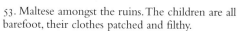
53. Maltese amongst the ruins. The children are all barefoot, their clothes patched and filthy.

54. Denis Barnham in his Spitfire at Luqa. By this time in 1942, there were no fuel bowsers so refuelling had to be done laboriously by hand from four-gallon tins. Other groundcrew rearm the Spitfire's two cannons and four Browning .303 machine-guns.

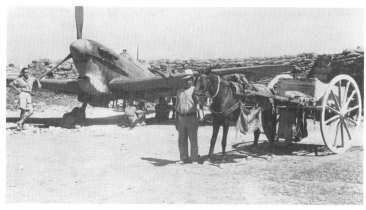
55. A Maltese, with his mule and cart, stands beside a Spitfire in its blast pen.

56. Christina Ratcliffe in a publicity shot for the Victory Kitchens. This particular one was in Castille Square, Valletta. Part of the sign is still visible on the wall today.

57. Denis Barnham's painting of the Air Battle for Malta. The underbelly of a Messerschmitt 109 flashes past a Spitfire. Two more 109s are right behind, while another Spitfire, chasing German Junker 88s, is also chased by a 109.

58. Warby, wearing his white scarf, grey baggy slacks and desert boots. Attitudes to dress were relaxed on Malta. It was an environment where a maverick like Adrian Warburton could shine.

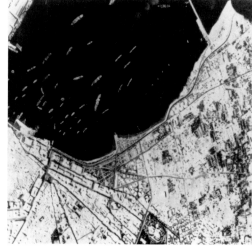

59. An aerial reconnaissance photograph of Tripoli Harbour taken by Warby.

60. Denis Barnham. By the time this photograph was taken, Denis had the necessary five kills that made him an 'ace' – four German and one Italian, painted on the side of his Spitfire.

Consequently, they were more exposed and the cargoes had to be taken out and put on to barges, which were then towed to the quayside and unloaded in turn, a slow and time-consuming business, especially as many of the barges had already been sunk.

Governor Dobbie had ordered the Maltese workers to start unloading immediately, which they had done despite being the target of a number of daylight attacks. Thanks largely to the gunners' relentless barrage and low cloud, neither ship was hit that first day or the following two, although there had been a number of close calls. Meanwhile, *Breconshire* had finally been towed into Marsaxlokk Bay on the night of the 24th, and was spotted and attacked the following day by bombers coming to hit Hal Far and Luqa.

The German bombers then returned to Grand Harbour with a vengeance on the 26th. By the law of averages, all the near misses were bound to become a direct hit at some point, and so it proved. *Breconshire* was struck once more and keeled over and sank. So too were *Pampas* and *Talabot*, and both caught fire. It was a heart-breaking sight. The plumes of dark smoke billowing above Valletta could be seen across the entire Island; three of the ships had tantalizingly reached their destination only to be struck on arrival. *Pampas* sank, and such was the threat of her ammunition supplies exploding, *Talabot* had to be scuttled.

By the end of the 26th, only 799 tons out of 7,462 had been salvaged from *Pampas*, 972 from *Talabot*'s 8,956, and none from *Breconshire*. This was a poor return after three days and three nights, particularly once it became clear the unloading process had been hampered by an appalling breakdown in management – and by those who should have known a great deal better.

From the outset, only the Maltese stevedores had been tasked with the unloading. The Army, used for just about every other job on the Island, had not been called in to help. Nonetheless, rather than wait for the stevedores, the station commander at Luqa, Wing Commander Powell-Sheddon,[12] had taken it upon himself to send down some RAF groundcrew to unload urgently needed aircraft spares the evening after the two ships had arrived in Grand Harbour. Peter Rothwell's Special Duties Flight, for example, had been grounded for the past fortnight due to the lack of aero engines and spare parts, and it was essential their Wellingtons became airworthy again at the earliest possible moment. Powell-Sheddon had also correctly guessed that with the drizzle and low cloud it was unlikely there would be much enemy activity that night. With groundcrews working from dusk until dawn, both at Grand Harbour and at the airfields, most of the aircraft spares were safely unloaded and eighteen Spitfires and Hurricanes were airworthy by the following morning.

Two nights later, on the 25th, Powell-Sheddon noticed all work on unloading the ships had stopped. He immediately telephoned Lloyd, who refused to believe him. So he then called the Harbour Master, who confirmed his fears. When he reported back to Lloyd, the AOC would still not accept what he was saying, so Powell-Sheddon went down to Grand Harbour himself. The place was eerily quiet. No one was about. Of the unloading parties, there was not a sign. He rang Lloyd yet again, but was tersely told to shut up and go to bed. But he felt this needed addressing *now*, so he rang the Governor. Dobbie, like Lloyd, dismissed him, insisting nothing more could be done until the morning. It turned out nothing had been unloaded the previous night either – the 24th – another period when there had been no enemy raids.

The following day – the 26th – with all three ships now sunk, George Simpson was on his way from Lazzaretto to Naval HQ when he met Lloyd. 'It's a disgrace, a most damnable affair!' Lloyd told him. 'Three whole days and nights of inaction and now they're both hit and on fire! It's disgraceful!' [13]

This was not quite true. Unloading had carried on throughout the night of the 23rd, and all through the daylight hours of the 24th and 25th, despite constant harrying by German bombers. Only on the nights of the 24th and 25th had the stevedores stopped working.

But why was Lloyd not fully aware of what was going on? As Air Officer Commanding and a member of the Island's Administrative Council, he should have been fully informed of precisely how the unloading was progressing. Powell-Sheddon could not have made his concerns clearer on the night of the 25th, yet Lloyd had chosen to do nothing about it.

But the fact that two whole nights – undisturbed by German bombers – were wasted was clearly bungling incompetence of major proportions. Admittedly it was dark and there was still a blackout, but with low cloud and no sign of any enemy action, an exception should surely have been made and illumination given to the unloading, even if this had just been lamps and torches.

Alongside Lloyd on the Administrative Council were the other two officers commanding, Vice-Admiral Leatham for the Navy, and General

Beak for the Army, as well as the Lieutenant-Governor, Sir Edward Jackson, and the Governor himself, General Dobbie. Each of them should have discussed the unloading process at great length. All would have known the dangers, and plans for all circumstances – weather patterns included – should have been put in place long before the convoy ever reached Grand Harbour. A large number of troops as well as RAF groundcrew should have been brought in for the operation. That none of them seemed to have thought of any of this was, frankly, astonishing. They, more than any others on the Island, knew how critical this convoy was, and the constraints and conditions in which they were obliged to operate.

While each member of the council should have carried his share of blame, the knives were now out for Dobbie. Lloyd, in particular, was only too willing to pass the buck, and wrote immediately to the Prime Minister demanding the Governor be relieved at once. 'The odds against our survival now seemed almost insuperable,' he wrote after the war, 'but it was a grim and murderous reflection at the time that it was not the fighting which had brought us to our present pass but sheer ineptitude, lack of resolution and bomb-stunned brains incapable of thought.'[14] Quite so – but one of these was his own. For Lloyd to claim he had no part in this was utterly shameless, to put it mildly, and a gross avoidance of his own responsibility.

Suggestions that the stevedores were not up to the task, or only too willing to run away when danger threatened, were totally unfair. The ships were damaged and many of the holds were waterlogged. During the day they were working through constant air attacks. John Agius saw the ships in the harbour and watched the stevedores working away. He did not envy them their task. 'It was not a case of danger money – it was a case of real danger every single minute.' Nor were they soldiers, trained to perform under fire; they were merely civilian dockworkers, which is another reason why troops should have been brought in to help. The biggest disgrace in this affair was the absence of strong, unified leadership when it was most needed.

Nonetheless, because the ships had sunk in shallow water, it was possible in the weeks that followed to salvage further supplies from *Breconshire* and *Talabot*. In the end, a grand total of 5,200 tons, out of a potential 26,000, were saved. This was better than nothing, and with those the Island could last a while longer yet. But Malta was reeling. The harbour installations were a mess. The airfields were frequently unusable. Her offensive capabilities had been brought to a standstill – 37 Squadron, a Wellington bomber unit, had been reduced to just one solitary plane. Seven more Spitfires arrived on the 29th, but the German attacks – heavy and prolonged, day in, day out – were taking their toll.

But there was worse to come. Much, much worse.

CHAPTER 13

Death's Door

APRIL 1942 – PART I

THE MARCH CONVOY proved to be the last operation to take place under ABC's direction. The First Sea Lord had decided to give him a rest and send him to Washington as head of the Admiralty delegation there. He was not best pleased, reluctant to leave the fleet at a time when it was at its lowest ebb, and hardly thrilled by the prospect of a desk job. Despite these reservations, he had always made a point of not questioning appointments, and did not do so now. On 1 April he lowered his flag, but not before concurring with Vice-Admiral Leatham, Wilbraham Ford's replacement at Malta, that all remaining surface vessels should leave the Island. It was a sad note on which to end his time in the Mediterranean. The victories – the opening salvoes in the summer of 1940, the Battle of Matapan, the successes of his submariners and Force K – must have seemed like distant memories. His appointment was kept secret until he had left, so as not to give the enemy forewarning – something he took as a great compliment – but he did write a message for the Maltese, faithfully published in the *Times of Malta:*

'The record has been magnificent, and I heartily thank every officer and man who has taken part, not forgetting those who have had the less spectacular, but none the less exacting, task of maintaining and bringing back into action our ships and aircraft to the discomfiture of the enemy ... The very extent of the success of the forces based on Malta has led to a ceaseless battering of the fortress, but one has only to think of the air effort the enemy is diverting to this purpose to realize that this is but another of the services that Malta is rendering to the Empire.'[1]

And so Malta had to face the beginning of April without one of her staunchest champions. By this time, the Island had suffered 117 days of continuous attacks, double anything suffered by London during the height of the Blitz. There had been 275 air raid alerts in March alone, an average of nearly ten a day. Governor Dobbie had broadcast to the people at the end of the month, admitting they had all been undergoing a 'pretty stiff time' – a considerable understatement. The loss of three merchant ships in harbour was, he said, 'a grievous disappointment', and, he added, 'we could not watch the burning of one of the ships without the deepest emotion.' He tried hard to look on the bright side, but there was nothing very encouraging to be said, except that Malta was at least playing a positive role in the Allies' fight against Nazism: the Axis air armada assembled against them in Sicily was substantial – aircraft that could not be used elsewhere, such as Russia or Libya; and many enemy planes had already been destroyed by the Island's gunners and fighter pilots.

But this was small comfort, and Dobbie could not hide the bleak outlook. 'Malta has suffered much and has been called upon to endure much, and this ordeal has been going on for a long time,' he concluded. 'But in the interests of Malta itself, of our Empire, and of the most righteous cause for which we are fighting, I call on Malta to endure still further and to continue to show the same courage which has won the admiration of the world.'[2] It was the rallying cry of a man staring down the barrel of defeat, and in a letter to the Air Ministry, he wrote, 'Malta can only continue to be useful if we are able to protect the ships and aircraft which operate from here … The situation thus disclosed is extremely serious and must at all costs be remedied.'[3] March's convoy had proved ships could battle their way across the Mediterranean, however great the risks. But over Malta itself, the Luftwaffe and Regia Aeronautica reigned supreme. Sure, it was a boost to morale to see Spitfires flying over the Island at last, but fifteen here, seven there, were simply not enough. Until there were sufficient quantities to adequately defend the harbour and airfields, the situation was hopeless. Sheer courage was not enough. Malta depended upon her vital resources of flour, ammunition and aviation fuel; when those ran out the Island would have to surrender.

But the horrifying truth was that Kesselring had not even begun his main assault, due to begin on 2 April. The Field Marshal had held a conference at Fliegerkorps II Headquarters in Sicily back in February, when he'd outlined the plan of attack on Malta. It was fairly simple: neutralize the Island's fighters – or at least put them out of action – so they wouldn't interfere with the bombers. The three airfields were to be attacked with heavy bombs, light anti-personnel bombs and machine-gun fire to destroy all aircraft on the ground and make the runways temporarily unserviceable. Other targets were the harbour installations and shipping; the town itself was to be spared. Daylight attacks were to be constant and incessant and with powerful fighter protection, so that any surviving British fighters would be kept from the bombers. At night, continual nuisance raids by single aircraft would be sent over with the aim of disrupting the clearing-up. Dive-bombers were to be sent over any shipping, and mines dropped outside the harbour entrance.

Once Malta had been neutralized, a decision could be made about whether or not to invade. Crete may have been preferred to Malta in the spring of 1941, but capturing the Island was still a feasible option and one that Kesselring, in particular, greatly favoured; consequently, General Kurt Student, mastermind behind the airborne invasion of Crete, had been asked to draw up a plan of attack, involving German and Italian parachutists, further air attacks and an Italian seaborne assault.

The Islanders, of course, knew nothing of this, although most were aware that invasion was a possibility. In early January leaflets entitled 'What to do in an Invasion' had been handed out by the Government, which, in a nutshell, amounted to taking cover and keeping off the roads. Ken Griffiths, now recovered from his wound, was also given regular anti-invasion training. 'We were expecting an invasion any time,' he says. 'We trained with little weights on our backs representing kit and we also had to learn to swim with these weights in St George's Bay in case we had to swim out to a boat.' Pete Watson at Takali was also given weapons training and put through his paces, but he admits that 'looking back, these were farcical to say the least.' Nor was Frank Rixon spending all his time filling in bomb craters and building blast pens. When not on duty at the airfield, he was being sent out into the field. One night they slept in a graveyard, another a goat shed. They would patrol the coast, build more defence posts – or 'sangars' as they were known – and carry out large anti-invasion exercises. But while Frank knew there was a *threat* of invasion, he had no idea how likely or unlikely this might have been. 'We weren't told anything about what was going on. You'd be given orders to go somewhere or carry out some exercise and you'd go off and do it without ever really bothering to think about it too much.'

Kesselring had ordered the main attack to start on 2 April, but even on the first day of the month the morning raid had been over a hundred aircraft strong, and as usual had made straight for the harbour and airfields. For once the anti-aircraft gunners and RAF fighters managed to inflict considerable damage. New supplies of anti-aircraft shells had been delivered and the gunners sent up a ferocious barrage against the incoming raiders. Nonetheless, the number of enemy bombers was daunting. 'It was like flies on a jam jar,' remembers Ken Griffiths, 'there were so many of them.' He and the rest of his team kept firing furiously, lugging across the tins of rounds and frantically feeding them into the Bofors. They'd all been feeling a bit more vulnerable in recent days – the heavy ack-ack battery next to them at Spinola had received a direct hit on 25 March. 'Bits of bodies all over the place,' says Ken. 'It was terrible.' And while firing, they still had to watch their backs for shrapnel and debris falling out of the sky.

Hugh Pughe Lloyd managed to have eight Spitfires and nineteen Hurricanes available that first day of April, and they found the slow Stukas comparatively easy prey. 'Luftwaffe's Heaviest Casualties in Return to Mass Attacks,' announced the headline in the *Times of Malta* the following day. 'Malta's Guns and Fighters Destroy and Damage 27 Raiders; No British Aircraft Lost.' But the fighter pilots weren't fooled by such bravado, and a few days later, when Raoul Daddo-Longlois took to the skies again, there were only nine fighters available. Raoul cut that number by one when, having attacked and damaged a Junkers 88, his plane was then struck in the radiator by the bomber's rear-gunner. He managed to land safely although somewhat 'hastily', and then his Spitfire was taken away to be repaired. There were now so few fighters left, he didn't fly again for ten days. For the four fighter squadrons on the Island – around sixty pilots – there were frequently less than ten serviceable aircraft. Even in the Battle of Britain, when the RAF had been battling against the odds, one squadron of sixteen pilots was using sixty planes every fortnight. But on Malta, there were five separate days in April when there was just one Spitfire available. On two days there were none at all.

Not that Raoul was idle. Like every other spare set of hands, he and the other pilots were roped into repairing the airfield and lugging blocks and sandbags to make more blast pens. One day he and the rest of the flight had been spending the afternoon building pens at the south-east of the airfield, when another assault arrived. All four of them flung themselves into the nearest slit-trench. Huddling together, they were just about sheltered from the worst of the blast. Once the bombers had passed, they gingerly stood up and began dusting themselves down until suddenly they noticed two 109s hurtling towards them. In seconds, the fighters were almost upon them and spitting machine-gun bullets along the ground. Hastily ducking back down, they only emerged once the fighters had gone. Standing there, brushing off the dust and debris for a second time, they realized they were all shaking – the shock had been quite overwhelming. At least when they were flying they had a machine and guns with which to fight back; on the ground, they had been defenceless. It made them appreciate even more the work of the groundcrews and the Army boys deployed around the airfield.

With so few serviceable Spitfires and Hurricanes, the Axis aircraft had almost total air superiority. Despite the unrelenting barrages flung into the air from the anti-aircraft gunners, their massed bomber formations were able to cause damage on a scale not yet seen by the civilian popu-lation. Kesselring, writing after the war, says they deliberately avoided civilian targets,[4] but no one in Valletta or the harbour areas on Tuesday, 7 April, would agree with him. The attacks that day were not stray bombs or poor aiming, but deliberate, designed to crush the will of the people below.

Meme Cortis had been given the day off and had gone to Sliema with a friend. Aware that it might take a while to get back to Imtarfa, they had decided to leave in good time and so had taken a ferry across the harbour to Valletta. It was around six-thirty in the evening when they began climbing the steps up towards the centre of town. Just then, the air raid siren sounded once more, but they hadn't reached a shelter by the time the bombs started falling. The Auberge d'Aragon took a direct hit and Meme and her friend were knocked over by the blast. Both were covered in dust and her friend's coat ripped across the shoulder. They hurried on and ran down the steps of the Lascaris public shelter. By this time the whistling of bombs and the explosions all around them was near-constant. Meme thought they would never get out again. She felt the whole world was falling in on top of them.

But eventually the noise subsided and the All Clear rang out. As they clambered up the steps, their first sight was of the Royal Opera House – or rather, what remained of it. This magnificent theatre, considered by many to be the finest building in Valletta, now lay in ruins. 'It was just a heap of rubble,' says Meme, 'not one wall was standing – just a few arches left. I couldn't believe it. The Royal Opera House was like Covent Garden to us.' Meme had even performed there once in a special school play.

Stunned by what they had seen, they stumbled on through the debris and on towards Floriana. Houses and shops had collapsed blocking all the roads and so they clambered over the fallen masonry until they eventually found a bus headed to Rabat at the Porte de Bombe, the gateway to Floriana and Valletta. Meme wondered whether the Germans were trying to bury them all alive. Nor could she help thinking about what would happen if they surrendered – presumably all of them would be taken off to camps in some unknown place. Her father was getting old and she couldn't bear the thought of him having to go through that. She would just have to pray even harder.

John Agius had arrived back home at around six o'clock that evening. He put his bicycle underneath the staircase and sat down for some tea with the rest of his family. Only his sister May was missing; now working as Mabel Strickland's secretary at the *Times of Malta*, she wasn't yet home.

Not long after, the air raid siren blared out and so they all immediately left the house and hurried to the shelter further along the street. Down there, John heard the explosions of the bombs detonating. Gradually they became louder and louder. He'd been in a shelter earlier that afternoon when a bomb had landed nearby, and he now judged one had struck a similar distance away. He began to worry their home might have been hit.

Eventually the All Clear sounded and John ran up the steps and out into the street. Looking towards his house, all he could see was a large cloud of dust. Slowly it cleared, and where there should have been walls and windows there was now a gaping hole. The family home he had lived in all his life was nothing more than a pile of smouldering rubble.

'I was very upset and I started shouting,' says John. There were two priests with another man standing in the street, men who were known to be pro-Italian. 'It's all your fault for being friendly with Mussolini!' John yelled. His brothers thought he was going to punch them.

Soon police arrived on the scene wanting to know if anyone was missing. No, John told them – all the neighbours were present. Then they were left alone to look at the remains of their house. In a trice, they had been made homeless. John now owned little more than what he was standing in. His beautiful bicycle was gone, but so were most of the contents of a large family home: clothing, furniture, bedding, books, tools, pictures, family treasures. Because of Double Summer Time during the war, it was still quite light and so they immediately began picking through the debris.

John's sister May had been working in Mabel Strickland's office when the siren began. Her boss was usually quite blasé about taking cover, but on this instance had a strange hunch and insisted May and she go down to the shelter underneath the newspaper offices. Safely underground, they heard the bombs start falling. For some reason, May had an uncontrollable feeling of impending doom. Closing her eyes tight, she hoped her fear would not get the better of her. Then she suddenly remembered the following day was her birthday; she would be 21. She hardly dared believe she would still be alive. Moments later, the building was hit and a choking column of dust filled the cave, accompanied by the now familiar stench of cordite. Panic-stricken, the children in there with them began crying.

But they were all still alive and not trapped in the shelter, although the damage to the building above was considerable. Once the All Clear had been sounded, May followed some of the others up the steps and through the dust, feeling her way. Her coat and handbag had been destroyed, so she borrowed the bus fare to go home. Once outside, she saw their office was far from being the only place to be hit. The Castille, where Suzanne Parlby had first worked for Intelligence, was nothing but a shell, and on the square in front there were huge craters. Every-where were bits of shrapnel, stones and debris. People stood around, stupefied – stunned by the level of destruction wrought upon their capital.

May stumbled towards the bus station, watching people with bundles of bedding making for the shelters. She found a bus and saw similar bomb damage all the way to Sliema. As soon as she stepped down on to the street, she began walking as fast as she could. Dusk had begun to fall and she just wanted to be at home, with her things around her and her family. She desperately wanted to tell them all that had happened.

But the closer she got, the more agitated the people on the street seemed. A policeman told her there had been a hit down the road, but she walked on, her heart thumping in her chest. As she turned into her street, she met some friends who tried to hold her back. Then she saw. Her home had gone. No one was hurt, she was told over and over again, but she could say or think of nothing. '*I* was hurt beyond healing,' said May. 'In my home I had lost a companion of my school-days and all the sweet surroundings of childhood.'[5]

John and his brothers had begun the task of rummaging through the rubble, but then one of their neighbours, who had a large house, told them to leave it until the morning and then anything they recovered they could keep safe in his house. They were all tired and hungry, and wondered what they were going to eat that night. Joseph, John's eldest brother suggested they buy some cheese pastizzi – soft cheese surrounded by dough. 'We'll buy three each and someone will give us a cup of coffee.'

They had just finished eating the pastizzi when, at nine o'clock, the sirens began yet again, and they all headed back to the shelter for the second time that evening. For the time being this cavern, some eighteen feet below ground, was to be their home; they simply had nowhere else to go. The German bombers now dropped incendiaries, one of which struck a furniture warehouse on the other side of the street. Once the All Clear had been sounded, John and his brothers spent the rest of the night helping to contain and put out the fire.

Anyone bombed out of their home was allowed three days' compassionate leave from work. During this time, John and the rest of the family picked through the debris, relieved when they discovered a treasured possession. On the third day, they found the cat behind a collapsed door. Pulling him out, they were delighted to see he was still alive.

In the following days, Valletta and the surrounding areas were to suffer again. On the 8th, Meme Cortis's local church, the Sacred Heart, was hit, along with its adjoining convent. Two priests were killed. It was the third church in Sliema to be struck. 'The pilots of the "Luftwaffe" enjoy destroying churches,' wrote the *Times of Malta* the following day. 'The enemy knows that our churches are dear to us. Families have been brought up in the shadow of their spires for generations – and it is the intention to hurt us where it hurts most!' Meme lost other friends and family too: a cousin was killed, leaving six children, including a baby of six months. Another friend lost his life during an attack – he left a wife and three children under the age of seven. Fortunately, her family home remained unscathed, but all around the rubble was piling ever higher. She continued to pray hard. Like many others, she maintained great faith in Our Lady, the 'Star of the Sea' – after all, she had saved Malta before during other sieges, and, Meme believed, would do so again.

On Thursday 9 April, Valletta and the surrounding areas suffered again. The Rotunda church at Mosta, not far from Takali, was hit. With the third-largest suspended dome in the world, it was considered one of Malta's most treasured buildings. At about 4.40 p.m. in the afternoon, during a service, and with three hundred people worshipping, a bomb pierced the dome, bounced twice off the wall, skidded the length of the nave and came to a halt – without exploding. Not a single person was injured and it was immediately hailed as a miracle. Others were not so lucky: a shelter at Luqa was also hit that day and totally destroyed, killing 25 people.

The bombing brought mayhem. The Island's electricity supply was now invariably cut off, as was the water system. Telephone lines were down too, and so was the Rediffusion system. Many roads were blocked with rubble and debris, and much of the Island's means of communication was cut. This caused major problems, not least with food distribution, and so the Government was forced to make an announcement in the *Times of Malta*, which, despite the bombing of the Press, was still producing its four pages daily. On the 10th, a notice was printed assuring the population they had not yet run out of food, but, because of the breakdown of communications, the problem of distribution was more complicated than ever before. 'When a lorry is sent to take goods from one place to another,' ran the notice, 'there is no guarantee that it will be able to reach its destination.'[6] There had even been an incident where a laden lorry received a direct hit. Dispatch riders were now being sent to relay a message where before a simple phone call would have done the job. Many shops, too, had been destroyed, while everything was further slowed down by the sheer length of the raids, during which people took shelter and normal life ground to a halt. One of the large bakeries on the Island was also hit, causing further problems in producing bread, the one staple still not rationed.

Before April, Islanders had been losing houses at a rate of around eight hundred a month, but this figure was now increasing. Many schools and other public buildings were being used as Refugee Reception areas, but there were still not enough to deal with all the homeless. More people needed to take refugees into their homes. 'Now,' the notice urged, 'when the Protection Officer comes or sends his representative to ask you to take in refugees, help him.'[7] Anyone reading it would have taken small comfort. The gist was, 'we're doing the best we can, but please be patient'; but this was hard for those who were homeless, hungry and with families to feed.

The dockyards had taken the worst of the attacks. HMS *Penelope*, the Force K cruiser, had been damaged during the attacks on the March convoy, and had been undergoing urgent repairs, which was why she hadn't left with the remainder of the surface vessels at the end of March. The Luftwaffe had singled her out for particular attention, so it was decided to get her away despite her obvious battle scars. HMS 'Pepperpot', as she had been nicknamed, crept out of Grand Harbour on the night of 8 April, many of her holes temporarily plugged with bits of wood.

But the harbour lay in ruins. Once the pride of the British Navy in the Mediterranean, it was now a heap of rubble, tangled metal and semi-submerged ships. A message from Naval HQ, Malta, to the Admiralty on 7 April is telling:

'No. 2 and 3 boiler yard machinery shop demolished. Santa Teresa tunnel completely wrecked. Church tunnel partly collapsed and completely blocked. Sewage system and water supplies almost completely out of action. Temporary engineering and electrical departments. Drawing Offices and many other offices and storehouses have been destroyed. The residences on top of Sheer Bastion and buildings on St Michael's Bastion are completely wrecked. The problem of finding alternative accommodation is acute but will be solved. Numerous large craters in roadways and on wharves and large masses of masonry on roadways which have brought practically all wheeled traffic to a standstill. These are filled in or cleared as soon as possible but seldom possible to attain clearance before further similar damage is caused by next raid. Joiners shop, ship repair shop, chain smithery and smithery sustained considerable damage. Further extensive damage to electric cables. At present there is practically no light anywhere in the dockyard except in 4 and 5 dock area. Shortage of cables etc., for the effecting of repairs is acute and supplies of cables are almost exhausted. Very few of the most essential telephones are in operation. Visual communication employing Naval signalman has been established across French Creek.'[8]

A catalogue of destruction and carnage, in which the desperation and exasperation felt are abundantly clear. Three days later another similar cipher was sent – only this time the damage was even worse.

Life for the Tenth Flotilla was also becoming intolerable. On 1 April, the Magic Carpet submarine *Pandora* was hit while unloading in Grand Harbour. The conning tower spouted a mass of roaring flame. Four minutes later, she sank, killing two officers and 23 ratings. A naval officer had watched the attack and was running to help when the next wave of bombers arrived. 'I was conscious of my forearm being knocked straight off and a fountain of blood when my artery was cut.' He landed on top of another wounded officer. After a colleague gave him a dose of morphia, they were carried to a tunnel where a naval doctor took care of them until they could be taken to hospital. 'We were in a rare old mess. A hunk of steel through my thigh almost took off my left leg. Another hunk went through my chest. Both my eardrums were blown out.'[9]

The same day, the U-class submarine *P.36* was sunk while berthed at Lazzaretto. Suzanne Parlby's friend, the Polish Boris Karnicki, was also having a rough time. Not only had he lost his flat, but then his submarine, *Sokol*, was badly damaged and they spent an arduous few weeks ducking and diving to avoid the bombs while repair work was carried out. Engineers laboured throughout each night, while during the day she would move and then be covered with camouflage netting. By 13 April she was sufficiently repaired to be able to dive during daylight hours. On the 15th she damaged a propeller and so it was finally decided she should leave Malta altogether. Simpson was sorry to see the Poles and *Sokol* go, but assured Karnicki they would see each other again soon. 'Captain, when you come to Poland after this war,' Boris told him, 'just ask for the office of the Commissar for the Socialization of Women and walk right in!'[10] But Simpson was worrying about all his crews even more than usual, and so long as *Sokol* was operating at half-capacity, she would be more vulnerable than ever. Furthermore, the Germans had also been helping the Italians lay minefields just outside Malta, making the shipping channels around Grand Harbour and Sliema so perilous they threatened to halt submarine activity altogether. So it was with great relief that six days after *Sokol*'s departure, Simpson received the message '*Sokol* to S.10. Proceeding.' 'It was all I wanted to know,' he wrote.[11]

Simpson's force was diminishing fast, and even *Upholder* was due for a rest. They had arrived back from their twenty-fourth combat patrol from Malta on 26 March, and Wanklyn had noted in his report, 'An epidemic of flu which kept 3 men on the Sick List almost permanently, made conditions hard for those who remained healthy, and most of these suffered from a heavy cold.'[12] Much as Simpson was loath to lose his champion crew, he recognized it was time for them to head back to England for a break, and so he told Wanklyn that after the next patrol they would be leaving Malta. 'Well, darling,' Wanks wrote to his wife just before his departure, 'count the days, they are not so many. Only 59.'[13]

Upholder sailed on 6 April. On board were two Arab agents and an Army officer. The plan was to drop off the agents in the Gulf of Sousse in North Africa, the Army officer paddling them ashore in a folbot (a collapsible canvas canoe). This was completed successfully on the night of the 9th/10th, and then Wanklyn was ordered to rendezvous with *Unbeaten* who was on her way back to England ahead of *Upholder* and would take the Army officer with her. This also happened without incident, and *Unbeaten* sailed towards Gibraltar while *Upholder* continued her patrol.

Some time on the 15th, *Upholder* was supposed to have been in position on a patrol line to intercept a convoy along with *Urge* and *Thrasher*. She never made it. An Italian reconnaissance plane sighted a submarine on the afternoon of the 14th. This news was relayed to an Italian destroyer *Pegaso*, who sighted a periscope and spotted the submarine on her echo sounder. The destroyer immediately attacked with a number of depth charges. *Urge*, not so far away, heard the distant explosions of heavy depth-charging. It was almost certainly this attack that hit *Upholder*. At any rate, nothing was ever heard of either her or her crew again.

Tubby Crawford had completed most of his CO's training and was now in charge of a training submarine carrying out escort work in the Irish Sea. 'I wasn't surprised,' says Tubby about hearing the news, 'but it caused me great sadness.' In Tubby's opinion, the strain of operating for so long and in increasingly impossible conditions, must have taken its toll. 'Wanklyn did have two patrols off [whilst at Malta] but I suspect all the time he was worrying about what was happening to his submarine and ship's company.' Basil Embry had suggested fighter pilots should only serve short stints on the Island – a maximum of six months, which was soon to be cut to just three. Wanklyn and most of his crew had been serving for sixteen months. Moreover, as Tubby points out, 'I don't think one can compare the CO of a submarine with a fighter pilot. The CO has thirty officers and men to look after, a fighter pilot only himself.'

In her career, *Upholder* had sunk two U-boats and damaged another, damaged a cruiser and a destroyer, and sunk or damaged a further nineteen supply ships, amounting to 119,000 tons. She was the most successful Allied submarine of the entire war, and Wanklyn the highest-scoring commander. In a note to Simpson, Admiral Harwood, the new C-in-C of the Mediterranean Fleet, wrote, 'Her brilliant career was an inspiration, not only to the Mediterranean Fleet, but to the people of Malta as well. The loss of her skilled and experienced company and in particular of L.C. M.D. Wanklyn, VC, DSO★★, Royal Navy, her Commanding Officer, is deeply regretted.' [14]

CHAPTER 14

George Cross Island

APRIL 1942 – PART II

O N FRIDAY 17 April, John Agius looked at his father's copy of the *Times of Malta* and read the stunning news that the entire Island had been awarded the George Cross, the highest civilian award for gallantry. 'To honour her brave people I award the George Cross to the Island fortress of Malta to bear witness to a heroism that will long be famous in history,' ran the citation from King George VI. The George Cross, like the Victoria Cross, was not handed out lightly, and although the significance of such medals might diminish somewhat in peacetime, the importance of this award was keenly felt at the time. For such an honour to be bestowed on an entire island population was unprecedented in British history, and made front-page news in Allied newspapers around the world. John certainly felt both proud and happy at the news. The award was undoubtedly a much-needed morale booster, and messages of congratulation soon started flooding in from all around the world. Malta had become the 'George Cross Island', a name it is still known by to this day. 'The Island has been an inspiration to many,' ran an editorial in the paper the following day. 'It has proved that by determination and fortitude and by the courage of the people and of that of the Services, the theories "that Malta would prove untenable" were utterly shallow and false.'[1] But were they? The Island was slowly dying. Constant bombing was beating the population further into the ground, just as the shortage of food and supplies weakened the appetite for the struggle. They could not eat the George Cross. Frank Rixon found the demoralizing job of repeatedly filling in bomb craters was made all the worse by seeing men blown to smithereens right before his eyes. 'You didn't get counselling then for picking up bits and pieces of your mates,' he observes.

Naval operations had ground to a halt, the Tenth Flotilla was barely operating, and the two Fleet Air Arm squadrons – Nat Gold's 830, and 828 – were so depleted they were formed into one, the Naval Air Squadron, Malta. Most of the Wellington bombers had gone since the beginning of the year – three squadrons in all. It was a similar story with the twin-engine Bristol Blenheims: in carrying out anti-shipping attacks and coastal operations during daylight against impossibly high odds they had suffered appallingly, although as many were destroyed on the ground as in the air. Four squadrons had either left or become inoperable since January.

In other words, Malta's offensive capabilities, once so effective, had almost ceased to exist. Burnt-out wrecks littered all three airfields. Groundcrews had desperately tried to keep their aircraft airworthy and despite the chronic lack of spares, cannibalization of damaged planes had kept them going longer than might otherwise have been expected. But the attrition rate had become too great.

The reconnaissance pilots were still at Luqa, however – albeit without Adrian Warburton – as were Peter Rothwell and the Special Duties Flight. The Flight had stopped all operations for the best part of a fortnight during March, hampered once again by a shortage of spare parts. During this time they had been sent up to the RAF rest camp in St Paul's Bay in the north of the Island. A quiet fishing village, it was supposedly the site where St Paul first came ashore after his shipwreck. Although nowhere on the Island was free from attack, this was a quieter spot than most and exhausted RAF pilots were given a chance to relax, sleep in a proper bed and swim in the sea.

This breather was not enough for the Flight's CO, Tony Spooner, who was by now suffering from malnutrition and blood poisoning. A Wellington arrived *en route* to Egypt, and Spooner commandeered it and flew it off the Island instead; the pilot was none too happy when he found out what had happened. Before he departed, Spooner asked Peter Rothwell to take over command of the Flight. Only 21, Peter could not have taken charge at a more difficult time.

With the arrival of the convoy, they had their much-needed spares and so became operational again. Peter flew on three different missions on 27, 29 and 31 March – hardly 'special' duties, but rather as the Island's main strike force. On the 31st they attacked the airfield at Catania in Sicily, in which they hit the dispersal hut and a couple of hangars. They were then attacked by two night-fighter Junkers 88s, but succeeded in slipping away.

As with Nat Gold and the Swordfish pilots, Peter always landed at night. And because he never knew what state the runway would be in, this was a scary exercise. Unlike the Swordfish, they did have the Army to help light flares briefly along the runway, but these gave off little light and the fact that a Wellington was far heavier and larger than a Swordfish made night-time landing on a bomb-cratered runway even more problematic. Peter was always greatly relieved once he'd safely landed his plane and the engines were switched off.

Conditions for the Flight were becoming increasingly hard. They used to have a tiny Fiat, in which they would drive themselves from Kalafrana to Luqa, or during days off to St Paul's or Ghajn Tuffieha. But by the beginning of April, there was no longer enough petrol on the Island to justify their keeping it and so they had to let it go. On 7 April, the same day John Agius lost his home, the Mess at Kalafrana was also bombed. The dining-room on the first floor was literally sliced in half, but Peter and the other pilots decided to carry on using it anyway, even though one end was now open to the elements. Whenever they could, they would still use the best china and silver, and dress as formally as the remains of their limited wardrobes allowed. By making an effort, the bully beef and tack biscuits somehow tasted better.

Without the Fiat, the pilots had to walk the four miles to Luqa. They were usually there by about ten in the morning. Refuelling was now done entirely by hand. Groundcrew and pilots alike would climb up ladders placed against each wing and fill the tanks from four-gallon cans. Since each wing needed a hundred gallons, this took a considerable time, especially if there were raids as well. Surprisingly, they had remarkably few engine failures, which says much about the abilities and determination of the groundcrews. Once the Wellington had been fuelled and prepared, they would carry out a brief air test, keeping an eagle eye out for marauding 109s. Peter hated these pilots – the way they would arrogantly fly over the airfield, lazily rolling their aircraft before shooting at anything that moved. He had several close calls while walking across the airfield, but reckoned he was safe as long as he could dive into a bomb crater in time. After the air test, he and other pilots would loiter in the Operations Room at Luqa, waiting to be told their mission.

There was now little they could do during their time off. They played cards and chatted with the two Army boys who'd been seconded to them as their Intelligence Officers. And they drank a lot of whisky – until their stocks became another bomb casualty. One day, Peter even took out a dinghy into Marsaxlokk Bay. He and his companions had just rowed out a small distance when another raid arrived. Shrapnel started landing on the water all around them, and they were terrified they were going to sink. A little jaunt out to sea had seemed a good idea at the time, but even that had turned into a potentially fatal situation.

Although fighter planes were one of the most precious commodities of all, such were the conditions on the Island that it had never been easier to damage them. On 16 April, Buck McNair was just taking off when he heard a bump. It sounded as though he'd hit something, but it didn't feel that way – and the plane became airborne without problem. A few moments later the air-controller came over on his radio and told him he'd lost a wheel. Buck's heart sank. The Spitfire he was in had only just been repaired after much work, and he knew the ground engineers were working miracles – without proper tools or equipment – salvaging parts from wrecks and working inhuman hours to make the surviving machines airworthy. Buck wondered about his options. If he landed with one wheel, the plane would be impossible to control, and he might go into a pot-hole and wreck the machine. A belly-land was the only answer.

Tightening his safety belt, he braced his knees against the instrument panel and stopped the engine as he came over the edge of the field at about 90 miles per hour. Miraculously, his only injury was a badly bruised knee; but he felt sick at heart. 'I felt so badly at having smashed the Spitfire that tears came to my eyes,' said Buck.[2] When he finally pulled himself out and looked at his aircraft among the three-foot high weeds and grass, he thought it looked pathetic, squat and forlorn. Later he discovered what had caused the wheel to break: as he'd been taxiing down the runway, he'd hit an unexploded bomb. These now littered the airfields and were marked by a little flag until the bomb disposal team had a chance to get rid of them. Between the wrecked aircraft and other debris, these little flags fluttered, a sign that the airfields now had their own kind of minefields too.

★

Having been told there would be another attempt to sail a convoy in April, Dobbie was distraught to hear these plans were evaporating almost by the day. On 4 April, Sir Dudley Pound announced the operation was being postponed until May, but asserted they would then send ships from both Gibraltar and Alexandria. Then, on the 15th, he decided a convoy from the west would be impracticable. Three days later, he announced that plans for the May convoy were being shelved too; some time in June was the best the Island could hope for. The Governor appealed to the Chiefs of Staff once more: 'The decision materially reduces our chances of survival not because of any failure of morale or fighting efficiency but because it is impossible to carry on without food and ammunition ... it is obvious the very worst must happen if we cannot replenish our vital needs especially flour and ammunition and that very soon.' He was particularly worried about the bread situation because one of the largest mills had been bombed and was currently out of action – and lying at the far end of Grand Harbour, it was highly vulnerable to attack. Assuming the mill was up and running again within the week, and that it wasn't struck again, there was enough flour – at current rates of use – to last until the end of May, while Dobbie reckoned they would be out of most other food by the end of June. It was a similar picture with the ammunition. Although the gunners had been told to fire only at the bombers, such had been the size of formations coming over, the expenditure of shells had been phenomenal. Heavy anti-aircraft ammunition would be exhausted by the end of June too, and light AA by the end of July. The fuel situation was slightly better: with few aircraft on the Island, he estimated aviation fuel would run out by mid-August. But the overall picture meant a Target Date for surrender in a little over ten weeks' time. After that, there would simply no longer be enough supplies on the Island for them to avoid capitulation. The Governor concluded, 'If Malta is to be held, drastic action is needed now. It is a question of survival.'[3]

But Churchill was determined not to let Malta fall. If the main obstacle in getting Spitfires to Malta was a lack of aircraft carriers, there was a way round the problem. They had an ally now, and a powerful one too. President Roosevelt had given Churchill fifty destroyers back in 1940 and that was before America entered the war. The Prime Minister wrote to Roosevelt, asking for the use of USS *Wasp* to help ferry Spitfires to the Island. If he agreed, then 'a powerful Spitfire force could be flown into Malta at a stroke.'[4] Roosevelt concurred. Launched only in 1939, *Wasp* had the capacity to carry 84 fighter planes, and was already in British waters at the beginning of April. And so she steamed into the River Clyde in Scotland, where she was loaded with 47 Spitfires – the best that could be managed – and two whole squadrons of pilots. Then, with all haste, *Wasp* set sail for the Mediterranean.

Steaming from Greenock aboard the mighty American aircraft carrier was 22-year-old Denis Barnham, and he was in the dog-house. Orders had come through so suddenly that there had been no time for embarkation leave, but on his own initiative the CO, Squadron Leader John Bisdee, had allowed his pilots 48 hours' leave. 'But don't let me down,' he told them, 'I need you back on time.' It had been particularly important that Denis, as new Flight Commander in 601 Squadron, set a good example, especially since Bisdee, a former colleague at 609 Squadron, had specifically asked for him to join 601; but he had failed his first test. Although he had allowed himself a three-hour margin to get from Glasgow Station to the airfield at Abbotsinch, this was used up and overrun by the late running of his train from Preston.

His disgrace only added to his misery. Married just a few weeks, it had been a terrible wrench to leave his wife Diana behind and set off towards an uncertain and dangerous future. Standing on deck, he watched as the ropes that bound them to the shore were untied and dropped into the sea, and then, gradually, the stevedores on the quayside shrank from view. Denis felt sick at heart.

Although only 22, this dark-haired, strikingly good-looking young pilot was in many ways more prone to introspection than many of his colleagues. Brought up in Feltham, Middlesex, he was the son of a long line of farmers. With no brothers – but two older sisters – he was expected to take over the farm one day, especially since his father was now quite elderly. But Denis's first love was painting. At an early age he had demonstrated a precocious talent as an artist, and for his seventeenth birthday his mother had given him a present of a studio, a room above the garages at home that had once been a chauffeur's quarters. There he had hidden himself away to paint whenever he could. At seventeen he'd won a scholarship to the Royal Academy School of Art, and began to think he might even be able to make a career as an artist.

Such plans were abruptly halted with the outbreak of war. Joining the fight had caused a certain degree of soul-searching. Both he and a friend at the Royal Academy had joined the Peace Pledge Union, but, on the other hand, he strongly believed Hitler was evil and should be stopped. With some misgivings, he joined the RAF, as soon as war was declared. If painting was his first love, flying was his second. He'd learnt to fly at sixteen, and well before war broke out had already gained his civil pilot's licence and joined the RAF Volunteer Reserves. This helped him enormously when he was sent off to Rhodesia for training, although he was a naturally talented sportsman and pilot and gained his wings with the highest of marks. From there he was posted to fly fighters, but the moral conundrum of having to kill remained unsolved, and was still causing him some anxiety two and a half years later as he headed for the ferocious combat zone of Malta.

And Denis was also afraid. Afraid that he would die and never see Diana, England, or his family and friends again. He knew something of the situation in Malta: that the Island was besieged, surrounded by the enemy and facing 500 German and Italian aircraft based just 60 miles away and that the odds were stacked against them. But that was if he ever got there. First, he had to take off from what appeared to be a very short runway, weighted down with extra fuel, and travel 700 miles – the distance from London to Venice. This task alone seemed fraught with dangers.

On the surface, Denis came across as a confident and controlled individual, but this cloaked his true fears and emotions, which he tended to confide with brutal honesty to his diary. He was also very realistic about the situation he was in; every time he took off on a combat sortie, for example, he knew that at some point within that hour he could be shot at, and his body burnt or mangled. The fear of this was particularly acute just before take-off, as he was walking over to his plane, and strapping himself in. This passed once he was in the air, but then reappeared sharply and drastically just before and during combat in the form of sheer terror. Once the bullets and tracer had passed it would fade for a moment, before lurching back again as another plane was engaged. This had happened on every one of his 64 fighter sweeps over occupied France, where there had been plenty of planes and they had been on the offensive. He wondered how on earth he was going to cope.

He spent the long journey to the Mediterranean writing his diary, long letters home – and sketching. One of those who sat for him was Squadron Leader 'Jumbo' Gracie, the only man among them who had already seen action on Malta. He already had something of a reputation

– dogged and resourceful, but also ruthless and hard-hearted. RAF electrician Pete Watson had once seen a Junkers 88 crash near the airfield. One of the German crew staggered out and collapsed on the wing. 'He could easily have been saved, but Jumbo Gracie refused to allow anyone to get him – and so he died,' says Pete. Another time he shot a dying airman in the head – a mercy killing, but an act which most would have balked at carrying out.

From him Denis at least learnt a bit more about what lay in store. Gracie had been sent by Lloyd to secure the safe passage of the new Spitfires and so here he was, ready to fly with them back to the beleaguered Island. Their bomber force, Gracie told him, lay wrecked on the ground. The Germans were now bombing them at a rate of 6,000 tons a month. 'If you're lucky enough to fly,' he said, 'then you're generally outnumbered forty or fifty to one.'[5] Denis tried not to look worried.

He still loved flying, and this was a source of solace. As a child he had always wanted to fly and his passion for planes had never wavered, not even now. If he was honest, this had considerably helped in his decision to join up at the outbreak of war. But, as he wandered through the hangar deck, looking at all the Spitfires tightly packed together, he couldn't help wondering how many would be left in a week's time and felt sure his chances of surviving the days and months ahead were slim.

Monday 20 April was a long and eventful day for Denis Barnham. Woken at 3.45 a.m., he breakfasted half an hour later with the rest of 601 and 603 Squadrons, after which they were given their final briefing. By 5.15 a.m., he was strapped into his Spitfire, with his illegally packed bag of painting things under his arm, waiting in a line to be hoisted by the lift on to the flight deck. On the signal, he started the engine, the roar even louder in the enclosed environment of the hangar deck. Then he was on the flight deck, opening the throttle and speeding off into the wide blue beyond.

Some four hours later he was approaching Malta. As he turned to land he noticed a harbour with a ship low in the water and thick black smoke rising from it. Further inland he spotted another column of red cloud rising into the sky, although at the time hadn't realized he was looking at a trail of bomb-dust.

Once he'd touched down and reached the end of the runway, two brown-faced airmen leapt on to his wings and cheerfully told him he'd just missed the 9 a.m. raid. With bayonets at the ready, they then began opening the gun panels to retrieve the cigarettes and tools Denis had been carrying in his wings instead of ammunition and guns. Moments later, a clapped-out bus, already full of other pilots arrived to collect him. With a grinding of gears and a cloud of dust, the bus headed off towards the Mess, dodging the newly formed craters and piles of rubble.

This was Luqa airfield and Denis was shocked by what he saw: potholes and craters all over the place, piles of rubble, crushed glass twinkling in the sun. Above them, the 109s were already beginning to circle like vultures.

Once out of the bus, he desperately wanted to run for cover, but both their guide and the CO continued to stroll unhurriedly down the dusty road and so he tried to amble too, keeping his inner panic to himself. They passed an airman busily hacking away at the ground by a post with a small flag. An unexploded bomb, Denis was told. Only when a red flag was hoisted by the dispersal did they all finally run for it, tumbling into the entrance of 'G' Shelter, the Luqa Control Room, carved into the rock below the edge of the airfield.

In fact the raid was headed for Takali. Raoul Daddo-Langlois was already in the air, flying for the first time in six days along with Buck McNair and four other pilots from 249. It was one o'clock, and they climbed as fast as they could to 17,000 feet. South of the Island, Buck spotted a number of Stukas heading for Hal Far and he ordered his flight to close in to attack. As ever, though, the 109s were not far away and immediately dived on them to split up the Spitfires. Raoul 'squirted' his guns at a Stuka, then a Junkers 88, before managing to shoot down a 109. Up there it was pretty hectic, the sky awash with swirling, turning aircraft. Buck saw another Messerschmitt start firing at Raoul, and so turned to attack in turn. As it passed, Raoul clipped the German fighter before it dived and fell into the sea. For a split second he thought he was going to die, but despite a huge crash and a large chunk being sliced off the end of one of his wings, his Spitfire was still flying, albeit with some difficulty. Getting himself safely back on to the ground was going to be tricky. He'd already seen bombs falling over Takali, so the airfield was likely to be full of craters, but with a damaged Spitfire and plenty of 109s still hovering about ready to pounce, he wondered if he was ever going to make it.

Raoul dropped out of the fray and approached Takali. Up above him he could still see the 109s, and so he circled the airfield waiting for a favourable moment to land. But with no ammunition left and almost no fuel, he was going to have to come in pretty soon. Briefly looking round, and praying for a slice of luck, he lowered his wheels and prepared to touch down. His wing had lost about eighteen inches, making it look square like that of a 109 rather than the classic elliptical shape of the Spitfire. But as he approached the runway, a Messerschmitt came in after him and his plane was hit. Dropping faster than he wanted and worried the whole plane would tip over, he then pulled up the wheels once more, and whistled past the other pilots watching from the dispersal hut. With a loud crunch and a screech of grating metal, he skidded along the ground on the plane's belly, eventually coming to rest in a large cloud of dust. Apart from sore shoulders where his harness had dug into him as he'd hit the ground, he was fine, but soon wouldn't be if he didn't get out of there fast. With frantically fumbling fingers, he undid the harness, ripped off his mask and radio wires and leapt out of the cockpit, running as quickly as he could for cover, machinegun bullets bursting dangerously close behind him. 'Collided with 109 head on. Pranged on landing! One 109 confirmed,' he wrote in his logbook later, betraying little of the action, adrenalin, terror and sheer danger of that brief sortie over the Island.

Another raid was approaching by the middle of the afternoon. Two Spitfires had been left on the ground, so Denis and another 601 pilot had volunteered to take them up to protect the other planes as they landed. They were told they would find one of the planes in North Siggiewi Blast Pen and the other between E and F Pens, and with a hastily sketched map, set off in a battered car to find them. Despite circling round the airfield three times they saw no sign of their particular planes. There were plenty of blast pens, but none of them were marked and when they did find a Spitfire, there were airmen around them who had never heard of Siggiewi or E and F pens and told them flatly to 'fuck off'. By chance they eventually found one of the planes, and then the other; but there were neither groundcrew nor starter trolley in sight. As Denis drove off to get help, another raid arrived. He only just made the shelter in time.

Later that day, he watched sixty bombers attack Takali. Black bomb bursts gushed back up from the ground in huge oily globules of smoke, some rolling off long stalks like mushrooms. Layers of smoke merged into one another, building into one monstrous cloud, which shrouded everything. Eventually the fog disappeared, leaving black pin-points, each streaming a dark column up into the sky. The new Spitfires were burning into the ground.

But his long day was not over yet. He and the rest of the squadron had been taken in the standard rickety old bus up to the Xara Palace in Mdina, where Hugh Pughe Lloyd had assembled all his fighter pilots for a pep-talk. He had just begun when yet another raid started. Several bombs landed close by, blowing in the window shutters, and causing the assembled gathering to stumble and fall over.

'As I was saying,' Lloyd continued once the bombers had passed, 'the Germans are bullies and incredibly foolish – the manner in which they are conducting their offensive against the Island shows us that.' Denis couldn't see there was anything wrong with their offensive – first impressions suggested the complete opposite.

Lloyd continued, 'Malta is like the famous statue of Achilles in Hyde Park, London. Our bombers, torpedo-carrying planes and submarines are our striking power, like Achilles' sword. Our sword has been blunted but we will sharpen it. Until then Achilles must rely on his shield. The anti-aircraft defences and you pilots flying your Hurricanes and Spitfires are that shield; Malta relies on you.'[6]

Feeling less than inspired, Denis boarded the bus once more to be taken to their new quarters in Naxxar, some four miles to the north-west of the airfield. Travelling at night in a bus with no windows and no lights was another new experience for him. Having been deposited at a large empty stone palace, they all stood in darkness in a stone hallway, which stank of drains and cooking fat, hastily striking matches in an effort to get their bearings. Eventually Denis was shown a bed, and spent the rest of the night lying there in his tin hat, gripping the sheets and trying hard to keep calm as bomb after bomb shrieked overhead.

Within 48 hours of Denis's arrival, only seven of the new shipment of 47 Spitfires remained serviceable. For Lloyd and the fighter pilots based there, it was the lowest ebb.

John Agius was feeling pretty low too. And he was sorely missing his bicycle. Getting to and from work was now often a lengthy and risky business. One time he decided to risk it and with some others persuaded a boatman to take them back from Valletta across the harbour to Sliema. Half-way across, the guns opened up on Manoel Island and

Fort Tigné. Everyone in the *dghajsa* began furiously paddling with their arms, trying to hurry the boat across the harbour. They made it, but John had been given the fright of his life. On another occasion, he'd been just about to board a boat when an air raid began. He rushed to a shelter, and when he re-emerged, saw that where he'd been standing before on the quayside, there was now a large hole.

Friday, 24 April, was a bad day. In the middle of the morning, John had been taking shelter and afterwards was walking back to Scots Street when he saw a lady lying face-down on the street. Her back had been ripped open. John could imagine what had happened: running for the shelter, she simply hadn't made it in time. And he knew her – she was Petra Dingstad, a 30-year-old Norwegian who was living with a friend of his. He felt terrible, seeing her like that.

That same day, one of the typists from Scots Street was also killed. She was Aida Kelly, a lively character who had been rather enjoying the excitement of the siege. She attracted plenty of attention from a number of young officers and would regularly go up on the roofs or on to the bastions to watch the raids. 'I've seen a terrific raid!' she would breathlessly announce on her return to the office. After the big attack of the 24th, however, she never came back. John's boss told him to go to the ARP Centre and see whether he could find out what had happened to her. Fortunately, John knew the man in charge there and asked him, 'What have you got about this girl?'

'Nothing,' he told him. 'All I have is three sacks full of bits and pieces. If you want to have a look at them I'll get somebody to open them one by one.'

John had no desire to rummage through bags of body parts, and was saved from doing so when he spotted a blue-and-white striped shoe. It had been discovered on the top of the bastion at St John's Cavalier, and he was positive it was Aida's. John was not surprised she'd got herself killed, and rather felt she'd been asking for it. Everyone had a responsibility for taking cover as soon as a raid approached. When someone like Aida exposed herself to danger, she was putting other people at risk too.

Two days later, John had another close call. Although it was a Sunday, he was at work again in Scots Street. It was 2.30 p.m. when the air raid siren sounded, and so he headed for a nearby shelter, underneath the Valletta Telephone Exchange on the corner of Old Bakery and Cavalier Streets. There were two entrances to this shelter – one through the Telephone Exchange, the other down a spiral staircase accessed from the street. John found himself down there with a handful of others – a few women and children, and about ten men from the Cheshire Regiment, all dressed in denims. They had been brought into Valletta to help clear away the debris.

Suddenly there was an enormous explosion nearby. Screams, coughing, cursing – and the lights went out. The Telephone Exchange had taken a direct hit. John immediately shouted, 'Don't anyone light a match!' Gas pipes might have burst, and then they would have been burnt to death. Instead, with his electric torch he looked to see what the damage was. Fortunately, he could still see daylight at the top of the spiral staircase. Pretty soon people arrived to help and they all escaped. John had been wearing a black suit, but when he emerged back into daylight he was white from head to toe. A man offered to brush him down – 'Everyone was so helpful to one another at that time. People would bend over backwards to lend a hand,' says John. Eventually, he made his way back home to Sliema. His brother looked at him and said, 'Has someone roughed you up a bit?' 'Yes,' said John, 'the German bombers.'

The destruction never seemed to end. One by one the famous buildings he had known all his life – buildings that represented Malta and the Maltese – were hit. He had been at work early on the 28th and after the first raid heard that the famous church of St Publius in Floriana had been hit. Standing in front of a large square, it was a sight familiar to anyone entering or leaving Valletta. John rushed up to the top of Kingsgate to see the damage for himself. The St Publius had a clock in each tower – one of which was never repaired. To this day it is kept at 7.50 in the morning, the time the great church was struck.

Even the hospital at Imtarfa was coming in for regular attack. Like everyone else on the Island, Meme was exhausted but still working long hours with few breaks and little sustenance. 'It was so hard to keep going,' says Meme. 'One just felt so drained of all energy. I had headaches all the time, my entire body ached, and at times I could barely even stand up. But you just carried on. We all did.'

One night it was the turn of the Sisters' Mess to be hit. When the sisters came out of their rooms, darkness hid the fact that their communal verandah had been destroyed, and so several of them fell twenty feet on to the rubble below. One broke her arm, another her back. Such casualties meant others had to work even harder. The hospital was hit almost every day at the end of April. The kitchens were destroyed on the 20th. A 1,000-pound bomb and two smaller ones bounced near the main hospital but failed to explode. One of the patients was from Bomb Disposal, and so despite a number of blast injuries and a fractured skull, he hobbled out in his dressing-gown and defused them himself. The following day, the Imtarfa Club and Infants' School were also ruined and the football ground and tennis courts, underground water tank and parts of 'A' and 'H' Blocks all damaged. More bombs fell on the 22nd and on the 25th. On the 30th, a pilot in a 109 even dropped a hand-grenade over Imtarfa.

There was only one small consolation amid this carnage and suffering. The gunners were doing well – really well. A crew member from a Junkers 88 was interviewed on German radio and testified to their success at defending the Island. 'Malta is one huge battery of anti-aircraft guns,' he said. 'Heavy and light AA guns are at every important point. Shells come up like a thunderstorm of steel. When the guns cease, the Spitfires and Hurricanes hang on to the tails of the German dive-bombers, trying to shoot them down during the dive. The gunners shoot well and the German aircraft need the highest skill and courage to get through.'[7] All this was writ large in the *Times of Malta*, as was the gunners' mounting score. On 29 April, their tally stood at 99 enemy bombers destroyed for the month. Could they make it one hundred?

On the 30th, the last day of the month, they claimed three more. The final figure for April was 102.[8] Ken Griffiths and the rest of his crew were certainly keeping track of the score. For much of the month, they'd been at Takali. They'd seen the Spitfires arrive and then be shot up, and, like everyone at the airfield, they had found this particularly soul-destroying. Day after day all they'd seen were more and more bombers, so to know they were inflicting considerable damage gave them a much-needed boost in confidence. Firing was not indiscrim-inate – they did train their gun on to a particular aircraft and try to shoot it down, and they certainly knew when they'd hit one. But there was usually little time for watching it descend, or much of a chance to celebrate – they were too busy lining up the next one and watching their backs.

Ken and his crew rarely paused all month. Barrels were worn out through overuse and mountains of empty shell-cases soon piled high. He and the rest of the gunners fired the massive total of 160,829 rounds in April – in January, they had used just 28,788. It was a staggering amount and says as much about the grim determination of those firing them as it does about the hordes flying over from Sicily every day. Inevitably, however, they could not keep up that kind of expenditure forever. By the end of the month, ammunition was running dangerously short, as were supplies of replacement barrels. They would not be in a position to repeat the performance in May.

Kesselring's plan to grind Malta into the dust was succeeding. He'd lost a lot of planes, but with the Island on its knees, the job was virtually done. During April alone, 6,728 tons of bombs were dropped on Malta – compared with 18,000 tons dropped on Britain during the entire Blitz. Thousands of buildings were destroyed or damaged. Meanwhile, in North Africa, Rommel was marshalling his forces for the push towards Egypt. With 99.2 per cent of the men and supplies he needed for the month reaching him safely, he could smell victory blowing towards him across the sea from Italy.

CHAPTER 15

Spitfire Victory

MAY 1942

B Y THE END of April, ten days after his arrival, Denis Barnham
was already feeling exhausted. Although he had only flown three
times since his arrival, life for the fighter pilots was lived at a
furious pace. The CO, Squadron Leader John Bisdee, was not dead but
badly injured and in hospital, so Denis was temporarily leading the
squadron. Another pilot had been killed, and four out of five had either
been hit or damaged their aircraft in some way. Nor was Denis getting
any sleep. His diary records the nightly bombing raids: on 30 April, for
instance, 'Bombs and bombers screeched all night long – seemed as
though all pillars of air were being flattened violently, one against
another, until they crushed our ear drums and left our ears ringing –
couldn't sleep.' Nor on 1 May, 'Same again – no sleep at all,' or the 2nd,
'Third night without sleep.' Or the following night, 'Yet another night
without sleep.' And it was hard to get comfortable when lying in bed
with a tin hat on his head.

Despite this, the last few days of April had brought a lessening in the
number of attacks. On 30 April, Dobbie signalled the Air Ministry warning them that they were expecting the comparative lull to be nothing
more than a respite before an invasion was launched. Reconnaissance
planes from 69 Squadron had photographed signs of large glider strips
being prepared near Gerbini airfield in Sicily on the 21st, and subsequent pictures taken over the following days only seemed to confirm
this. Significantly, they were all near railway lines, which suggested
airborne forces and easy-to-assemble gliders would be brought in with
comparative speed. To those on the Island, the threat of invasion after

such an intense period of bombardment seemed not only possible, but very probable.

The Chiefs of Staff back in London seemed less concerned. 'We have as yet received no evidence of preparations to carry out an airborne invasion of Malta,' was one response from the Chief of Air Staff, Air Marshal Sir Charles Portal. 'We believe that if such an attack was intended we should by now have seen some signs. There is also no evidence at present pointing to a seaborne invasion of the Island.' On the other hand, he continued, they had now received reliable information pointing to the withdrawal by the Germans of both a bomber and fighter *gruppe*, with further withdrawal planned for the near future. This 'reliable information' had been provided by Ultra decrypts intercepted on the 26th.[1] The Chiefs of Staff had assessed the threat of a German invasion at the end of March and had at that time concluded there was little likelihood of this happening.

In fact, Kesselring had every intention of invading. He'd repeatedly urged Hitler and Göring to stabilize the Axis position in the Mediterranean by taking Malta, even persuading Rommel to support him, and had been making preparations for several months. Finally, in February, he'd had his plans approved. After a highly charged meeting with Hitler, the Führer had grabbed his arm and told him, 'Keep your shirt on, Field Marshal Kesselring. I'm going to do it!'[2]

By the middle of April, Kesselring had told Hitler the task of 'eliminating' Malta's defences was virtually completed and that the Island was now totally cut off from any reinforcement from the sea. The Führer then invited Mussolini to his mountain retreat in Berchtesgaden to decide upon the timetable for further strategy in the Mediterranean. The Italians, like Kesselring, put the capture of Malta ahead of any other priority, but insisted they could not do it alone. In fact, the Field Marshal, already well aware of this, had always intended it to be a joint operation.

Two major factors stopped Hitler giving the project the green light there and then. The first was Rommel, who, thanks to Kesselring's pounding of the Island, was now in the ascendancy once more in North Africa; although he agreed Malta should be invaded, he argued that the conquest of Egypt was the major priority. The second was Hitler's gut instinct. Since the Battle of Crete, he had been nervous about the use of airborne troops, and his earlier reluctance to invade had not lessened. Kesselring groaned with frustration: it was precisely because the capture of Egypt was so critical that Malta needed to be taken first; it was imperative there should be no interruption in the passage of supplies.

Hitler proposed a compromise. Assuming Rommel reached the Libyan-Egyptian border in the next couple of months, they could then invade Malta sometime in the middle of July or, at the latest, mid-August, when a full moon would provide ideal conditions for a landing.

Although frustrated by Hitler's reluctance to launch an immediate invasion, Kesselring took comfort from the fact that the plan had only been postponed rather than shelved entirely. Nor was he too bothered about the transferral of so many of his air units – after all, they'd done the job asked of them, and he believed there were still sufficient forces left on Sicily to keep Malta in check. And even if the British did try to fly in more aircraft, experience had shown these forces could soon make light work of such reinforcements.

The news that the massed bombing attacks were at last coming to an end was a great relief to those running Malta's war, and gave them just the faintest glimmer of hope. If they could successfully bring in some more Spitfires, they *might* even be able to win air superiority. And if they could do that, the chances of successfully seeing in the June convoy would be increased considerably.

But the sorry saga of the March convoy and the destruction of the Spitfires on the ground showed that without sufficient leadership and preparation, fighting on would be a lost cause. If they were to make the most of another large consignment of Spitfires, a major re-think was needed in a number of areas.

Preparation of the Spitfires both before and after they reached Malta was the first problem to overcome. Most of the 47 that had flown in on 20 April, for example, had arrived in poor flying condition. Although they'd had their tropical air filters already fitted, the time lag between arrival and getting them back in the air had been too long to prevent most being destroyed on the ground.

Clearly this slow turn-around was not good enough. Even a submariner like Shrimp Simpson could see this was crazy. To him it was crystal clear that the dominance of the Axis air forces was so complete that unless the total consignment of Spitfires was back in the air almost immediately, there was little point in flying them to the Island in the first place. In mid-April, he had spoken to a friend of his in the RAF about the 48 Spitfires due to arrive on the 20th and had been stunned to hear that only twelve would be sent into the air at any one time. 'You don't understand the problems,' his friend had told him, 'of servicing on arrival, refuelling, ammunitioning, plus the long passage just flown, plus briefing and all these problems. To imagine we can have any more than twelve airborne at one time is just wishful thinking.'[3]

Simpson had gone straight to Admiral Leatham and told him such complacency spelt doom. 'Please, sir, will you go and persuade AOC to organize things so that all 48 can go up and fight?'[4] No, the Vice-Admiral had told him. It wasn't up to him to interfere with Air Vice-Marshal Lloyd's arrangements. So, on 19 April, Simpson had tried another friend at Air Headquarters. Again he'd been told that getting all the Spitfires straight back into the air simply couldn't be done.

On his arrival back at Lazzaretto, Simpson had been given a message to move the Tenth Flotilla to Alexandria. 'The decision,' he'd replied, 'has already been made. The Spitfires arrive tomorrow and will be eliminated, chiefly on the ground, then I shall leave with a clear conscience.'[5] Of course, this is exactly what happened, and during the last few days of April, the Tenth Flotilla departed Malta, one by one, the Royal Navy's role on the Island well and truly finished.

There was a final sting for Simpson. On the 27th, HMS/S *Urge*, under Lieutenant-Commander Tomkinson, hit a mine as she left Malta, and sank. All her crew were killed. *Urge* had been second only to *Upholder* in terms of enemy tonnage sunk, and Tomkinson one of Simpson's most beloved COs. April was for Simpson – as it had been for the whole of the Island – truly the *mensis horribilis*.

Simpson's assertions about getting the Spitfires airborne immediately had been absolutely right. Fighters had been refuelled and rearmed in the Battle of Britain within fifteen minutes, and although conditions and facilities were considerably worse on Malta in 1942 than they had been in southern England in 1940, it was more a question of having plenty of people and the necessary fuel and ammunition on standby as the planes landed. Plenty of new aircraft had reached Malta since June 1940, and by the time Denis Barnham and the other April Spitfires arrived, Lloyd and his men should have learnt from experience and long since devised a plan for getting them airborne again promptly. It seems that Lloyd was not admonished in any way for the loss of so many Spitfires on 20–21 April, but just as Simpson had foreseen what would happen, so it must have been equally crystal clear to the AOC. Yet neither he nor Leatham, nor any of the other Administrative Council for that matter, did anything to prevent it.

They were now faced with one more chance. This time, they needed to work out a system whereby newly arriving Spitfires could be put back into the air in less than twenty minutes. Either that, or the operation would once again be doomed to failure.

A second concern was with the pilots themselves. It had been noted that many of the new pilots of 603 and 601 Squadrons had been short of experience, with over half their number having never flown in action before. As Lloyd correctly pointed out, Malta provided the most intense and arduous theatre of war for any fighter pilot, and was simply not the place to send green recruits who had never fired their guns in anger. Even Denis Barnham, a veteran of numerous fighter sweeps over France, reached the Island with little idea about the tactics needed or the conditions under which they were expected to fight. *Offensive* flying – which is what such sweeps were – was very different from the kind of *defensive* flying the fighters were performing over Malta. When flying offensively, aircraft were rarely scrambled, but took the fight to the enemy at a time of their choosing. Nor were they waiting for the enemy and trying to second-guess where they were. Finally, the fighter sweeps usually involved massed layers of aircraft – several squadrons of planes at once – rather than just three or four single Spitfires or Hurricanes.

This difference in fighting conditions was starkly demonstrated when, on his second day, Denis Barnham had volunteered to fly up to intercept an incoming raid along with his CO and Squadron Leader Gracie. Before take-off, he quickly spoke to Gracie. The conversation went something like this:

Denis: 'Sir, what are the best tactics to use?'

Gracie: 'You'll learn, but don't go chasing the bastards all the way to Sicily.'

Denis: 'If we are separated from you, with formations of 109s around, what's the best technique then?'

Gracie: 'If you're by yourself weave around at nought feet all over the Island, or better still do steep turns in the middle of Takali aerodrome, inside the ring of Bofors guns, but don't take any notice of their fighters, it's the big boys we've got to kill.'[6]

This was his only preparation for fighting in an air battle completely different from anything he had experienced before.

After nearly colliding with Gracie on take-off, Denis climbed to 15,000 feet with the other two pilots before spotting a large formation of Junkers 88s. They dived and Denis opened fire, although he had no time to see whether he'd hit anything. Then he drew up behind another and, with the Spitfire shuddering from his cannon-fire, saw smoke start to pour from the starboard engine of the German bomber. A second before he'd not been able to see any 109s at all, but suddenly there were orange flashes whipping past his cockpit and the crackling of machine-gun fire in his ears, although he couldn't see where they were coming from. Then two Messerschmitts were diving at him from the left, and more tracer curling across his Spitfire. Denis turned in towards them, but his helmet was slightly too big for him and the pressure of the turn caused it to fall over his eyes. Frantically, he pushed it back up only to see two more 109s, this time attacking from the right. Again, he turned in towards them, and managed to get on the tail of another. Pushing his helmet off his face again, he was about to fire when his view was completely blotted out by the underside of another Messerschmitt, streaked with oil, flashing past him. A split-second later it was gone and he was firing a long burst of machine-gun bullets into the 109 in front, his Spitfire shaking and shuddering once more from the recoil, until the German started belching black smoke and toppled over on its side. But more German fighters were zipping in from the right and Denis flipped his plane over, the Island rotating from below to above him. Then, an ear-splitting crack and smoke burst from the engine and flooded back into the cockpit. Upside down again, then he was spinning, the control column limp in his hands. He was falling out of the sky, his plane out of control and smoke billowing behind him. Desperately, he tried to pull off his oxygen mask and radio leads. Too low now to bale out, he realized death was unavoidable. A moment of strange calm, then he felt the controls respond after all. A glance upwards told him the 109s were still above, watching him, but hopefully they would now leave him alone. Briefly climbing over some sheer cliffs, the engine finally died with another burst of smoke. Having noted the large number of small stone-walled fields with a sense of renewed horror, he saw Hal Far just ahead of him, although he was still travelling too fast to avoid over-shooting. His only hope of stopping before crashing into another wall beyond the airfield perimeter was to belly-land. Turning in over the skeletal shell of a hangar, he tightened his harness and hoped for the best. Like Raoul Daddo-Langlois the day before, Denis ground to a halt only to see 109s swooping in behind. He jumped on to the wing, then to the ground, and ran for his life.

When he finally made it back to Luqa, he discovered his CO, John Bisdee, was missing, presumed dead. Gracie was there, but had already reported Denis as being killed too. 'So you're alive are you?' he said. 'You nearly pranged us both on take-off.'[7]

This flight – from the moment he started his engine to leaping from the crashed Spitfire – lasted just half an hour. Denis had done as ordered and gone for the bombers, but had immediately lost sight of Gracie and Bisdee. Within moments of the dogfight beginning, he was on his own fighting for his life against overwhelming numbers of 109s. Every time he avoided one attack, another pair seemed to be gunning for him. And the Messerschmitts always worked in pairs – a leader and his wingman. Denis had no such luxury, and by constantly performing tight defensive turns into the enemy, he was losing speed, and with it manoeuvrability, increasing his chances of being hit. It was only his skill *and* experience as a pilot – his visual awareness and ability to perform effective defensive manoeuvres – that prevented him from being shot down earlier.

Pilots with little or no combat experience stood small chance of survival. There was no opportunity for spending a quiet fortnight acclimatizing, as Tommy Thompson had done when first joining the Battle of Britain. Nor was there even time for a practice flight. New pilots arriving on Malta were ordered into their aircraft and told to get on with it. Since every minute wasted on the ground was roughly equivalent to 3,000 feet of height, a pilot simply ran to his plane, jumped in, took off, gunned his throttle and climbed as high as possible before intercepting the enemy.

Most pilots were arriving totally unprepared for the conditions on the Island. Both Raoul and Denis had been completely taken aback by what was waiting for them. As one pilot newly arrived on Malta said, 'The tempo of life here is just indescribable. The morale of all is magnificent – pilots, groundcrews and army – but it is certainly tough. The bombing is continuous on and off all day. One lives here only to destroy the Hun and hold him at bay; everything else, living conditions, sleep, food, and all the ordinary standards of living, have gone by the board. It all makes the Battle of Britain and fighter sweeps seem like child's play in comparison.'[8]

★

271

The final cause for concern was nothing to do with the planes and their pilots, but over the matter of leadership. For whatever reasons, the Administrative Council was no longer working as a team. Responsibility for key aspects of Malta's war effort was not being shared; a blame culture had emerged. In short, the management crisis that had reared its ugly head after the arrival of the March convoy had not gone away. For Malta to survive, this breakdown needed to be resolved quickly, decisively, and with the minimum of fuss.

In response to Lloyd's criticism of the Governor, Air Marshal Tedder, the AOC-in-C Middle East, and Sir Walter Monckton, the Minister of State, were sent to Malta on 12 and 13 April to judge the situation for themselves. Both also met with Lloyd, General Beak and Vice-Admiral Leatham, as well as the fifth member of the Council, the Lieutenant-Governor, Sir Edward Jackson. Tedder then also took the opportunity to tour the airfields and visited Raoul, Buck and the other Takali pilots. Standing on the balcony of the Xara Palace, he was able to watch a couple of 109s roar across the airfield raking the pens with machine-gun fire. One of the Luftwaffe pilots even made a pass right in front of them, leaving the AOC-in-C in no doubt about the drastic air situation.

Hugh Pughe Lloyd clearly still had the confidence of his men. Tom Neil and Denis Barnham may have been underwhelmed by him, but he was liked and trusted by most, despite his shortcomings. By making a point of regularly visiting the pilots and airfields and finding time to talk to all, whether an erk or station commander, he endeared himself to those under his command. He was also sensible enough to realize there was no place for the kind of rules and decorum practised elsewhere in the RAF, and consequently the likes of Warby thrived under his command. His gung-ho spirit also seems to have been appreciated. 'He'd come down to the Mess with his long cigarette holder and a gin in his hand,' recalls Peter Rothwell, 'and he'd say, "Right, what I want you to do is kill the Hun, all right? Kill the Hun!"' Air Marshal Tedder had no doubt that Lloyd was doing sterling work under impossible circumstances.

The commanders of the other two services were holding less critical posts at this point. General Beak was working well with Lloyd in ensuring his men were on hand at the airfields, while Vice-Admiral Leatham had little under his direct control now that the Royal Navy had all but left the Island.

Neither Tedder nor Monckton had any concerns with them, but both agreed with Lloyd that Dobbie needed to be replaced. Leatham and Beak, when pressed, also felt the Governor had lost his grip. So too, it emerged, did Sir Edward Jackson. In other words, a unanimous verdict had been reached: Dobbie should go.

But despite drawing these conclusions – made on 13 April – it wasn't until the 20th, a week later, that Monckton signalled his recommendation to Churchill. On hearing this news, Lord Cranbourne, the Secretary of State for the Colonies, and a friend of Dobbie's, then wrote to the Prime Minister expressing his concern. The Governor, as far as he was concerned, had been doing an admirable job, maintaining the high morale of the people. To replace him at this 'critical juncture is likely to be exceedingly bad.'[9]

But Cranbourne was missing the point. Far more harmful would be prevaricating over the decision at such a critical time in the siege, and, for that matter, the Mediterranean theatre. If Dobbie was to go, then he should do so immediately and with the minimum of fuss. Monckton had already held up the process, and now Cranbourne was throwing a spanner in the works by turning the issue into a question of differing factions.

Matters were made worse when Dobbie then discovered Mabel Strickland had been intriguing against him. The editor of the *Times of Malta* had been convinced Dobbie was about to surrender the Island as early as spring 1941, although there is little evidence to support this. Nor does it seem likely that he was about to throw in the towel in April 1942. Dobbie's appeals to the Chiefs of Staff were always based honestly on his assessment of the situation at the time. Quite simply, he intended to hold out as long as supplies lasted. Mabel Strickland was convinced otherwise, but having got nowhere with her letter to Churchill the previous year, she had more recently contacted Lord Mountbatten, in whom she had confided before. Somehow, Dobbie had seen a draft of this letter. Hurt by her betrayal, the Governor then wrote to Cranbourne demanding an explanation from Mountbatten and asking that the Prime Minister be informed.

Had Monckton known about this Strickland Intrigue, the Prime Minister asked? Yes, he replied, but he had deliberately made a point of not seeing her during his visit, so as to not be influenced in any way. That Dobbie should be replaced was entirely his own – and Tedder's – judgement. But the Prime Minister, who had also been slightly startled by Dobbie's sudden bad press, decided Cranbourne should now visit

Dobbie and judge for himself whether the allegations were justified.

This was wasting more precious time, Monckton argued. On the 26th – nearly two weeks after Monckton's visit to Malta – Churchill replied, pointing out that it had taken the Secretary of State a week to inform the Chiefs of Staff of his opinions in the first place and that if anyone was wasting time, it was him.

In the meantime, the Prime Minister asked Lord Gort to stand by, to take over from Dobbie, if necessary, at a moment's notice. Gort, awarded a Victoria Cross in the First World War, had been Commander-in-Chief of the British Expeditionary Force in France in 1939–40. Recently, he had been Governor of Gibraltar, where he had performed well. A tough and uncompromising soldier, but with experience of civilian administration, he was a man without foibles or obvious quirks of character. In a nutshell, he was the ideal choice to replace Dobbie.

Cranbourne duly flew to Malta, and signals continued to hurry to and fro between London and the Mediterranean, so that it wasn't until 4 May that Dobbie was finally sacked and Gort told to set forth for Malta – three whole weeks after Monckton's and Tedder's visit, a disgracefully long time considering this period coincided with the worst episode of the entire siege to date.

To minimize any damage to morale by this sudden change of command, Dobbie left without issuing a farewell message and with the minimum of fuss. Gort arrived by flying boat at around 9 p.m. on 7 May, predictably in the middle of another raid. Dobbie and his wife and daughter were waiting for him in the Station Commander's house at Kalafrana, along with a number of officials ready to carry out the swearing in of the new Governor. A bomb exploded nearby, and although no one was hurt, the ceremony was carried out with haste and a noticeable lack of pomp. Then the Dobbies hurried to the same flying boat that had brought in the new Governor, and left.

The first the rest of the Island knew about it was when the change-over was announced on the Rediffusion system – now up and running again – and in the *Times of Malta* two days later. Dobbie, they were told, had left for health reasons only, while listeners and readers alike were reminded at every opportunity that Gort had earned a Victoria Cross for extreme valour and had brought with him the Island's George Cross. Despite Cranbourne's fears, Dobbie's sudden departure had no noticeable effect on morale. This was not because he had been unpopular – for the most part, he had been well-liked and had done a difficult job extremely well. It was just that for most people, the Governor was a somewhat distant figure; and governors came and went, even in peacetime. Even so, the change-over had been handled well; what could have been a public relations disaster turned into something of a coup instead.

Meanwhile, Churchill had once again persuaded Roosevelt to lend the USS *Wasp*, this time to operate alongside HMS *Eagle* in flying off an even larger consignment of 64 Spitfires, to be followed soon after by a further seventeen Spitfires from *Eagle* on a second run out of Gibraltar. The first batch was due to arrive on Saturday 9 May, while the fast minelayer, HMS *Welshman* would reach Grand Harbour with much-needed supplies of fuel and ammunition at dawn the following morning. Having established where they'd gone wrong before, it was now essential to work out a plan that would ensure the operation was carried out with maximum chance of success.

At the end of April, Group Captain Woodhall arrived at the Xara Palace from Fighter Control in Valletta, and called together five pilots from 249 Squadron, Raoul Daddo-Langlois and Buck McNair among them. Having given each man a drink, Woodhall took them to the top of the balcony overlooking Takali and told them about the plan to bring in the Spitfires on 9 May. It was essential, he told them, that the next reinforcements should be led in by men with experience of Malta; and so they were to fly out the following day, 30 April, on a transport plane to Gibraltar, where they would later join the aircraft carriers and the new consignment of Spitfires. The new pilots, he told them, at least had plenty of experience, having already cut their teeth against German 109 and Focke-Wulf fighters over France. 'I don't have to tell you fellows what is at stake with this operation. Everything will hang on it. It's make or break and it has just got to succeed.'[11]

Raoul Daddo-Langlois spent a week on Gibraltar, eating steaks and drinking beer and wine, indulging himself in a way he had almost forgotten about since leaving England. It was a much-needed respite, marred only by the news that Norman McQueen – one of his closest friends, and with whom he had flown out in February – had been killed. Six of their original sixteen who had left Plymouth back in February had already died, and a further four invalided out through wounds, disease or exhaustion. The statistics brought no comfort.

Neither Raoul nor Buck McNair was flying with the main batch on

9 May, for they were due to return to the Island a week later with the second flight from HMS *Eagle*. In the meantime, rigorous plans had been put in place for the safe arrival of the initial 64 planes. They were to be split into three batches and between airfields, so that the first arrivals would be already airborne in time to provide cover for the second and third batches. Woodhall had told the crews that the newly arrived Spitfires must be ready to take to the air within no more than half an hour of landing; this time, they were promised, the guns would already be harmonized, the radio sets properly tuned and each aircraft in the best possible condition.

Each aircraft was to be clearly numbered, and on touch-down the station controller would shout out the number of the aircraft and a groundcrew would run out to the plane, jump on the wing and direct the pilot to the corresponding blast pen. There, five groundcrew and Army helpers – Frank Rixon included – would be waiting with a stash of four-gallon petrol cans and ammunition to refuel and, if necessary, rearm. Other more specialist groundcrew – electricians like Pete Watson – would also be waiting to carry out any necessary servicing and quickly remove the extra fuel tanks. Finally, experienced Malta pilots would be standing by to take over each plane, and to be scrambled at a moment's notice.

The gunners also had a key part to play. Ken Griffiths and his crew were temporarily sent back down to Takali, as it was agreed that the three airfields should be given priority for barrages during the next few days. All target restrictions were also lifted – 109s could no longer expect to be immune – and the men were placed on constant duty.

Lloyd was expecting the enemy raids to be frequent and heavy, and even if they managed to get Spitfires airborne almost immediately, was counting on a number of casualties. Denis Barnham was told to expect to fly at least six or seven times during the day. While waiting to be scrambled he was not to leave his aircraft; food would be brought to him. If he damaged his Spitfire in combat, he was not to return to his normal pen, but to taxi down newly laid strips to repair pens in the rear. By this time, Army and RAF personnel had built no fewer than 358 blast pens on and around the airfields – a labyrinthine network, and often well away from the main runways. Having delivered his damaged plane, and if unwounded, Denis was then to return straight to the main dispersal point and pick up another machine. Lloyd, and especially Woodhall, who masterminded the plan, had left no stone unturned.

On the night of 8 May, Denis tried to write a letter to his wife, but was struggling to find the right words. He was still reeling from the mêlée he'd found himself in earlier that day – a jumble of 109s outnumbering them five to one, hurtling over the Island at low level. Unable to sleep through the night-time bombing, he was still exhausted; and as he sat there, pen poised over the sheet of paper, he was aware this fatigue was heightening his fear about the day ahead. Then bombs burst nearby, and overhead he heard the roar of aircraft followed by the clatter of machine-guns. A Maltese waiter running across the room knocked into his table, making him drop his pen. Denis cursed – the nib had broken and it was the pen he had been using for sketching. Briefly, he felt anger replace his fear.

The following morning he was waiting patiently at Luqa, his Mae West lifejacket already strapped around his neck and waist and clutching his helmet and goggles. He looked at his blast pen, newly constructed from petrol tins, the silvery metal glinting conspicuously in the morning sun, and then saw the first Spitfires glide in towards Takali. It was a little after 10.30, and already the 109s were following in behind – straight into an intense barrage of flak.

All the first sixteen touched down safely, and all were ready in under ten minutes. The Station Commander, the newly promoted Group Captain Gracie, was in his new plane within six. So far, Woodhall's plans seemed to be working like clockwork.

Luqa's first batch of Spitfires were approaching the airfield just after eleven o'clock. Denis was due up after they had safely arrived, but they were still circling over the airfield and preparing to land when another alert was sounded. Over thirty Spitfires from Takali took off to intercept, but the attack was on Hal Far this time. The airfield was made temporarily unserviceable and huge brown clouds of smoke and dust drifted into the air, hanging listlessly for several hours.

Despite mistakenly forming up over some 109s, all the first batch of Luqa Spitfires landed safely, and shortly afterwards, Denis was strapped into the cockpit of his new aircraft, waiting for action and once more pondering his mortality.

Many men in wartime simply could not imagine death ever happening to them, regardless of how much death and destruction they saw; it was too big a concept to deal with. Tubby Crawford, despite knowing the odds were stacked against any submariner, always believed it would be 'someone else' who was killed rather than him. So too did Tommy Thompson. Denis, however, was one of those men who thought a great deal about his imminent destruction; it was what had prompted him to try to write a farewell letter to his wife the previous evening. Even sitting in his plane that morning, waiting to be scrambled, he couldn't help wondering which parts of the cockpit would puncture his body if he crashed.

He remained sitting there, wracked with nerves, waiting for the word to take off, through two more alerts and two more All Clears. Where were all the enemy bombers? He had even clambered down to stretch his legs when he heard sudden gunfire and roaring engines, then watched Stukas and Spitfires dancing overhead. One of the dive-bombers suddenly burst into flames and plunged into a nearby field. Two more batches of 109s appeared high above at different stages during the after-noon, but they were ignored. The Spitfires remained on the ground, gleaming in the sun, their engines clicking gently in the heat. Denis, like most of the pilots and crew, found the wait agonizing. Takali was bombed just before five o'clock, but that was it, and at dusk Denis was stood down, having not flown once all day. The furious never-ending air battles for which he had mentally prepared himself never came.

But all the carefully laid plans had worked beautifully – 61 of the Spitfires had landed safely, and, although four more had been lost during the day, there were still over fifty Spitfires available to take on the Axis aircraft in the ensuing days.

Churchill was delighted and immediately signalled the captain of the USS *Wasp*, 'Who said a Wasp couldn't sting twice?'[11] So too was Lloyd. That evening, he called his pilots together once more in the Xara Palace. The next 24 hours would be crucial, he told them, and men-tioned that 9 May was his lucky day, for on that day in 1915 he'd been knocked off his motorcycle by a shell, but had survived. Just as he said this, yet another bomb dropped nearby, and the party hurriedly broke up while their commander's luck still held.

The minelayer, HMS *Welshman* arrived at 5.25 a.m. on the 10th, and half an hour later the first enemy planes arrived in force. But a surprise was waiting for them – a smoke-screen had been laid across Grand Harbour. Furthermore, there were plenty of Spitfires, and the most intensive anti-aircraft barrage ever developed over the Island. Despite the continuing attacks, working parties from the Royal Artillery, RAF and Royal Navy all helped unload the cargo in five hours flat. The contrast with the fiasco in March could not have been greater.

Throughout the night, Denis Barnham had been feeling increasingly lousy. For the first time since his arrival, he was not kept awake by relentless bombing, but by an encroaching fever. By dawn he had a rising temperature and was shivering as the bus jolted through the blue-grey darkness to the airfield; normally, the cool air through the smashed windows was a welcome relief.

Having had to rush behind a nearby rock on several occasions, Denis realized he'd come down with the dreaded Malta Dog. Clearly in no fit state to fly, he miserably watched the morning's events from the edge of a large bomb crater. What he saw was a fog of green-grey smoke spreading up from huge canisters, covering Grand Harbour and shielding the *Welshman* from view. At the sound of the bombers, the anti-aircraft guns began pounding and pumping, shell-bursts, like black puffs, spattering the sky. Denis sat mesmerized, watching the Stukas and Junkers 88s peeling down into the smoke. Cutting through the roar and exploding bombs came the Spitfires, twisting and turning as they hurled themselves at the enemy bombers. Looking up, he spotted black dots dropping like stones on to the Spitfires: the Messerschmitt 109s. Meanwhile, across the Island at Luqa, more Spitfires and Hurricanes were surging down the runway to join the fight. Away from the harbour, high in the blue, ever more enemy planes were appearing – and even more Spitfires behind them. Planes twirled and zig-zagged across the sky, and then two plummeted into the sea, long tails of black smoke following them. Denis watched a parachute open and calmly drift downwards away from the fury of the dogfight. A motor launch sped out seawards, hurrying to pick up a wounded airman. Another Stuka dived over the harbour, but this one was hit, a ball of orange flame rising up through the smoke-screen, so that all that remained were fragments of the disintegrating plane dropping behind the hill.

In the Plotting Room at Lascaris, Christina Ratcliffe, part of 'D' Watch, was frantically trying to keep pace with the furious battles raging above. She had grown weary in recent months of plotting the same one-sided contest. 'Forty plus bombers approaching Island,' or even more had been a regular feature – depressing one-way tracks all headed for Malta and with little to come out and beat them back. They'd even made fake plots to try to fool the enemy, hoping the Axis controllers had been listening to their British counterparts exchanging messages with non-existent pilots. The ruse had worked on several occasions but it showed how desperate the British situation had become.

All that had suddenly changed. 'On the morning of the Tenth, it was almost as if a magic wand had been waved over the Operations Room,' wrote Christina later.[12] The cavern became a hive of activity, with so much traffic on the plotting table that it was almost impossible to keep track of what was going on. Christina quickly glanced up at the Controller, 'Woody' Woodhall, and saw he was beaming with satisfaction. Now, at last, Woodhall had a large amount of fighters and they were immediately making their mark. Christina considered it a great stroke of luck that her watch happened to be on duty that morning. They could all see how well the fighter pilots were doing – they probably knew more about what was going on than those swirling around the sky. She felt proud to be doing her bit on such an occasion.

This had been just the start of the day's raids, but for the first time since the outbreak of hostilities, the RAF was able to meet the bombers in equal or superior numbers. Fifty Spitfires and Hurricanes greeted the heaviest raid of the day – some thirty Stukas and Junkers 88s – which arrived mid-morning. There were further enemy attacks during the afternoon and evening, but on every occasion the Spitfire Vs were able to climb quickly and to a height that ensured they were waiting in the best possible positions. The remaining Hurricanes, now able to concentrate on the bombers at lower altitudes, were once again effective. Despite their terrifying scream and ability to bomb with precision, the Stukas proved no match for fighters. It was a rout.

Now feeling marginally better, Denis joined the rest of the squadron in the Mess at Naxxar that evening as they tuned in to Rome Radio to compare their own claims with the losses admitted by the enemy. Thirty-seven Axis aircraft had failed to return from operations over Malta, announced the Italian broadcaster. Unusually, this was a figure slightly higher than those claimed by the RAF. The defenders had lost just four Spitfires.

10 May marked a turning point in the Siege of Malta. Sixty-five Axis aircraft were lost or damaged in the day's fighting. With fewer than two hundred aircraft remaining on Sicily, this was a major blow. 'The last two days have seen a metamorphosis in the Battle of Malta,' wrote the *Times of Malta*:

'After two days of the fiercest aerial combat that has ever taken place over the Island, the Luftwaffe, with its Italian lackeys, has taken the most formidable beating that has been known since the Battle of Britain ... It has always been known that man for man, and machine for machine, the RAF were infinitely superior to the Hun and everybody looked forward to the day when he could be met on terms of parity ... That day has arrived – the RAF even had numerical superiority over its fighter opponents for the first time – and the results have excelled the most optimistic expectations. Our fighters have formed, with the AA Artillery, a team which has dealt out appalling destruction on the enemy.'[13]

The *Times of Malta* could be forgiven its moment of triumph. Although supplies were still desperately short, air superiority had at last been regained by the RAF, and as long as the Island had fighter cover, there was always hope.

There were even more Spitfires coming. Missing all the excitement in the skies above Malta were Raoul Daddo-Langlois and Buck McNair, who were still in Gibraltar and waiting to escort the next batch of aircraft over to the Island. Both had initially enjoyed a much-needed rest, but soon were champing at the bit to get back and annoyed to have been assigned to the second flight off *Eagle*. Wing Commander McLean was in charge of the preparations in Gibraltar, and so Buck had worked on him relentlessly to allow him to leave with the first batch on 9 May. One morning on the airfield under the Rock, he exploded, shouting, 'Let's get on with it and get ourselves a slice of this fucking piece of goddam cake.' His anger had been in vain; McLean had kept him on the second shuttle.

Although there had been nothing to compare with the size of raids that had appeared on 10 May, there had been plenty of air activity in the following days. Certainly Denis Barnham had been kept busy. By evening on the 11th, he'd been feeling much better and returned to the Mess just in time to hear about an Italian who had baled out only to land on top of a fountain. 'The spike went through his arsehole and impaled him there,' one of Denis's fellow pilots told him cheerfully.[14] Denis confided to his diary that this apparent lack of respect for a fellow human being depressed him greatly. He felt as though they were all being conditioned into becoming merciless killers, all sense of humanity discarded. But this disgust was largely misplaced. The banter between pilots – or soldiers or sailors for that matter – was a defence mechanism. If they thought too much about the men they were killing and who were being killed, they would not have been able to carry on. Ask any pilot how they dealt with the loss of colleagues, and they all reply in much the same way as Tommy Thompson: you didn't dwell on it, and tried to put it to one side; in wartime, there were practical reasons for maintaining a stiff-upper-lip attitude. Combatants may have felt they hated the enemy – but if so, they hated them as a whole, rather than as individuals; it was simply easier not to think of them as young men like themselves with mothers, lovers, wives and children.

The following morning, Denis was down at Luqa, sitting on a pile of sandbags waiting to fly. He was chatting to one of the new pilots who'd arrived three days before and been posted to 601 Squadron. A sergeant-pilot, Charles Graysmark was just twenty, but looked even younger. Despite his youth, he revealed that he too had a wife back home. They had been married just two weeks ago, a few days before he left England. Denis offered the new boy some of his thoughts about flying over Malta, remembering his own experiences on arrival on the Island. Graysmark listened eagerly, then they watched a Spitfire spiral out of the sky and crash-land into a stone wall on the far side of the airfield.

Later that afternoon, Denis was scrambled to intercept an enemy raid. Leading the section, he was amazed by the number of Spitfires taking off at the same time amid great clouds of dust. They certainly weren't all in his flight, so someone somewhere had made a big mistake. Denis had taken off and was turning back over the airfield when he saw two Spitfires below crash straight into one another. 'What are the orders?' he asked the Controller. 'Land immediately,' he was told.[15] This was unusual, but no sooner had he done so than he discovered the rest of the flight were still steadily climbing towards the interception. The new boy, Graysmark, was supposed to have been his wingman. Cursing, Denis immediately took off again, hoping to catch up with his now leaderless flight. By now, though, it was hopeless; they were too far ahead. Long before he was ever close to catching them, they had already engaged. In the ensuing dogfight, Graysmark was shot down.

But he'd been seen baling out and drifting down into the sea, so Denis landed once again and, collecting another member of the squadron, took off yet again to provide air cover for the rescue boat sent out to find him. Four 109s were attacking the launch, so Denis and his companion circled around trying to harry them as they came into attack; had they gone chasing a German each, there would have still been two left to shoot up the launch. Their tactics saved the rescue boat, but not Graysmark, who was dead by the time he was picked up. Although he'd managed to get himself into his inflatable dinghy, his wounds had been too bad. 'He made the error of lagging behind, of being inadequately covered by the others, shot down because, like the rest of us, he had never flown the line abreast formation before and had had no opportunity ever to practise,' Denis wrote later.[16] And he was also a victim of an error on the ground: had Denis been with him, he would most likely still be alive. As a Flight Commander, Denis had never lost a pilot when he'd been leading. Always erring on the side of caution, his spatial awareness was exemplary and he would have ensured Graysmark had not been left out on a limb. As it was, this young pilot became yet another casualty of the brutal air war – a young bridegroom who would never be seeing his wife again.

Raoul Daddo-Langlois and Buck McNair finally arrived back on Malta on 18 May, along with fifteen other Spitfires. The tempo had slowed considerably since they'd been away, especially in the last day or so. Fewer raids in fewer numbers. When they'd left, Takali's fighter planes had been tired, battered and thin on the ground. By comparison, the place was now heaving with Spitfires. The defenders were fighting back – and at last on something like an even footing.

On 10 May, the defenders' best day of the war to date, Kesselring reported to the OKW – the German High Command – that Malta had been neutralized. 'There is nothing left to bomb,' he insisted (ignoring, of course, the exceptionally beautiful headland palace which he had earmarked as his official residence after the Allies' surrender), and so the removal of Fliegerkorps II continued. Malta would never again see the intensity of attacks that it suffered during March and April.

Kesselring had repeated the mistakes of the Battle of Britain: bringing an enemy to their knees, then failing to kick them into the dust.

PART V

Starving

'I have never been to a place before or since that had such a visible atmosphere of doom, violence, and toughness about it.'

AMERICAN RAF PILOT LEO NOMIS

CHAPTER 16

The Island Starves

JUNE–JULY 1942

T HE MALTESE WERE bearing up well, but were being tested to the absolute limit of their endurance; for although the worst of the bombing was, for time being, over, now the threat of starvation loomed. The Governor, ever mindful of this, was also fully aware that most Islanders would have a far better existence under the Italians. Although the majority remained fervently pro-British, the wind could easily change, and so it was felt that the slightest hint of dissent should be stamped on very firmly. Those with strong Italian connections had been interned at the start of the war, but in February, forty-two had been deported to the Sudan – the former Chief Justice and President of the Court of Appeal, Sir Arturo Mercieca, among them.

Not long after Lord Gort's arrival, a Maltese Italian spy, Borg Pisani, was caught landing on the Island. Pisani had been a member of pro-fascist movements on the Island before the war. Having been granted an Italian scholarship, he had studied in Rome, and it was there that he had joined the Fascist Party and offered his services to Mussolini. His mission to Malta, ostensibly to check on the levels of morale and defence capabilities, was a disaster from the start. On arriving by sea beneath the towering Dingli Cliffs, he immediately lost most of his supplies when they were washed out of his reach, and he found himself trapped between the cliffs and the waves. Only after shouting for help was he rescued and taken to hospital where, under questioning, he soon confessed all. His capture caused a considerable stir on the Island, where his family still lived, but despite his farcically bungled efforts, Lord Gort was determined to make an example of him. Tried and found guilty, Pisani was eventually hanged for treason on 18 November, the Governor having refused any appeals for clemency.

Gort feared the Maltese would find the increasing food shortages harder to bear even than the bombing. Trying to make the Island's supplies last as long as possible without breaking the resolve of the people was one of his most difficult tasks. One of General Dobbie's last acts as Governor had been to announce the rationing of bread, to just ten-and-a-half ounces per person per day. Pasta, rice and tomato paste had already been rationed in April. These were the staples of most Maltese food, and it was feared that restrictions on bread would be seen as one cutback too many.

In fact, most Maltese accepted the decision with stoic fortitude, although after ordering a stock-take of all essential commodities, Gort announced a number of further cuts. Sugar and rice were rationed further, while entitlements of kerosene, coffee and soap were also reduced once again. Because of the shortage of fodder, cuts in livestock needed to be made. Most horses were spared, as were a few goats supplying the Milk Marketing Department, a few cows, and some chickens for egg production. Pigs, sheep and the rest of the Island's goats were all slaughtered. Consumption of water was another area that needed drastically redressing. Several reservoirs had been emptied, and bomb damage to pumping and distribution pipes added to the difficulties, and so the people were urged to use as little as they possibly could. 'Endurance and Fortitude' were now Malta's watchwords, the Government stated in the *Times of Malta*. 'When the history of the defence of Malta comes to be written, the endurance of the public in putting up with all the shortages will not be forgotten.'[1]

Going hungry was bad enough, but the shortage of just about any everyday commodity brought other miseries. Those supplies that did arrive were inevitably those most urgently needed: flour, oil, fuel, ammunition, aircraft spares. Replacing worn-out clothes became almost impossible; there was simply no more cloth or leather. Clothing had to be darned, patched and stitched up again. Curtains were sacrificed and made into dresses or a pair of trousers instead. Parachute silk was greatly cherished; those who floated down from the aerial battles above would land and find themselves accosted by women scrabbling to claim their parachute. People began using rubber from now unused car tyres to replace worn-out soles of shoes. John Agius was forced to re-sole several pairs of shoes in this manner. Endless queuing became a regular feature of daily life. After the All Clear, the people would emerge from their catacombs to queue for water – or for kerosene, or for bread. By an inevitable process of strangulation, one shortage led to another: when there was no more coal, so the power stations faltered and there was no more electricity. People cooked using kerosene, but by June that was not only rationed but had run out entirely. Cooking a hot meal, however small in quantity, became very difficult indeed. Then the only fuel left was wood – from furniture, as there were few trees on the Island – but the furniture supplies were soon exhausted too.

For those who had been made homeless, life was even harder. After his house had been destroyed in April, John Agius discovered first-hand the discomforts this caused. In the days that followed, his mother and sisters would go to one of their neighbours to use their washroom and toilet. His father used a friend's chemist shop to carry out his ablutions, while John visited the home of someone he'd known in the Scouts. It was both embarrassing and awkward. After a week or so, they saw a house to let in Sliema, not far away. The agent dealing with it lived in Balzan, near where John's oldest sister, Gemma, was teaching. In fact, he had two houses for let and gave Gemma both sets of keys, although he refused to go down and show them round himself – Sliema was far too dangerous a place to be. The following day, John's sister returned to Balzan, reporting to the agent that they liked one house more than the other, but it had fewer beds. 'Look, I've told you I'm not coming down to Sliema,' the agent told her. 'Take whatever you want from Number 78 and put it in Number 80. Do what you like! Take whatever you like!' So this was what they did.

But the Agius family were fortunate to find such a house comparatively quickly and easily. The Montebellos were still stuck in their underground cubby-hole. Poor living conditions and insufficient food had led to disease becoming rife. Michael Montebello was rarely free of fleas and suffered from scabies, a skin infection caused primarily by a lack of subcutaneous fat. 'But most of us kids had that,' he says. In April, the *Times of Malta* had run a piece entitled 'Tackling the Flea'. These mites increasingly sprang on to human bodies as the numbers of animals on the Island diminished. The article was staggeringly unhelpful, suggesting the best means of combating the flea was by keeping as clean as possible. The author recommended spraying everything in sight with a solution made from three parts common soap, fifteen parts water and

82 parts kerosene. But the Montebellos, for example, living in their underground cave, had little soap, and not much water, and, if they ever laid their hands on kerosene, it was not going to be used for making unreliable anti-flea concoctions. Nor did they have the equipment with which to start spraying themselves. Like most people, they scratched and put up with it.

Another problem was that those left homeless had little means of cooking for themselves even when there were still supplies of kerosene. To resolve this, the Communal Feeding Department was established. In January, they had begun the Victory Kitchens, which provided hot meals not only for the homeless but for anyone else who wanted to subscribe. It was hoped these would help people to economize further. The idea was a simple one: subscribers forfeited a portion of their rations, or paid sixpence, in return for one hot meal a day consisting of a meat or vegetable stew, which could be taken either at midday or in the evening. A kind of minestrone soup could be bought for threepence. Another proviso was that people had to register for at least a week at one time.

Most loathed the Victory Kitchens, but necessity meant they were soon to be found all over the Island, and numbers of subscribers increased steadily as rationing became stricter. During July and August, goat meat was served every single day – a stringy, normally inedible meat that simply could not be stomached without even the smallest variety. The standard of cooking was generally poor. The meal was very often a 'stew' only in the loosest possible meaning of the word. More frequently, it was little more than coloured water with a few bits in it. Portions were invariably meagre and insufficient. Many also complained vociferously about the service. People were once more forced to queue, not just for their meal, but also to subscribe for the following week. Finding people to run and manage the kitchens was another major problem. Most able-bodied men and women were already involved in vital war work and those who weren't had families and children to look after. It was left to the Island's nuns to run a number of the Victory Kitchens.

By June, most adult civilians were lucky if they ate 1,500 calories a day, less than half of what they should have been consuming. It was often as little as 1,100 calories. Children received even less. Servicemen were given more than the civilians, but not much more, and because of the intensely physical nature of their work, most were constantly hungry. Pete Watson spent much of his day thinking about food as he worked on the aircraft at Takali. He imagined tucking into a juicy steak and rice pudding, although such dreams had to remain in his imagination. When the food cart came around, the soup they were given was so thin he could see the bottom of the pan. He was sick of corned beef too: corned beef hash, corned beef stew, chopped corned beef and dry biscuit, or just plain corned beef. However it was dressed, it was still boring and insubstantial.

He did discover one way to supplement his rations. Anyone given the day off was handed a pass, which also acted as a ration card while off-base. Pete and two of his mates discovered these passes were fairly easy to forge, and so they'd walk into Mosta and present their official pass at one place, then their forged one somewhere else. They were rumbled once, but while the store keeper was on the telephone checking up on them, they scarpered. Another time they stole out at night and pinched a chicken and a couple of potatoes. 'They were delicious,' says Pete.

Frank Rixon had two people to look after now: his wife Mary and their unborn child. He tried to bring her what rations he could – a slice of corned beef, a small amount of sugar and sometimes some tea, but it wasn't much. One time Mary had been in a shelter with Frank and had smelled the aroma of an orange – all fruit was now very scarce. A woman was eating one in the entrance-way above. Mary had a sudden craving for a taste, and so Frank went back up the stairs of the shelter and asked the woman if she could spare a segment for his pregnant wife. 'Here,' she said, handing him a piece. It was the last time Mary would taste orange for a long while.

There was always the black market. Frank used to buy eggs and bread from a nearby farmer at hugely inflated prices. 'The bread looked more like a cake, but with a couple of eggs it was quite tasty. Many of us used to do that.' They also used to pinch melons from a farm near Marsa. It was not uncommon to see farmers patrolling their plots with a gun. 'When you're hungry you do all kinds of things you'd never normally think of doing,' admits Frank. Ken Griffiths was also tempted by the black market on one occasion, when a man offered him an egg sandwich. He paid the equivalent of a week's wages for it – an exorbitant sum. 'But, boy, did I enjoy it,' he says.

For much of 1942, Ken was rationed to just three cups of tea a day – one at breakfast, one at midday and another in the evening. Tea was considered an essential part of daily life for most servicemen. 'If the supplies had ever failed the morale of the army would have been reduced more than by a major defeat,' said one soldier,[2] so just three mugs a day was sailing dangerously close to the wind. Despite the endless bombing, despite his wound, and despite the heat and appalling conditions, Ken's worst moment during his entire stint on Malta occurred over a tiny piece of food. His daily ration had dwindled to just two Number Nine biscuits – dry hard tack – and a meagre piece of bacon for breakfast; a thin piece of corned beef for lunch; and for tea he'd have the remaining part of his biscuit and a bit of jam. That summer, Ken was hungry nearly all the time. 'I'd go to bed hungry, wake up hungry, feel hungry all day,' he says. He and his mates would try to put each other off their food so they could eat it instead. Not that the ploy ever worked – the food was boring rather than rotten in any way. Then, one day, Ken saved half of one of his Number Nine biscuits. He was hungry and desperately wanted to eat it, but the prospect of having an extra half biscuit the following morning stiffened his resolve, and so that night he carefully placed it under an up-ended orange box, with his tin helmet on top of that so the rats could not get at it. Despite such precautions, by the morning it had gone. 'A rat had somehow got underneath, even with me lying there right beside it. I felt soul-destroyed,' says Ken, 'it was absolutely devastating.'

The promised convoy, with ships arriving from both Gibraltar and Alexandria, was finally planned for June. It was hoped that with fewer enemy aircraft now on Sicily and with strengthened air defences on Malta, a large part of both ends of the convoy would make it through. Even so, it was still a highly risky operation: the Mediterranean Fleet was now much depleted and the war in the Pacific had claimed the services of some of the Western Mediterranean Fleet and precluded any American involvement. On the evening of 14 June, Lloyd came over to the new 601 Squadron Mess to give the pilots another of his pep-talks. Denis Barnham and his colleagues had recently been moved from their billet in Naxxar to a new and large house in Sliema, which with its carpets and homely furniture was considered a great improvement.

The two convoys were, Lloyd told them, already under way. The one from Alexandria had soon come under heavy attack from Axis planes in North Africa, while the one from Gibraltar had already lost several merchant ships. By the following morning, most of the naval escorts would have to turn back to port, leaving both parts of the convoy dangerously exposed, and at a time when attacks were expected to be heaviest. Seventy miles from Malta, the convoys would come under the protective umbrella of the Island's fighters, but they needed to extend that umbrella, and so Lloyd wanted 601 to fly with long-range fuel tanks. But there was a snag – only four Spitfires could be flying over the convoy at any one time because, from a squadron of twelve, the other eight would have to be either on its way out or on its way back. Furthermore, if the convoy was attacked just as a section of four fighters was about to leave, they were to stay on and fight. If fuel then became low, they would have to ditch their aircraft and hope they would be picked up by one of the ships.

At dawn the following morning, Denis sat in his cockpit feeling certain his end was near. He could not possibly survive such appalling odds. Fighting over sea at such distances from land was dangerous enough, but four Spitfires against countless enemy aircraft with no quick return to the Island was little short of suicide. He had never felt so expendable in his entire life. His worst fears were confirmed when, about to lead the third section to fly off, he was told that the first two had already been shot down.

Having mentally prepared himself for certain death, however, he once again saw little action that day. They found two Italian cruisers on course to attack the convoys, and were fired at, but of the convoy there was little sign. Some oil stains on the surface, but nothing more. It turned out the convoy from Alexandria was miles south of its expected position. After an hour in the supposed battle area, they returned to Luqa. Nor had the other two sections been shot down; this had simply been a cruel piece of misinformation.

Another section from 601 had more success, but by the time it was Denis's turn to fly off again, the Gibraltar convoy was now within normal range of the Island, and Spitfires from Hal Far and Takali took over. Two of those involved in the escort work were Raoul Daddo-Langlois and Buck McNair. Raoul flew three times that day, covering Fleet Air Arm Albacores and then finally attempting to intercept some enemy bombers, although without any success. Landing again, the pilots excitedly reported how they had seen Italian ships hit time and again by the torpedo-bombers they were escorting – Raoul thought Albacores had hit two Italian cruisers – but in fact most had missed. Newly arrived Beauforts from Malta had successfully torpedoed an Italian heavy cruiser and damaged a battleship, but it had not been enough to prevent the failure of the Alexandria convoy. Late on the 15th, the decision was made to turn back. The Italian fleet had finally withdrawn, but the convoy and its escort only had twenty per cent of its ammunition left, an amount considered insufficient to see them into Malta. Two of the eleven merchant ships and three destroyers had already been sunk, and the cruiser *Hermione* was also destroyed on the return trip. Denis Barnham was bitterly disappointed, as were all the other pilots who had battled so hard. Having come so far – almost within fighter range – it seemed a terrible blunder to turn back, even with a shortage of ammunition. All their efforts, Denis felt, had been a failure. In addition to the seamen lost, sixteen Malta pilots were killed while trying to bring the convoys safely into Grand Harbour. From the combined operations, only two merchant ships from the seventeen that had started ever made it to Grand Harbour. At least this time the ships were rapidly unloaded under the protection of smoke-screens and a large fighter force, but 25,000 tons of supplies was nothing like enough.

On the evening of the 16th, Lord Gort broadcast to the Island. He was, he told them, going to speak with complete frankness. 'The truth never hurts and we are always at our best when we know the worst.' But he had bad news – the convoys had largely failed. Nonetheless, he said, 'Every effort will be made to replenish our stocks when a favourable opportunity presents itself. Meanwhile we must stand on our own resources and everyone of us must do everything in his or her power to conserve our stocks and to ensure the best use is made of all the available resources that remain to us.' The prospects were grim; life was tough enough as it was, and Gort knew it. After warning people against resorting to the black market and becoming unwitting Fifth Columnists, he did as Dobbie had done before him, and looked to divine salvation. It must have seemed their best hope. 'We have the sure conviction that our cause is just,' the Governor concluded, 'we have trust in ourselves and we have a still greater belief – our faith in Almighty God. Strong in that faith let us all go forward together to Victory.'[3]

Shortly after the convoy arrived, John Agius's older brother turned up at their new home with an entire loaf of bread. 'But it's inedible,' he told them. It had been made with flour contaminated by engine oil. It smelled awful, but they sliced it up all the same, and decided to toast it. There was no wood as such for a fire, so they burnt some furniture instead and toasted the bread on a piece of wire across the fireplace. There was nothing to put on it – no butter, no jam – but John still ate a couple of slices. 'It didn't kill me,' says John. 'When you are hungry, you would even eat a rat. I was hungry morning, noon and night.'

But living like this was taking its toll. General Dobbie had been concerned that the constraints of living on an island might have a bad effect on the morale of the servicemen, and, of course, it did. The isolation, the constancy of their situation and the lack of any chance to get away from it all slowly ground people down. Raoul Daddo-Langlois was either flying or doing very little. In May he wrote to his sister, 'I look forward immensely to coming home; I only hope it won't be too long now … As you can imagine, our everyday life is pretty dreary, with no company except other service types. I hope you will have a beautiful girl all lined up for me when I come home – there are almost no European women here. We certainly miss them an awful lot.' A few sentences later, he returned to the theme: 'How we long to see English women and everything English again – one gets quite worked up over Dorothy Lamour on the "Flicks"; and what a desolate place to spend a birthday.'

Raoul had just turned twenty. In a letter to his mother he wrote, 'I find at the moment that books on modern affairs are about the only things with which I can amuse myself. As you can imagine, the Island is pretty dead as regards mental activity outside flying.' In another he told her, 'A large number of your letters have arrived recently and I have been very interested to hear what was going on at home. It is amazing how interested one gets in domestic affairs as soon as one goes abroad – at least I do.' As the supply situation became worse, it is not surprising that Raoul had more and more time to brood. Thoughts of home, girls and the future were obvious topics for a young man who felt he was far from home and facing extreme danger every day. To his sister, with whom he could be considerably more frank than his parents, he said, 'I often stop for a moment and wonder what I shall do after the war. I'm afraid the prospect is rather blank at the moment … I think all my friends have disappeared all over the place. A lot have been killed judging by recent casualty lists. Don't think there is anything more to say at the moment.'

It is easy to picture him sitting at a table in the Mess at Xara Palace; although it was high summer, the room would have been dark and cool, the heat rising to the top of the high stone walls. What more could he say? His was a dangerous occupation and his chances of ever returning home were not good. Censorship prevented him writing about any operations, but would his sister really want to hear about how he'd circled round and round above a colleague who'd baled out into the sea, while he waited for the rescue boat? And how when the launch finally arrived the pilot was dead anyway? Or about the time he attacked a number of Italian fighters who were searching low over the water for one of their own colleagues? Closing in on one, he'd opened fire, his Spitfire juddering as hundreds of bullets drummed out from the wings, the slower cannon – bom-bom-bom-bom – curling towards his target; he'd watched as bits of the plane flew off, smoke started pouring from the engine and it plunged into the sea, the pilot almost certainly killed. Then moments later, Raoul's section had been 'bounced' in turn by four 109s. Swirling, turning, frantically trying every trick in the book to shake them off, Raoul and his three colleagues had then been involved in a running dogfight all the way back to Malta. By the time he'd landed his plane he would have been shaking with the rush of adrenalin, from the knowledge that he had literally been fighting for his life. But he could tell Angela nothing of this. Nor how he'd clambered out of his cockpit, his back drenched with sweat, scraped his flying helmet off his head, and stumbled over to the dispersal hut. 'Those yellow-nosed boys certainly know their stuff,' he'd commented to the other pilots. An understatement, of course, but they would have understood the terror of those desperate moments out over the sea.

The pilots, too, were suffering from the worsening conditions. There was no longer any form of transport to take them from Mdina to the airfield, a walk of two miles each way. So they remained at Takali all day, regardless of when their flight was on duty. The food was almost inedible. Even the bread was now being made with – among other things – potato skins. For Buck McNair it was the vast armies of flies that made life so hard. 'There were always flies and bugs in the damn stuff. We would swat flies all day long. If we tried playing cards while on Readiness, it really became a fly-swatting exercise.'[4]

Unlike the camp-beds, armchairs and record players of the dispersal huts in England, there were no such comforts at Takali. The hut built by Maltese labourers the previous year was still standing, but the roof had gone. Inside there was just rubble. The pilots made themselves chairs from rocks and a card-table from the wrecked wing of a plane. Conditions weren't much better for Denis Barnham and his colleagues at Luqa, where the Airfield Headquarters were underground, carved into the rock and illuminated by a single light bulb, and known as 'G Shelter'.

61. A page from Denis's diary, 14 June 1942, and his sketch of the ruins of Sliema, home of John Agius and Meme Cortis.

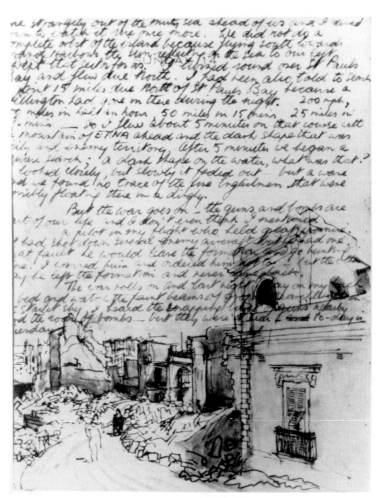

62. Frank and Mary Rixon with their baby daughter, Betty. Imtarfa was bombed just after Betty was born, and Mary was lucky to survive. The parents were so worried about their new-born child, they had her christened almost immediately.

63. George 'Screwball' Beurling's signed photograph that he gave to Pete Watson.

64. A Spitfire flies over the cathedral at Mdina. The Xara Palace, home to many of Takali's pilots, lay just to the left of the cathedral.

65. The inspirational and brilliant Air Vice-Marshal Keith Park, strapping himself into a Spitfire Mark V. Within two weeks of his arrival in July 1942, daylight bombing had all but stopped.

66. Meme Cortis. She continued to work at Imtarfa throughout the siege, later following the troops to Italy, which is when this photograph was taken.

67. Freddie Treves. At seventeen, he had only just left school when he joined the *Waimarama* as its youngest officer for Operation Pedestal. It was to be a voyage that would haunt him all his life.

68. The Californian Art Roscoe. Art joined the RAF after being rejected by the US Military Academy at West Point for having a slight stigmatism in one eye. He joined 71 Eagle Squadron in England before being sent to Malta.

me + my "Spit:"

69. Fred Jewett, an Able Seaman on the gunnery team of the destroyer HMS *Ashanti*. Fred was a veteran of a number of Arctic convoys before the escorting force for Operation Pedestal.

70. The first victim of Operation Pedestal. At 1.15 p.m. on 11 August 1942, the aircraft carrier HMS *Eagle* was hit. Freddie Treves felt 'numb with horror' as he watched this mighty ship sink in just a few minutes.

71. Operation Pedestal. HMS *Indomitable* comes under attack. The black puffs of smoke are from exploding anti-aircraft shells.

72. The end of *Waimarama*. Freddie Treves was one of only 19 from a crew of 109 who survived when the ship was hit.

73. Maltese children cheer in the surviving ships of Operation Pedestal.

74. The tanker *Ohio,* straddled by the destroyers HMS *Penn* and HMS *Ledbury,* inches into Grand Harbour.

75. Unloading *Rochester Castle*'s precious cargo onto barges to be taken to the quayside. No stone was left unturned this time, with plenty of troops brought in to help the Maltese stevedores.

76. Some of *Rochester Castle*'s crew with RAF staff at Luqa. Joe McCarthy is standing on the far left. Unlike most who found themselves stationed on the Island, Joe enjoyed his time there.

77. The four 'B's standing on the wing of their Beaufort. From left: Ron Brockett, Fraser Carlisle-Brown, Stan Balkwill and Bob Buckley.

78. Headline of the *Times of Malta,* Thursday 15 October 1942.

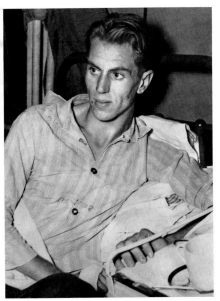

79. *Below* Tubby Crawford leading two of his officers off his submarine, HMS/S *Unseen*. His journey back out to Malta was a hazardous experience that tested the newly promoted commanding officer to the full.

80. *Above* George Beurling, one of the most natural and gifted fighter pilots of the war. No other Allied fighter pilot shot down as many enemy aircraft in such a short space of time as 'Screwball' Beurling did over Malta in 1942. For him, Malta was the fighter pilot's paradise, and a place where he reigned supreme. Sadly, he would never find such glory or fulfilment again. This picture was taken while he was recovering in hospital in England after being flown out of Malta, but even here his pale eyes show something of the intensity of this brilliant but ultimately flawed man.

81. HMS/S *Unseen* in Marsamxett Harbour.

82. *Above left* Fraser Carlisle-Brown (left) and a friend sailing in St George's Bay, Malta some time during the spring of 1943. By this time, the siege was over and the Axis forces had almost been beaten in North Africa.

83. *Above right* Tubby Crawford marries Margaret Lewis at Blythe in Northumberland on a wet English summer's day, August 1944.

84. *Left* John Agius, sixty years on. Behind him, just to his right, is the house rebuilt on the site of the family home, destroyed by German bombers on 7 April 1942. He is standing near to where the air raid shelter would have been. This photograph was taken on 19 April 2002.

Nor were the pilots given particularly privileged status. Everyone was expected to pitch in to help. The fuel bowsers had by now all been destroyed. 'All petrol had to be lugged by hand to refuel every Spitfire dispersed all around the airfield – we could not spare the gasoline to truck it around,' said Buck McNair. 'And it takes a lot of petrol to fill even a fighter when you have to manhandle every drop.'[5]

Comradeship with his fellow pilots and a close friendship with Laddie Lucas was just about Raoul Daddo-Langlois's only source of comfort. It was the same for Ken Griffiths, now back at Spinola. 'For those who weren't there it is impossible to explain the comradeship forged then,' he says. He was as close to those men in his gun crew as he'd been to anyone. They all had their foibles and quirks of character which, under normal circumstances, might have proved irritating, but because they were living and working together so intensely these were ignored. 'We never really argued with one another,' says Ken. 'There was no point. We got along about as well as is possible among a group of lads. There was an unbreakable bond between us.' There needed to be, for after the massive expenditure of ammunition throughout April, there was now such a shortage that Ken and his mates were restricted to only a few rounds a day – an amount that could be fired in well under a minute. Although there were fewer raids, this was an extremely testing time. The guns still had to be manned as normal, and the crews were expected go through the motions of sighting and training their guns on to targets.

Denis Barnham drew less comfort than most from the intense camaraderie of squadron life. He liked many of his fellow pilots well enough, but had no particular group of friends. It seemed to him that none of them shared his anxiety about the morality of what they were doing. A major comfort to him was his painting, although most of his pictures were confiscated and torn up when he was discovered sketching some ruined buildings in Naxxar. Another batch which he had packaged up and put on a mail plane had also been destroyed when the aircraft crashed on take-off.

The inconsistency of mail was another factor that wore down the servicemen on Malta. Raoul received nothing for ages, then a whole bundle of letters all together. Denis suffered the same frustration. From the moment he left England, he was desperate for a letter from his wife, Diana. The days, then weeks passed and there was still nothing. Other men in the squadron had been given letters, which had confused him even more. Why had Diana not written? Had she wandered off and left him already? He knew this was quite common – many of the groundcrew who'd been out for nearly two years had received 'Dear John' letters from their wives telling them they'd gone off with someone else. Then a note arrived from a friend of his saying Diana was well and that he'd been taking her out a fair bit. This was almost too much – he was feeling low enough as it was without the added paranoia of wondering whether his wife was having an affair. It wasn't until Saturday 6 June, that he finally heard from her – a whole batch of letters suddenly arrived, the first written the night he left England, the last just a few days ago. But waiting for them had been a cruel form of torture.

Malta Dog plagued most servicemen at some point or other and affected its victims with varying seriousness. Stomach cramps, temperatures, vomiting and diarrhoea were its symptoms. There were plenty of jokes about pilots being caught out at 18,000 feet.

CONTROLLER: How's the dog up there?

PILOT: Not too bad.

CONTROLLER: But is he barking?

PILOT: Not so far.

CONTROLLER: If necessary, get him down to the kennel.

After a bout of the Dog, pilots reckoned the litmus test for flying again was whether they could fart without danger. Denis Barnham suffered from it not only on 10 May, but on several other occasions, and each time it prevented him from flying.

Nor did the war ever go away. There may have been a lull, but there were still daily raids, and intruders to intercept. Raoul Daddo-Langlois, for example, flew nineteen times in June – compared with the five occasions in April – including twice on the 3rd, the 6th, the 10th, three times on the 15th and then three times on 2 July.

Peter Rothwell was also kept busy with the Special Duties Flight. On 5 June, he destroyed the Italian merchant vessel, *Reginaldo Giuliani* – the first ship to be sunk by a Maltese-based aircraft in months. As the sole Wellingtons on the Island, the Flight was sent to bomb Taranto on three separate occasions in June. Flying through intense anti-aircraft fire was 'a bit hairy', but no more terrifying than having bombs falling right next to him, or landing at night when he didn't know whether there were craters on the runway or delayed action bombs about to explode. Following his efforts over Taranto, he was sent to illuminate the Italian fleet as it came out of harbour. At the mercy of the fire-power of the entire fleet, this was another extremely dangerous task. As Peter was discovering, commanding the Island's sole Wellington unit was quite a responsibility for a 21-year-old.

And the bombs kept falling. One evening, when Denis Barnham's 601 Squadron had been given a rest, the CO announced they were all going on a trip into Valletta. The first club they went to was shut. So was the second. They thought they'd try the Mayfair Hotel and were making their way towards it when they heard a bomber overhead. Moments later came a whistle of bombs and an enormous crash from the neighbouring street, followed by the usual avalanche of tumbling masonry. They eventually found a bar that was open, but it was a sleazy joint smelling of sweat and stale wine. The ceiling was stained black from candle smoke, and the atmosphere was hardly one of convivial boisterousness. Denis didn't stay long.

Ken Griffiths also had a close call. One day he and a friend were standing on the opposite side of the road from his billet. Pausing to watch a dogfight they then heard the whistle of bombs. Both rushed across the road to the billet, wedging themselves in the doorway as they both jumped in at the same time. Such instances did nothing for his nerves. After avoiding the bombers for a few days he would feel a bit more confident; but then something would happen that would shatter his confidence, and he would again go back to feeling scared most of the time. But as Suzanne Parlby confessed, the shame of admitting, or even showing, you were frightened was often worse than anything the Germans could throw at them. In March, a notice was posted at all gun sites warning about giving into fear. 'Anxiety neurosis is the term used by the medical profession to commercialize fear. Anxiety neurosis is a misnomer which makes "cold feet" appear respectable. To give way to fear is to surrender to the enemy attack on your morale. To admit to anxiety neurosis is to admit a state of fear which is either unreasonable or has no origin in your conception of duty as a soldier. If you are a man, you will not permit your self-respect to admit to anxiety neurosis or to show fear.'[6] But, inevitably, people did suffer from anxiety neurosis – or shell-shock as it is more commonly known. It was hardly surprising, with death and destruction hurtling down from the sky day and night. Most who survived the siege admit to jumping at loud noises, still, sixty years later. Meme Cortis saw a number of cases at Imtarfa. 'We had one sailor in particular who'd been on a merchantman.

I heard him say, "I'd rather die than go through it again." But we also had pilots with anxiety neurosis. They were still casualties of war.'

Frank Rixon had not stopped worrying about Mary and his unborn child, and with reason. One day in June, when Mary was eight months' pregnant, she was on her way to an air raid shelter when the bombs started falling. One landed nearby, the blast blowing her off her feet. She got up again, dusted herself down, then ran into the nearest house and hid under a table. Whose house it was, she had no idea; she was too distressed about the possibility of losing the baby to worry. Not long after, she had just entered another shelter and gone down some steps, when she heard aircraft overhead. One man was leaning against the entrance, watching what was going on. Then there was a loud rattle of machine-gun fire and he tumbled backwards down the steps past Mary. He had been severed in half. Mary was so shocked, she fainted.

Then her home was bombed. Frank rushed over to Sliema as soon as he could, but thankfully Mary, the unborn baby and his mother-in-law were all right. Some of the walls were still standing, but the roof had gone and a large girder was blocking their attempts to retrieve any of their belongings. Frank moved it out of the way but badly hurt his leg in doing so. Miraculously, two holy pictures were still hanging on a wall, entirely untouched.

That same day, Frank asked to be given some married quarters at Tigné Barracks and had his request granted. It was the fourth place they'd lived in since marrying eleven months before.

Although a large Red Cross had been painted on the Sports Ground, the 90th General Hospital at Imtarfa also continued to suffer from the effects of bombing. At the centre of the complex, in 'D' Block, was a large and distinctive clock tower, a landmark the bombers would use when attacking Takali from the north. On 6 June, Imtarfa was hit once again. Meme was on duty at the Families Isolation Hospital, a separate block just behind the main hospital. She was looking after an eighteen-month-old baby girl suffering from bronchopneumonia and being nursed in an oxygen tent, when there were several explosions nearby, the blast causing all the windows around her to shatter. Rushing out of the nurses' office to see whether the baby was all right, she heard the whistle of another bomb falling. With no chance of escaping to safety, she wedged herself tightly into the corner of the ward. Seconds later, the building shook, plaster, dust and glass showered around her, and she felt a sharp blow – a piece of shrapnel had become lodged in her arm. Although the raid was still on, she was soon placed on a stretcher and taken straight to the operating theatre, where the jagged piece of metal was removed. 'Someone up there was looking after you,' one of the nurses told her; yards from where she had been hit, the walls were peppered with holes from the blast.

Although her wound was not serious, many of her friends were not so lucky. One such was Edwin Cafiero, a former neighbour of hers who had lived opposite her aunt. They'd gone to school together; Meme was a good friend of his sister's. Now he was serving with the King's Own Malta Regiment, and had suffered serious shrapnel wounds. 'His legs were like a colander,' says Meme. She went to visit him as often as she could, then one day she was in the kitchen of the Senior Officer's Ward and she saw him hobbling towards her. He was taking some exercise but had hoped to see her: he was going back to his unit and wanted to say goodbye. 'But you still can't walk properly,' said Meme. 'Why are they letting you go back to base?'

'Duty, isn't it?' he told her.

Three days later, on his twenty-seventh birthday, he was blown up and killed. 'I will never forget his face when he said goodbye,' says Meme. 'He looked so sad – I suppose he knew what he was going back to.'

Conditions for the pilots were recognized to be so bad that it was decided to cut the tour of duty from the six months prescribed by Basil Embry back in January to just three. The same did not apply to the hapless groundcrew or the Army, some of whom, like Frank Rixon, had now been on the Island for over two years. Soon after, on 21 June, Hugh Pughe Lloyd called in Peter Rothwell and told him that since he'd completed a six-month tour of duty, he was being posted to Egypt. There was a Wellington that needed a major overhaul, so he was to take that with a number of fighter pilots and other passengers on board and fly to Cairo.

Peter was quite relieved – he was feeling run-down and in dire need of a break. Like Tony Spooner before him, he had a number of boils and before he left had been to see the doctor. 'Just lie outside stark naked and the sun should sort those out for you,' he was told. The following day, after formally handing over the Flight to his successor, he took off from Luqa. After about one and a half hours, one of the engines caught fire. Peter activated the extinguisher, but this only worked for a short while and the engine reignited. They were in serious trouble: travelling over the sea, some 200 miles south-east of Malta in a twin-engine plane with only one engine working. Peter told the crew to jettison anything they could – all baggage, anything loose in the hold – and then he turned back towards Luqa. They were losing height and speed all the time. It was exhausting work: the torque from the working engine was pulling the aircraft to one side, and only by applying hard rudder on the other – rather as Tom Neil had discovered on his flight to Malta the year before – could Peter keep it flying straight. Although desperately tired, he just managed to make it, and with one engine still on fire, he landed the Wellington safely back on Malta. It was an experience he never wished to repeat.

By the following day Peter was beginning to feel seriously under the weather. By lying out in the sun as the doctor had suggested, he'd caught sandfly fever, and soon had a raging temperature. He finally left the Island on a Dakota transport plane, a sick passenger in need of a hospital bed.

Shortly after the June convoy, a rumour started that 601 Squadron was to be posted to Egypt. On the 21st, Tobruk finally fell to Rommel, and the loss of Egypt now looked increasingly probable. Then rumour became fact – 601 were moving, and Denis Barnham was given the task of supervizing the fitting of long-range fuel tanks on to their Spitfires. But he was still struggling with bouts of Malta Dog. A few days before, he'd begun vomiting behind a stone near his aircraft and had then been taken to Imtarfa for an examination. He felt a shadow of his former self and as though Malta was defeating him. As a fighter pilot, he was told to be a killer – 'Kill the Hun!' Lloyd had repeated – but he struggled to accept this role. A few weeks before, he'd begun drawing a picture of himself – hollow-eyed, gaunt, a dazed expression on his face. 'The future? What?' he'd written underneath. He was, he knew, burnt out, and wondered how much use he would be to the war effort in Egypt.

Group Captain Woodhall could see this too. He had personally taken Denis to Imtarfa on the 19th and had recognized his pilot was in dire need of a rest. On the 22nd, as the squadron were preparing to leave, Woodhall rang through to Luqa and told Denis he would not be going to Egypt with the others. Having flown 200 operational hours, he was told he was now 'tour expired'. Denis was going home – back to England and to Diana and away from the Island that had brought him close to Hell.

As ever, some would leave, and others would arrive. George Beurling, for instance, had flown off HMS *Eagle* on 9 June and then joined 249 Squadron. He came with a mixed report. One of the other pilots of 249 had flown with him in England earlier in the year and apparently Beurling had been something of a loner. No team player, on fighter sweeps over France he had often gone off on his own, behaviour that created major tension with his fellow pilots, particularly as he ignored all criticism. On the other hand, he had proved beyond doubt that he could certainly fly – fly *and* shoot with deadly effect.

The replacements arriving from the *Eagle* were to be allocated to 249 and 603, both based at Takali. The two squadrons decided to toss a coin for who had first pick – Laddie Lucas won and chose George Beurling for his Flight. A few days later, Lucas became CO of the squadron and Raoul Daddo-Langlois finally agreed to take command of a flight – 'A' Flight, with the new boy, George Beurling, under his charge.

Raoul soon recognized his ability, but also noticed that George refused to obey orders and, as before in England, kept disappearing off on his own and ignoring commands in the air. Lucas had a word with him. Clearly, he had the potential to achieve great things, 'but,' the new CO added, 'if you don't toe the 249 line, then let's be quite clear about this. You'll be on the next aeroplane into the Middle East.'

'Boss,' said Beurling, 'that's OK by me. I'll play it your way.'[7] Neither Raoul or Lucas ever had cause to caution him again.

Raised in Verdun, a province of Quebec in Canada, Beurling had been a single-minded loner from childhood onwards, always getting into trouble and performing badly at school until the epiphany of a visit to a nearby airfield when he was fourteen. From then on, flying became a passion; a passion he funded by taking several menial jobs in return for a couple of hours' tuition each week. When the war broke out he was eighteen and a fully qualified pilot. Joining the fight seemed to him the perfect way in which to test himself, but with no academic qualifications he was refused by the Royal Canadian Air Force.

Undeterred, he secured a passage to Britain by working on a merchant ship, heading straight for the RAF recruiting office on arrival at Glasgow. However, as he hadn't brought his birth certificate with him from Canada, he was refused. Six weeks later he presented himself again, having sailed back and forth across the Atlantic just to fetch it, and was at last accepted into the Royal Air Force. During his training, his natural ability and flair were honed into shape by the Battle of Britain ace, James 'Ginger' Lacey.

On completion of his training he'd been posted to 403 Squadron, and then to 41 Squadron flying Spitfires on fighter sweeps and bomber escorts over to France. When he refused to stay in formation and took himself off to hunt for enemy aircraft on his own, his colleagues accused him of desertion. Telling them to 'go jump at themselves',[8] he went straight to the CO and asked for a transfer. It took the best part of a month to come through. In the meantime, he was ignored by the other pilots and deliberately left out of the daily operations.

Like Adrian Warburton, George Beurling was a misfit: a non-smoking, teetotal loner, but someone who was not afraid to speak his mind. His sole obsession in life was flying, which he viewed as a precise science; he also believed he knew more about it than most. Unlike Denis Barnham, he had no crisis of conscience about killing, despite a healthy respect for God; nor had he joined up because he believed the cause was just and right; he'd done so purely and simply to fly and shoot down planes. He didn't care a fig for authority and respected people only for what they did, not their rank. Unsurprisingly, he did not care much about his appearance either: his shorts appeared too big, and his socks, like those of a schoolboy, were always rolled down. His blond hair was kept long – but his eyes were as pale and as piercing as a hawk's. Everything to George was a 'goddam screwball' – the food, the enemy, the planes, the bombs, the flies. He'd only been on the Island a week when his colleagues decided 'Screwball' should be his new nickname, something he never complained about. Somehow it appealed to his ego.

Given his individualism, Malta was the ideal place to test his theories. As he said himself, 'On Malta, you'd get Jerries by going up and shooting them man to man. No more of these beautifully executed fighter sweeps. No more massed wings of Spitfires, maybe two hundred strong.' On Malta, George was expected to rush to his plane at a moment's notice. 'Then,' he said, 'card tables would go over like ninepins, cards and cash would hit the floor, pilots would jam the windows to get to those aircraft. You'd grind up there to meet them as if the fate of mankind depended on the time you could make reaching 20,000 feet and picking yourself a handful of Jerries and Eyeties with odds of five, seven and even ten to one against you.'[9]

He had a short while to wait. Although he'd flown a couple of days after his arrival – and badly damaged a 109 – it wasn't until the beginning of July that his true ability began to show itself. After the arrival of the Gibraltar convoy, the air activity quietened considerably. By July, however, Fliegerkorps II in Sicily had once again been reinforced, as had the Regia Aeronautica, and so launched another offensive. This time, however, there were plenty of Spitfires to meet them, in one of which was George 'Screwball' Beurling. His moment to shine had finally come.

By eight o'clock in the morning on Monday 6 July, he was frantically climbing into the sky along with seven other Spitfires from 249 to intercept three Italian bombers and 30 fighters headed for Luqa. Having been told to stop the bombers first, they tore into the formation. George singled out one and peppered it with bullets, killing the pilot and leaving the observer to try to fly the stricken plane back to Sicily. Moments later, he had swept past and was climbing to attack an Italian Macchi 202 fighter. 'A one-second burst smacked him in the engine and glycol tank,' said George. 'He burst into flames and went down like a plummet.'[10] He then saw another Macchi on the tail of a Spitfire, so after a quick climbing turn opened fire once more. Another brief burst sent a second Italian fighter into the sea.

He flew two further patrols that day without seeing anything, then in the evening was scrambled with Raoul Daddo-Langlois – 'Daddy Longlegs', as George called him – and two others to intercept seven Junkers 88s and their 109 escort. While Raoul was attacking the bombers, George went for the Messerschmitts. Attacking one of them at an angle and from the long range of 800 yards, George gave it a few seconds of fire and hit it in the glycol tank.

This was an extraordinary shot. Deflection shooting was mastered by very, very few pilots. As with a submarine firing a torpedo, it meant calculating the speed of both aircraft, and aiming sufficiently far ahead so that the aircraft and bullets converged. Bullets also drop, so George would have had to aim high as well as ahead. Most fighters had their guns synchronized to meet at around 250 yards, but the rule of thumb was only to fire when one could see the whites of a pilot's eyes. 800 yards – some 750 metres, or nearly half a mile – is a phenomenal distance. But this was no embellishment on George's part; he followed the 109 almost down to the sea until it burst into flames and dropped into the water. Four days later he shot down another 109 and a further Macchi. The day after that he claimed another three, including two inside ten seconds. In just three days of combat, he'd destroyed eight enemy aircraft. Few pilots had made such a devastating impact in such a short time, and for his efforts he was awarded a Distinguished Flying Medal (DFM).

George had agility in the air, innate judgement of distance and position, excellent eyesight, and an ability to shoot very accurately and with deflection, a combination shared by no more than one per cent of all fighter pilots. He also carried with him a small black notebook in which he made calculations about the angles, speeds and shots he had made, so he could see where he had missed and where there was room for improvement. His ability to shoot successfully with deflection was helped by a number of equations he developed and committed to memory.

It was a hectic time for Raoul Daddo-Langlois too. Unlike George Beurling, Raoul had never managed to master deflection shooting; he was an above average pilot, but not the greatest shot, as he himself admitted. Even so, on 2 July he chased a Junkers 88 forty miles out to sea before it finally went down in flames. It was the squadron's hundredth enemy plane destroyed since they'd transferred to Spitfires in March. Two days later the squadron were out in force and shot down three Italian bombers in one action, Raoul sharing one. Two of the airmen survived, and the following day he went with Lucas and a couple of the others from 249 to visit two of the wounded Italian pilots, now at Imtarfa. As they approached, one of the Italians looked at them forlornly, then slowly lifted an arm. His hand had been blown clean off by a cannon shell during the attack. All were sickened by what they'd seen – none of them wanted to witness so blatant a demonstration of their handiwork. The practice of visiting wounded prisoners had to stop.

On the 11th, Raoul hit another 109 and watched the pilot bale out on to land. This was to be the last action of his tour on Malta. In the first two weeks of July, over a hundred enemy aircraft had been shot down, a rate of loss the Axis could ill afford to sustain. Raoul, Buck and Laddie Lucas had more than done their bit to help, but by then they'd been on the Island for six months, double the prescribed tour. It was time for them to go home.

★

Hugh Pughe Lloyd was also on his way. Now there were sufficient Spitfires on Malta – and more flying in – it was at last felt that a man with greater knowledge of fighters was needed to command the RAF there. They might have made this change earlier in the year, as soon as the Island's bombing capabilities ceased and the principal role of the RAF on Malta became fighter defence. Lloyd's successor was certainly quick to demonstrate what a man with a successful fighter background could achieve.

On 14 July, Air Vice-Marshal Keith Park arrived by flying boat. Ordered to circle until a raid had passed, he soon became weary of this and landed anyway, much to the irritation of Lloyd, who admonished him for taking an unnecessary risk. A New Zealander who had been a highly successful fighter pilot during the First World War, Park had, by 1940, taken charge of 11 Group of Fighter Command during the Battle of Britain. His tactical skill and resolve in managing the whole of the south-east of England – the front line during the battle – ensured the adoration and respect of most Allied fighter pilots.

His opposite number during the summer of 1940 had been none other than Kesselring, and now the two faced each other again. Two years before, the German Commander had been hampered by his superiors – notably Göring – and by faulty intelligence; by July 1942 he found himself in much the same situation as, once again, the Axis had failed to deliver a killer blow. The invasion of Malta, which Kesselring had so repeatedly urged, had by now been called off. Hitler used the capture of Tobruk as an excuse to scrap the plan altogether and found a yes-man in Göring, who feared another massive loss of forces as had happened in Crete. Despite continually stressing that the two islands were in no way comparable and that, after the bombing offensive, Malta could have been taken with genuine ease, Kesselring's arguments fell on deaf ears.

It was now left to Park to complete his old adversary's humiliation, although, the new AOC had suffered his own fair share of disappointments, having been at the centre of a major tactical row during the Battle of Britain. He had then favoured using fighters in small numbers of no more than squadron strength, sixteen planes at most. There were several reasons for this preference. First and foremost, it meant there could always be fighters in the air covering those refuelling and rearming on the ground. Secondly, smaller numbers were easier and quicker to manoeuvre together. Thirdly, it ensured the preservation of his planes

– the fewer planes in the sky, the smaller the target for the enemy. Trafford Leigh Mallory, his counterpart for the north and north-east of London, believed otherwise, favouring 'Big Wings' of several squadrons at a time. By sticking to his guns, Park had come to be seen as inflexible and pig-headed: a reputation that cost him his job, despite having played a major part in saving Britain.

On Malta, Park soon proved such accusations unfounded, and was quick to re-establish the Island's offensive role. Under Lloyd, the Spitfires had still been acting defensively, taking off and generally heading south to gain height, then returning to intercept the bombers and 109s over the Island. Park thought this tactic was ludicrous, and said as much to Lloyd. With plenty of Spitfires to play with, the new AOC thought it made much more sense to try to intercept enemy bombers before they reached Malta, the idea being not only to shoot them down but also to break up their formations and thus encourage them either to turn back or to drop their loads at sea – a plan which would, in theory, save lives, time, aircraft and labour. The Island's radar was now much improved, and by insisting on a much quicker take-off time – two or three minutes – and by working in three squadrons, this was, in theory, quite possible. The first squadron would climb into the sun, then turn with it behind them to attack the high enemy fighter cover. The second squadron would intercept the bombers' close fighter escort or, if unescorted, the bombers. The third would make a head-on attack on the bombers as they approached, some ten miles north of the Island. Even if the bombers were not hit, it was important to break up their formation and force them to jettison their bomb loads in an effort to improve their chances of escape. Park also insisted the Air Sea Rescue was improved.

He issued his 'Forward Interception Plan' on 25 July, and its results were almost immediately apparent. By the end of the month the Axis had virtually given up daylight bombing; nor were Stuka dive-bombers used any more. It was also known that at least one Luftwaffe bomber squadron had been forced to stand down. Enemy fighter sweeps intended to regain the initiative were now arriving even higher. Park retaliated by insisting his own fighters did not climb over 20,000 feet. While this obviously gave the Axis fighters crucial height advantage, it did mean that if they wanted to fight, they would have to do so at levels more suited to the Spitfire V than the 109.

Offensive bombing operations from the Island were also slowly beginning to get under way again, largely due to the enterprise and determination of a small number of Beaufort bomber pilots. Although new four-engined aircraft were being developed and built, there was still a place for smaller, twin-engine bombers, especially if, like the Beaufort, they were highly manœuvrable; they had proved their worth during the battles to bring in the June convoy, and more arrived in the following weeks. By the end of July there were three squadrons as well as more Wellingtons, and offensive operations could begin again in earnest.

The RAF was slowly clawing its way back.

CHAPTER 17

Pedestal

E VEN THE MALTESE found the summer heat unbearable. For the fighter pilots, waiting to be scrambled, or for the men out in the fields or manning the guns, it was just another affliction and burden to be borne in this Maltese battle. It had rained at the beginning of June, but since then there had been nothing but deep blue skies and a sun that bore down relentlessly day after day after day. With the beginning of August, the sirocco arrived, blowing the heat and sand of the North African desert over the sea and adding to the discomfort of the Island. Kesselring had promised to pound Malta into dust, and he had been true to his word. Dust was everywhere: on all the houses, in the streets, covering the piles of rubble, swirling about the air whenever there was the slightest breeze; it made food and drink taste gritty, caused eye infections, clogged the back of one's throat, caused blisters on one's feet. The pilots were covered in the stuff every time a plane took off. Raoul Daddo-Langlois described watching a section of four take to the air. 'Then they were all away, roaring across the parched field until they were lost to sight in a dense cloud of dust which got into one's hair and eyes and from which there was no escape, except to get off the Island.'

Much of the Island lay in ruins, a constant reminder of how Malta had suffered. And the population was now even hungrier. The bread ration had been cut again, and at the beginning of July pasteurized milk was restricted to hospitals and children between the ages of two and nine. Farmers had been ordered to hand over all their crops to the Government, a necessary move but one that caused deep suspicion.

Supplies of potatoes were also now exceedingly short. As Lord Gort pointed out in a letter to the Prime Minister, 'Nations at War have managed to ration either bread or potatoes, but not both. It does not matter whether the calorific or vitamin content of a diet is sufficient scientifically to maintain health if the psychological side of the diet is wrong. To be told you will not starve, but to be conscious at the same time that your stomach is an aching void, is apt to leave the average person discontented.'[1] Gort understood this only too well: as Governor, he'd decided he needed to set an example and so was living off the same rations as everyone else. For the most part, he also refused to travel by car, instead riding a bicycle and even carrying it over the piles of rubble.

On 15 July, Mary Rixon was taken to Imtarfa Hospital. Frank accompanied her in the aged ambulance along a road so pitted with pot-holes and bomb craters that he worried she would give birth before they reached the hospital. But they made it in one piece and shortly afterwards Mary gave birth to a baby girl, Sarah Elizabeth, to be known as Betty. Their daughter was just two days old when the hospital was bombed. The nurses and midwives rushed in and took away Betty and the other five babies on the ward to a nursery downstairs where they could be better protected. The mothers were left alone and terrified in their beds. Sick with worry, Mary suggested they crouch under their beds until the bombing had stopped. No sooner had they done so than a huge explosion rocked the building. When they finally crawled out, they saw all the windows had been blown in and that their beds were covered in glass. They could all have been killed.

It was an extremely worrying time for both Mary and Frank. Frightened, unsure of what they should be doing, and desperately worried about their precious child, they decided to have her christened straight away, in the hospital. That she might die seemed a very real possibility with bombs falling around them and the terrible shortages. Nor did life get much easier once they were allowed back home. Feeding was still a problem and there were no nappies, so Mary had to make do with strips of white towelling. The shortage of water and soap also made it hard to keep the baby clean. Betty was such a tiny defenceless little thing; her mother worried all the time.

On 2 August, General Alan Brooke, Chief of the Imperial General Staff (CIGS), visited Gort *en route* to Cairo to assess the situation for himself and to brief the Governor about future strategy in the

Mediterranean. Although Gort had told Churchill at the end of July that morale remained good, Brooke had been shocked to see shoeless children gazing at him plaintively and rubbing their tummies as they had driven past. 'The destruction is inconceivable and reminds one of Ypres, Arras, Lens at their worst during [the] last war,' he noted in his diary.[2] Brooke spoke at length with Gort, Vice-Admiral Leatham and Keith Park. The Target Date for surrender had now been put back to the end of September thanks to the June convoy and the Magic Carpet services. But for Gort, managing the Island's meagre stocks was a never-ending and thankless juggling act. Because it was now high summer the lack of kerosene was less of a problem than it would be once winter arrived, when a whole host of further difficulties would arise. With this in mind, he was eager to keep reserves of potatoes for use as seed rather than for eating. But there was a limit to how much could be home-grown, and attempts at using human faeces to fertilize the soil had backfired badly, causing a small typhoid epidemic, and killing 99 people.

There was also the issue of the Island's military role. While Park might have currently held the upper hand in the air war, this could change in no time. All would be well as long as his Spitfires continued to intercept the bombers, but, if they were left stranded on the ground because of lack of fuel, the Axis would soon make short work of them, as they had on 20–21 April. A difference of opinion had also emerged between Gort and Park. The Governor favoured conserving fuel and this meant concentrating purely on defending the Island. Park, on the other hand, believed it was important to build up Malta's offensive capabilities and to continue chipping away at Axis supply lines while they were in a position to do so. To this end, he was anxious for the torpedo bombers to continue their work and to bring more bombers back to the Island.

The Tenth Submarine Flotilla was also gradually congregating back at Malta. Shrimp Simpson had arrived on 22 July; Lazzaretto was still in one piece – just – with tarpaulins acting as roofing where necessary. By the time Brooke arrived, there were six U-class submarines ready to continue their work. As Park knew, they could also work very effectively in conjunction with the Beauforts. But these too required fuel.

Despite the desperate shortages, Park had a strong case. The situation in North Africa was once again at a critical stage. On 1 July, the British Army had fallen back to a small railway junction sixty miles west of Alexandria, called El Alamein. Since then, Rommel had gained no further ground. The British commander, General Auchinleck, had even counter-attacked on 22 July, although the ensuing battle had ended in stalemate.

But Rommel was now in a potentially vulnerable position. Although Tobruk was his closest port, it was still more than 300 miles behind his front line and within range of the RAF and now US Air Force bombers operating from Egypt. Furthermore, it had insufficient unloading facilities to cater to his supply needs. Most of these, therefore, still came from Tripoli, 1,300 miles away. Logistically, this made the German Field Marshal's life very difficult. If the British could just stop him reaching Alexandria, the tables might well be turned. The best way to achieve this was by Malta-based aircraft and submarines sinking as many of the Axis supplies as possible. Having survived the Axis blitzes of the first part of the year, it was time for Malta to play an important role once again.

But if Malta made an all-out effort to help the Allies in North Africa, Gort feared the Island would be risking imminent capitulation, and very possibly before she had done enough to make a serious impact on Rommel's forces. The answer to this conundrum lay in the successful arrival of another convoy, bringing not just food, but plenty of aviation fuel. Without these supplies, Kesselring could yet have the last laugh. More than ever, the futures of Malta and North Africa were inextricably linked. They would either sink or swim together. The entire fate of the Mediterranean and the Middle East now depended on whether another convoy could reach Grand Harbour soon.

The Chiefs of Staff had already approved a plan for 'the largest possible convoy to be run into Malta from the West'[3] during a meeting on 15 June — before the disappointments of the last convoy had occurred. That they could even contemplate such a plan was partly due to the twenty-four-hour summer daylight in the Arctic, preventing convoys from running there, which meant there were potentially ships to spare. Furthermore, the American naval victory against Japan at the Battle of Midway on 4–7 June had also relieved the pressure to send British naval ships to the Pacific. But the Arctic convoys would be starting again in the autumn, so if they were to mount a large-scale operation, there were really only two opportunities when this could happen: either the middle of July or the middle of August, during the dark period when the moon was at its smallest. Since there was simply not time to get everything ready for July, it would have to be August. It was the narrowest of windows.

★

The planning of Operation Pedestal, as it was code-named, began in earnest in the middle of July. The officers of the naval forces involved were brought over to London and, working closely with the First Sea Lord and his staff at the Admiralty, began the process of assembling the largest ever convoy to Malta and the most heavily escorted Allied convoy of the war. Finding suitable merchant ships was, as ever, no easy matter, especially since speed would be a key factor if it were to succeed. Losses of merchant ships in the North Atlantic and Mediterranean were enormous and had proved a considerable drain. But eventually twelve large merchantmen capable of the required fifteen knots were ear-marked for the operation, and began assembling at Glasgow, Liverpool and Bristol. All these ships were to be given the same cargoes – fuel, ammunition, food, mechanical spares, and medical supplies in crates and carboys – and divided between each of the ship's holds, so that a proportion of each of the supplies would get through even if one or more of the ships was sunk. Unfortunately, these vessels did not have holds suitable for carrying fuel and so it had to be loaded in four-gallon cans. Some of the ships even had these cans stashed away on the decks.

This would not be enough, however, and to supply the Island with anything like the amount of fuel needed the convoy *had* to have an oil tanker among its number. The problem was that the British merchant fleet no longer had any oil tankers left that were of sufficient size or speed. Only the Americans had such ships, and they were needed by the US Navy. Fortunately for the future of Allied operations in the Mediterranean, someone in the Ministry of War Transport had already foreseen this problem and had asked the head of the British Merchant Shipping Mission in Washington to see if he could 'borrow' any American tankers that might fit the bill. Although there was consider-able opposition to the request, the United States Maritime Commission had generously allocated two such tankers for use by the British. One had been the *Kentucky*, sunk during the June convoy; the other was the *Ohio*, built in 1940 for the Texaco Oil Company. This was to be the operation's only tanker. With her rode the hopes of Malta's fuel-starved forces. A fourteenth ship – another American vessel – was added to the fleet at the end of July, and so began the process of adding anti-aircraft guns, loading and preparation for the task ahead.

'A Life on the Ocean Wave' was the final march played at Freddie Treves' passing-out parade at the Nautical College, Pangbourne, in

Berkshire. Four days later, he was standing on the quayside of Number Two, Victoria Dock in Birkenhead gazing up at the pride of the Shaw, Saville & Albion Line, the merchant vessel *Waimarama*. Freddie was seventeen years and four months old. Officially, he was to be a junior officer on the ship, although as Cadet Treves it was a shock to suddenly find himself a lowly apprentice on a large ocean-going ship after being top dog and Head of House at Pangbourne Nautical College.

Having been shown around the ship, Freddie watched the loading: torpedoes, high-octane fuel, machine-guns, larger guns, grain and other food. An air raid occurred while they were loading. Freddie had never seen people move so fast in all his life, but he was stuck in the ship and had to stay where he was — an alarming taste of things to come.

He'd been told little about the forthcoming voyage, but he had noticed crates stamped with 'Malta' on them. 'Doesn't mean a thing,' one of the other apprentices told him. 'Probably a trick to fool the Jerries. We'll probably end up in Russia.'[4] Whatever their destination, Freddie was at war now, and something niggling at the back of his mind warned him he was in for a torrid time.

Joe McCarthy was Third Engineer on the SS *Rochester Castle*. He'd not been on a convoy before, as the *Rochester Castle* tended to sail alone, usually on runs down to the Argentine to bring back meat; but she'd been called up to the Clyde because of her comparative speed. Despite the supposed secrecy of such convoys, they all knew they were headed for Malta — he, too, had seen crates and carboys loaded on to the ship stamped with their destination. On leave before the trip, he even told his father that was where he was being sent next. He was excited about it too — the war was nearly three years old now and he still hadn't seen any action. 'It sounds stupid, I know,' he says, 'but I really wanted to see just something of the war.'

It very nearly didn't happen. Carboys of sulphuric acid were being lowered on to the deck when one broke and a fire started. All the fuel and ammunition had already been lowered, so there was a rush to extinguish the flames as quickly as possible before the whole ship blew up.

Born in Wigan in 1915, during the first Zeppelin air raid on the Wigan Coal and Iron Company, Joe had left school at fourteen for an apprenticeship making diesel motor lorries and mining machinery. He was good with his hands, and enjoyed working with engines; and, as most of those he worked on were exported, he would often go to the Liverpool docks to see them loaded up for shipment. Life on the sea appealed – by joining a ship he could see the world and still work on engines – and so he wrote to Union Castle and was given an engineer's job on the *Cape Town Castle*, a mail boat. Once war had broken out, Joe's ships took to ferrying not just mail but anything they were asked, from meat to men.

Now loading up on the banks of the Clyde, he knew he was bound to see some action, for the assembling ships further up the river had already come under fire. And had he been in any doubt, the amount of guns being bolted on to *Rochester Castle's* decks was enough to tell him they were in for a rough ride.

Also on the Clyde was the destroyer, HMS *Ashanti*, preparing for her role escorting the merchantmen. The naval escort was to be split into two: Force Z under Vice-Admiral Syfret in his flagship – the battleship *Nelson* – was to provide heavy gun cover and air support from the four aircraft carriers. They would only accompany the convoy as far as the Sicilian Narrows, at which point they would need to return to Gibraltar to refuel. The remaining escort was Force X, comprised of cruisers and destroyers, which would accompany the convoy all the way to Malta. *Ashanti* would, all being well, go the whole distance.

On board was Fred Jewett, an Able Seaman who was part of the ship's gunnery team. Now nineteen, he'd entered the Navy as a boy sailor and been sent to join the crew of the cruiser HMS *Phoebe*. He'd been a First Class Boy back then, the lowest of the low in the Royal Navy. In those two years he certainly saw some action, and had his fair share of luck. Once, after bombarding the Norwegian coast, the cruiser was sent back to England to rearm and refuel. While reloading, Fred was accidentally hit by a crate of ammunition and was sent to hospital in Glasgow. *Phoebe* sailed without him. Shortly afterwards, a torpedo struck the Boys' Mess, killing many of Fred's old shipmates. In the meantime, he'd been posted to *Ashanti*, a destroyer made up entirely of professional rather than volunteer sailors. Most of their work had been escorting the Arctic convoys, an unforgiving task. 'If your ship sank up there you had about four or five minutes to live,' says Fred. He'd watched plenty of men drown in those freezing waters.

Now, it seemed, they were heading for the Mediterranean and Malta – at least that was the rumour filtering around the crew. Apparently the

Island had been having a tough time, and this convoy was of major importance – death or glory, they were saying. He didn't feel particularly afraid. 'I was so hardened by wartime conditions and discipline,' says Fred, 'that I didn't really feel any fear.' He also had enormous confidence in the men of his ship, and was proud to be serving on *Ashanti*. They were a bunch of crack sailors, and they would see this convoy safely through. He was certain of that.

Throughout July, Lloyd and then Park had been losing Spitfires at a rate of around sixteen or seventeen a week. Because of the improved Air Sea Rescue service, nothing like that number of pilots had lost their lives, but it did mean the Island needed regular supplies of more Spitfires – as Tedder had advocated back in April. Churchill and the Chiefs of Staff had been true to their word: 59 had arrived in June and the same again in July. Now, as part of Operation Pedestal, a further 38 were due to be launched from HMS *Furious* as the convoy entered the Western Mediterranean, and then a week later it would return for another fly-off of 32.

One of those singled out for the first batch was a 21-year-old American named Art Roscoe. He was born in Chicago, but his parents had separated and his mother remarried. At the age of thirteen, he had moved with his mother and older sister to California. He'd been captivated by flying at an early age. Down the road from where he lived there was a bakery run by a German émigré who had been a fighter pilot in the First World War. Behind the counter was a picture of the aircraft he had flown, a Fokker D.VII biplane. Art had read a number of novels about the fighter aces and was somewhat in awe of this ex-pilot baker, and so decided he would make a replica model of his plane. It took him six months. Painstakingly, he carved the wood and sanded it down, making it as detailed as he possibly could. He even painted on the exact same colours and markings. Then he took it to the German shopkeeper. 'Here,' said Art. 'I made this for you.' The German was stunned. How much did Art want for it? 'Nothing,' he replied. It was a gift. 'Then you must have all the money in this till,' he told him. No, Art insisted, he didn't want any money. The German had never known such a kind gesture. 'Then at least have as much candy as you want in return.' Art accepted the offer. 'I wasn't going to turn down free candy,' he says.

Art began hanging out at the nearby airfield, the Los Angeles Metropolitan, washing planes, sweeping up and taking on any other chores that needed doing in return for flying time. He soloed at sixteen, and spent as much time as he possibly could at the airfield. After high school, he joined the aircraft manufacturer, Lockheed. He was now living and breathing aeroplanes, and he and two friends bought a small plane of their own. Working for Lockheed was all very well, but what he really wanted to do was fly professionally, and so applied to the Military Academy at West Point. He was turned down flat – a slight astigmatism in one eye meant he failed the medical; his flying experience counted for nothing.

Then he heard about the Clayton Knight Committee, who were screening young pilots like himself and helping them to join the Royal Air Force. Britain's war might not have been his, but the prospect of flying big powerful aircraft like the Hurricane and Spitfire with engines of over 1,000 horsepower was too great an opportunity to miss; in California 225 hp was about as big a plane as he was ever going to fly. With his mother working and his father out of the picture, Art had no parental opposition and so immediately applied, turning up for an interview at the Hollywood Roosevelt Hotel. Successfully screened, soon afterwards he found himself on a ship heading to England.

After completing his training, he joined 71 Squadron at North Weald in Essex, flying Spitfires. This had been the first of the American – or 'Eagle' – squadrons, commissioned on 19 September 1940. As with most fighter pilots prior to reaching Malta, Art spent most of his time carrying out large formation fighter sweeps over France. He'd acclimatized to life in England pretty quickly. It had been cold when he'd first arrived in February 1941, but he'd been 'too damn excited' to worry about that.

Art had volunteered for this new overseas posting. Word had got out that the Eagle squadrons were going to be transferred over to the US Army Air Force, and he was pretty sure they'd give him a medical then throw him out because he didn't have twenty:twenty vision. And he didn't want that: he wanted to keep on flying. Initially, he had no idea where he was headed, but turned up to Greenock in the Clyde and reported to HMS *Furious*, a former First World War cruiser converted into an aircraft carrier. It had never been used for flying off Spitfires and had a particularly short flight deck. Compared with the mighty USS *Wasp*, it was positively antique. Nonetheless a practice flight was successfully carried out and so Art shrugged to himself and supposed all would be well.

★

The early stages of the convoy's journey proceeded without incident. Art Roscoe thought it was like being on an ocean cruise. What *Furious* lacked in terms of state-of-the-art facilities it more than made up for with its food — freshly baked bread, real butter and plenty to drink. He and his fellow pilots put on their tropical kit and laughed at one another's white knees.

Freddie Treves, on board the *Waimarama*, was given an action station under the fo'c'sle, towards the prow of the ship. He was officer in charge of the Forward Fire Fighting Party, with a crew of one man, Able Seaman Bowdory, aged sixty. Both Bowdory's sons had joined up, and, deciding he could not sit back and let them fight without doing anything himself, had joined the merchant navy. Although he was the youngest person on the ship commanding the oldest, Freddie soon made friends with his avuncular charge.

By Sunday 9 August, the entire convoy had assembled and before turning towards the Mediterranean a final exercise was carried out with the whole fleet practising emergency turns and responding to simulated air attacks. Freddie had never seen anything like it. The whole sea seemed to be covered with ships. He looked at the four aircraft carriers and the huge battleships, *Nelson* and *Rodney*; the cruisers, *Sirius*, *Nigeria*, *Charybdis*, *Manchester*, *Kenya*, *Cairo* and Fred Jewett's old ship, *Phoebe*; and the destroyers: 32 in all, plus the accompanying oilers and corvettes. A mighty fleet indeed. It was hard to believe he was now a part of all this, and that he'd still been at school just a few weeks before.

That night, Freddie was out on deck. The whole fleet was blacked out, but drifting out from the cabin near the chart house he could hear Tchaikovsky's Second Piano Concerto and the calm orders from the bridge: 'Steady as she goes, steering 096 degrees, 74 revolutions.'

On the night of 9–10 August, they sailed past the narrows of Gibraltar and into the Mediterranean, travelling slowly so that *Ashanti* and the other destroyers would have a chance to enter port and quickly refuel before rejoining the fleet for the rest of the voyage.

Freddie Treves was on watch on the bridge when suddenly he saw a string of lights across the front of the convoy. It was a Spanish fishing fleet. Observer planes had been spotted earlier in the day, and now the Spanish had seen them. Although neutral, they were fascist, and Freddie realized this information would be sent straight to Berlin. Throughout the whole of the 10th, however, the sun burnt down without a single enemy submarine or aircraft in sight. Neither Freddie nor Joe McCarthy knew what to expect, but for the more experienced, this period of calm, waiting for the inevitable attack, was stretching fragile nerves.

While the waters were warmer than those of the Atlantic, there were a number of disadvantages for convoys sailing through the Mediterranean. It was a much smaller stretch of sea and thus a much harder one in which to hide. In the middle of the Atlantic, thousands of miles from aeroplane range, and with only U-boats to contend with – however dangerous that may have been – it was possible for convoys to slip through the net. In the Mediterranean, where the Allies were sur-rounded by enemy forces, ships faced attack from all directions and from above and below. In fact, the Axis had already received intelligence of the convoy and had amassed an enormous force of planes, ships and U-boats to ensure not a single ship made it through. Along the route were 659 front-line aircraft, six cruisers, fifteen destroyers, nineteen E-boats, sixteen Italian and three German U-boats. It was in fact an Italian spy in Spanish Morocco, rather than the Spanish fishermen, who confirmed the moment the convoy entered the Mediterranean.

'A beautiful day,' one of the other sailors called out to Freddie Treves. 'Costs money in peacetime and here we are for nothing!' Freddie laughed and waved back.

CHAPTER 18

Pedestal

WHEN THE ATTACK came, it sent shock-waves through the entire convoy. On 11 August at 1.15 p.m., the aircraft carrier HMS *Eagle* was hit by four torpedoes from a German U-boat south of the Balearic Islands. *Eagle* was a vast ship, yet in a matter of minutes the massive hull was on its side and about to sink from sight for ever. As an engineer, Joe McCarthy spent most of his days on the *Rochester Castle* below decks in the engine room, but had been taking a break on deck when the *Eagle* was hit, and watched in amazement as the ship turned over. Men were sliding down the side of the flight deck along with the Sea Hurricanes, their screams carrying across the water. 'It was a terrible sight,' says Joe. 'Not just the men being killed, but we had been depending on those Hurricanes for protection. And if they'd got the *Eagle* as easy as that, we all knew the rest of us stood little chance.' He looked out at the rest of the convoy — ships seemed to stretch as far as the eye could see, spaced out a quarter of a mile apart on the calm blue waters of the Mediterranean Sea — and realized they were sitting ducks.

Fred Jewett's action station on HMS *Ashanti* was on the bridge, just a few yards from the Captain. With a radio and head-set, it was his job to relay the orders from the Captain to the Gunnery Officers. This also meant he had a grandstand view of all that was going on, and he too had seen the *Eagle* go down. 'An almighty big aircraft carrier was there one minute and then she was gone. I could hardly believe my eyes.' He also picked up some of the frantic calls from the pilots on the SRE

(Ship's Radio Equipment) – some of whom had just taken off and others who had been in their planes when the ship was hit.

Freddie Treves, on board the *Waimarama*, felt absolutely sickened. He'd watched the flight deck alive with the distant dots of men sliding, jumping and falling into the water, and heard their screams across the calm sea. 'I felt numb with horror,' he says. The whole fleet immediately turned ninety degrees, while destroyers dashed about dropping depth charges.

Another who watched the *Eagle* sink was Flying Officer Art Roscoe. He was on deck about to lead the fourth flight off the *Furious. Eagle* was sailing a parallel course to his left and Art was watching her aircraft flying off on an anti-submarine patrol. Then suddenly four towering spurts of water burst into the air – clearly it had been hit. It was time for him to take off. With his engine already running, he was flagged off. As he sped off the bow, he watched in horror as the white wake of a torpedo passed directly underneath him, barely missing the *Furious.* 'I could see the damn thing – it was just creaming along,' says Art. 'Clearly there was a submarine out there somewhere. I was glad to get off that ship. There might have been a couple more coming.' Circling over the *Furious*, he told his group to get a move on and join him. It was still 680 miles to Malta, and Art wanted to get there just as soon as he could.

Eagle was the first casualty of Operation Pedestal, going down in eight minutes along with 163 of her crew. She would not be the last.

Later that evening, Axis aircraft caught up with the convoy, but although there were a number of near misses, no other ship was sunk that day. But all the while the convoy was inching closer to the Sicilian Narrows. By the morning of the 12th, they were south of Sardinia and north of Tunisia and within easy reach of a whole host of Axis airfields. Attacks arrived throughout the day. *Deucalion* was the first merchant vessel to be hit, straddled by a four-bomb stick from some Junkers 88s at 1 p.m. This was her second Malta convoy run, and although she had survived the first, this time she was not to be so fortunate. Three bombs narrowly missed, but the fourth hit, seriously disabling her.

The destroyer *Bramham* was immediately sent to her rescue. On board was Sub-Lieutenant Ted Fawcett, one of two Gunnery Control Officers. Aged 22, he had joined the Royal Navy Volunteer Reserve (RNVR) just before the outbreak of war. At the time, he had been working as an apprentice in the family firm of accountants in Glasgow, but his father had been a lieutenant-commander in the Navy in the last war and Ted was determined to follow in his footsteps, particularly as he loathed accountancy. Initially joining as an ordinary seaman, he later became a cadet rating and was eventually commissioned. He joined *Bramham* at the end of 1941.

As Gunnery Control Officer, it was his job to decide where the ship's guns should be aimed. Operating from the Gunnery Director behind the bridge, he had to assess the speed and direction of the enemy vessel or aircraft, and so where the guns should be pointed. This was no easy task and usually the first broadside – all guns firing together – would be off the mark. By watching where the shells exploded in relation to the target, he would make adjustments, until, all being well, he got it right.

By the time they reached *Deucalion*, the merchantman was still picking up those among her crew who thought she'd been mortally hit and had jumped overboard. When they finally got under way again, the stricken vessel could only manage eight knots and they were way behind the rest of the convoy.

They were attacked again at around 7.45 p.m. – the Luftwaffe was showing no mercy. As two Junkers 88s swooped in low to attack, *Bramham*'s guns began firing furiously. Training guns on to aircraft was especially difficult because they were considerably more manœuvrable than surface vessels. 'To hit an aircraft was really a matter of luck,' says Ted Fawcett, 'although a torpedo-bomber had to fly straight and level at some point during its run-in, so then one might score a hit.' Even if the guns continually missed, their barrage probably put the bombers off their stride.

Both guns and bombers missed their targets on that occasion, but just after 9 p.m., two Heinkel bombers attacked again, this time with complete surprise. Having cut their engines, they glided out of the dusk and struck *Deucalion* with two torpedoes. Unable to save the ship, *Bramham* circled until all the survivors had been rescued. By the time they sailed on their way, the merchant vessel was low in the water, the sea sweeping over her decks. The destroyer made off at full speed and not long afterwards they all heard a loud explosion – it was the end of *Deucalion* and her cargo.

Meanwhile the rest of the convoy had been suffering the heaviest aerial attacks of the day. Freddie Treves on the *Waimarama* watched as Stuka dive-bombers flew towards them out of the sinking sun. These were the first he'd ever seen. 'It was absolutely petrifying, like a Banshee from Hell,' he recalls. Peeling off one after another, they singled out a second aircraft carrier, HMS *Indomitable*, for attack. Sensibly, the German bombers were aiming to neutralize the convoy's fighter protection first. Despite a ferocious response from the Royal Navy escort and the newly armed merchantmen, there were three direct hits on the ship. Freddie watched part of the deck collapse and fires burst out. One of the strikes hit the twin turrets just forward of the bridge, killing everyone in sight.

By now they were facing attack from above and below, as they were sailing through the enemy submarine patrol zones. The U-boats had been lying in wait. Joe McCarthy was briefly up on deck on the *Rochester Castle* when he saw the battle cruisers HMS *Cairo* and HMS *Nigeria* sustain torpedo hits.

Ohio, the former Texaco Oil Company tanker, was also struck. A torpedo smashed into her alongside the pump room, causing an explosion upwards that ripped open a large section of her decks. A huge column of flame shot into the sky as part of her cargo ignited. There was chaos in the pump-room and her steering gear was damaged. All the crew expected her to blow up at any second and were preparing to abandon ship when the Captain told them to hold firm. Immediately stopping her engines, the men then set about trying to put out the fire. Ironically, it was the hole in her side, 27 by 24 feet wide, which saved her — sea-water rushed in and helped quench the flames. An hour after she'd been hit, the flames were brought under control and she steamed ahead once more.

At this point, the heavy escort, Force Z — which included the remaining aircraft carriers — left the fray and began the trip back to Gibraltar, leaving the convoy without any fighter protection. Of the remaining force, two of its cruisers were now out of action: *Cairo* had to be scuppered, and *Nigeria*, the flagship of Force X, had to return to Gibraltar. Rear-Admiral Burroughs, the commander of Force X, then transferred his flag to Fred Jewett's ship HMS *Ashanti*, no easy task as *Nigeria's* rudder was jammed and she was going round in circles with the destroyer following after her on the outside.

Beyond the range of fighter protection from Malta, the convoy was now at its most vulnerable, especially since the evening attacks had caused the fleet to become quite spread out. Wave after wave of enemy bombers were arriving, but although they now had few heavy naval guns to call upon, both escort and merchantmen could still send up a considerable anti-aircraft barrage. The noise of the ongoing battle was so deafening, Joe McCarthy could hear it from the depths of the engine room of *Rochester Castle*, where he was still desperately trying to ensure the ship continued to steam at fourteen knots. During the day, the sky had been mottled with puffs of black flak from the ships, and shards of shrapnel and sea-spray rained down across the decks. Occasionally an aircraft would plummet from the sky trailing fire and black smoke. Now, with the light fading, the sky was lit up with hundreds of orange flashes and massed lines of criss-crossing tracer.

Freddie Treves watched two merchantmen ahead of them, *Empire Hope* and *Clan Ferguson*, go down. *Clan Ferguson* was hit with a massive explosion and it seemed impossible to think anyone could have survived. A sheet of flame leapt into the air, brilliantly bright in the fading light. Men were burning alive on deck as the ship slithered deeper into the water. Moments later she had gone, leaving behind a ring of flame on the surface and a mountain of smoke streaming high into the air. Miraculously, though, some sixty crew were picked up.

By 11 p.m., Freddie was sitting huddled under the fo'c'sle, frightened out of his wits and unable to stop shaking. He'd brought a buoyancy suit with him and had at last overcome his shyness about putting it on. He'd initially feared he'd be laughed at, but now found himself envied. Three merchant ships had been sunk and two more damaged, and Freddie had seen much of it. Thinking Bowdory was asleep, he began to pray. But his companion was still awake. 'I'd pray too,' Bowdory told him, 'but can't get down on my knees – old age.'

As though in some hellish survival game, the rest of the convoy had passed through the U-boat zone only to creep round the headland of Cape Bon into the E-boat zone just before midnight on the 12th. With the lighthouse from Kelibia at Cape Bon in Tunisia guiding them, these fast motor-torpedo boats wasted no time. It was a dark night, but suddenly motor launches were heard rapidly surging towards the Allied armada, and the sky lit up with tracer and fire and explosions. On board *Bramham*, Ted Fawcett missed the ensuing carnage – they were still some distance behind – but he could certainly see Dante's inferno raging ahead of him and was glad he was out of it.

Joe McCarthy, on *Rochester Castle*, was lying exhausted on his bunk, still in his oily boilersuit, when he heard a massive explosion and was thrown right into the air. A torpedo from an E-boat had struck the Number Three hold ahead of the engine-room bulkhead. Each hold was separated by a thick iron wall – the bulkhead – that spanned the cross-section of the ship, so although Number Three hold was flooded, the ship was still able to continue at thirteen knots. Joe was soon back in the engine room, desperately trying to help keep up the speed of the engine.

In the same attack, a fourth merchant ship – *Glenorchy* – was sunk, and the cruiser HMS *Manchester* hit, almost at point-blank range, by two torpedoes. The engine-room flooded and the ship stopped dead in its tracks. Fred Jewett saw it happen. 'What people don't realize is that the engine-room doesn't just propel the ship forward, it also provides power for everything else – lighting, heavy guns and so on. With her engine-room out of action she was as good as useless.' The *Manchester* had been hit the previous year, and on that occasion her crew had managed to get her going again and to limp back to Gibraltar. After the best part of an hour, it became clear there would be no repeat performance. The Captain ordered them to abandon ship and, not wishing to leave her for the Axis forces to drag into port at a later stage, scuttled her.[1]

The E-boats may have suffered their most humiliating defeat during their attack on Grand Harbour just over a year before, but they certainly had their revenge that night. In all, four merchantmen were sunk, the biggest loss ever in the Mediterranean from one attack: *Glenorchy*, *Wairangi*, *Almeria Lykes* and *Santa Elisa*. HMS *Bramham* reached the battle scene just before dawn and in time to pick up many of the survivors of the *Santa Elisa*. As the junior officer, Ted Fawcett was given the task of saving as many men as he could. With a crew of five, he was lowered over the side of the destroyer in their whaler, a 22-foot rowing boat, since there was neither time nor enough light to use the side netting. The *Santa Elisa* had been an American ship and, unlike the *Ohio*, had kept her American crew. Most of the survivors were wearing life-jackets with lights on, so Ted found them quite easily. The E-boats and aircraft had now gone and there was an eerie quiet across the sea, broken only by shouts for help and whistle blasts to attract attention. Ted couldn't help feeling anxious – he could no longer see *Bramham*. Then, having picked up over thirty men, to his great relief he spotted his ship once more. Having disembarked the first bunch of survivors, however, he was told to go and find some more. By the time his whaler was full again, first light was creeping over the Mediterranean. Soon the

Axis bombers would be back. Ted was glad to finally get back on board his ship.

When Joe McCarthy staggered on to deck the following morning he could barely believe the sight that confronted him. Two days before they had been a massive armada, the sea full of Allied ships in every direction. Now, all he could see were four other merchant ships all in a line behind them and a handful of destroyers – and they were still 85 miles from Malta.

A sixth surviving merchant ship was the *Dorset*, whose captain had taken her on a more northerly route. She was attacked and had to be abandoned later that morning. The seventh was the *Brisbane Star*. Struck by a torpedo around 9 p.m. the previous night, she was left with a large jagged hole through her bow. Because of this, she could no longer keep up, and so Captain Riley, her skipper, decided to leave the rest of the convoy and take her down the edge of the African coast in the hope that it might offer a bit of protection.

By the next morning the ship was off the Vichy-controlled Tunisian coast and was ordered into harbour – orders which Riley ignored until a warning shot was fired across the bow. Alone, and near the enemy coast, they were in a precarious position, so Riley stopped the engines while a French launch came out to meet them. Somehow, the captain managed to talk his way out of trouble and the *Brisbane Star* continued on her own towards Malta.

Joe McCarthy was still on deck when the klaxons around the ship rang out their warning. That was his signal to hurry back down to the engine room, but in no time the bombers had reached them and the ear-splitting artillery barrage began. He watched as two Junkers 88s dived in low towards the *Waimarama*, the ship directly behind them. The first scored a direct hit on the deck cargo of tinned petrol, causing a massive explosion. 'It was incredible,' says Joe. 'The fire-ball was so intense and sudden, the second bomber was blown up mid-air from the blast.'

Having finished picking up survivors, *Bramham* was catching up with the rest of the convoy when *Waimarama* was hit. Ted Fawcett watched the fireball with a sickening sense of horror. Surely, he thought, no one could possibly survive such a holocaust.

Freddie Treves had been with Bowdory at their action stations on the fo'c'sle when the ship was hit. Fortunately there was no fuel nearby and he was blown through a doorway in the bulkhead and on to a bag of lime, with Bowdory landing on top of him. He felt very numb and thought he was going to die, and strangely, despite his earlier fear, didn't care. Then the feeling came back into his body. Bowdory lifted himself up and ran out on to the deck and Freddie followed. Through thick brown smoke he looked up at the bridge – it was listing badly to starboard, and then Freddie remembered a premonition he'd experienced the previous evening: the ship had also been listing then, but to port. He rushed over to the port side and looked down at the clear water and hesitated for a moment, wondering whether to jump. Then the ship groaned and sank further and Freddie dived, head-first, still in his buoyancy suit and tin helmet. Smacking the water, he swam away as fast as he could.

Eventually, he paused to catch his breath. He was surrounded by debris and could hear the cries of panic-stricken men drowning. More planes roared overhead machine-gunning the water. The *Waimarama* was sinking, although the flames were still billowing upwards and the smoke rising in a dark column high, high into the sky.

Then he saw Bowdory. His friend couldn't swim and was standing on a raft, silhouetted against the huge flames burning on the surface of the water, his arms outstretched, pleading for help. Freddie wanted to save him, wanted to haul him out from the carnage, but there was nothing he could do. The suction from the sinking ship was pulling the raft closer to the flames; Freddie could feel it pulling him too. As Bowdory fell into the fire, he screamed. Freddie watched his friend – this kindly old man – burn to death. 'It has haunted me ever since,' he says.

But there were others whom he could help. Another man was in trouble nearby. John Jackson, the Third Radio Officer, had been chatting to a colleague in the chart room as the bombers had approached. When they heard the aircraft they started to move towards the port-side bridge, just before the explosion. As his companion went out on to the bridge from the chart room, Jackson stepped back and suddenly a wall of flame separated them.

Recovering quickly from the initial blast, and coughing and choking through the thick smoke, he'd jumped straight overboard; he'd already been wearing his life jacket. But having never learnt to swim – like so many sailors – he hated being in water and began to think he might drown, or even burn to death in the flaming oil on the sea's surface.

Then Freddie Treves spotted him struggling in the water, and swam over, telling him to keep calm and to allow himself to be paddled away. Fortunately there was a great deal of debris floating about, so once they were safely away from the flames, Freddie grabbed hold of a bit of spar for Jackson to hold on to.

Freddie had been very lucky. He should have dived over the side nearest the water, but his strange premonition had made him do otherwise. The wind had also suddenly changed, blowing the flames away from him. The destroyer HMS *Ledbury* tried to close in towards the survivors, but the Germans were attacking her. The Captain, Roger Hill, was shouting to the men in the water through a loud hailer, telling them he would be back but had to try to shake off the German air attack first. The Captain was as good as his word; shortly afterwards, a junior officer approached them in a small wooden boat and Freddie and Jackson were hauled aboard, then later taken on to the *Ledbury*. Having been pulled out of his buoyancy suit — which had not worked and was heavy with water — Freddie went up to the bridge, and there the enormity of what had happened to him began to sink in. Nearly all his comrades had been killed — only nineteen out of 109 had survived. He crouched down and shook. Had he been on dry land, he would have been whisked away and taken to hospital, well out of the firing line. But there was no let-up in the attacks, and the *Ledbury*, part of the close escort for the convoy, was very likely to be hit too. At any moment, Freddie might have to relive his experiences on the *Waimarama* all over again. He felt absolutely petrified.

After watching the *Waimarama* go down, Joe McCarthy decided to keep wearing both his tin hat and life jacket at all times. He began to think he would probably die. Although scared, he wasn't really worrying about death — rather he thought about his mother and how upset she would be.

The *Ohio* was singled out again, this time by the Stukas. The *Ashanti* had drawn up alongside her, and from the bridge Fred Jewett could see the dive-bombers swooping down over her, coming in from all directions. 'We were about a hundred yards away from her and trying to put up an umbrella barrage above her,' he recalls. *Ashanti*'s gunners were firing away madly, Fred relaying the skipper's orders through the colossal din, when they hit one of the Stukas. It was still screaming as it hit the water — but then it bounced off again, like a skimming pebble and landed right on the deck of *Ohio* in a shower of flames. By a miracle, the tanker did not explode, although because of the blast and two further near misses, her boiler fires went out and she stopped dead in the water.

On Malta, the progress of the convoy had been followed closely and with mounting despair. In the Operations Room at Lascaris, Christina Ratcliffe was nervously watching the plotting table and listening to the controller. Recently promoted, she was assistant to Woodhall's Number Two, the 'Op's B', and so was working up on the shelf with the rest of the controlling team. On the morning of the 12th she had not been on duty, but had gone into work anyway, unable to sit at home while such momentous events were unfolding out at sea. Many others had obviously felt the same way, because the place was heaving with people anxious to know how the convoy was faring. Although tobacco was another commodity in short supply, almost everyone seemed to be smoking 'V' For Victory cigarettes that day, and the cavern was thick with the smell of smoke and sweat and soap-starved khaki.

Suddenly a large brown paper parcel dropped in front of her, and she looked round to see a tall, tanned, blond-haired man standing behind her. Warby. He was back.

Not only was he back, he was now a squadron leader and CO of 69 Squadron. Before coming to see Christina, he'd already taken a Spitfire over Taranto to take pictures of the Italian Fleet preparing to leave harbour. 'See you at six at Captain Caruana's,' he whispered to her, then slipped away again.[2]

The parcel had been a gift from an old Malta girlfriend, now in Cairo, and passed on to Warby before he flew back. It was a survival kit of goodies: toothpaste, soap, a facecloth, a jar of cold cream, several bundles of hair curlers and a comb. There was also a box of face powder, lipstick and a small bottle of Coty's *L'Aimant* scent. Christina was thrilled – such luxuries belonged to a distant and bygone age. The package was a treat that outclassed any Christmas stocking.

Later, as planned, she met Warby at Captain Caruana's. It was one of the few bars that had any drink left. She'd been hoping for his return ever since he'd left five months before, and now here he was, looking fit and well – which was more than she could say for herself. Like everyone on the Island, she'd lost weight. Feeling her ribs, Warby whistled. 'My word, you are thin. We'll have to do something about this. Can't have you dropping down the plughole,' and so he suggested they see his old friend Tony who ran Monico's nightclub and the recently acquired Mayfair Hotel.[3]

Christina could barely believe her eyes when they walked into the Mayfair a short while later – she'd never been there before, nor even knew of its existence, but the restaurant was heaving, and waiters were rushing by with plates of food. Ushered to Tony's private table, they were then plied with large bowls of rabbit spaghetti, cheese and biscuits and coffee, and even Players cigarettes, stamped with 'HM Ships Only'. She'd tried to keep off rabbit, having heard that at the Victory Kitchens 'rabbit' was often a euphemism for 'cat', but that night the spaghetti tasted delicious. It was typical of Warby, after months away, to find on a besieged island a meal fit to celebrate their reunion.

But while Christina and Warby were tucking into their cheese and biscuits, Park and Vice-Admiral Leatham were planning an elaborate game of bluff with the Italian navy, which, as Warby's pictures had shown, was clearly heading to intercept the convoy, most likely at first light. Further reconnaissance had shown this to be the case, and so an ASV Wellington had been sent up by Park to track the Italian ships and to illuminate them every half-hour, an action designed to suggest a large air attack was on its way. A second Wellington also joined in and Fleet Air Arm Albacores were flown off to attack. Just before 2 a.m. on the 13th, the ruse finally seemed to be working. Shadowing aircraft reported that the fleet had now turned away from the convoy. Fully aware their radio traffic was being listened to, Woodhall and his controllers then began talking to non-existent Liberator bombers. The Italian fleet continued sailing back towards Italy.

The Albacores were then recalled, but Shrimp Simpson's submarines were lying in wait, and one, HMS/S *Unbroken*, struck two of the Italian cruisers with four torpedoes, immediately immobilizing them.

In fact, it wasn't just the bluff that had made the Italians turn back. Since they would be operating so close to Malta, the Italians had demanded air cover. Kesselring refused: his air forces were already fully occupied in attacking the convoy and in protecting their own shipping. On hearing of this decision, Mussolini personally ordered the fleet back to port. For the remaining merchant ships, at last coming into range of the Maltese Spitfires, this was a decisive moment.

★

Art Roscoe had arrived safely on Malta on the 11th and been posted to the former 1435 Flight, now given full squadron status. Because of the lack of fuel, he was given no familiarization flight and put on immediate readiness. By the 13th he was flying his first convoy patrol, alongside just one other pilot. When they found the convoy, it was already under attack from six Italian bombers. The two Spitfires dived just as the Italians were beginning their bomb run. All six scattered, dumping their bombs in the sea. Art's flight leader shot down one, while he managed to damage another. Their job well done, they flew back to Malta. Air cover made all the difference.

It was just as well, because the convoy was still in a bad way. *Rochester Castle* suffered a number of near misses that morning. Down in the engine room, Joe McCarthy heard the explosions continue around him, an experience he likened to being in a big metal tin that someone was whacking with a stick. The sound of bombs dropping either side of them clunked and reverberated around the iron hull. But even near misses caused their fair share of damage – shrapnel and other splinters riddled the sides. The decks were also covered with bits of shell and jagged metal embedded into the wood. Another near miss at around 10 a.m. had lifted her right out of the water and put her engines temporarily out of action. Fires had started and were spreading, so they had to flood one of the magazines. Her steering mechanism was also damaged. By the time she was fixed, she was 36 feet below the water-line at the front and 30 at the stern. There were leaks in every hold and in the engine room.

Incredibly, despite this damage, she continued to make good progress. With the Italian navy far away and with the Spitfires above, they were within sight of the Island by the afternoon, and the Malta escort force had come out to meet them. At 6.25 p.m. on the 13th, *Rochester Castle* was the first to reach Grand Harbour, followed shortly after by the *Port Chalmers* and *Melbourne Star*. Allowed above decks, Joe McCarthy was there to witness their reception. Happy and relieved to have survived, he watched the people lining the docks and Barraccas, cheering and waving flags; only then did he understand what their arrival meant to the Islanders. It was a sight he would never forget.

The following day, and completely unexpectedly, the *Brisbane Star* reached Malta. Captain Riley's lonely detour had paid off. Four out of fourteen had now safely reached port.

★

Meanwhile the remainder of the convoy was still struggling at sea. Earlier on the morning of the 13th, *Bramham* had been sent to the aid of the *Dorset*. Once more, Ted Fawcett had been lowered in the whaler to scoop up the survivors. The desperate search for his ship the previous night had been an unsettling experience, but at least now, in broad daylight, there was little chance of them losing each other. His captain was not so sure: as Ted was rowing away from the destroyer, the skipper leant over the edge with a megaphone and shouted, 'Ted, if you can't bloody well get alongside us this time you can take them back to Gibraltar on your own!'

It was not looking good for the *Ohio*, and her precious cargo of fuel. A large piece of her side was sticking out, which, when the destroyer *Penn* tried to tow her, acted like a rudder and turned her in circles. She was then attacked again, and another near miss caused even more damage. With the tanker looking almost certain to split apart and with her engines completely dead, it was decided to abandon ship.

The *Penn* circled the stricken tanker, waiting for further reinforcements. Then, despite her fragility, they could make another effort to move her. But miraculously, the *Ohio* did not sink. A large number of enemy aircraft arrived throughout the afternoon, but with a constant patrol of sixteen Spitfires protecting her, the tanker, although standing still in the water, was only hit once. This time, the bomb wrecked the engine room and the rudder. The crew, having gone back on board during another attempt in the afternoon to shift her, abandoned ship for a second time.

By evening, the Axis had pretty much called a halt to their attack on the convoy and were now concentrating on the returning force to Gibraltar. *Bramham*, having picked up the survivors of *Dorset*, was sent to search for the *Manchester*, but finding no trace of it, returned to the *Ohio* the following morning. *Ledbury* was also on hand to help.

Freddie Treves was still crouching on *Ledbury*'s bridge. He'd barely moved since boarding the destroyer, although on the first night he'd stayed with a badly burnt gunner from another ship, who'd mistakenly thought his ship had been hit and had dived overboard straight into some flames. The following morning the man had died and he was buried at sea in a canvas bag. Freddie then went back on to the bridge. Every time another attack appeared he hugged himself more tightly and prayed he might be spared. 'I was totally out of it,' he says now, 'completely paralyzed with fear.'

★

Another plan was hatched to get *Ohio* moving. They were going to try to straddle the tanker (i.e. attach a vessel to her on either side to keep her heading straight) and bring her in that way. But before they had done so, a final air attack appeared. Most of the planes were seen off, but one Stuka still managed to drop a 1,000-pound bomb dangerously close, jolting the tanker forward with its concussion and smashing another hole in her stern.

Everyone was now feeling pretty desperate. Then suddenly music drifted across the decks, gradually growing louder. It was the Glenn Miller number, 'Chattanooga Choo Choo'. Someone had picked it up on the radio and was broadcasting it through the Tannoy. Light and frivolous, it was just what the crew needed as they reached their lowest ebb.

With *Bramham* tied to one side, *Penn* to the other, and with *Ledbury* ahead to act as a rudder, the *Ohio* finally began to inch forward. Survivors from the other merchantmen volunteered to board her and man her remaining guns, while a number of minesweepers had arrived to help pave the way. Food on all four ships had become very short, so the crew of the *Ohio* raided the Christmas lockers and pulled out party hats, chocolate and rum.

Travelling at no more than walking pace, the final part of her journey was tantalizingly slow. 'There was no sudden arrival into Grand Harbour,' says Ted Fawcett. 'We seemed to be looking at the breakwaters for hours' – and expecting another air attack any moment. But by 8 a.m. on the 15th, they finally passed into the harbour. Although the *Ohio* was barely afloat, her precious cargo was saved. The band played and the bastions around Valletta were once more lined with crowds cheering, shouting and waving flags and hats. 'The relief was absolutely unbelievable,' says Ted. Watching the people waving and cheering was, he says, 'undoubtedly one of the greatest moments of my life.'

John Agius was one of the many waving a handkerchief on the Barraccas. He'd seen the *Ohio* at seven o'clock, just by the breakwater at the harbour entrance, and then, at nine, had rushed down again from the office, as excited as everyone else on the Island. Michael Montebello, down by the water's edge had watched all the ships arrive, but the biggest crowds had been waiting for the *Ohio*. 'There were so many people, you wouldn't have been able to put a needle between them,' he recalls. 'Everyone knew exactly what was on the *Ohio* and how important it was, more so than the other four.' For Meme Cortis, on duty at Imtarfa, the news came as an incredible relief. 'We were all so excited,' she said. 'Excited and happy – it was as though a miracle had occurred.'

George 'Screwball' Beurling, recovering from a particularly bad attack of Malta Dog, decided the time had come for a display of victory aerobatics and so flew his Spitfire upside down the length of Grand Harbour.

Anthony Kimmins, a naval war correspondent on board the *Ohio* (and who had been on patrol with *Upholder* the previous December), wrote in the *Times of Malta*, 'If ever there was an example of dogged perseverance against all odds, this was it. Any one of those hundreds of bombs in the right place and she would have gone up in a sheet of flame.'[4]

But she didn't, something that says much for American shipbuilding. The Maltese preferred to think of it as a miracle, but then again, to them, God had always been on their side. As it happened, 15 August was one of the Island's most important feast days – the Feast of Santa Maria. Clearly, an act of providence had allowed the Santa Maria Convoy to fight its way through. The safe arrival of these five ships caused widespread celebration on the Island. Malta had not been forgotten.[5]

Of the five merchant ships that reached Malta, *Port Chalmers* was the only one not to sustain any significant damage. Nor was the destroyer *Ashanti* hit – Fred Jewett's confidence had been well-founded. But nine of the fourteen merchantmen and four Royal Navy ships had been sunk, and most damaged one way or another, with terrible loss of life. Crucially, however, 55,000 tonnes of supplies had been safely delivered – enough to set back the Target Date another couple of months. And Air Vice-Marshal Keith Park now had plenty of fuel for his Spitfires, Beauforts and Wellingtons.

It was time to take the fight to the enemy.

PART VI

Malta's Triumph

'Malta has the lives of many thousands of German and Italian soldiers on its conscience.'

FIELD MARSHAL ERWIN ROMMEL

CHAPTER 19

Fightback and the Final Blitz
SEPTEMBER–OCTOBER 1942

TWO WEEKS AFTER Operation Pedestal was over, a lone Bristol Beaufort torpedo-bomber was flying low over the Mediterranean on its way to Malta. The crew of four had only just finished their training and on the morning of 17 August had flown off from Portreath in Cornwall – Raoul Daddo-Langlois's old airfield – to Gibraltar in a brand-new Mark II machine. There had been a few hitches on the way: as they neared the north coast of Spain, they flew over thick cloud and then discovered their ASV – Air-to-Surface Vessel radar – set was faulty. The idea was to skirt round the edge of Spain and Portugal, then drop into Gibraltar, but they couldn't see whether they were over land or sea. Then through a brief gap in the cloud they saw they were above land, probably Portugal, so they turned due west towards the Atlantic. After a few minutes, the pilot decided to descend through cloud, something that was strictly forbidden, so they could quickly get their bearings. Breaking into the clear at about 800 feet, they realized Lisbon and the Tagus Valley – with its high mountains on either side – was just a few miles behind them. Pure chance had saved them from crashing into one of those peaks. Having breathed a collective sigh of relief, they then found Gibraltar without any further problems, except that as they were about to land, they discovered the hydraulics on the undercarriage were also faulty and so had to furiously hand-pump the wheels down instead. All in all, it had been quite a nerve-wracking journey.

These faults had held them up for a week at Gibraltar, but now, finally, on 24 August, they were drawing close to Malta. With the deep blue sky and dazzling sun above them, there was thankfully no low cloud to worry about, only enemy aircraft; which was why they were flying just fifty feet above the sea, below the range of any Axis radar.

They were the four 'B's: the pilot, the Canadian Stan Balkwill; the two Wireless Operators/Air Gunners (WOP/AGs), Ronnie Brockett from Luton and Bob Buckley from Durham; and the navigator/ observer, Fraser Carlisle-Brown, a 22-year-old from Wembley, in North London. Fraser had originally joined the Army, before the outbreak of war. He'd previously hoped to be taken in by the RAF, having always enjoyed the annual Hendon Air Shows near where he lived, but had been told there was an enormous waiting list. In September 1939, his Territorial Army infantry regiment was transformed into a searchlight regiment and he'd spent the Battle of Britain in Norfolk, manning a searchlight on the coast. It had been pretty boring – there hadn't been much activity over Norfolk – so when he heard the RAF was now looking to recruit more aircrew, he applied, and this time he was accepted. At first he'd thought he was going to be a pilot, having never really considered the RAF needed non-pilot crews as well, but during his initial training was told he'd been earmarked to become a navigator. He met the rest of the crew at his Operational Training Unit, where pilots, WOP/AGs, and navigators all intermingled for the first time. After chatting and getting to know one another, they formed themselves into crews of four.

The four 'B's had only been together a few weeks, but were already firm friends, and Fraser was glad they'd all be sticking together, no matter what lay in store. With a smiling face, wavy brown hair and thin moustache, Fraser was a good-natured man who enjoyed the humour of his colleagues. There was Bob with his northern expressions and Stan's strange one-liners. 'That's the way the cookie crumbles,' was one of his favourites. Fraser had never heard such a phrase before. He had lived in London all his life, and travelling to different parts of the world with a bunch of mates from all over was just what he'd hoped for when he joined the RAF.

For much of the route, they'd noticed bits of debris floating on the surface, then suddenly they saw a large patch of orange. Fraser took out his binoculars and had a closer look. They were, in fact, oranges, hundreds of them, bobbing about on the surface – the remnants of Operation Pedestal.

The four of them were typical of the crews being sent out to the

Middle East: ordinary young men, drawn from different parts of Britain and her dominions, and, in their case, all sergeants rather than commissioned officers. They knew something of what lay in store for them, since two of the instructors at their OTU had already served in the Mediterranean. Of the situation in Malta, Fraser only knew what he'd read in the paper – that the air attacks had been beaten off and that the Island was holding up well under the siege. Was he scared? Not especially; he was just glad to be doing something useful at last. After all, he'd left the searchlights because he'd felt he wasn't doing much to help the war effort.

Before leaving Gibraltar they'd been armed with sandwiches and Thermos flasks of coffee, as though they were heading for a weekend hike in the hills rather than off to war. Perhaps they would all have been a bit more apprehensive if they'd known their chances of survival stood at less than one in six. And if they were lucky enough to make it through their first tour of duty, the odds of surviving a second were slashed to just one in thirty-three. As they munched their sandwiches on their way to Malta, the likelihood of them ever seeing their homes and family again was very slight indeed.

The development of the Beauforts on Malta as an effective strike force was largely due to one man. Patrick Gibbs had been a pre-war regular in the RAF, winning a scholarship to the RAF college at Cranwell in 1934. After completing his course he was almost immediately seconded to the Fleet Air Arm, flying Swordfish and serving on, among other ships, the aircraft carrier *Furious*. Then came a spell instructing at the Torpedo Training School in Gosport. His first wartime posting was with Beauforts, but in 1941 he had suffered a number of injuries during a flying accident and found himself stuck with a desk job at Group Headquarters in England.

His experiences with the Navy and at Gosport led him to form firm ideas about how to use coastal torpedo-bombers, views he was only too happy to voice at every available opportunity. This did not win him any friends and so he was posted out of the way to Middle East Command HQ in Cairo. Once again he was away from the action. Only after consistently badgering his seniors was he finally posted to 39 Beaufort Squadron, in April 1942. By June he had brought his rusty flying skills back up to scratch again and was taking part in active operations.

One of his first missions was to attack the Italian fleet during the June convoys to Malta. This was something of a disaster. Over half their number were lost to enemy fighters *en route*, and although the surviving Beauforts found the fleet and dropped their torpedoes, not one struck home. All five aircraft were damaged in the attack, and they flew on to Malta with their confidence seriously shaken.

Although the remnants of the squadron were sent back to Egypt two days later, that brief visit was something of a revelation for Gibbs. He realized that, with fighter protection, Malta was the perfect place from which to use the Beauforts, and believed they could make a real dent in the Axis shipping. Since arriving in the Middle East, it had become clear to him that success or failure in this theatre depended on who got the most supplies through. In a meeting with Hugh Pughe Lloyd he poured out his heart: his plans, his ideas – and his frustrations. Lloyd agreed with him wholeheartedly and at once asked Tedder if 39 Squadron could remain on Malta. He also detained 217 Beaufort Squadron, which had landed *en route* to the Far East and which had already been responsible for crippling the Italian cruiser *Trento* and sinking the *Reichenfels*, a German tanker loaded with fuel, vehicles and men for one of Rommel's panzer divisions.

By the end of June, Lloyd had been granted his wish, and Gibbs, with five other remaining aircraft, flew back to Malta, this time for good. By the end of July, they had not only been joined by another Beaufort squadron, but were also working closely with a squadron of Beaufighters. These aircraft were similar to the Beauforts but, as their name suggests, primarily fighters. Heavily armed with four cannon and six machine-guns, Beaufighters could be sent ahead of the torpedo-carrying Beauforts to heavily strafe – and bomb – enemy shipping, and so improve the chances of the torpedo-bombers.

Now commanding all three Beaufort squadrons, Gibbs asked the recently arrived Keith Park if the Beaufighters could be fully integrated into his Beaufort wing. This sounded like a good plan to the new AOC, who was only too anxious for his strike forces to be used to their full potential.

Nonetheless, these men were paying dearly for the few successes achieved: of the 28 Beaufort pilots and crew who had reached the Island, only ten were left by the end of July. But Gibbs was careful to vary tactics, and to ensure all his men were fully briefed for every operation, and gradually their experience and achievements grew, and with important side-effects. The Beauforts and Beaufighters had greater range than Fleet Air Arm Swordfish and, once again, Axis convoys were forced into taking a much longer route to North Africa. Crucial to the mounting success of the torpedo-bombers was their unfailing ability to find any Axis shipping that came their way. British Intelligence now knew about almost all Axis convoys before they'd even finished loading their ships in harbour. Interception of Italian naval signals was important, but it was undoubtedly the cracking of the German Enigma codes that was of most value. Rommel, now desperate for more supplies, was kept informed of every single merchant ship setting sail from Italy. These signals were intercepted, decoded at Bletchley Park in England, and forwarded to the Middle East. Four Special Liaison Units (SLU) had been set up specifically to handle the influx of Ultra information – three in North Africa and one in Malta, which was housed in Lascaris. Information about the size, quantity and shipping course of each enemy convoy was passed straight on to Park and the other commanders on the Island.

As ever, it was essential the Germans never discovered their codes had been broken, and so it fell to 69 Squadron to continue carrying out the very overt and necessary reconnaissance work high above the intended targets. The pilots of 69 Squadron, now using high-altitude blue Spitfires and twin-engine American Baltimores, were as busy as ever; without them, offensive operations in the Mediterranean would have been impossible. Warby, for example, had been involved in an attack on an Italian tanker, the *Pozarica*. That particular convoy had left Messina for Benghazi and consisted of the tanker and the German steamer, *Dora*. Warby had photographed the two ships and their escort on the 20th. An attack, led by Wing Commander Patrick Gibbs, had been launched soon after. There was invariably a price to pay – in this case, two Beauforts and a Beaufighter were shot down, and two other Beauforts damaged. One of these Beaufort crews had been on their first operational flight. A 69 Squadron Baltimore then photographed the aftermath of the strike, which showed that although a Beaufighter strafing run had killed a number of sailors on board one of the escort destroyers, neither of the merchant ships had been hit.

At first light, Warby again flew over the convoy, which during the night had sailed further east down the Greek coast, a much longer route. Another strike force, of nine Beauforts and four Beaufighters, once more led by Gibbs, set off later that afternoon. Twelve miles from the Greek island of Paxos, they found the convoy and went in for the attack. This time they hit their target – Gibbs's torpedo smacked into the side of the *Pozarica*, while the Beaufighters dropped a bomb on one of the destroyers and shot down several assorted enemy aircraft accompanying the ships. Another Beaufort, again with a crew on their first combat flight, was lost in the action, as was a Beaufighter. A 69 Squadron Baltimore then confirmed the success of the attack. The loss of the *Pozarica* was keenly felt in Benghazi, where the Italians had to plead with Rommel for more fuel, even though he was desperately short himself.

It was into this frenetic, high-risk world that Fraser Carlisle-Brown and his crew were flying. They landed at Luqa on 24 August. Clambering out, they saw a squadron leader approaching, rubbing his hands together with glee. 'Ah, a brand-new Mark II,' he said admiringly, 'I think I'll have that.' Annoyed to have had their aircraft requisitioned, they were also, like most new arrivals, somewhat shocked by the number of wrecked aircraft and bomb-damaged buildings. They were ushered off to the Sergeants' Mess, where each of them was given a pint mug of tea and a slice of white bread. Fraser started drinking the tea, then noticed a groundstaff maintenance sergeant watching him intently. 'Do you want your slice of bread?' he was asked. 'No,' said Fraser – he was still full from all the sandwiches they'd eaten *en route*. 'Can I have it then?' asked the man. 'By all means,' said Fraser, and then watched him gobble it down. He'd known the Island was besieged, but hadn't realized they were all *that* hungry.

But Fraser and his crew were not to be fed to the hounds just yet. They had reached Malta without any torpedo training, and so were told they were being sent on a course at Shelufa, near the Suez Canal in Egypt. Two days after their arrival, they were off again, dispatched to Cairo on a Dakota transport plane.

Although Force Z, the heavy escort ships for Operation Pedestal, had been harried all the way back to Gibraltar, both Ted Fawcett on *Bramham* and Fred Jewett on *Ashanti* had barely heard a squeak out of the enemy on their return. After pausing in Malta for refuelling and rearming, they had headed back to the UK via Gibraltar.

Ledbury, however, had remained in port for several days. Soon after their arrival, Freddie Treves had been put ashore, with nothing but the clothes he stood in, which by that time were rigid with dried salt. The air raid siren had begun wailing almost immediately, and he and the other survivors from the *Waimarama* ran to the nearest shelter. After the All Clear had sounded, the remaining seamen were ushered away, while he, the only surviving Upper Deck officer, was taken to a small hotel in Sliema. Having been given some khaki drill to wear, he was told to remain there the night and await further instructions. He was placed on hotel rations, and remembers being given a special meal of one tiny square of bully beef, two Brussels sprouts and three potatoes.

Shortly after, he was told to board HMS *Ledbury* once more. The thought of going through the same experience all over again filled him with horror, but although he spent an agonizing few days waiting for an attack at any minute, he too had a bomb-free journey back to Gibraltar. Freddie's ordeal was over.

Rochester Castle was in a terrible way and needed months of repair work before she had any hope of being fit again for duty. Joe McCarthy didn't mind. There was work to be done in the engine room, but he was given plenty of time off too. Joe had always enjoyed walking, and in the ensuing weeks gained something of a reputation among his shipmates for wandering all around the Island. He also went swimming in Sliema and was once invited to the Officers' Mess at Luqa. And despite the lack of drink, there were also a few dances. The Marquis Scicluna would sometimes open up his house, the Dragonara Palace, and invite service-men over. With music playing on the gramophone, there would be dancing in the ballroom. It was on one such occasion that Joe met an attractive nineteen-year-old girl called Yvonne, the daughter of an eminent dental surgeon on the Island. They soon started dating and even became engaged. Joe was one of the few servicemen enjoying his time on Malta.

Rochester Castle was berthed in French Creek, in Senglea. Michael Montebello's home town now lay in total ruins. 'It was in a dreadful state,' says Joe, 'one big heap of rubble.' From their shelter across the harbour, Michael saw the remains of Senglea every day. With each raid on Grand Harbour, it suffered a bit more. All the buildings he'd known so well had gone – even his old school. His education had abruptly ceased when they'd left their home, but Michael was still keeping himself busy. He now had a little canoe and would paddle around any ship in harbour, keeping an eye on things as he'd been asked to do as a Boy Scout, and talking to the sailors. *Melbourne Star*, one of the Pedestal merchant ships, was anchored nearby – just a few barges lay between her and the quayside where Michael lived. Whenever there was an air raid, the crew used to run to his shelter. Michael soon got to know some of them and they invited him aboard. 'Next time bring back some food!' his mother told him. So on his following visit, he went to the pantry of the Officers' Mess and asked if he could have some of the leftovers in return for some help. Even the scraps were better than the meals the Victory Kitchens offered.

After Operation Pedestal, Art Roscoe had been transferred to 229 Squadron at Takali and promoted to Flight Lieutenant. His squadron was not billeted at the Xara Palace, but in a monastery in Mdina, where he was sharing a room with Eric Hetherington, a Flight Commander from 249 Squadron. Theirs was a small stone room off the main staircase on the first floor, while on the next level was the Mess where they ate their morning and evening meals. Unlike George Beurling, who had become susceptible to Malta Dog, Art was feeling quite fit and healthy and not especially bothered by the bully-beef and jam diet. A number of small improvements had been made to the life of the pilots in recent weeks. There was once again a truck to take them to and from the airfield, and Takali even had some more petrol bowsers. There were fewer unexploded bombs left lying around. 'The sappers came and dealt with those right away,' says Art.

There were also plenty of aircraft; the days of one or two battered fighters straining across the airfield had long gone. Spitfires were now taking to the air in squadron strength and more. With the newly arrived fuel, Park had been given permission to resume offensive action, and so decided to take his Forward Interception Plan one step further. On 20 August, eighteen Spitfires – including those of Art Roscoe and George Beurling – took off for the first ever offensive sweep over Sicily, led by the resourceful Group Captain Walter Churchill, a relative of the Prime Minister's. 'Not a Jerry stirred,' recalled George Beurling. 'Not a drop of flak was poured up at us. We rolled along, coming out over Cape Scaramia and beetled home. Nothing much to it, bar the pleasure of sticking your nose into the enemy's country for a change.'[1]

They tried it again three days later. 'It was just like the fighter sweeps we used to do in 71 Squadron over France,' says Art Roscoe, 'trying to get the Huns up to fight. But there was nothing – no fighters, no flak.'

Getting into the air in such large numbers could also be quite hazardous. 'With no runway, you just took off in lines as many as you wanted,' says Art. One time, he was taking off and blew a tyre, causing the aircraft to slew round through 180 degrees so that he was facing back the way he came. Another Spitfire had been taking off behind him and suddenly emerged through the dust. Sitting strapped into his aircraft, Art watched the Spitfire speeding straight towards him. Luckily, the other pilot pulled up in the nick of time, missing him by inches. 'The only damage was by his wing clipping off my radio antenna, which stuck up into the air right behind the cockpit,' says Art. But both pilots could easily have been killed. 'It was close! It all happened so quickly. I would've been scared if I'd known what was going to happen.'

On 27 August, they decided to go in low and shoot up the airfields instead. They attacked Biscari, Gela and Comiso, shooting up a few planes on the ground and strafing a number of buildings and huts. This time, however, they did finally come up against heavy anti-aircraft fire, and Group Captain Churchill was shot down – Art saw him go down in flames. At 35, he'd been old for a fighter pilot, and had been suffering badly from sinus problems and poor eyesight. Refusing to give up flying, he'd paid the ultimate price. It was clear, meanwhile, that these sweeps were achieving little, apart from wasting petrol, ammunition and lives, and so, for the time being at any rate, they were abandoned.

If August had been a quiet time for the fighter pilots, September was even more so. From the non-stop, round-the-clock bombing of earlier months, enemy raids dropped to just 57 for the whole month. Art still had to be on duty and fly off on occasional scrambles, but he tried to make the most of the respite. It was difficult; there was very little to do, but on days off he visited Valletta, wandering through the rubble, and stopping at a little café for some tea. The waiters always apologized for the sparse menu – 'Next convoy, sir.' He also talked to some of the gunners there. 'Their skin was the colour of dark leather. They didn't know about skin cancer in those days – they just wore a helmet and shorts. They had those guns polished and the ammo stored, and then they brewed tea. We had some interesting chats with those guys.' On another occasion, he even took his whole flight over to the neighbouring island of Gozo to swim and sunbathe. Much smaller than the main island, Gozo had avoided the worst of the war, but up until now the crossing had been considered too dangerous to allow anyone to make regular trips there. 'It was like a different country,' says Art. The Gozitans were suffering from rationing just like everyone else, but there was barely a piece of rubble on the entire island.

Art would often just stay at the Mess, reading and getting some rest, or watching the enemy raids from one of the balconies. He rarely met anyone other than other service types. 'Just how one would date a girl on Malta, I never found out,' he admits. 'There was no place to go, no way to get there, and nothing to do when you arrived.'

But the Luftwaffe never let them relax for long. Art was pretty sure they knew the Takali pilots were billeted in Mdina, because one day a Junkers 88 came roaring past the airfield and headed straight for their monastery home. Art was on the balcony at the time with some of the other pilots, and saw they were the target. All of them ran for it, but had it not been for another stroke of luck, they would have probably all been killed. Piercing the roof, the bomb dropped straight down a stairwell and lodged in the courtyard outside the front door – without exploding. They had to evacuate the building until the bomb disposal team arrived and defused it.

They also held a big party that month. More planes were flying between Malta and Egypt now, and so occasional stashes of booze would appear. Warby also made several trips to Egypt at this time – mostly for strategy meetings at Middle East HQ – and made sure he never returned empty-handed. It was with such a supply that the fighter pilots held their party. Other squadrons were invited as well as the girls from Lascaris. 'Some sort of protocol existed that required the presence of a local Maltese official,' recalls Art. 'He brought his two daughters. These beautiful, young Maltese girls had the infamous title of the "death sisters". Past flying types that had socialized with these ladies had all been shot down, or met with other unpleasant fates – or so it was said. So we left them to the non-flying types.'

Art's room-mate, Eric Hetherington, was George Beurling's flight commander. 'Beurling was a great shot, but no tactician,' says Art, 'so Hether would lead him into position and then tell him to do his stuff.' Although in different squadrons, George and Art were both based at Takali, and got to know each other well enough. 'He was OK, but a bit of a weirdo,' says Art. As a member of the 249 groundcrew, Pete Watson often looked after George's Spitfire. 'I got on very well with him,' he says, 'and always called him George. There used to be a fair few stray dogs about the place and Beurling used to say, "I wonder if I can get this goddam screwball between the eyes," then take out his revolver and shoot them.' George would also shoot lizards. Standing alone and stock-still, he would wait for one to get to a range where he reckoned it was roughly the size of a 109 at two hundred and fifty yards, then try to hit it with a single shot. 'He was a loner,' says Pete, 'very friendly, but he would usually sit on his own away from the other pilots.'

But this oddball was already becoming something of a legend on the Island, having steadily added to his mounting score. By September, he had already shot down more planes than any other fighter pilot on Malta. On 27 July, he had even claimed four in one day, a staggering achievement.

Barely one in five Allied pilots ever shot down the prescribed five air-craft that entitled one to be labelled an 'ace'. Less than half of those then went on to reach double figures. Of the remainder, less than fifty per cent ever scored a thing. To make it as a successful fighter ace, pilots needed stamina, intense concentration, good co-ordination and fast reflexes, and excellent eyesight. George worked hard to train his eyes to take in the whole sky in one searching and regularly repeated glance. 'You've got to do that constantly when there may be enemy planes about,' he said. 'Especially you've got to watch the sky above you – that's the dangerous place – and when you look, make sure there's nothing there, or if there is, *what* it is.'[2]

Getting a confirmed kill on Malta could be quite difficult – at least one witness had to corroborate any claim; otherwise a pilot was only credited with a 'probable'. Even a crashed aircraft on the ground was not necessarily enough evidence because it was hard to prove who had caused its destruction. Quite often two or more pilots would claim they had shot down the same aircraft, in which case it would be shared. In England, fighters were fitted with cine-cameras, but supplies of film were understandably never available on Malta. Denis Barnham certainly found this frustrating. On 14 May, for example, he shot down two Junkers 88s, but later noted, 'The 88 I've just destroyed has been credited to the ack-ack gunners – credited to them despite the wing snapping off just where I hit it, despite the rear-gunner, who baled out by parachute, confirming that I, the Spitfire Leader, shot him down. Not only that but the earlier 88, the one that I, and Ingram flying the Spitfire behind me, destroyed after circling above St Paul's Bay, the one that fell on Takali – it has been credited to a Takali pilot.'[3] Both were, in fact, later awarded to him, but Art Roscoe certainly lost out on several occasions because of this ruling. On one occasion he shot down two

109s, but because he'd had no witnesses and had not hung around to watch them crash, had been unable to make a claim. 'I once had a Macchi 202 going down at an angle, in an inverted dive, with its engine flaming at seven hundred feet,' says Art. 'No one saw that crash either. Alas, our job was to defend the Island – not to worry about big scores.'

George Beurling was a slightly different case, largely because of the accuracy with which he described every kill. One time he'd disengaged from the fray and spotted a lone Macchi 202, which he then attacked and shot down. No one else had seen it, but on his return he told the Intelligence Officer (IO) that he had delivered a short burst of cannon fire and had seen strikes all along the fuselage, in the wing root and along the side of the engine. Shortly after, a Macchi was reported crashed on Gozo, heavily damaged by cannon-fire along the port side of the fuselage, in the wing root and up to an area just below the engine. Clearly it was the same aircraft, and George was credited with a 'confirmed' kill. Even so, he was annoyed. 'Dammit, I was certain I had hit that goddam screwball in the engine!'[4]

He also learnt to watch the enemy pilots and pick out the really good ones. 'After a pilot has made one or two turns you can tell if he is really good,' he said.[5] Those were the greatest risk to him and his fellow pilots, and so he would always try to hit those first. This is what he'd done on the 27th, when he singled out the Italian ace, Captain Furio Niclot, the first of his four victims.

Generally speaking, the Italians and Germans were viewed as different species entirely by the Malta-based pilots. George thought the Italians brave and obviously skilled pilots, but not good marksmen. The Germans, on the other hand, tended to fight only if they held a superior tactical position; if the odds were against them, they soon made themselves scarce. There was also a belief that the Italians were, broadly speaking, reluctant combatants. Denis Barnham recalled an incident where one of his pilots had been chased all around the sky by an Italian fighter. Throwing his Spitfire every which way, the pilot had been unable to shake off the Italian and was expecting to be shot down at any moment. Instead, his adversary pulled up alongside him, and, waving, fired his guns into the air, then headed off home. There were also a number of reports of Italian bombers scattering and unloading the bomb loads at sea, then turning for home; as long as their guns had been fired and their bombs dropped, it was easy to get away with it. This may also partly explain the grossly inflated claims announced on Rome Radio; it was not just propaganda, but Italian fighter pilots trying to convince the authorities they were more aggressive than they actually were.

By September, Rommel's position was critical. The front was now stagnant, but this lull heavily favoured the British, who were able to resupply their forces far more easily than the Axis ever could now that they were such a massive distance from their ports. Aircraft, fuel, ammunition, and the new American Sherman tanks were pouring into Egypt in a steady stream. Rommel reckoned that if he were to have any chance of continuing his charge to Cairo, he would need to attack by the middle of September at the latest. But he could not do anything until he had received more fuel and ammunition. The loss of the tanker *Pozarica* to Patrick Gibbs' Beauforts had therefore been very bad news. 'Unless I get 2,000 cubic metres of fuel, 500 tons of ammunition by the 25th [of August] and a further 2,000 cubic metres of fuel by the 27th and 2,000 tons of ammunition by the 30th, I cannot proceed,' he told General von Rintelen, the German Military Attaché in Rome.[6]

A plan to send more fuel-carrying ships to North Africa was hastily put into action. Nine vessels were to leave Italy over a period of six days starting on 28 August. Once again, Ultra information enabled those on Malta to know every detail of the Axis shipping plans, and once again, reconnaissance work by 69 Squadron provided confirmation, and the necessary corroboration. On the 28th, Warby photographed Taranto and Brindisi as the first fuel-ships set sail. The situation of the previous six months had dramatically been turned on its head: now it was up to the Malta-based aircraft and submarines to stop Axis convoys getting through.

Gibbs's Beauforts and Beaufighters sank two of the first three ships the same day, and later on the third was torpedoed and sunk by one of Shrimp Simpson's submarines. Despite this blow, Rommel decided to go ahead and launch an attack on the Alam Halfa Ridge at the southern end of the British line, praying that the next tanker due in – the *San Andreas* – would successfully deliver her cargo of 3,198 tons of fuel.

But by the time the German tanks and guns opened fire on the evening of the 30th, the ship was already at the bottom of the Mediterranean. Earlier that day, Patrick Gibbs had flown off with his team to attack the 5,000-ton tanker. It was just south of Taranto, in an area notoriously well defended, but Gibbs dared not delay his attack: it was obviously imperative to hit the ship as soon as possible. Usually, if striking north of Malta, they would fly sixty miles due east, then turn on to a northerly course to avoid passing within range of the Sicilian fighter airfields and radar. On this occasion, such a detour would have made them increase the length of flight beyond their own range, and so the Beauforts had to rely on the accompanying Beaufighters to protect them on their way to the target. The weather helped – a thick haze shielded them from the view of the coastline – and they reached the open waters of the Gulf of Taranto without incident. Then the haze cleared, and Gibbs could suddenly see for miles and miles. The heel of Italy reminded him of a lion's mouth, two jaws stretched wide to engulf them. But there, down below – just two narrow dots – were the tanker and its escort.

Although there were three Axis airfields just a few miles away, Gibbs turned his Beauforts towards the coast, while the Beaufighters climbed higher to patrol overhead. Then, glancing upwards to check for any enemy fighters, he turned back to attack head-on from the shore. Barely able to control his finger hovering over his release button, he swooped in low and steady, and then, at the shortest range possible, dropped the torpedo. Bombs from a Beaufighter exploded at the same time, obscuring the tanker in a mountain of spray, and as he flew over it, his aircraft rocked and buffeted so badly, he thought he'd been hit. In fact, it wasn't him, but his torpedo striking the *San Andreas*. An enormous explosion had erupted, blowing bits of the tanker high into the sky; it was this that had jolted Gibbs's Beaufort. A second torpedo had also struck home. The tanker burst into flames, her cargo burning high into the Mediterranean sky. Not that Gibbs and his force had much chance to admire their handiwork. Enemy fighters had now appeared, and for ten minutes the Beauforts struggled to keep them off their tails, although the Macchis' short range prevented them from pursuing the British aircraft for long. Gibbs landed back safely at Luqa, but he had lost his most trusted and experienced officer in the attack. News of their success had already reached the Island. Warby, flying over Taranto, had seen dense black smoke rising almost to the height of his Spitfire, some 20,000 feet above.

The Beaufort Wing was starting to have a devastating impact on the changing situation in the Mediterranean. Thanks to them, the Axis forces in North Africa were getting almost no fuel whatsoever. 'Petrol was already scarce,' Kesselring wrote later, 'and the loss of a 4,000–6,000 ton tanker meant an almost irreparable gap.'[7] The German commander was forced to transfer some of the Luftwaffe's fuel over to Rommel's

Panzers. But there was worse news for the Germans. Although a further tanker and two supply ships had reached Tobruk, it was discovered the fuel in the tanker had been contaminated and was therefore useless. The following day, 31 August, two more tankers left Taranto and although one made it through, the other, full of fuel, paraffin and gas oil, was bombed by Malta Wellingtons and exploded. Of the nine ships sent to relieve Rommel, five had been sunk, all by forces operating from Malta. On 1 September, the German Panzers, having barely gained a yard of ground, were ordered to retreat.

The action had cost Rommel precious tanks and, of course, more fuel, while giving considerable heart to the British Eighth Army in North Africa, and Malta had played a crucial part in that defeat. So had Patrick Gibbs. When he had first taken command of the Beauforts, he had resolved to always lead any attack himself. With so much of his time taken up with planning and organization, this self-imposed rule had become impossible to follow, but even so, he had flown more times than most. But the burden of responsibility, especially with so many losses, was taking its toll, as was the strain of working non-stop under such stressful circumstances. The heat, and the lack of food – especially sugar – had played havoc with his health. By September, he had become so physically and mentally ill that he had to be sent back to England. And although he was awarded the Distinguished Service Order and a Distinguished Flying Cross and bar for his work on Malta, he was a shadow of his former self by the time he flew off from Luqa for the final time. 'I had died the death I never dreaded in Malta,' Gibbs wrote shortly afterwards.[8] There were many on Malta who had reason to mourn his passing.

In North Africa, Rommel was preparing to face General Montgomery for a large-scale – and potentially decisive – battle. Like those on Malta, his Army, beaten at Alam Halfa, was suffering from a lack of food and water, and disease among his forces was rife. Meanwhile, despite the loss of eleven Axis supply vessels in September, ships had been steaming across the Mediterranean almost constantly, and not all could be sunk. That month, 11,200 tons of fuel was safely unloaded in North Africa, as well as more ammunition and other supplies. Nonetheless, the loss of any merchant ship was now critical, and while Montgomery waited to make his move, it was essential the Axis bolstered their forces with as many reinforcements as possible.

Malta was proving a major thorn in the Axis side, and Kesselring was determined to do something about it. Although there was now no question of invading the Island, the blitzes of the first part of the year had for a time rendered her useless as an offensive base. Another concerted effort would probably do the same, even if again only temporarily. From his base in Italy, Kesselring knew that despite the August convoy, Malta was still struggling, and reasoned that after two years of siege, the Island had to be vulnerable to another all-out air attack. He began reinforcing Sicily once more for another sustained onslaught. In partnership with the Regia Aeronautica, the German commander soon amassed over 700 bombers and fighters with which to deliver a final knock-out blitz, a force that included his highly experienced, battle-hardened Fliegerkorps II. This, Kesselring hoped, would make all the difference between winning and losing North Africa.

George 'Screwball' Beurling knew, just *knew*, the enemy was going to make another attempt to 'blow Malta into the sea'. Nor was it just him – such talk was on the lips of every 'man and woman on the whole damned Island'.[9] George had been trying to look after himself, but he'd been suffering from bouts of the Dog since late July and knew he was physically well under par. What he hated most was the wait – kicking his heels about the airfield, feeling groggy and having to listen to talk of whether and when the next convoy might arrive. He was relieved when the attacks came. At last he could be flying all day again, keeping himself busy and taking his mind off everything else.

On 10 October, he was flying over Takali, testing his newly serviced Spitfire, when he was warned of two Messerschmitt 109s that had sneaked over the Island from the south. He spotted them soon after – they were travelling well below him at around 1,000 feet – and so he dropped down for the classic 'bounce', with the twin advantages of height and speed. Swooping in behind the right-hand plane first, he peppered the vulnerable under-belly and the German fighter flipped over and crashed on to the Island. Then he attacked the second, executing a perfect deflection shot that caught the German pilot unawares. Both plane and pilot were blown up as cannon-fire pierced the Messerschmitt's fuel tank. Having already been awarded a second DFM – a bar to his first – he was about to be awarded a DFC as well. Both his awards and tally were mounting steadily – these two kills lifted his score on Malta to an extraordinary 21 confirmed destroyed.

The renewed Axis blitz began at twenty past seven the following morning, 11 October, when seven Junkers 88s, escorted by 25 Macchi 202s and four 109s, approached Malta. With over a hundred Spitfires on the Island, the five Malta-based fighter squadrons were able to face the new attacks at full strength. Implementing his Forward Interception Plan once more, Park scrambled nineteen Spitfires – eight from 1435 Squadron, seven from 126 and four from Art Roscoe's 229. The entire enemy formation was intercepted before they reached Malta, and the few bombers that did make it through caused little damage. There were a further five raids that day and two night-time attacks. The lull of the previous weeks had been spectacularly shattered.

Art Roscoe was suddenly ordered to be on 'alert' all day. There were three stages of readiness: Mess Readiness, which meant being immediately available to go down to the airfield; Dispersal Readiness, when he needed to be at Takali, wearing his flying gear, with his parachute in the cockpit and ready to go; and lastly, Cockpit Readiness, for which he had to be strapped into his aircraft, helmet on the stick, plugged into the battery trolley with the groundcrew standing by, and ready to be airborne right away. Unfortunately for the pilots, it was still hot, and Art found sitting in the cockpit with all his kit on extremely uncomfortable. His erks fashioned cardboard and cloth sun-shields to drape over the Perspex canopy, but this brought little relief. Art felt as though he were sitting in a metal sauna. At mealtimes, food was brought to the aircraft. 'If the red Verey flare went up during a meal, over the side with it, finished or not, and off you went,' says Art.

Generally, aircraft were sent up in flights of four. A typical scramble from Cockpit Readiness had a flight in the air and climbing at full throttle in less than half a minute. As a flight commander, Art would call, 'Oxo Red Leader, airborne.' From Control, he would hear Woody Woodhall's voice through his earphones reply, 'Roger Oxo Leader, fifty plus at angels twenty, fifty miles north, Buster.' In other words, he was to try to intercept an enemy formation of over fifty aircraft flying at 20,000 feet and currently fifty miles away to the north of the Island. Interception would be about ten minutes later, but depending on the time of day, Art would try to manoeuvre his flight so that the sun was always behind them when they attacked. Unlike in the Battle of Britain, when British fighters flew in a tight arrowhead of three planes known as a 'vic', Malta fighter pilots used a formation of four aircraft rather like the German finger-four, or *rotte*, except that instead of staggering them-selves, they flew line-abreast. Although this was not as manœuvrable as a vic, it meant they could all watch out for one another and that no one lagged behind in the vulnerable 'tail-end charlie' position – the death of many a new and inexperienced pilot.

The enemy formation never arrived as one mass of aircraft – the bombers were generally at around 15,000 feet, with the fighter escort some 5,000–10,000 feet above. The job of the Malta fighters was to get at the bombers, preferably to shoot them down, but also to break up the formation and to encourage them to jettison their bomb loads before they reached the Island. But any swarm of enemy aircraft was quite hard to miss in the short distance between Sicily and Malta, and so Art would be left to direct his flight towards an interception without further radio contact from Control. Woodhall and his team of Controllers were key to any successful interception. 'Woodhall was a great Controller,' says Art – and there seems to be no one who would disagree. 'He was the voice that we heard at all times, but he wouldn't bother you in the air. So many Controllers in England would do everything except actually fire your guns, and sometimes they got to be a nuisance. But Woody would give you all the basic information – he'd tell you what they had on radar, its position and the altitude – but he didn't tell you *how* to do it. He left that to the flight commander.' Once the bombers were spotted, they would try to get in at least one pass: a short burst of fire at one, another few seconds at another, speeding through their formation from front to rear. There was seldom any time to ever observe positive results. As soon as they made their attack it was every man for himself. They tried to work in pairs, but in the ensuing mêlée this rarely worked for long; there were few who worked as well together as George Beurling and Eric Hetherington.

If the enemy fighters were on the ball, they would be down among them by this point. Art would then have a choice – to have another crack at the bombers or tangle with the Macchis and 109s. Often, it was a combination of both – he would be desperately craning his neck on the look-out for anyone attacking him, while at the same time trying to line up a clear shot on the nearest enemy aircraft. With his ammuni-tion finished, he would corkscrew down to the deck and head for home. By this stage another flight of Spitfires would have arrived to relieve them, and relays would continue to attack until the raid was broken up. Any bomber that did make it through then had to face the formidable anti-aircraft barrage put up by Ken Griffiths and the rest of the Island's gunners.

For Art Roscoe and George Beurling, the action was almost continuous. They would land, jump out, have their planes rearmed and refuelled and then be at either Dispersal or Cockpit Readiness again. Late that first day, Art was climbing with three other new pilots who'd recently arrived on a transport plane. For once Art found himself above some 109s. 'I thought, oh boy! This is heaven!' he recalls. Looking down, he could see the bombers beneath the fighters – it reminded him of stair steps. By his reckoning, they should all get at least one each. Art peeled off and dived, followed in turn by the rest of the flight. Pulling up right behind the closest 109, he closed until its wingtips filled his gunsight, then pressed down on the gun button. 'His engine kind of came apart, smoke engulfed the plane, he flipped over and went straight down,' says Art. Then he lined up another, fired again, knocking off the canopy and bits of the plane. That was two – all in a matter of seconds. He hoped the other guys were doing well, but briefly glancing around couldn't see a single Spitfire anywhere. 'Then I suppose one of the Germans must've said, "Achtung Spitfeuers!" because they immediately broke [formation].' Art was now on his own and among a mass of angry 109s. 'I shoved my stick forward and went down through the lower tiers of fighters right to the bombers. Every Ju88 I got my sights on got some of my ammo until it was all gone, when I headed for the deck without having a shot fired at me that I knew of.'

Art landed back at Takali to discover all three of his flight were there already. The first said his windscreen had got oil on it and he couldn't see. The second claimed his engine sounded rough and thought it best he get it back quickly. Only the third admitted that against fifty-plus enemy aircraft the odds had seemed too long and so he had scuttled back to base. Art sighed; Malta was still no place to send inexperienced pilots.

He'd been lucky on that occasion, but his good fortune did not last. On 12 October, Art was scrambled to meet the fifth raid of the day at around half past three in the afternoon. Eight of them this time had made an initial attack on the escorting fighters, when Art suddenly felt a thump on his back, as though someone had come up to him and hit him on the shoulder. Instinctively, he turned hard right. A 109 had attacked him from slightly above and at an angle. Art cursed himself for not watching his tail properly, but at least his Spitfire seemed to be still running fine. With his anger mounting, he decided he was going to get this 109 if it was the last thing he did. An instructor at his OTU in England had told him a trick he'd learnt in the Battle of Britain: by pulling back the throttle and kicking on a 'yard' of right rudder, the Spitfire practically stopped. The plane behind then had to either detour round or collide. 'So this guy went round and suddenly he's in front of me,' says Art. Immediately ramming forward the throttle and applying left rudder, he now had the 109 in his sights at almost point-blank range. 'He was fifty yards in front and I didn't miss. He went straight down.'

Only then did Art realize he'd been badly hit. He was bleeding profusely, although he felt no pain. A cannon shell had gone right through him, just missing the petrol tank in front of his instrument panel. He turned for home, but half-way there he was attacked again by a lone Messerschmitt. Art turned hard again and after a few wild circles the 109 flew off. This time, however, his Spitfire had been hit in the engine and cooling system. Smoke was billowing out in front of him, and although he couldn't see any flames, there were loud clanking noises and the whole plane was juddering. There was nothing for it but to bale out. Disconnecting his oxygen mask and radio leads, and releasing his harness, he rolled his aircraft on to its back and pushed forward on the stick as he'd been taught. But nothing happened – he didn't budge. Meanwhile the engine, although spluttering, was still going, so he righted the plane and continued on his way to Takali.

'The last thing I remember was flying low over a blast shelter. I must have hit the top of it, because the next thing I knew, I was lying on a table in the Mess up at the monastery,' says Art. He had crash-landed. His Spitfire had been on fire and he'd been flung out of the cockpit, landing some way away with a broken shoulder, broken arm, and weak from the loss of blood caused by his cannon-shell wound.

Meanwhile, George Beurling was still fighting his one-man crusade against the Axis air forces. On 13 October, he saw a Spitfire spin past him just as a German pilot opened his parachute. A couple of nearby 109s, thinking it was the Spitfire pilot who had baled out, circled the parachutist and one after the other gave him a burst from their machine-guns. George watched as the murdered man plummeted into the sea. 'I damned nearly vomited into the cockpit,' he said.[10] The same day he had been scrambled to intercept a formation of 109s and Junkers

88 dive-bombers and had met the formations three miles north of St Paul's Bay to the north of the Island. He attacked eight bombers, shooting down one, then turned on two faster and more manœuvrable 109s, shooting one at a 90-degree angle and another moments later. Returning to Malta, George saw that just four of the German bombers had reached the Island, where they dropped their bombs on Takali and the neighbouring village of Attard. He was able to score his third kill of the day as the Junkers turned back towards Sicily.

Then, on the 14th, his luck ran out too. George had shot down another bomber when he saw one of his colleagues with a 109 on his tail. Racing past the flaming bomber, he hit the 109 but then was attacked himself by the tail-gunner of the burning Junkers. Bullets nicked a finger and also his arm, but even so he managed to shoot down another fighter before being hit again by cannon-fire that shattered his right heel and wounded him again in the arm as well as his chest. Somehow he managed to bale out, landing in the sea, but by the time he was rescued the bottom of his inflatable dinghy was full of blood and he was rapidly losing strength. He was safely picked up, but his wounds ensured there would be no more fighting for him for a while. Both he and Art Roscoe were sent to Imtarfa along with a mounting number of pilots.

On the 15th, the headline in the *Times of Malta* ran: '82 IN FOUR DAYS – Malta's Answer to Luftwaffe's New Bid' and then revealed that 'the Axis lost its 1,000th aircraft over or near Malta soon after dawn on Tuesday to 20-year-old Canadian ace fighter pilot, Pilot Officer Beurling.'[11] The blitz lasted for two weeks, although the most intense period of enemy action was already over after three days. Art and George had more than played their part in that victory. 'The assault in the middle of October had not been the success we hoped for,' wrote Field Marshal Kesselring after the war. 'I broke it off on the third day because, especially in view of the expected [Allied] landings [in North Africa] our losses were too high.' The Malta fighters, he conceded, 'had indeed considerably refined their methods of defence.'[12] Large numbers of further raids did, in fact, continue for another ten days, but by the end of the month enemy action had trickled to a standstill, and Kesselring had ordered what was left of his Fliegerkorps II back to North Africa and Greece. Over 350 German and Italian aircraft were damaged or destroyed during this time – half the assembled force; and although losses of Spitfires had been quite high, few of the pilots had lost their lives.[13] Park's men had overwhelmingly won the day. Captured German pilots confessed that they found the Malta of October 1942 stronger than ever before and that this had surprised them. An airman brought down in a Junkers 88 said of their attacks on the Island, 'Malta drove us to the limit.'[14] These losses suffered by the enemy on the eve of the Battle of Alamein were significant, for when Montgomery finally launched his attack on 23 October, it was against a force whose air protection had been severely depleted.

The German gamble had failed.

CHAPTER 20

From Besieged to Bridgehead

NOVEMBER 1942–JULY 1943

G EORGE BEURLING SAT out the rest of October in hospital feeling increasingly twitchy. The battles were raging on without him, and he would sneak out of bed to a window and just sit there forlornly watching the sky. 'The real lucky guy on the ward, however, was Art Roscoe,' he wrote later. Few survived that kind of crash-landing, especially not with a hole through the shoulder. But as more pilots steadily reached the hospital, a clear picture was emerging. 'Everybody came back bearing the same tale. We were handing it back to Jerry five for one.' George just wanted to get back in the air and shoot down some more. Then, on the 25th, Park came up to see him and the other pilots. He'd been awarded a DSO, Park told him, and then came the bad news. There was no chance of him flying again for at least two months, and the Canadian Government wanted him back to help out with recruiting. He was being sent home. 'And that was that,' said George. 'So long, Malta.' [1] Art, meanwhile, had been awarded a DFC. He too would be leaving the Island.

Shortly afterwards, Art and George found themselves down at Luqa hobbling on to the same RAF Liberator. Normally a four-engine bomber, this plane had been converted into a cargo carrier. Without any seats or safety belts, it was not really designed as a transport plane, but nonetheless, 39 boarded the plane on that last day of October: a crew of six, a few civilians – including four women and two babies – and the rest pilots, either wounded or tour-expired, heading back to England.

Art bedded down in the bomb bay along with the others and slept most of the way. He awoke the following morning at dawn, feeling hot, so he moved to the waist gunner's position where there was a cool draught blowing through. George Beurling came down to join him, and watch their landing on to the strip at Gibraltar. Touching down too far along the runway, the pilot tried to take off again in order to make another attempt, but unfortunately he was unable to make it into the air again and, overshooting, ran into the sea. Luckily, the sea was quite shallow and as soon as the plane came to rest on the seabed, both Art and George escaped through the gun ports. A few others followed suit, but most were trapped in the wreckage. 'Art Roscoe was hanging onto a chunk of wreckage,' said George. 'His fractured collar-bone made swimming impossible.'[2]

But Art was okay, and seeing two life-rafts, inflated them and helped another pilot into one and pushed him towards shore. George was in the water nearby and offered to help, but Art told him he could manage. Both safely made it back to dry land, but sixteen were killed, including both babies and Eric Hetherington, George's old partner and Art's roommate. 'One of those things,' says Art. 'He was a really nice guy.' George, too, was upset at losing a good friend. 'I lay abed that night and looked out of the window on the lights of Gibraltar. So this was how it had to end … I'd never go roaring up to 28,000 again with Hether, both of us proud as hell that we could beat any team in 249 to get up where the Jerries were.'[3]

Surviving the months of hard aerial combat only to be killed in a flying accident was a not uncommon irony of war, although Art certainly believes he knows why they crashed. 'It was crew fatigue. They'd flown to Gibraltar to Malta to Cairo to Malta to Gibraltar with no crew rest, so he must have been seeing two or three runways by the time he got to Gibraltar again.' Art made it to shore, only to be put back in hospital. His mood was not improved when his room-mate, an Army officer, died during the night. Shortly afterwards, both airmen were flown back to England – George to go on to Canada, Art to stay in the country he had chosen to fly for. After recovering, there would be further battles to fight for both of them – but nothing to compare with the intensity of the previous few months. For George 'Screwball' Beurling, in particular, Malta had been the fighter pilot's paradise.

There was not much room in a pilot's logbook to write detailed descriptions of action in the sky, but Warby tended to be more succinct than most, rarely betraying the drama and danger of many of his flights. With small, neat handwriting, he wrote of 14 October: 'Shot at by 6 Macchi 200s. Took DR [in this case destroyer] to dinghy. Rescue okay.' If ever Warby was to demonstrate his fearlessness, it was on this particular occasion.

In sharp contrast with the earlier German and Italian blitzes, throughout October the Maltese offensive operations never ceased. With Montgomery about to strike, it was as important as ever that Axis shipping be prevented from reaching North Africa. So it was that, as George Beurling was making his final claims in the raging air battles over the sea, Warby was taking off in his PR Spitfire to take pictures of a Beaufighter strike on a 2,000-ton Axis merchant ship and its destroyer and motor torpedo boat (MTB) escort.

Circling above, Warby watched as the three Beaufighters approached the merchant vessel at mast height and flew into a torrent of fire from the destroyer and MTB. The first plane was blown up in mid-air, while a second was unable to release his bombs. Despite the vicious barrage, he made a second run, then headed back. The third dropped his bombs but missed, and was badly shot up in the process. The pilot was forced to ditch his aircraft four miles to the north-west.

Warby saw it all, including the crew of the ditched Beaufighter scrambling into their dinghy. They had survived the crash, but he knew that unless he did something, this would only be a stay of execution. In that wide open expanse of sea, miles from the nearest coast, those men were finished. No Allied ship would come to their rescue, but an Italian prisoner-of-war camp had to be better than dying of thirst on an unforgiving sea.

Warby dropped down and swooped over the destroyer and MTB, which understandably opened fire. Ignoring the flak, Warby repeatedly circled round the two ships, flying alongside at sea level, and waggling his wings in an effort to convince them he had no hostile intentions.

He continued like this for twenty minutes, flying past low, then risking flak and gunfire as he circled round them again. But Warby would not leave – he *had* to make them understand. Eventually they did. Having stopped firing, the MTB set off towards the ditched crew, Warby flying ahead to lead them to the spot. As the ships approached the dinghy, six Macchi 200s suddenly appeared. In his unarmed blue PR Spitfire, his only defence was his superior speed, but he still refused to make good his escape. Weaving and circling, he managed to dodge the machine-gun fire of the Macchis until he'd seen the two Beaufighter crew safely pulled on board the MTB. Only then did he fly off as quickly as he could. For this action, Warby was awarded a second bar to his DFC.

There were many who thought he should have been awarded a Victoria Cross. John Agius, still at the RAF HQ at Scots Street, saw a signal arrive for Keith Park, suggesting Warby be given a VC. 'Apparently Park didn't see it this way,' John recalled. 'Perhaps he was finding Warburton difficult enough at times without such a prestigious award. In any event none of the Battle of Britain aces such as Bader, Tuck, Malan et cetera had been so honoured.'⁴ Nor was Warby especially keen on the idea. When one of his crew had mentioned it to him, he replied, 'There is a nasty word called "posthumous" usually associated with that one.'⁵

Four minesweepers had been sent to Malta and were doing sterling work clearing the shipping channels outside the harbour. It certainly made entering and leaving port a much simpler proposition. Sufficiently repaired, *Rochester Castle* finally left Grand Harbour in November. She was to sail for Alexandria, then round the Cape and on to New York, where she would undergo a major refit. Joe McCarthy was sorry to be leaving. 'I made some good friends while I was there,' he says. And he would miss his fiancée, Yvonne. Still, there was a war on, and both ships and experienced seamen were needed elsewhere now.

The minesweepers, however, were particularly appreciated by the submariners, as was the introduction of smoke canisters. Although there were still plenty of air raids, a number of these devices had been placed along the shore of Manoel Island and, when set off, quickly covered the base in a dense fog. Canisters were also placed on the casing of any submarine moored alongside the Lazzaretto – if a bomb hit them now, it had to be a very lucky shot.

Of the pioneers of the Tenth Flotilla, only *Utmost* had returned to Malta. Not a single one of Simpson's original COs remained with the Flotilla, although he was given a boost with the arrival of Commander Ben Bryant, Tubby Crawford's first CO, now commanding a new S-class boat, HMS/S *Safari*. Between his arrival in September and the moment he relinquished command in April 1943, he sank no fewer than 29 vessels of all kinds, amounting to around 40,000 tons. Although this may seem like a modest amount of tonnage, most of the larger merchant ships – such as the *Conte Rosso* – had now been sunk, and since the Axis were not building large merchant vessels at the same rate as the Americans, they were relying on the shipment of supplies in smaller merchantmen. Bryant sank four ships in October alone.

ABC was now back in the Mediterranean, based at Gibraltar. He had been working closely with the Americans planning the proposed Allied landings in French North Africa. Operation Torch, as the invasion had been labelled, would take place on 7–8 November. At the end of October, ABC told Shrimp Simpson that he was to be in command of all submarines operating in the central Mediterranean and asked for his suggestions about how best to use this force. The top priority was to stop the Italian fleet interfering in any way, so Simpson proposed keeping all thirteen submarines at his disposal on patrol lines around the heel of Italy and south of Sardinia. 'You will be glad to know that submarine operations in the central Mediterranean at this decisive moment are in the competent hands and the long experience of Captain G.W.G. Simpson, Commanding the Tenth Submarine Flotilla based at Malta,' ABC told all his naval commanders prior to the launch of the operation.[6]

As it turned out, Simpson and ABC might almost not have bothered. The Italian fleet was by now largely finished as a fighting force. Hampered by the shortage of fuel and with their confidence still shaken after the damage caused to two of her cruisers during the Pedestal convoy, the fleet remained in port for the whole operation. An Italian U-boat was sunk, as was a German U-boat depot ship. Another Malta submarine blew the bows off a new Italian light cruiser that did dare show its face. By 11 November, Simpson was ordered to carry on as normal. For the first time since the war began, American ground-troops were now deployed in the Mediterranean theatre. With Montgomery pushing Rommel back through Egypt and Libya, and with the Americans and Allies pushing from the west, a pincer movement to drive the Axis out of North Africa had begun.

There was plenty more work for the Beauforts, however. 39 Squadron had been temporarily moved to Egypt at the end of September to provide a chance for the crews to take some leave in Cairo and for their remaining aircraft to be repaired and serviced. They were supposed to return a couple of weeks later, in October, but this plan was changed when they were called upon to help out with the attack on Axis shipping arriving at Tobruk before and during the Battle of Alamein. They finally returned to Malta in November.

Having completed their torpedo course, Fraser Carlisle-Brown and the other 'B's flew back with the rest of the squadron. Luqa looked much the same as it had done when they'd first arrived at the end of August, except that most of the crashed aircraft had now been tipped over the edge of a ravine at one end of the airfield. The Army was building ever more blast pens, and unhurried Maltese with their donkeys and carts carried stones and boulders back and forth. The four of them were billeted in the Balluta Buildings in Balluta Bay, on the northernmost edge of Sliema. An ornate five-storey building overlooking Ballutta and St Julian's Bays, it was an awkward distance from Luqa, and once the bus had taken them there, they never left the airfield again until it was time to go back to their digs.

Fraser soon discovered he had little spare time. The crews were worked in shifts, each of the three flights – 'A', 'B' and 'C' – standing by for eight hours at a stretch. If a message came in from one of Warby's 69 Squadron reconnaissance planes, they would be ushered into the Briefing Room and told the size of the target and where it was. Fraser only ever went on a handful of day strikes, since by now most of the Axis shipping within range of Malta was travelling at night. Instead of flying in groups, they would take off individually.

When on a mission, all four of the crew were fully concentrating on the job in hand – which left little time for feeling frightened. Stan Balkwill, the pilot, had to fly them at fifty feet above the sea – the height of a four-storey building – which was extremely demanding. The two gunners were busily sweeping the skies all the time just in case anything was around, while Fraser was fully occupied in making sure they reached their target without mishap.

Crew losses remained high. One of Fraser's good friends from Observer School had reached Egypt too and had flown over to Malta with the rest of the squadron. On one of their first missions over Palermo, he was shot down along with the rest of the crew. Fraser had been quite upset about it, although news came through later that his friend had been rescued and made a prisoner-of-war. Despite these losses, morale remained high. This was due in part to their CO, Wing Commander Maurice Gaine, who Fraser believed was an outstanding leader, and in part to the changing situation – after all, the Axis were now on the back foot. Fraser was also aware of a strong sense of team spirit, not just within the squadron, but throughout the whole Island. On Malta, they might have been set apart from the rest of the world, yet Fraser felt a deep-rooted sense of belonging too, as though their successes were the result of a combined effort of every man, woman and child on the Island.

More reinforcements were being sent out to the Tenth Submarine Flotilla, and one of Simpson's trusted officers from the early days on Malta was now making his way back. Having completed his CO's course in Britain, Tubby Crawford was given command of a new U-class submarine – *P.51* – being built at Barrow-in-Furness in the north of England. Joining his new crew and boat in July, he was immediately sent to join the Third Flotilla in Scotland, where he was to spend six weeks checking all was well with the new submarine and acclimatizing the crew. Even then, he knew they would shortly be sent to Malta, and on 20 September, he set sail from Portsmouth, arriving in Gibraltar on 4 October.

Some bad weather on the way meant that by the time *P.51* reached Gibraltar a few repairs were needed. Nonetheless, his first major voyage had gone well enough. With the North Africa landings about to be launched, Tubby was ordered to stay in Gibraltar, from where he would carry out his first Mediterranean combat patrol as part of the naval operations of Torch.

It was a traumatic first trip. On 6 November, Tubby spotted a destroyer entering Toulon in the south of France. With orders to report the movement of any Vichy French vessel seen, Tubby moved well out of range then signalled his sighting. The problem was that in doing so, he revealed their presence, and the following day a number of French anti-submarine ships were patrolling the area. *P.51* was detected, and then attacked, five depth charges dropping uncomfortably close. The boat swayed and rocked, bits of corking fell from above, and Tubby found himself crouching once more. He'd not suffered such an attack for the best part of a year, but there was a terrible familiarity about the experience. The force of the explosions caused the quick-diving emergency tank – Q Tank – to flood, causing the submarine to begin sinking rapidly. Tubby had never seen the needle on the depth gauge going round so fast, and realised some drastic action was needed quickly. To be depth charged on his first patrol in the Mediterranean – and with the explosions horribly close – was as stiff a test of his resolve and leadership as he was ever likely to get. Now, everyone was looking at him, watching his expression and waiting for his command – there was no Wanklyn to turn to. Ordering the Numbers One and Two Main Ballast Tanks to be blown – i.e., releasing the water from the two of the tanks encasing the body of *P.51*, part of the normal process for rising – he hoped he could halt this terrifying dive.

Finally, the boat steadied at 345 feet below the surface; the U-class was not supposed to be able to dive lower than 200. They could easily have sunk to their graves. But their difficulties were not over. The problem now was that with the two ballast tanks blown, they began to rise to the surface once again. Air trapped in the tanks would force out more water, making the submarine even lighter and liable to come to the surface like a cork. The only option was to open the vents in a short burst and hope that the escaping air would not cause too many air bubbles and disturbance on the surface and give their position away. Fortunately, they were not spotted, and were able to make good their escape. 'It wasn't very pleasant,' says Tubby of this attack, 'although it did give us great confidence in our submarine to know it could safely dive to such a depth.' Already, he was discovering that commanding a submarine was very different from being the Number One officer. Getting command of a boat had been his goal since first volunteering for service in submarines, but the war had given him this responsibility much earlier than would have been the case in peacetime. In 1942 he was just 25. 'Of course, it was a great thrill to get a command, but a fairly awesome responsibility too,' he says.

This first patrol also taught him that orders from above needed to be handled with a certain degree of discretion, something Wanklyn had always understood. Because the Vichy ship had been *entering* port, and therefore posed little threat to the Torch operations, Tubby was criticized for making his report and revealing his presence. Nonetheless, the recently promoted Rear-Admiral Raw was happy now to give *P.51* a new name – *Unseen* – an irony lost on no one.

After further repairs, *Unseen* finally left Gibraltar on 4 December, arriving in Malta fully laden with stores just after midday on the 13th. Tubby had mixed feelings about being back. 'There was always a wonderful spirit in the Malta squadron under Simpson,' he recalls, 'so it was good to be back under his command.' And it was good, too, to discover his old friend Margaret Lewis was still on the Island. But life on Malta was grim, the shortages far from over and the effects of two-and-a-half years of siege were taking their toll on a war-weary population. 'Glasses in the mess were sawn-off beer bottles – it was pretty basic,' says Tubby. 'Foodwise, we submariners were all right, but it certainly wasn't much fun ashore any more.'

There were few Maltese who would have disagreed with him. While Montgomery was beating back Rommel at El Alamein, Malta was facing one of its most critical stages of the entire war. Despite the victories in the air and at sea, the Island was starving. Operation Pedestal had moved the Target Date for surrender back several months, but her cargoes had been principally fuel, ammunition and essential foodstuffs such as flour and potatoes. True, the Magic Carpet Service was still bringing in more supplies, but again, these tended to be aviation fuel and essential medical supplies. Of virtually every other basic commodity, there was nothing left. Goats, pigs, chickens and sheep had all gone; they'd been eaten along with just about any other animal on the Island. And although there were more subscribers to the Victory Kitchens than ever, this says more about the desperation of the people than anything else. On 1 September a letter to the *Times of Malta* reported:

'The midday meals supplied from the Victory Kitchens of Valletta and of several other districts had to be thrown away *en masse* today. The meal was composed chiefly of liver in a sort of stew. It was hard and had a bitter taste, which made it unpalatable and uneatable. This suggests that the gall had not been removed from the liver either before it was put in cold storage or before it was cooked ... A slice of corned beef was passed round hours later.'[7]

Ken Griffiths had lost so much weight, he could count all his ribs. In October he was promoted to sergeant and invited to the Sergeants' Mess. 'What would you like to drink, Taffy?' he was asked. 'Whisky, please,' he replied. 'You'll be bloody lucky,' he was told. 'You'll have gin and like it!' In fact, he was 'bloody lucky' to be offered even that; the only drink on the Island now was that brought in by RAF crews and the Navy. Even Warby's friend, Tony, had been caught and locked up for black market profiteering. By the beginning of November, Ken was living on three boiled sweets, half a sardine and a spoonful of jam a day. They were given powdered milk to go with their tea, but it sank to the bottom of the mug. Bread was sawn off a loaf, weighed, then handed over. Each slice was riddled with fleas and bugs, so he brushed them off, picked out the particularly bad bits and ate the rest. Bomb damage still lay strewn throughout the Island's towns and cities: no one had much strength left to do anything about it. Even the submariners, used to fighting with full stomachs, were struggling with the shortages like everyone else. There were no more pigs to be reared on Manoel Island now.

On 6 October, the new Acting Lieutenant-Governor broadcast to the people; he had little of comfort to say, but defended the necessity and good intentions of the Victory Kitchens, pointing out that the bread ration had increased in August – albeit by a tiny amount – and announcing that they had received 'certain small amounts of chocolate, Bovril, biscuits and currants'. They were not of sufficient quantity to make a regular issue, but a single, small issue would be added to the ration. 'You, for your part, must continue to look forward to better days, remembering that the food front is the battle front in Malta.'[8]

The only way there would be better days was for convoys to start arriving at regular intervals. By November, Tobruk had been retaken and the Eighth Army was advancing towards Benghazi. The problem was that Tunisia and Tripolitania, the parts of North Africa closest to Malta, were still in Axis hands, as, of course, were Sicily, Sardinia and other surrounding islands. With the British fleet busy with the North Africa campaign, this made sending another convoy through to Malta highly problematic.

Nonetheless, approval to try another convoy from Alexandria was given, and on 15 November, a week after American troops had landed in Algeria, four merchantmen, loaded with 35,000 tonnes of food and supplies, and escorted by five cruisers and seventeen destroyers, set sail for Malta. Although the convoy was attacked by torpedo bombers *en route*, only one of the ships suffered any damage. With their hands full in North Africa, the Axis had been unable to assemble more than a token strike force. At 3 a.m. on the 20th, all four ships pulled safely into Grand Harbour. Salvation had come in the nick of time: the Target Date had been set for 3 December, just thirteen days away.

On 1 December, four more merchant ships left Egypt, later joined by a 7,000-ton American tanker from the newly reoccupied Benghazi. The ships arrived five days later. The crews were greeted by 'a memorable reception … early on a fine crisp morning. There were thousands of people lining the battlements cheering each ship as it passed through the narrow entrance. Soldiers at various points stood to attention as each ship passed. Never have we seen such gratitude.'[9] This was the last convoy of supplies ever to be sailed to Malta, and it had arrived entirely unscathed.

The longest siege in British history was over.

But Malta's misery was not over yet – not quite. As Meme Cortis says, 'Malta was hit not just by bombs but by epidemics as well.' After such a long time being underfed and living in less than sanitary conditions, it was only to be expected that the majority of people's resistance to disease had been weakened. Many were suffering from tuberculosis and dysentery, which made Meme's work much harder. Imtarfa had become so full that a number of cases were transferred to a sanitorium in Mdina. Two of Meme's former school friends had been sent there, as she'd discovered whilst accompanying some patients from the hospital. Both had been engaged to be married, and both died shortly after being admitted. Polio epidemics had ravaged the Island from time to time throughout the year, but now, with the Island saved, it was attacking the survivors once more. Meme nursed an Irish Guardsman struck down by the disease. For many months he hung on, supported by an iron lung, eventually recovering to spend the rest of his life in a wheelchair.

Frank and Mary Rixon's daughter, Betty, was doing well in spite of all their worry and anxiety. But many weren't so fortunate. In 1942 the infant mortality rate rose to almost one in three. The weak and old also suffered, and for the first time since records had existed, the Island's population went down.

Nor did the arrival of the convoys bring instant relief. Just before Christmas, ration increases in all basic foodstuffs as well as soap, matches and kerosene were announced, but frustratingly were not put into effect until the third week of January, nearly three months after winter had set in. The Island's servicemen were the first to really benefit, although in many cases they simply couldn't digest what they were given. At Christmas, Ken Griffiths and the other gunners at Spinola were all issued with a tin of steak and kidney pudding. 'Just a small tin, but by God, that was good!' says Ken. 'But a lot of them couldn't eat it because their stomachs had gone so small.' Ken was offered half of someone else's tin, which he readily accepted, but found he couldn't finish it. 'I'd eaten too much by then.'

Because the servicemen were receiving more rations than the civilian population, the Royal West Kent Regiment held a Christmas party for local children at St Andrew's Barracks on 2 January. The men gave up part of their rations so they could lay on enough food for a decent buffet. Frank Rixon was only too happy to help out; now he had a child of his own, he appreciated more keenly than ever the importance of giving the children a treat.

As time went on, life gradually began to improve. Rations were increased again on 6 February and twice in March, and as the population gathered its strength, so its health improved. Enemy raids had almost ground to a halt: from 153 in October, there were just 30 in November, 25 in January and a mere five in February. Those who still had homes were able to sleep in their beds again, free from the damp and the sand flies. Cinemas were full once more and dances were being held. On 21 January, an advertisement in the *Times of Malta* announced that 'A dramatic repertory company is to be formed. Services personnel and Civilians interested are invited to send their names, etc, to Captain Crossley, Command Fair, Merchants Street, Valletta.'[10] And for a change, the news from abroad was almost consistently good. On 24 January there was a spontaneous popular demonstration on Kingsway, at the heart of Valletta, to celebrate the Eighth Army's entry into Tripoli. The Germans were also in retreat in Russia, having finally surrendered at Stalingrad on 2 February. In the Pacific, the Allies were back on the offensive too, taking the island of Guadalcanal the same month.

ABC had been involved with planning the Allied invasion of North Africa. So far, all seemed to be going well and he was now summoned to join the Chiefs of Staff and Allied leaders – Churchill, President Roosevelt and the Allied Supreme Commander in North Africa, General Dwight Eisenhower – at a conference in Casablanca to discuss the next stage of the war. The American and British forces were now working ever more closely, and appointments about who was commanding who in battle needed to be resolved. As a result of the position shuffling, Tedder was appointed Commander-in-Chief of a united Allied Air Force, something he had long advocated, while ABC was to remain as overall Commander-in-Chief of the Allied Naval Invasion Forces. He was also promoted to Admiral of the Fleet. There was no higher active command. 'I considered myself extremely fortunate at having been lucky enough to reach the highest rank in His Majesty's Navy,' wrote ABC later.[11]

At the Casablanca Conference, it was also agreed that the invasion of

Sicily should proceed as quickly as possible after the defeat of the Axis in North Africa, and planning began in February. Malta would have a key role: from there the invasion would be launched. Its proximity to Sicily meant it could be used as the bridgehead, a solid aircraft carrier which could be built up with supplies and forces until D-Day – the moment of invasion – arrived.

In the meantime, Malta had an important part to play in the ultimate defeat of the enemy in North Africa. The Allied advance had paused at the end of 1942, and the Axis had used this opportunity to reinforce their forces with troops, fuel, ammunition and other supplies. Rommel was not going quietly. Shrimp Simpson's submarines and the Beaufighters, Beauforts and Wellingtons of Malta were as busy as ever.

On his first patrol from Malta in December, Tubby noticed an alarming change in the enemy. Although there had been two nights with no moon, *Unseen* was detected on no fewer than six occasions by enemy aircraft. They were bombed twice and once a surface vessel was led towards them and a hunt developed. As he was discovering, the Italians now had ASV radar in their aircraft. From now on, Tubby would have to be even more vigilant.

Unseen sailed off again on 8 January to patrol the western approaches to Tripoli, which were already being evacuated by the Axis forces. On the 17th, they spotted a merchant vessel escorted by a motor torpedo boat. Closing in for the attack, Tubby gave the order to fire three torpedoes, two of which hit. In between scooping out survivors, the MTB escort hunted for *Unseen*, dropping a number of depth charges. Once again, Tubby's skills were tested to the full. Six were close 'and shook the crew alarmingly,'[12] but caused no serious damage to the boat. Eventually, after two hours, the MTB sailed away, and Tubby gingerly raised the periscope to see the remains of his victim. All that was left was a raft, a few oil drums and petrol containers, a lifeboat and a sole corpse, floating on the water. 'It was a great relief to get a hit,' says Tubby, 'and, of course, it was good for the morale of the whole crew.' His good touch continued in the next patrol, too, when they sank another small merchant vessel.

But Tubby's reunion with Shrimp Simpson was to be short-lived. On 23 January, the indefatigable commander of the Tenth Flotilla relinquished command. He was exhausted and confessed to 'the gnawing anxiety every hour of every day and night over how my men were standing up to the strain of operating within a narrow channel with barely sea room to manœuvre.'[13] Tubby had nothing but the highest esteem for Simpson, and like the other COs was sorry to see him go. A quarter of a million tons of Axis shipping had been sunk or damaged during his command, a considerable figure. Admiral Harwood wrote to him, 'The 10th S/M Flotilla has distinguished itself in a branch of the Service whose reputation has never stood higher than it does today. The great achievements of the S/Ms operating under your control are a reflection of your resolute and inspiring leadership.'[14] There was not a man in the Tenth Flotilla who would disagree.

Mines were increasingly being used by the Allied Forces as well as torpedoes. With the Axis vacating a number of ports along the North African coast, laying minefields was a particularly effective way of sinking enemy shipping in the rush to leave harbour. The Tenth Flotilla's minelayer *Rorqual*, for example, no longer needed for the Magic Carpet Service, could lay no fewer than fifty mines at any one time. The Beauforts were also used for such duties.

On 9 January, Fraser Carlisle-Brown and his crew were ordered to lay mines off the Tunisian port of Sfax. They were heading back, having completed their task, when they realized they were being followed by a German night fighter – they could see the orange glow on its nose. Stan Balkwill immediately dropped back down as close to the sea as he dared, but every time they looked round, the enemy plane was still there. They couldn't understand why it hadn't tried to shoot them down. It was a nerve-wracking trip back. Only when they were ten minutes from Malta were they finally left alone. It was the Intelligence Officer back at Luqa who explained why they'd been spared. Because they'd flown so low, the night fighter would have known it was all too easy to crash into the sea.

Meanwhile, Frank Rixon had spent much of his time since Christmas helping with the unloading of cargo ships. To safeguard all the supplies, this was carried out as quickly as possible, then the goods were taken to a number of dumps which had been set up all over the Island. From there they were taken to civilian stores and to Royal Army Service Corps (RASC) stores. 'Pink' Dump at Floriana was where the Royal West Kents were deployed, the men working in twelve-hour shifts. Even so, there had been time for an inter-regimental football tournament, where the Kents had acquitted themselves well – their greatest triumph being a six-nil victory over the 7th Heavy Anti-Aircraft Regiment. Frank, though, was more interested in running and boxing, and in any case, spent any time off with Mary and Betty. 'She always knew when Frank was coming down the steps,' says Mary, 'because she used to start chanting "Da-Da, Da-Da".'

By March, with the Axis collapse in North Africa ever closer, the Island began its preparations for the invasion of Sicily. On the 3rd, the Royal West Kents started a period of intensive training. Frank was sent to Gozo for a week, then to Manoel Island to practise combined operations with the Navy.

Tubby Crawford was also preparing for the invasion. In May, he was ordered to undertake top secret reconnaissance work along the beaches of Sicily. He was to work with a number of men from the Combined Operations Pilotage Parties (COPP), and was to leave Lazzaretto at dusk with a couple of Coppists (as they were known) on board. Attached to the submarine, just aft – or behind – the conning tower, would be a 'chariot' – a two-man underwater human torpedo, to be used in this instance in an alternative role. After dark, *Unseen* would surface and sail towards Sicily, diving again before first light. At daybreak, Tubby would carry out a periscope reconnaissance of the beach concerned, pointing out landmarks to the Coppists. Then it was a question of waiting underwater until dark. At this point, *Unseen* would surface again, about a mile from the shore, and the two Coppists would clamber out with a small collapsible canvas canoe – a folbot – and unhook their chariot. In the folbot, the Coppists would lead the chariot to a position half a mile from the beach. Then one of the men, wearing diving kit, would clamber on to the chariot and dive to about forty feet, finishing the journey to the beach along the bottom of the seabed. Just short of the beach, he would swim ashore, attached to the chariot by a wire. Then, having carried out his reconnaissance, he would return to the submarine by the reverse procedure.

Tubby was to spend four months carrying out such missions, and although they never lost a single chariot in that time, these were not the sort of operations he enjoyed. Lying all day on the bottom of the seabed just a mile from shore, and with ASV-equipped enemy aircraft buzzing overhead, was an uncomfortable experience, to say the least.

★

By the end of April, the war in North Africa was nearly over. On the evening of the 23rd, Fraser Carlisle-Brown and his crew took off from Luqa to hunt down an Axis merchant ship that had been struck earlier in the day by US Army Air Force bombers but not sunk. Both he and Stan Balkwill had been commissioned, but although that meant that the two moved out of the Balluta Buildings and into different digs, the four of them were still spending most of their time together; apart from a week's leave, they had been on almost non-stop operations. And, incredibly, they were *still* together, a complete crew unchanged since the moment they'd left England. They'd had a few close calls, of course. On one occasion, they'd been attacking a convoy of one tanker and one merchant vessel on a bright moonlit night, but because of the proximity of the ships to the Marettimo Islands off the western point of Sicily, they'd been obliged to attack with the moon behind them. Silhouetted against it, their approach could not have been clearer had it been in the middle of the day, and anti-aircraft fire was soon bursting all around them. Just before they dropped their torpedo, their Beaufort was hit, damaging both the rudder and the elevators. Although they'd dropped their torpedo and hit the merchant vessel, they were in serious trouble. Fraser had tried to send out an SOS signal, but there had been no reply. Somehow, Stan had managed to get them back, and with Fraser pumping down the undercarriage manually, they'd landed in one piece. Stan was to be given a DFM for that night's work.

The night of the 23rd was a different proposition. They found the damaged ship, already dead in the water and abandoned, the escort long since gone with her crew. A large 5,000-ton vessel, she was a sitting duck. Stan made sure they did not miss – as their torpedo struck, the ship exploded, and it sank in less than five minutes. Fraser did not know it then, but they had just scored the last ever torpedo hit by a Beaufort in the Mediterranean.

Meanwhile the Malta Spitfires had been keeping busy. Keith Park had sent out his first bomb-carrying Spitfires the previous October, but in recent months his 'Spit-Bombers' had been continually buzzing over Sicily and Italy, bombing airfields, trains and anything else they could see. On 28 April, they shot down their 1,000th aircraft. The *Times of Malta* was enjoying the Island's revenge.

'The score was still 999 when the two Spitfires took off early today,' it reported the following day. 'Their pilots were Squadron Leader J.J. Lynch, of Alhambra, California, and Pilot Officer A.F. Osborne of Reading. The Spitfires went to the coast of Sicily and began to search for the thousandth Hun. Squadron Leader Lynch saw it first – a Junkers 52 flying near the coast just above the smooth sea. He made one attack and saw strikes along the starboard side of the fuselage. The Junkers began to trail petrol, hung in the air for a few moments while its pilots attempted to get to the beach, then went straight into the sea. In the meantime, Pilot Officer Osborne had found another Junkers 52 a little distance away. "As soon as my Junkers had crashed, I went off to see how my No. 2 was doing," said S/Ldr Lynch. "I found him attacking his Ju. 52 and we finished it off together." That made one thousand and one enemy aircraft destroyed by the RAF in Malta since the war began.'

Adrian Warburton was now a Wing Commander, and leading the newly formed 683 Squadron of PR (Photo Reconnaissance) Spitfires. In March he'd been given a couple of weeks' leave. This was the first time he'd been back to the UK since leaving with Tich Whiteley and 431 Flight in September 1940. Back then, he'd been in debt and in serious trouble, so it was a nice surprise to discover the fund Whiteley had arranged for him had never been stopped. For two-and-a-half years a proportion of his pay had been going into this account. The debt had long since been paid and the account was now comfortably in credit. Having arranged to meet his old mentor – who was still in England – Warby gave him a sealed envelope, asking him not to open it until he'd gone. But Whiteley tore it open right away. Inside was a large wad of five-pound notes – half the balance of the account. Knowing Warby would never take the money back, Whiteley arranged for it to be redeposited once his friend had left for Malta again.

Despite being a Wing Commander, Warby never stopped flying and he never stopped getting his pictures. Pantelleria, Lampedusa, Sicily – Warby photographed them all. John Agius, who saw him a good deal, remembers one story. Warby had been flying over Sicily in his unarmed PR Spitfire, and had been shot at by anti-aircraft fire. 'Naturally Warburton was very annoyed, seeing he could do nothing about it. So the moment he landed in Malta, he asked for an armed Spitfire and went back to Sicily, swooped down on the gun site and gave them all he had. He was still not satisfied and went back once more, this time with his PR Spitfire so that he could show what he had achieved on his second expedition.'[15]

John Agius had been following the developments in North Africa. The *Times of Malta* never failed to report the good news, but at the RAF office in Scots Street he heard things, and could see for himself the number of Spitfires and pilots arriving on the Island. It didn't take much to work out Malta was winning her war.

The Axis forces in North Africa finally surrendered on 12 May. Since 1 December, around 230 Axis ships had been sunk in the Mediterranean, mostly by Malta-based submarines and aircraft. In the weeks to come, plans for the invasion of Sicily were stepped up. Ships, aircraft, men and provisions poured into the Island. Malta had begun her war with a handful of obsolete biplanes; by July 1943, she was heaving with over 600 aircraft.

The pace had at last slowed for Fraser and his mates, and they made the most of it by swimming in the bays and hiring a small boat to go sailing. He enjoyed hearing the *dghajsa* men singing opera tunes by the Sliema landing; even with the amount of destruction still so evident, he felt there was a kind of haunting beauty about the Island.

There were now a number of American gunners on Malta. Ken Griffiths never had a chance to meet any of them, but he and his friends were annoyed at the way the Yanks, with their better pay, were pushing up the price of everything. As far as he was concerned, the sooner they were in Sicily, the better.

Higher-ranking Americans were now at Lascaris, which had been transformed into the nerve-centre for Operation Husky, the invasion of Europe. Just a year before, Malta was one of the worst postings in the world. Now, it was swarming with Allied leaders: Eisenhower, Montgomery, General Clark, General Alexander, Air Vice-Marshal Park; all had offices down in the Hole.

Even the King wanted to go to Malta; he had told this to ABC while on a visit to Algiers. Now re-appointed C-in-C of the Mediterranean as well as being Admiral of the Fleet, ABC knew more than anyone how much such a visit to the Island would be appreciated. George VI arrived on Malta on the morning of 20 June, aboard HMS *Aurora* and accompanied by Malta's favourite Admiral. A fighter escort of Spitfires roared overhead, but although the visit had only been announced at 5 a.m. that morning, the Barraccas, quayside and any other vantage-point were all thick with cheering people. 'I have witnessed many memorable spectacles; but this was the most impressive of them all,' wrote ABC. 'The visit produced one of the most spontaneous and genuine demonstrations of loyalty and affection I have ever seen.'[16]

The King even managed to visit the hospital at Imtarfa. 'All the doctors, sisters and nurses filed outside to have a good chance of seeing him and to wave as he went past,' recalls Meme Cortis. He passed by just a few yards from her, which was a great thrill. For Meme Cortis, the lack of bombs overhead seemed like a miracle. She still found herself ducking when low-level aircraft flew overhead, but seeing the Royal Navy filling Grand Harbour brought back happy memories of the Island before the war. The wards were quieter now, and once the invasion started, she wondered whether she might be more use in Italy.

The Royal West Kents, on the other hand, were not part of the invasion plans. After three years on the Island, filling in bomb craters and surviving the worst of the blitzes and shortages of the siege, Frank Rixon and his colleagues were posted to Egypt in June. The move meant a painful separation from his wife and baby daughter, but such were the hardships of wartime. It would be nearly two years before he saw them again.

Fraser Carlisle-Brown and the rest of his crew also left Malta in June. Posted to North Africa, it seems they were the only Beaufort crew to have survived a tour of duty in the Mediterranean together.

With its airfields heaving with aircraft and harbours wedged with ships of all shapes and sizes, Malta had become home to the biggest amphibious invasion force the world had ever seen. It was a remarkable turnaround in the Island's fortunes. Nowhere in the world had suffered such persistent and concentrated bombing. And while the bombs fell, her people had endured starvation, death and disease. Brought to her knees, the Island had never fallen. Now, as the Allies prepared to invade Sicily, Malta's triumph was complete.

A Short Engagement over Sicily

12 JULY 1943

ONE OF THE many fighter pilots on Malta at the beginning of July 1943 was Raoul Daddo-Langlois, having recently returned to play his part in the invasion. He had become a quite different person from the eager, fresh-faced young man who had arrived on the Island eighteen months before. How could he be otherwise after what he'd been through?

On their return from Malta in July 1942, Raoul and his friend Laddie Lucas had at last been split up. Lucas took up a staff job at Fighter Command HQ, while Raoul was sent to become an instructor at RAF Chedworth in Gloucestershire. This was the fate of many pilots after an intense operational tour of duty, but Raoul struggled to come to terms with this sudden and drastic change of pace. The countryside around Gloucester was, he admitted, lovely, and the flying not *too* bad, but he was feeling rather depressed about the new situation. 'I can't get settled down to this "peaceful" flying,' he admitted to his sister, Angela. 'Get so fed-up occasionally.'

Whenever he could, he travelled up to London – there he could meet up with Laddie and other friends, men who'd been through similar experiences; men who understood what it was like to tear about the sky, fighting for your life, a 109 on your tail. On one occasion he met a girl – Patience Welstead, known as Paddy – at a club where she had her own song and dance routine. It was Paul Brennan, an Australian pilot who'd been in 249 with him on Malta, who introduced them. That night Raoul and Paddy sat at one of the club's tables and drank three-quarters of a bottle of whisky. Raoul returned to Chedworth thinking the two of them were an item, but several weeks passed and he heard nothing more from her. When he tried to call her on his next leave, she told him she was about to go off on holiday for a month and had been suffering from bronchitis. He never saw her again.

In April 1943, Laddie Lucas was posted to command 616 South Yorkshire Auxiliary Squadron and immediately wrote to Raoul asking him to come and join him as a flight commander. He refused. Without mentioning anything to any of his friends or family, Raoul had applied to join a photo reconnaissance unit. A month later, in May 1943, he was ordered to fly a new blue PR Spitfire Mk IX to Castel Benito, near Tripoli in Libya.

Although he'd suffered some engine trouble *en route*, he managed to land safely in Gibraltar. Having had his aircraft checked over, he took off again the following day for Castel Benito. All went well to begin with, but soon after crossing into North Africa he discovered his long-range fuel tanks wouldn't work. By this time he was flying over the desert, a vast and inhospitable wasteland. There was no chance he'd make Castel Benito, but he figured he might just make Sfax on the east Tunisian coast. Then the cloud came down, and although he picked up a ground station he was sent back in the direction he'd just come from. Flying on until he ran out of fuel and his engine cut, he then spotted a small area that looked fairly level. Wheels up, amid a cloud of dust, he landed.

Fortunately, he was not too far from civilization and with the help of some Arab tribesmen, was able to reach a small French desert outpost. From there, he eventually made it to Castel Benito, some nine days late and without his brand-new Spitfire.

After a couple of days' hanging about, he was told he could take passage in a transit plane to Malta, where he was due to join Adrian Warburton's 683 Squadron. But just as he was about to board the plane, he met Warby himself, 'the kingpin PRU man in Malta'. Raoul explained what had happened, but Warby suggested he go back to England for another PR Spitfire, rather than fly on to Malta. Raoul wasn't having any of that. He'd had nothing but trouble since leaving England and on his long journey through the desert had decided to try to get back on to a fighter squadron. Raoul told Warby this, 'and he was pretty annoyed – naturally enough. After a short argument, mainly one-sided, it was agreed that I would go on to Cairo and try and get a posting from there.'

From Cairo, Raoul was posted back to Malta, to join 93 Squadron as a supernumerary flight commander. He landed back at Luqa on 30 June.

By July 1943, the Island had also changed since he'd last been there. With the lifting of the siege, Malta was now swarming with aircraft, ships and supplies in preparation for the invasion of Sicily. The days when there'd been so few planes the pilots had been able to count them on the fingers of one hand, or when they'd survived on scraps of sardines and insect-infested bread, had long gone.

Despite the turn-around in the Island's fortunes, Raoul was not happy to be back, and thought his new squadron, 93, a disorganized joke. On his first sortie on 1 July, for instance, half the squadron had turned home early, behaviour that would previously have landed them in serious trouble. Despite the fact that an imminent invasion was being planned, there seemed to be little method to their flying: he'd never seen such a lack of discipline in the air. A more haphazard squadron would have been hard to find.

Raoul had desperately wanted to rejoin his old squadron, 249. They were still on Malta and still based at Takali, the airfield where he had spent so much of his time the previous year, but his Group Captain had told him it was impossible. It was hard to believe it had been almost a year since he'd first left the Island; it was even harder to believe what they'd gone through then: the endless bombing, the long and desperate days, under the ever-present threat of invasion, flying battered Spitfires against an enemy of vastly superior numbers, day in, day out. Constantly falling ill through lack of food and sleep, they had fought on despite those appalling conditions and facing relentless and overwhelming enemy forces. Many of his friends had been killed — some shot down into the sea, others bombed on the ground. But a fellowship had been forged in the teeth of death, a fellowship so close as to be inexplicable to anyone who'd not shared the experience. And together they'd somehow clawed their way back, until victory in the air was theirs and the whole balance of the Mediterranean war had begun to turn.

When he returned, it was to find a new squadron complaining about the threat to the Wing from as few as 20 enemy fighters. Wings! A wing meant three whole squadrons – as many as 48 aircraft in one formation. In the old days they'd sometimes had as few as four Spitfires to take on a hundred! This new crew knew nothing of what air-fighting was really like. And he also missed his old comrades. Friends who really knew him. Friends from all walks of life and from all across the English-speaking world whom he would never normally have come to know: friends with whom he had forged a cast-iron bond and who were now either dead or far away in different arenas of the war.

On 4 July 1943, American Independence Day, Raoul had watched wave after wave of American bombers fly beneath him towards Sicily. It felt as if the Island of Malta had been transformed into an enormous aircraft carrier. Three new airfields had been built: Safi, which lay between Hal Far and Luqa in the south; Qrendi, in the west, recently opened by Air Vice-Marshal Sir Keith Park flying in the first Spitfire to land there; and another on the smaller, neighbouring island of Gozo, built by the Americans in an incredible nineteen days. Of the 608 planes on the Island, over 500 were fighters, and most were Spitfires. And whereas fuel and ammunition had been precious commodities a year before, the Island now had all the supplies it needed.

A few days after his return to Malta, Raoul had bumped into John Lodge, an old friend from his first spell on the Island. Previously the Intelligence Officer at Takali, John was now a squadron leader, and the two had had a long talk about the old days. Despite everything they'd endured, Raoul left him feeling 'very sick' for those times.

Now D-Day had finally arrived. Operation Husky, the Allied invasion of Sicily, was under way. On this day, 10 July 1943, just over three years after Italian bombers first attacked Malta, the Allies would re-enter Europe.

Raoul was flying a patrol over Sicily on 12 July, two days after the invasion, when a dozen German Junkers 88s attacked the bombers flying below him. Peeling off from the rest of the formation, he ordered his section of four to follow. Like most such dogfights, the engagement was fast, furious and hard for its participants to follow; and Raoul was soon lost to view in the mêlée. Moments later his fellow pilots heard him say on the radio, 'I've got a Ju. 88, but am hit and will have to force-land.'

He aimed for a field near the south-east coast of Sicily. Despite having crash-landed before and survived unscathed – even on his first flight on Malta sixteen months before – his luck now deserted him. On impact, he so badly damaged himself and the plane that his rescuers had difficulty cutting him out of the wreckage. Examined by a naval surgeon shortly afterwards, he was diagnosed with a 'compound depressed fracture of the frontal bone of his skull and minor injuries of both arms and legs'.

After temporary treatment on a Navy landing craft, arrangements were made for Raoul to be transferred that evening to a hospital ship waiting off-shore. But American friendly fire mistakenly attacked the launch taking him to the ship – and it was sunk, with him on it.

The story of Raoul Daddo-Langlois is in many ways symbolic of the experience of those living through the Siege of Malta. Like most who fought in the war, he was young – only eighteen when he joined up – and, again, like most, indelibly scarred by what he had witnessed.

To his friends, he was 'a delightful man, straight, courageous' and 'possessed a most attractive personality; everyone liked him.'[1] And he was dependable, too. Quiet, but always cheerful, everyone in 249 Squadron had known they could rely on 'Daddy-Longlegs'.

But by the time of his death, Raoul had an old man's world-weariness. The difference between his handwriting two years before, and that of the days before his death, is telling. In a letter to his mother from Cambridge in the autumn of 1940, his words are high-looped and free-flowing. It is an eighteen-year-old's letter, full of life and humour, in which he thanks her for sending through the cricket gear and tells her he thinks they will shortly be posted elsewhere. But perhaps, he asks, she could send through some fruit? '(M)any' apples from the orchard at home would be 'hugely appreciated'. It is also a letter that underscores the extreme youth of men such as Raoul: fresh from school, still subject to his mother's attempts to look after and protect him.

Raoul's mother would undoubtedly have been shocked by the changes war had wrought in him. A letter written from Africa three years later, *en route* to his second posting to Malta, betrayed no hint of excitement or *joie de vivre*. Even taking the censors' work into account, it was an especially anodyne note, and his handwriting, once so fluent and full, had become tiny and flat, a barely legible scrawl. By the time he'd reached Castel Benito, he had been feeling lonely and miserable. He'd always had a low boredom threshold, but since leaving Malta the previous summer, these bouts of frustration had increasingly been replaced by dark, 'insidious' moods. 'Another of those terrible moods of despondency has settled and I have given way to it,' he wrote, '... there seems no light ahead to guide one's groping hands; no sense in the ordaining of one's moments; nothing to look forward to.' Yet this was a change which had occurred in little more than a year, for the diary he wrote during his first weeks on Malta, in February 1942, revealed the same unmistakable hand of the eighteen-year-old recruit.

Raoul Daddo-Langlois's story condenses the paradoxes of war. During his months on Malta in 1942 he witnessed destruction and hardship on a scale that, today, we cannot possibly comprehend. But while every day was a struggle for survival, he had, nonetheless, never felt more alive. This was both the most exciting and traumatic period of his life: he was part of a small band of men fighting against appalling odds for a cause in which they believed. Nothing could ever equal the intensity of that experience of the 'old days' to which he repeatedly referred in his diary.

By the time of his return to Malta in July 1943, the Island had become the bridgehead for the biggest amphibious invasion in the history of warfare. Of course he was not able to relate to his new comrades in arms, who, aside from their youth and inexperience, had never seen the Island during its darkest days. They could never live up to the memory he carried of his fallen colleagues. The irony is that the posting he was refused to his old squadron might well have left him even more disappointed.

A fighter pilot can be killed at any moment. Even the greatest aces can be hit by a chance bullet, suffer unaccountable engine failure at any time, or momentarily lose concentration. Those who survive need their share of luck.

It is hard to say why Raoul had to die in an air battle in which the Allies, at last, enjoyed total air superiority. But it does seem clear that on 12 July 1943 Raoul Daddo-Langlois was already living in the past, psychologically wounded by the burden of his brief experiences. The youthful vigour, that of a young man with everything to live for, had already been extinguished.

Raoul's body was never recovered. Instead, he is remembered on

Panel 6, Column 1 of the Malta Memorial, an imposing column crested by a Golden Eagle, standing outside the City Gate, the main entrance to Valletta.

He was twenty-one.

POSTSCRIPT

The last air raid over Malta was on 20 July 1943, the 3,340th alert since that morning on 11 June 1940. On 3 September, the Italians surrendered, and on the 11th, ABC signalled the Admiralty, 'Be pleased to inform their Lordships that the Italian battle fleet now lies at anchor under the guns of the fortress of Malta.'[1]

Churchill visited the Island in November. As one of their staunchest supporters, the Maltese had reason to welcome him warmly, and although his visit had been kept secret, there was still a sizeable crowd to cheer him as he toured the wrecked streets of Valletta. In December, President Roosevelt also visited Malta. 'In the name of the People of the United States of America, I salute the Island of Malta, its people and its defenders, who in the cause of freedom and justice and decency throughout the world, have rendered valorous service far above and beyond the call of duty,' he said during his address at Luqa. 'Under repeated fire from the skies, Malta stood alone but unafraid in the centre of the sea, one tiny bright flame in the darkness – a beacon of hope for the clearer days which have come.'[2]

But Malta lay in ruins. Its harbours were still a tangled mess, the quaysides wrecked, her waters littered with sunken or disabled ships. The war continued – but Malta's part had been played and she was left with the wreckage of the siege. For years, the bomb damage remained, the towns full of collapsed buildings like scars unable to heal, and the countryside strewn with smashed and burnt-out aircraft. It was too much for Michael Montebello. 'The Army was leaving, the Navy was leaving … it was like a ghost town,' says Michael. At sixteen he joined the merchant navy, and, when in port in Australia, decided he liked the look of the place and jumped ship. He was flung in prison, but after two months was let out and has stayed there ever since. His mother sent his father over to bring him back to Malta, but he, on his arrival, reckoned his son had been very sensible and decided to stay there too. The whole family emigrated for good shortly after. Michael returned to sea, joining the Australian Merchant Navy and it was whilst his ship was at Adelaide that he met his wife Jean – also brought up on Malta. They married in 1955 and have two children. Michael retired in 1986 – as a Chief Steward on the Australian National Line – and now lives in the small town of Rosebud in Victoria. He still visits Malta from time to time, as he did in April 2002, sixty years after the worst of the Blitz. The shelter where he lived for three and a half years is still there, as is the fish market and the Wills cigarette factory, although the building now lies empty. The quayside, in fact, looks remarkably unchanged. Any visitor now would recognize Grand Harbour as much the same place it was in 1940.

Dom Mintoff became Labour Prime Minister in 1955 and immediately called for integration into the United Kingdom. Crippled by the war, the British government vetoed the idea despite a referendum overwhelmingly in favour. Defence cuts also hit the Malta dockyards hard. Soon afterwards Mintoff began a crusade for full independence, continued by Prime Minister Dr George Borg Olivier, and finally granted in 1964. Malta became a republic in 1974, although British military services were allowed to continue to use specified land under the Military Facilities Agreement, until 1979.

John Agius was sorry to see the British go. After all, they were his employers and continued to be so after the war. He retired on 3 February 1978, having worked for the RAF for forty-two years. Never marrying, he continued to live in the family home with his brother Emanuel and sister May. After his retirement, he undertook the task of accounting for every single casualty of Malta's war. With patchy wartime records it was a considerable achievement, for which he was awarded an MBE. Every year, on 7 April, the family ate cheese pastizzi, just as they had the night their home was destroyed. Emanuel died in 1993, but John and May still observe this family tradition.

Meme Cortis did go to Italy. After the war she decided to go to London for further training and there she qualified as a Registered General Nurse (RGN) and State Certified Midwife (SCM). On returning to Malta, she met Les Turner, a sailor. They married on the Island, then moved back to London, where she continued in nursing. Now living in Northolt, she has two daughters and four grandchildren.

Sadly, few who flew from Malta during those days are still alive today. George Burges stayed in the RAF, attending Staff College and then joining the Air Ministry in 1944. He held a number of posts before retiring in 1959. After that he joined a retired Navy captain and Army colonel to set up and run a large painting contracting firm until he retired for good in 1980. He died of cancer ten years later.

Denis Barnham spent much of the remainder of the war as an instructor. He left the RAF once the war was over, and became the art master at Epsom College in Surrey, and a painter of some note. There he stayed, painting, teaching and running the RAF section of the school cadet force, but otherwise putting his military days behind him. His love of painting and architecture never diminished and he spent many school holidays travelling abroad, including a number of trips to Malta, the Island that had left such an indelible mark on him. In the 1970s, he developed a brain tumour, which forced him to retire early and leave Epsom. He and his wife Diana then lived in Dorset until his death in 1981. The day I visited Diana, she had just received a letter from one of his old pupils at Epsom saying what a very great influence Denis had been on his life.

George 'Screwball' Beurling did his bit for Canada, but depression soon struck. During speeches and interviews he began to make more and more outrageous comments. In one interview he gave this description of an attack on an Italian fighter: 'I could see all the details in his face because he turned and looked at me just as I had a bead on him. One of my cannon shells caught him in the face and blew his head right off. The body slumped and the slipstream caught the neck, the stub of the neck, and the blood streamed down the side of the cockpit. It was a great sight anyway.'[3] After a full recuperation, he was sent back to Britain, but life after Malta just wasn't the same. Uncontrollable, he tested the authority and patience of one after another of his commanders, including Johnnie Johnson and Buck McNair. Having been transferred to the RCAF, he brought his tally up to 32 confirmed kills before being given an honourable discharge. He applied to join the US Air Force, but was rejected. After the war, he was lost, and was even reduced to begging on street corners, until in 1947 he was asked by the Israeli Government to lead an international squadron of fighter pilots in their war with Palestine. On 20 May 1948, the transport plane taking him from Rome to Israel crashed, and he was killed.

Buck McNair returned to the UK and after taking part in the infamous Dieppe Raid in August 1942, took command of 421 Squadron RCAF, rising to become a wing leader in 1944. An earlier injury, when he'd been forced to bale out of a burning Spitfire, ensured he was taken off operations before D-Day. He finished the war with sixteen confirmed victories, and afterwards remained in the RCAF, later commanding No. 4 Canadian Wing in Germany. As a result of treatment for his back – the result of twice baling out during the war – he contracted leukaemia. He died in 1971.

Tommy Thompson left Malta to become an instructor in the Sudan, but on discovering this was more dangerous than being in a fighter squadron, joined another night-fighter squadron in the Western Desert. He was flying over El Alamein as the night barrage opened up at the beginning of the battle. After a stint as a test pilot, he joined BOAC in 1944, remaining a commercial pilot until his retirement from British Airways in 1975, by which time he'd become the most senior pilot within their fleet. He now lives in Hampshire.

As 81 Group Tactics Officer in the UK, Tom Neil finally got to fly Spitfires. He went on to command 41 Squadron, and then, after a brief spell instructing, was seconded to the US Air Force as Flying Liaison Officer. He took part in the Normandy invasion and then briefly saw action in Burma. After the war, he became a test pilot and then for some years served in the British Embassy in Washington. He later returned to America as a businessman before retiring to Norfolk. Married with three sons, he is still fit and well and now has a successful career as a writer.

Peter Rothwell returned to the UK and completed twelve months' instructing in Northern Ireland. From there he was posted to a four-engine Halifax squadron carrying out Met. (weather) flying. It was another difficult period for Peter as the Halifaxes suffered from repeated engine failure – on five separate occasions he was forced to fly back to base with only three engines working. He left the RAF in December 1945 – with 158 operational sorties to his name – and went back to Imperial Tobacco, the company he'd started working for before the war. He left in 1947 and went into car sales, running a series of garages in Poole, the Isle of Wight and Stratford-upon-Avon, before turning to a highly successful career in ship-building, and selling his boats all around the world. Now retired, he lives in Bournemouth.

After leaving Malta, the four 'B's finally split up and Fraser Carlisle-Brown became an instructor, firstly at a Beaufort OTU in Northern Ireland, then at an Advanced Navigation School near Barrow-in-Furness. He grew tired of instructing and managed to get himself posted to Transport Command, where, working with Dakota transport planes, he was involved in dropping parachutists on D-Day and at Arnhem. He left the RAF after the war and worked as a civil servant, firstly with his local authority, then for central government. He is married and now lives in Norfolk. Sadly, his pilot, Stan Balkwill, having survived the Mediterranean, was killed in a flying accident in Canada before the end of the war.

Pete Watson didn't leave Malta until 1944. After the war he joined a refrigeration company, which took him to Italy, among other places. He remained an electrician all his working life. Married, with a son and daughter, he lives in South London.

Art Roscoe eventually recovered from his injuries, and after a spell of non-operational flying, passed his Central Medical Board and requested to go back on operational flying. Posted back to Malta after the invasion of Sicily, he then joined 322 Wing in Sicily as a Flight Commander. He remained with the Wing for the rest of the war, going on to become CO of 232 Squadron. After Italy he was sent to Syria and Palestine, before taking part in the invasion of southern France in August 1944. From there he was posted to Fighter Command in the UK and converted to jets. Once the war ended, he was offered an extended service commission, but that would have meant taking British citizenship and relinquishing his US passport, so he finally returned to the United States for good in August 1946, four years after he'd first left to join the RAF. Back in the US, he became a 'soldier of fortune' for a while before becoming an airline pilot. Eventually he inherited a family business – a talent agency in Hollywood. He sold it ten years ago, although he still works for an off-shoot of the company. 'I have to work,' he says, 'as I have no pension.' He looks well on it, though, and a lot younger than his 81 years.

Ken Griffiths was supposed to come home in November 1943, but that plan was cancelled and it wasn't until March 1944 that he finally left the Island. He hadn't been home long when he and the rest of the Regiment were sent over to France as part of the Normandy invasion force. After the war, he left the Army when his father suffered a stroke in 1946. Given compassionate leave, he returned to Llandrindod Wells in Wales and took over the family civil engineering business. He has remained in the area ever since.

After leaving Malta, Frank Rixon was sent to Egypt for further training, then the Battalion was sent to the Dodecanese islands of Samos and Leros. They were defeated on Leros and Frank escaped down the

Turkish coast on a British minesweeper. He eventually returned to the UK in March 1945, when he was at last reunited with his family. He stayed in the Army after the war, transferring to the Royal Electrical and Mechanical Engineers (REME) in 1948. Posted to Japan, Korea and Singapore, he was eventually sent back to the UK to join a REME training battalion. He left the Army as Company Sergeant Major (CSM) in 1957, having been awarded a British Empire Medal for service in Korea in 1953. Frank took a while to settle down after life in the Army and worked in a number of jobs before taking on a post as an Army barrack accountant at Tidworth in Hampshire. After a number of heart attacks, he was forced to retire in 1986. Another daughter, Margaret, and a son, John, joined their daughter Betty, and he is now a grandfather many times over and even a great-grandfather. Despite Captain Buckle's doubts back in 1941, Frank and Mary are still married, 61 years on.

Suzanne Parlby returned to the UK and joined Naval Intelligence, working on the preparations for the D-Day landings. Before the war, she had come to know a submariner, Michael Kyrle-Pope, but had been told he'd been killed. Her already crumbling marriage collapsed when she discovered Michael had, in fact, survived, and had been repatriated after spending the war in a POW camp. They married in 1947, and subsequently had two children, a son and a daughter. Suzanne accompanied Michael on various naval postings around the world. After he retired from the Navy in 1970, they returned to the UK and now live in Devon.

George 'Shrimp' Simpson remained in the submarine service, and after the war rose to become Rear-Admiral and then Flag Officer Submarines in 1952. After retiring from the Royal Navy, he moved to New Zealand, where he became a farmer, an interest fostered during his time at Lazzaretto in 1941. He died suddenly in 1972.

Tubby Crawford remained with the Tenth Flotilla until December 1943, after which he was posted to the submarine school in Blythe in Northumberland. Just before he left Malta, he became engaged to Margaret Lewis, but she was unable to join him in England until after the D-Day landings. They were married in August 1944. Tubby remained in the Royal Navy, returning to Malta in the 1960s. After leaving active service in 1968, he remained on the Submarine Service Staff as a retired officer until 1980. He returned to Southsea, where he and Margaret still live, and keeps himself busy by working tirelessly for the RNLI. In 1986, a second HMS/S *Upholder* was built by Vickers at

Barrow-in-Furness. Tubby was there to see her launched.

Nat Gold returned to England to work as an instructor, and was later posted to Trinidad to teach at the No. 1 Observer Training School. He left the Royal Navy after the war and went to the College of Estate Management and became a surveyor. He worked for a number of different companies before taking over a pub called, appropriately enough, the Lord Nelson. Neither he nor his wife enjoyed life as publicans, and eventually they retired to Oxfordshire, where they still live.

Of those who took part in Operation Pedestal, Fred Jewett remained in the Navy until after the war. He married a girl from Newcastle and moved to the north of England, where he spent the rest of his working life as a policeman. He and his wife still live in Northumberland. Ted Fawcett took part in the Allied landings in North Africa, but also left the Navy after the war. He worked in public relations for the Shell oil and Lucas electric companies, before joining the National Trust. He rose to become its first Director of Public Affairs, for which he was awarded the OBE. Now retired, he lives with his wife in London. Joe McCarthy never did marry Yvonne. After Malta, the *Rochester Castle* eventually made its way to New York for full repairs. There, Joe heard about the death of his father, to whom he'd been close. He felt that once war was over he would be needed at home and could no longer go back to Malta, and so wrote to her, breaking off the engagement. From the *Rochester Castle*, he joined another Union Castle ship, the *Durban Castle*. He then returned to the Mediterranean, where amongst other tasks, they transported 1,000 Yugoslavian refugees to Egypt. After the war, he married a nurse and so decided his life at sea was over. He went to college to study engineering and, after briefly working for a sugar company and then in a munitions factory, was invited by one of his old friends from *Rochester Castle* to join a small family engineering firm in Essex. He stayed there until he retired in 1986. After his first wife died in 1985, he remarried and moved to Cyprus, returning to England ten years later. He and his second wife now live in Dorset.

Freddie Treves made it back to England without further trauma, but shortly afterwards suffered a nervous breakdown. He recovered and joined the Royal Navy Reserve as a midshipman, and was posted to the Far East, where he took part in the bombardment of the Malayan coast. He returned to the UK, a sub-lieutenant, in 1946, and was offered a commission and promotion to Lieutenant in the Royal Navy. He turned it down, preferring to try his hand as an actor. His first job was with the Amersham Repertory Theatre, and in spite of being sacked for nearly killing the leading lady with a counter-weight, won the last full Korda Scholarship to RADA. He has remained an actor for the past fifty-six years, and, amongst others, has worked with Trevor Howard, Joan Plowright and Edith Evans. He has rarely been out of work, having acted in numerous films, plays, radio and television programmes, including *The Jewel in the Crown, Game, Set And Match*, and most recently *The Cazalets, Monarch of the Glen* and *Midsomer Murders*. For his actions during Operation Pedestal, he was awarded the British Empire Medal and the Lloyd's War Medal. 'It has affected my whole life,' he says now of those terrifying few days. 'Even now I sometimes wake up in the night and hear the screams.'

ABC was appointed First Sea Lord in October 1943, upon the death of Sir Dudley Pound, a post he kept until 1946, when he voluntarily retired. He had already entered the House of Lords. Admiral of the Fleet, Viscount Cunningham of Hyndhope, KT, GCB, OM, DSO settled into retirement with his wife Nona, the couple moving back to their house in Bishop's Waltham in Hampshire. Unsurprisingly, he kept himself busy, writing his memoirs and becoming Lord High Commissioner to the General Assembly of the Church of Scotland. He died, aged eighty, in 1960.

Adrian Warburton took command of No. 336 PR Wing in La Marsa, North Africa, on 1 October 1943. He now commanded four PR squadrons, but had also been working increasingly closely with the US Air Force's 3rd and 5th Photo Groups, for which he was awarded an American DFC to add to his other decorations. Soon afterwards he was badly injured in a motoring accident in Tunis, and, much to his disgust, was invalided back to the UK. He had by this time completed over 300 operational trips. Warby stayed in the UK during the first few months of 1944, itching to get back into action. On 12 April, he and an American pilot took off from a US air base in England in USAAF P-38s to photograph ball-bearing factories at Regensburg and Schweinfurt, recently bombed by the Allies. They were to split up, with Warby photographing Schweinfurt. Then he disappeared. He'd made plans to fly on to San Severo, where his old wing was now serving, but never showed up.

It will never be known for certain exactly what happened to Warby that day. The remains of a wrecked P-38 F-5B – the exact model Warby had been flying – were discovered near Comiso in Sicily. His planned visit to San Severo had been unofficial, and the burnt-out P-38 in Sicily did not correspond to any official flight. For many years it was believed that Warby had been on his way to see Christina once more, and the Island where he achieved his greatest triumphs. Then in August 2002, another P-38 F-5B was found in a field south-east of Egling in southern Germany. Amongst the wreckage was discovered a length of film as used by the standard American cameras. The crash had been witnessed by locals – boys at the time – who confirmed the aircraft had hit the ground at around 11.45 a.m. on the 12 April 1944. Human remains have also been discovered – and fragments of blue-grey RAF clothing.

Christina never got over her loss. She remained on Malta, living in her flat in Floriana. Nor did she ever marry. In her later years, she drifted into alcoholism. An old colleague of hers from RAF Control days tried to look her up a few years ago. When he rang her and asked to meet up, she sounded flustered. 'But there's an air raid on,' she told him. She died penniless in 1988, and was later buried in a pauper's grave. Months later, a relative of hers from Cheshire wrote a letter to the *Times of Malta* enquiring about her, to which Frederick Galea, Honorary Secretary of the National War Museum Association, replied. This led to her re-interment with a proper burial ceremony in a newly purchased grave and with a marble headstone. The inscription reads simply: 'Christina of George Cross Island.'

For the past 25 years, Malta's principal source of income has been tourism. Parts of the Island, particularly the north coast, have become unrecognizable, swamped by more and more housing, hotels and resorts. Other areas remain much the same. Valletta has been rebuilt, as have the Three Cities, but they are clearly one and the same place they were in the war. Kingsway, now Republic Street, is lined by modern shops, but Wembley Stores is still there on the corner of South Street. The War HQ at Lascaris is exactly the same, now preserved as a museum. The Opera House still lies in ruins, the only landmark not to have been rebuilt. Rumours constantly abound that one day it will be returned to its former glory, but in June 2002 its base housed a PVC marquee with large screens showing the Football World Cup. After three years of fund-raising, in 1992, the Siege Bell Memorial was erected. Built on the site of a Bofors gun emplacement, it overlooks Grand

Harbour. Every day, at twelve noon, the bell rings out its mournful toll. On calm days, it can be heard 35 miles out to sea.

The Lazzaretto building is still standing, although in a derelict state. But gazing across at it from Valletta it is still possible, with a little imagination, to picture the submarines moored alongside the familiar arches, and Tubby, Shrimp and the other submariners sitting above on the long gallery.

Mdina has also changed little. The Xara Palace is now a luxury hotel and Château-Relais restaurant, but it is possible to go up to the balcony where Tommy and Raoul and the other fighter pilots looked out and watched the action unfolding across the Island. Imtarfa Hospital is also still there, although now a school. Luqa has become the international airport, and Hal Far is still used, but Takali – never much more than an area of flat, open ground – is no more. A sports stadium has been built instead, and a craft market fills the Nissen huts built after the war. A small group of enthusiasts ensures that Takali is not forgotten, however. In an old hangar at one end of the former airfield, they have built an aviation museum. A static Spitfire has been rebuilt and now they are working on a Hurricane. On one trip, I was telling them about the letter from Alex Mackie's mother, when Frederick Galea stopped me. 'Look over there,' he said, pointing to a piece of grey engine cowling. 'That is from Mackie's Hurricane.' And so now, 61 years on from that fateful day in January 1941, new life is being breathed into the remains of Alex Mackie's plane. Somehow, this seems rather fitting.

From His First Operational Trip ...

by Raoul Daddo-Langlois

[This was written by Raoul while he was an instructor at Chedworth, Gloucestershire, after his return from Malta in 1942.]

Your career as a u/t [under training] pilot is coming to an end. You have been shown here as much as the instructors are able to demonstrate of modern air-fighting methods.

Perhaps you may have been guilty, when in the company of your girlfriend, or other doting companions, of expressing the opinion (your own of course) that you are fully operational.

This is fatal. It is so annoying to get to a squadron and discover that you won't be allowed to go on a sweep for at least a month. Especially if you happen to have promised your girlfriend a Hun in your first week.

If you go to Eleven Group you may find yourself on a sweep in your first week. During the winter, however, this is very unlikely. If you do, you have my blessing.

In the other Groups life is mainly a long succession of convoy patrols. Don't despise the old convoy patrol too much. Remember that many Huns have been shot down while attempting to sink our little coastal ships. Several of our pilots have been lost too, because they were flying around with their finger up.

You are all familiar with the inscription on the tombstone which runs ... 'From his first operational trip he never looked back.' Don't give anyone the chance of inscribing that on yours.

These are one or two essential qualities which go towards making the efficient fighter pilot. These are ...

1. *The ability to see things*

When you go on your first sweep at, perhaps, 25,000 feet, you probably won't see anything unusual at all. Unless you straggle and get bounced. You probably won't appreciate that either.

After two or three, when your experience has widened a bit, you will probably realize that the boys who reported seeing 190s on the last show weren't shooting a line after all.

Cultivate the habit of looking around in long visual sweeps. Not just a quick glance while you're weaving, but a cool, calm inspection of the sky around you. Remember that the Hun likes to come up on you very fast from below and behind. The Hun has great respect for the Spitfire, but chiefly for the front end. So don't give him a chance to be rude to the tail.

2. *The ability to fly your aircraft*

Get to know your aircraft inside out. In order to get the most out of your Spitfire you must know what it will do and what it won't. The more you know about it the easier it will be to put yourself in the right position to shoot the other bloke down. Which brings us to the third essential ...

3. *The ability to shoot*

Your whole training as a fighter pilot is designed for one purpose, and one purpose only. You are not put into the air to enjoy yourself or to waste petrol and ammunition. You are trained for the sole purpose of shooting.

Hurricane and Spitfire Production

NOVEMBER 1940–DECEMBER 1941

Figures show aircraft 'Ready to current acceptable standard', with accumulated monthly figures in brackets.

Date	Hurricane	Spitfire
1940		
Nov 1	158	50
Nov 8	126	60
Nov 15	114	77
Nov 22	137	125
Nov 29	139 (674)	171 (483)
Dec 6	166	184
Dec 13	168	213
Dec 20	162	238
Dec 27	167 (663)	258 (893)
1941		
Jan 3	173	269
Jan 10	213	292
Jan 17	229	276
Jan 24	226	282
Jan 31	231 (1072)	285 (1404)
Feb 7	198	274
Feb 14	194	298
Feb 21	203	304
Feb 28	187 (782)	303 (1179)
Mar 7	192	312
Mar 14	238	299
Mar 21	247	293

Mar 28	273 (950)	336 (1240)
Apr 4	211	359
Apr 11	208	415
Apr 18	225	433
Apr 25	238 (882)	354 (1561)
May 2	169	381
May 9	144	363
May 16	137	312
May 23	135	301
May 30	157 (742)	286 (1643)
June 6	147	287
June 13	148	317
June 20	122	345
June 27	149 (566)	187 (1136)
July 4	178	142
July 11	164	105
July 18	183	74
July 25	214 (739)	63 (384)
Aug 1	182	45
Aug 8	128	52
Aug 15	160	46
Aug 22	146	48
Aug 29	81 (697)	51 (242)
Sept 5	50	49
Sept 12	55	50
Sept 19	81	49
Sept 26	47 (233)	56 (204)
Oct 3	42	50
Oct 10	45	78
Oct 17	23	40
Oct 24	26	42
Oct 31	21 (157)	60 (270)
Nov 7	25	58
Nov 14	18	63
Nov 21	44	78
Nov 28	22 (109)	60 (259)
Dec 5	52	89
Dec 12	28	88
Dec 19	48	77
Dec 26	48 (176)	102 (356)
TOTAL	8,442	11,254

During this period 1,979 Hurricanes were sent to the Middle East and the Mediterranean, of which 10 were Sea Hurricanes.

16 Spitfires were sent to the Mediterranean on 13 February, and 16 on 16 March.

A NOTE ON PRONUNCIATIONS

The official language of Malta is Maltese, a blend of Arab and Mediterranean languages unique to the archipelago. 'X' is pronounced 'sh', 'q' is silent, and 'g' is pronounced 'j'. So, Naxxar is pronounced 'Nashar'; the Xara Palace, 'Shara' Palace. Luqa sounds like 'Loo-ah'. However, the British and Allied forces on Malta tended to pronounce or spell names as they should have been in English and so Ta'Qali became the harder sounding Takali and likewise the 'q' in Luqa was no longer silent. For the purposes of this book, then, I have reverted to the old British military pronunciations, as still used by the Malta veterans interviewed. I hope any Maltese readers will forgive me for this.

NOTES

The letter cited in full at the beginning of this book comes from the collection of letters and other papers of Maud Buckingham, Principal Matron at Imtarfa Hospital during the Siege of Malta, now archived at the Imperial War Museum in London. While every effort has been made to trace the relatives of Margaret and Alex Mackie, this has proved unsuccessful. If anyone would like to claim copyright, please do make contact and every effort will be made to redress this in future editions.

Notes have not been made for quotations from any of the people interviewed or from private papers, letters and diaries lent by the individuals and families of those written about in the book.

Chapter 1 – The First Day of the Siege: 11 June 1940

1. George Burges – interview for National War Museum Association, Malta
2. 'Carve Malta on My Heart', *Daily Star* March 1958
3. Ibid.

Chapter 2 – Britain's Dilemma – the Build-up to 11 June

1. *A Sailor's Odyssey*, p. 188
2. Nelson in a letter to the British Prime Minister, Henry Addington, 28 June 1803, cited in *Malta At War*, Volume 1, Issue 1
3. Cited in *Malta*, Insight Guide, p. 57
4. 'Carve Malta on My Heart', *Daily Star*, March 1958
5. Cited in the *Times of Malta*, 11/6/1940
6. PRO – in a letter from Dobbie to Lord Lloyd
7. *Times of Malta*, 12/6/1940

Chapter 3 – Faith, Hope and Charity: June–August 1940

1. *A Sailor's Odyssey*, p. 235
2. Corporal Harry Kirk, quoted by Roy Nash in 'The Unknown Air Ace', *Daily Star*, March 1958. This is the only explanation I have been able to find for the naming of the Gladiators. Certainly, they had become lore before the year was out

3. George Burges in an interview for the National War Museum of Malta
4. Ibid.
5. Cited in the *Times of Malta*, 18/6/1940
6. PRO CAB 120/624
7. *A Sailor's Odyssey*, p. 260
8. Ibid., p.262
9. PRO CAB 120/624, in a note to General Ismay on 12/7/1940
10. PRO CAB 120/624, in a note to Pound on 15/7/1940
11. Wing Commander R. Carter Jones cited in *Malta at War*, Volume 1, Issue 9

Chapter 4 – Gathering Strength: September–December 1940

1. PRO CAB 120/624, in a copy of a note to Cunningham sent by Churchill to General Ismay on 8/9/1940
2. PRO AIR 27/606
3. *A Sailor's Odyssey*, p. 269
4. Ibid.
5. Cited by Christina Ratcliffe in 'Carve Malta on My Heart', *Daily Star*, March 1958
6. PRO WO 169/912, the Queen's Own Royal West Kent Regiment War Diary
7. John Spires cited by Roy Nash in the *Daily Star*, March 1958
8. Ibid.
9. *A Sailor's Odyssey*, p. 285
10. Ibid., p. 287
11. *Times of Malta*, 6/12/1940

Chapter 5 – The *Illustrious* Blitz: January 1941

1. *Periscope View*, pp. 101–2
2. Cited by Warlimont in *Inside Hitler's Headquarters*, p. 128
3. *A Sailor's Odyssey*, pp. 301–2
4. 'Carve Malta on My Heart', *Daily Star*, March 1958
5. Ibid.
6. 'Obiter Dicta', *Complete Verse* by Hilaire Belloc
7. *Periscope View*, p. 111

Chapter 6 – The Tightening of the Screw: January–February 1941

1. PRO AIR 27/606
2. Adrian Warburton cited by Christina Ratcliffe in 'Carve Malta on My Heart', *Daily Star*, March 1958
3. Ibid.
4. 'A Very Brave Man' by Nat Gold, cited in *Malta Remembered No. 5*
5. According to official Italian records, between January and April 1941, 94 per cent

of supplies and 97 per cent of all troops and personnel sent to North Africa safely reached their destination

Chapter 7 – Success and Failure: March–April 1941

1. 'Carve Malta on My Heart', *Daily Star* March 1958
2. PRO AIR 27/606
3. Terence Horsley cited in 'Find, Fix and Strike'. Like most 'Stringbag' pilots, he was highly defensive about the aircraft
4. Cited in *A Sailor's Odyssey*, p. 319
5. Pilot Officer John Pain cited in *Hurricanes Over Malta*, p. 80. Pain survived Malta and the war, returning to his native Australia. He died in 1980
6. Flight Lieutenant Whittingham, cited in *Malta: The Hurricane Years*, pp. 150–1. Whittingham had arrived on the Island from North Africa on 29 January, and survived Malta – and the war – despite his fatalism. He retired from the RAF as a Squadron Leader
7. Cited in *A Sailor's Odyssey*, p. 319
8. Pound cited in *A Sailor's Odyssey*, p. 322
9. Cited by Commander Wilfrid Woods in *Cunningham: The Greatest Admiral Since Nelson*, p. 256
10. Ultra was the codename given for Special Intelligence decrypts, although the name was not coined until a few months later in 1941
11. Commander Geoffrey Barnard quoting Cunningham, cited in *Cunningham: The Greatest Admiral Since Nelson*, p. 142
12. Ibid.
13. Commander Geoffrey Barnard quoting Cunningham, cited in *From Dartmouth to War*, p. 106
14. *A Sailor's Odyssey*, p. 332
15. Ibid.
16. *Times of Malta*, 12/16/1941
17. PRO ADM 236/48

Chapter 8 – Valour at Sea: May 1941

1. Pound cited in *A Sailor's Odyssey*, p. 343
2. *A Sailor's Odyssey*, p. 344
3. 249 Squadron was reformed at Church Fenton in Lincolnshire in May 1940. On 14 July they moved to Boscombe Down near Salisbury in Wiltshire, and it was while there that James Nicolson won a Victoria Cross – the only one during the Battle of Britain – for his action over Southampton Water on 16 August. On 1 September 249 it moved to North Weald, where it remained until transferred to Malta in May 1941
4. Tom Neil had by this time shot down the following: a Messerschmitt 109 on 7 September 1940, a Heinkel 111 bomber on the 11th, two Dornier 17 bombers on

the 15th, and one Messerschmitt 110 twin-engine fighter and a shared Junkers 88 on the 27th. To be regarded an 'ace', a pilot had to have five *confirmed* kills to his name. 'Probables' and 'possibles' did not count to this score. A shared kill counted as half, so two shared kills made one complete kill

5. PRO CAB 120/624

6. Ibid.

7. Section L was the National Defence Section of the Oberkommando der Wehrmacht and was headed by General Walter Warlimont

8. *A Sailor's Odyssey*, p. 389

9. George Curnall cited in *Hero of the Upholder*, p. 106

10. This unfortunate man was one of the signalmen. Once safely back in Malta, Wanklyn recommended to Simpson that the man be taken off submarines. The man was very distressed about this and appealed to Simpson. 'Of course, I upheld Wanklyn's decision but I reassured the signalman that it was nothing for him to be ashamed of,' wrote Simpson later

Chapter 9 – Summer Calm: June–August 1941

1. Oberleutnant Joachim Müncheberg, a veteran of both the Battle for France and the Battle of Britain, went on to score a total of 135 kills. He was awarded the Knight's Cross and Oak Leaves and after Malta served briefly in North Africa, before being transferred to France where he became known as a specialist 'Spitfire Hunter', shooting down no fewer than 35 of the type. In July 1942 he was transferred to the Eastern Front before heading back to the North African theatre. It was here that the Spitfires finally had their revenge when several of them from the American 52nd Fighter Group shot him down on 23 March 1943. Luftwaffe fighters had a different approach to scores from their Allied counterparts. The RAF, for example, promoted the success of the squadron, while the Luftwaffe promoted the cult of the individual, and all efforts were made to ensure that a unit's ace continued scoring; his wingman, for example, was there purely to protect him while he got on with the business of shooting down aircraft. The leading German ace of the war was Hauptman Erich Hartmann with a staggering 352 kills to his credit – many of which were scored over the Eastern Front. The top-scoring Allied ace was Johnnie Johnson, with 38

2. George Burges, writing in *Malta: The Hurricane Years*

3. 'Carve Malta on My Heart', *Daily Star*, March 1958

4. Paddy Moren and Johnny Spires cited by Roy Nash in 'The Unknown Air Ace', *Daily Star*, 13/3/1958

5. Tich Whiteley cited, ibid.

6. Cited in *Periscope View*, p. 128

7. Simpson was given this advice by the Flag Officer Submarines, Vice-Admiral Sir Max Horton, the man who first approached him about the Malta job in September 1940, and is cited in *Periscope View*, p. 163

8. PRO ADM 199/1817

9. Cited in *Warburton's War*, p. 127

10. The timings of the attack are difficult to pinpoint accurately, owing to conflicting evidence. According to the Operations Record Book (ORB) of 830 Fleet Air Arm Squadron (PRO 199/108), the two flights of Swordfish left Malta at 6pm and the first flight made their attack at 7.20pm and the second flight at 7.40pm, with all aircraft landing back by 9pm. The ORB of 69 Squadron suggests all the Marylands left at 7.30pm and were back at 9pm. However, *Upholder's* patrol report says she surfaced at 9.25pm and saw an attack being made on the convoy and another at 9.45pm. Warburton's biographer, Tony Spooner, suggests that Warby arrived on the scene *before* the rest of the Marylands and the Blenheims, but this seems unlikely, especially considering that he flew with a number of Junkers 88s, who must surely have spotted him as British had it been before 8pm and still light. ORBs tended to be written up a day or two – or even later – after the events they describe, whereas the submarines make notes immediately of every movement including diving and surfacing times. Consequently, I think the timetable of events I have outlined is likely to be the most accurate

11. This picture of ABC and his Staff Officers comes from Commander Wilfrid Woods, cited in *Cunningham: The Greatest Admiral Since Nelson*, pp. 256–7

12. The CO of *Rorqual* was Lieutenant Lennox Napier. He was later awarded a DSO for his work on the 'Magic Carpet' service, and, in January 1943, sank the German oil tanker *Wilhelmsburg*, which, according to Admiral Dönitz, prompted Hitler to fly into a terrible rage. 'It has given me great pleasure ever since,' Napier later said, 'to think that I was responsible for making Hitler go red in the face.' Before the war was out, he had also been awarded a DSC. When I was younger, I played cricket against him on several occasions. He was still turning out for the village of Fovant well into his eighties. I knew nothing then about his wartime achievements; nor did the majority of his team-mates. He died in August 2001 before I ever had the chance to talk to him about his memories of *Rorqual* and the 'Magic Carpet'

13. *Onwards to Malta*, p. 123

14. Johnny Spires cited in 'The Unknown Air Ace', *Daily Star*, March 1958

15. Although all regiments were supposed to keep war diaries, these are no longer in existence for all the various regiments stationed on Malta. Consequently, the number of guns quoted is an estimate based on the basic make-up of each regiment. For example, Ken Griffiths' regiment, the 32nd LAA, which has no surviving war diary, was made up of three batteries. Each battery usually had three troops of four guns – making a total of 36. The 74th LAA had just two batteries, while the 3rd LAA also had three – so, 96 guns in total

Chapter 10 – Hurting Hitler: September–December 1941

1. Squadron Leader P.J.H. Halahan led No.1 Hurricane Squadron during the Battle for France, where he was awarded the DFC. He features strongly in Paul Richey's excellent memoir of that period, *Fighter Pilot*. Halahan survived the war

2. The RN Cinema Service had been initiated by Lord Mountbatten before the war

3. Lord Haw-Haw was known for his pro-Nazi broadcasts from Germany sent throughout the war and which aimed to stir up defeatist feeling among the British. Born William Joyce in New York of Anglo-Irish parents, he joined Oswald Mosley's British Union of Fascists, but moved to Berlin before the outbreak of war. His 'Germany Calling' broadcasts were considered a massive joke by most, but despite their ineffectiveness he was still executed for treason in 1946

4. PRO ADM 236/48

5. *A Sailor's Odyssey*, p. 420

6. *Ciano's Diary*, 9/11/41

7. Dennis Barnwell cited in *Hurricanes Over Malta*, p. 147

8. Harry Kirk was the camera mechanic in question. The story is related by Tony Spooner in *Warburton's War*, p. 66

9. Lloyd cited by Tom Neil in *Onwards To Malta*, p. 223

10. David Wanklyn, letter to his wife November 1941, cited in *Hero of the Upholder*, p. 129

11. *Times of Malta*, 24/12/41

12. *The Memoirs of Field Marshal Kesselring*, p. 105

Chapter 11 – Kesselring Unleashes Hell: January–February 1942

1. Vice-Admiral Wilbraham Ford, cited in *A Sailor's Odyssey*, p. 439

2. PRO AIR 23/1200

3. *A Sailor's Odyssey*, p. 438

4. Ron Hadden, cited by Corporal Cyril Woods in *Warburton's War*, p. 107

5. *Times of Malta*, 19/2/1942

Chapter 12 – Malta Sinking: March 1942

1. *Times of Malta*, 31/12/1941

2. Tony Holland, writing in *Thanks For the Memories*. Flight Lieutenant A.C.W. Holland served in 603 (City of Edinburgh) Squadron on Malta from April to June 1942, and later with 165 Squadron over Europe, covering the airborne landings at Arnhem

3. *Times of Malta*, 12/3/1942

4. *Periscope View*, p. 209

5. Ibid., p. 211

6. 'Carve Malta on My Heart', *Daily Star*, March 1958

7. Ibid.

8. Air Chief Marshal Sir Hugh Lloyd, cited in 'The Unknown Air Ace', *Daily Star*, March 1958

9. PRO AIR 23/1200

10. *A Sailor's Odyssey*, p. 452

11. Ibid., p. 439

12. Wing Commander Powell-Sheddon was the first CO of the Malta Night Fighter Unit when Tommy Thompson joined at the end of July 1941. He was promoted to Station Commander at Luqa in January 1942. Tommy Thompson remembers him as a likeable character, who, like a number of fighter pilots, had a bad stutter. 'He was desperate to get back to England. He needed to get home by a certain date in order to qualify for some vast inheritance. He made it just in the nick of time.'

13. Cited in *Periscope View*, p. 219

14. *Briefed to Attack*, p. 159

Chapter 13 – Death's Door: April 1942 – Part I

1. Cited in *A Sailor's Odyssey*, p. 460

2. General Sir William Dobbie, cited in the *Times of Malta*, 30/3/1942

3. PRO AIR 20/2428

4. *The Memoirs of Field Marshal Kesselring*, p. 122

5. May Agius, cited in *They Made Invasion Possible*, p. 86

6. *Times of Malta*, 10/4/1942

7. Ibid.

8. PRO WO 106/2113

9. Lieutenant Godfrey Style, first lieutenant of the destroyer HMS *Lance*, cited in *The Fighting Tenth*, pp. 168–9

10. Boris Karnicki, cited in *Periscope View*, p. 217

11. *Periscope View*, p. 218

12. PRO ADM 236/48

13. Wanklyn in a letter to his wife, 10/4/1942, cited in *Hero of the Upholder*, p. 162

14. PRO ADM 236/48

Chapter 14 – George Cross Island: April 1942 – Part II

1. *Times of Malta*, 17/4/1942

2. Ibid.

3. PRO WO 106/2113

4. PRO PREM 3/366/4

5. Cited in *One Man's Window*, p. 37

6. Ibid., p. 59

7. Cited in the *Times of Malta*, 24/4/1942

8. This score of 102 aircraft shot down by Malta gunners is a confirmed score. There were plenty of witnesses for every destroyed aircraft, unlike the confusion caused by the mêlée of a dogfight.

Chapter 15 – Spitfire Victory: May 1942

1. PRO PREM 3/266/4

2. *The Memoirs of Field Marshal Kesselring*, p. 109
3. Cited in *Periscope View*, p. 225
4. Ibid.
5. Ibid., p. 226
6. *One Man's Window*, p. 59
7. Ibid., p. 65
8. Pilot Officer Herbert Mitchell of No. 603 Squadron, cited in *The Air Battle of Malta*. Mitchell was shot down two days after saying this, on 12 May. He was heard to say to the Fighter Controller, Group Captain Woodhall, 'Bye Woody, I've had it,' before crashing into the sea at about 300 mph. His body was never found.
9. PRO PREM 3/266/1
10. Group Captain A.B. Woodhall, cited in *Malta: The Thorn in Rommel's Side*, p. 149
11. PRO PREM 3/266/4
12. Christina Ratcliffe in the *Sunday Times*, Malta, 18/5/1980
13. *Times of Malta*, 11/5/1942
14. *One Man's Window*, p. 141
15. Ibid., p. 146
16. Ibid., p. 146

Chapter 16 – The Island Starves: June–July 1942

1. *Times of Malta*, 14/5/1942
2. R. Farran, cited in *The Sharp End*, p. 286
3. Lord Gort's broadcast cited in the *Times of Malta*, 17/6/1942
4. Cited in *Buck McNair: Canadian Spitfire Ace*, p. 74
5. Ibid.
6. From the *Official History of the Second World War, Army Medical Services, Campaigns in General History*, pp. 631–2, cited in *Malta: Blitzed But Not Beaten*, p. 131
7. Cited in *Malta: The Thorn in Rommel's Side*, p. 232
8. *Malta Spitfire*, p. 106
9. Ibid., p. 123
10. Ibid., p. 138

Chapter 17 – Pedestal: August 1942 – Part I

1. PRO PREM 3/266/5
2. War Diaries 1939–1945, p. 288
3. PRO PREM 3/266/2
4. Freddie Treves noticing the crates were marked 'Malta' led to a major secret inquiry conducted by Justice Tucker. After returning to the UK, Freddie had been staying with the Hon. Mrs Talbot at Froyle House near Alton in Hampshire. Also staying was the Earl of Cork and Orrery, an Admiral of the Fleet. Freddie mentioned his observations to the Earl, who then raised the matter in the House of Lords. An inquiry was subsequently launched, leading to major changes in the marking of cargoes

Chapter 18 – Pedestal: August 1942 – Part II

1. HMS *Manchester's* skipper, Captain Drew, was later court-martialled for this, and his career ruined. In the opinion of Fred Jewett and many others this was a monstrous injustice
2. Cited by Christina Ratcliffe in the *Sunday Times*, Malta, 15/8/1982
3. Ibid.
4. *Times of Malta*, 24/8/1942
5. Soon after Pedestal arrived, the *Times of Malta* started the 'Malta Convoy Fund', an initiative to raise money for the families of those who had given their lives during Pedestal. For the most part, the Maltese were not wealthy people, yet money poured in from every town and village, and when the fund closed on 12 October, over £7,500 had been raised – about £270,000 by today's standards

Chapter 19 – Fightback and the Final Blitz: September–October 1942

1. *Malta Spitfire*, p. 190
2. Goerge Beurling cited in *Maclean's Magazine*, 15 January 1943
3. *One Man's Window*, p. 152
4. Cited in *Malta: The Thorn in Rommel's Side*, p. 237
5. George Beurling cited in *Maclean's Magazine*, 15 January 1943
6. Cited in *Supreme Gallantry*, p. 183
7. *The Memoirs of Field Marshal Kesselring*, p. 112
8. *Torpedo Leader*, p. 206
9. *Malta Spitfire*, p. 202
10. Ibid., p. 210
11. *Times of Malta*, 15/10/1942
12. *The Memoirs of Field Marshal Kesselring*, p. 135
13. The figures were as follows: 126 confirmed, 62 probables and 162 damaged. In addition, the night fighters were credited with 6:1:2
14. Cited in *The Air Battle of Malta*, p. 93

Chapter 20 – From Besieged to Bridgehead: November 1942–July 1943

1. *Malta Spitfire*, p. 226
2. Ibid., p. 232
3. Ibid., p. 234
4. John Agius cited in *Warburton's War*, pp. 136–7
5. *Warburton's War*, p. 124
6. Cited in *Periscope View*, p. 261
7. *Times of Malta*, 1/9/1942, cited in *Malta: Blitzed But Not Beaten*, p. 77
8. Cited in the *Times of Malta*, 7/10/1942
9. Reg Scott, 3rd Engineer on the merchant ship *Glenartney*, cited in *Malta Convoys 1940–1943*, p. 462
10. *Times of Malta*, 21/1/1943

11. *A Sailor's Odyssey*, p. 518
12. Jim Richards, Tubby Crawford's Telegraphist on *Unseen*, cited in *The Fighting Tenth*, pp. 268–9
13. *Periscope View*, p. 285
14. Cited in *The Fighting Tenth*, p. 272
15. John Agius cited in *Warburton's War*, p. 160
16. *A Sailor's Odyssey*, p. 544

Epilogue

1. Collection of W.R. Daddo-Langlois, RAF Museum, Hendon
2. Laddie Lucas in a letter to Raoul's niece, Zoë Thomas, 22/11/1982

Postscript

1. Cited in *A Sailor's Odyssey*, p. 565
2. Cited in *Malta: Blitzed But Not Beaten*, p. 199
3. Cited in *Hero* by Brian Nolan

GLOSSARY

AA	Anti-aircraft
Ack Ack	Anti-aircraft fire
Angels	Height
AOC	Air Officer Commanding
AOC-in-C	Air Officer Commander-in-Chief
ARP	Air Raid Precaution
Asdic	The acronym stands for Allied Submarine Detection Investigation Committee, but asdic is a form of sonar, or hydrophone
ASV	Air to Surface Vessel
AVM	Air Vice-Marshal
Ballast Tank	Hollow tank surrounding the hull of a submarine, filled either with air or water, or a combination of both, and the means by which a submarine is able to dive
Bandit	Enemy aircraft
Bounce	Surprise attack by aircraft, usually with the advantage of height and speed
Chariot	Two-man human torpedo
C-in-C	Commander-in-Chief
CID	Committee of Imperial Defence
CIGS	Chief of the Imperial General Staff
CO	Commanding Officer
COPP	Combined Operations Pilotage Parties
Coppist	Member of the COPP
COS	Chiefs of Staff
DA	Director Angle – the angle required to aim a torpedo so that it hits a moving object
DFC	Distinguished Flying Cross
DFM	Distinguished Flying Medal
Dispersal	Point at which pilots congregate at the airfield when on readiness
Dghajsa	Maltese boat, similar to an Italian gondola

DR   Destroyer

DSC   Distinguished Service Cross

DSO   Distinguished Service Order

E-boat   Italian motor torpedo boat

ERA   Engine-Room Artificers

Erk   RAF groundcrew

Flak   Bursting anti-aircraft fire

Folbot   Two-man collapsible canoe

Fruit Machine   A calculating machine into which all the relevant attack information is fed, and from which information is given to help carry out a torpedo attack

Gharry   Horse-drawn carriage available for hire

Gruppe   Luftwaffe equivalent of a squadron, although usually with more aircraft – often as many as 30 to 40

HAA   Heavy anti-aircraft

Hydroplane   Fin at either end of a submarine acting like a rudder but for vertical movement

IO   Intelligence Officer

ITW   Initial Training Wing

JDC   Joint Overseas & Defence Committee

LAA   Light anti-aircraft

MTB   Motor torpedo boat

OTU   Operational Training Unit

Plot   A single or number of aircraft picked up by radar or observers and tracked on the plotting table in the RAF Control Room

PR   Photo-Reconnaissance

PRU   Photo-Reconnaissance Unit

RAFVR   Royal Air Force Volunteer Reserve

RASC   Royal Army Service Corps

RDF   Radio Direction Finding (Radar)

Readiness   Ready to go into action at a moment's notice

RMA   Royal Malta Artillery

RNVR   Royal Navy Volunteer Reserve

Rotte   Luftwaffe formation of four aircraft, known in the RAF as the 'Finger Four'

R/T   Radio transmitter (radio)

Sangar   A defence post or small gun emplacement made from stone blocks

(S) 1   Captain First Submarine Flotilla

(S) 10   Captain Tenth Submarine Flotilla

Scramble	Orders to immediately take to the air
SLU	Special Liaison Unit (for receiving Ultra intercepts)
SRE	Ship's Radio Equipment
Stand Down	Come off duty
Stand To	Ready for duty
TAG	Telegraphist Air Gunner
Trim	The state of buoyancy – or balance – of a submarine
VAD	Voluntary Aid Detachment
VAM	Vice-Admiral, Malta
Vic	Arrowhead formation of three aircraft
Wing	Three squadrons
WOP/AG	Wireless Operator/Air Gunner
W/T	Wireless telegraphy

BIBLIOGRAPHY & SOURCES

I would like to make it clear that although the Prologue has been largely dramatized, it is as accurate a description of Alex Mackie's final flight as is possible 61 years on from that fateful afternoon. I visited the crash-site on two occasions – the wall around the orchard remains partially destroyed where the aircaft hit – with Tony Spiteri and Ray Polidano of the Malta Aviation Museum Foundation, and Frederick Galea, Honorary Secretary of the National War Museum Association. Having taken into account a number of factors, Mackie's final few moments, as described in the Prologue, are what we considered to be the most likely course of events.

Unpublished Sources

ARCHIVES
Public Records Office, Kew
ADM 199/108
830 Fleet Air Arm Squadron operations

ADM 199/1824
Combat patrol reports of HMS/S *Unseen*

ADM 236/48
Combat patrol reports of HMS/S *Upholder*

AIR 20/2428
Report by the Joint Intelligence Sub-Committee on the likelihood of an Axis attack on Malta, March 1942; and Memorandum by the Chief of the Imperial General Staff on the Malta Supply Situation, April 1942

AIR 23/1200 & 1201
Letters and ciphers relating to the number of aircraft flown to Malta, including requests from Lloyd and Park, and copies of Park's 'Forward Interception Plan'

AIR 27
RAF Operational Record Books for 249, 69, 39, 601, 229 and 93 Squadrons

AIR 41/26
Air Historical Branch Official Account of the Air Battle for Malta, January–June 1942

CAB 120/624
Documents and official correspondence relating to Malta's offensive potential

CO 967/87
Semi-official and personal correspondence of General Dobbie

PREM 3/266/1
Official correspondence relating to the dismissal of General Dobbie and his replacement as Governor by Lord Gort

PREM 3/266/4
Official correspondence relating to the supply of Spitfires to Malta in 1942

PREM 3/266/5
Correspondence between Lord Gort and Churchill regarding the situation in Malta

WO 106/2113
Situation reports and correspondence regarding bomb damage to Malta, spring 1942

WO 169
2nd Battalion Queen's Own Royal West Kent Regiment War Diary and notes of monthly Commanding Officers Conferences
    WO 169/912 – February–December 1940
    WO 169/3285 – January–December 1941
    WO 169/7432 – January–December 1942
    WO 169/14589 – January–June 1943

WO 216/114
Semi-official and personal correspondence of General Dobbie, May 1940–October 1941

The Imperial War Museum, London
Personal letters and papers of Maud Buckingham

The RAF Museum, Hendon, London
Diary and logbook of W.R. Daddo-Langlois

The National Library, Valletta, Malta
The *Times of Malta*, 1940–1943

The National Newspaper Archive, Colindale, London
'The Unknown Air Ace' by Roy Nash, in the *Daily Star*, 3–18 March 1958
'Carve Malta On My Heart' by Christina Ratcliffe, in the *Daily Star*, March 1958

The National War Museum of Malta & The Malta Aviation Museum
Interview with George Burges

Documents and articles relating to George Beurling
Documents and articles relating to Christina Ratcliffe
Documents and articles relating to Adrian Warburton

UNPUBLISHED SOURCES
Autobiography by Frank Rixon
The Letters and Personal Papers of Raoul Daddo-Langlois, c/o Zoë Thomas
Malta Remembered Nos. 1–5, edited by Frank Rixon
Malta VAD by Carmela Turner, RGN, SCN
Reflections On Malta – Summer 1942 by Arthur F. Roscoe
Royal Air Force Groundcrews – An 'Erk' on Malta by Jack Paternoster

INTERVIEWS & PERSONAL RECOLLECTIONS
John Agius, MBE, RAF civilian clerk throughout the war
Diana Barnham, wife of Denis Barnham
Elisabeth Beaman, British civilian on Malta 1939–42
Lieutenant-Colonel Chevalier Antoine Pace Bonello, MBE, officer in the Royal Malta Artillery
Antony Buhagiar, steward on board submarine HMS/S *Porpoise*
Denys Carden, officer on HMS *Nelson*
Fraser Carlisle-Brown, navigator/observer, 39 Squadron
Peter Cooper, SOE agent on Malta
Margaret Crawford, civilian working for Military Intelligence 1939–44
Captain M.L.C. 'Tubby' Crawford, DSC★, No. 1 of HMS/S *Upholder* and later Commanding Officer HMS/S *Unseen*
Edward Fawcett, Sub-Lieutenant on HMS *Bramham*
Douglas Geer, RAF, 1941–3
Bill 'Nat' Gold, Telegraphist Air Gunner 830 Fleet Air Arm Squadron, 1941–2
Jim Gray, DFC, fighter pilot, 93 Squadron, Malta June–July 1943
Ken Griffiths, 32nd Light Anti-Aircraft Regiment, Malta 1941–4
Jack Hubbard, 4th Heavy Anti-Aircraft Regiment, Malta 1941–4
Fred Jewett, Able Seaman on HMS *Ashanti*
Suzanne Kyrle-Pope (then Parlby), civilian working for Military Intelligence, living on Malta 1938–42
Joseph McCarthy, 2nd Engineer aboard SS *Rochester Castle*
Michael Montebello, Maltese civilian throughout siege, living on Malta 1930–45
Wing Commander Tom Neil, DFC★, AFC, AE fighter pilot 249 Squadron, Malta 1941
Malcolm Oxley, 10th Heavy Anti-Aircraft Regiment, Malta 1941–4
Frank Rixon, BEM, Queen's Own Royal West Kent Regiment, Malta 1940–43
Mary Rixon, civilian
Art Roscoe, DFC, fighter pilot, 229 Squadron, Malta 1942
Peter Rothwell, Wellington pilot, Malta 1942
Fred Shute, RAF Air Sea Rescue & Marine Craft Section, Malta 1942–4

Bob Spicer, RAF groundcrew

Edward St George, Maltese schoolboy

ARF 'Tommy' Thompson, DFC, fighter pilot, 249 Squadron and later Malta Night Fighter Unit, 1941–2

Ray Tow, civilian working for the Admiralty, Malta 1939–4

Frederick Treves, BEM, LCWM, Petty Officer aboard SS *Waimarama*

Meme Turner, RGN, SCN (née Cortis), VAD nurse 90th General Military Hospital, Imtarfa, Malta 1939–43

Daryl Tutt, able seaman aboard USS *Wasp*

Peter Watson, RAF groundcrew, 249 Squadron, Malta 1941–4

Robert Waxman, Cadet Midshipman aboard the *Almeira Sykes*, 1942

Squadron Leader Geoffrey Wellum, DFC, fighter pilot, 1435 Squadron, Malta 1942

Published Sources

DOCUMENTS, NEWSPAPERS, MAGAZINES & PERIODICALS

Malta at War, Volume 1, Issue 1–12 edited by John A. Mizzi

Maclean's Magazine, January 15 1943

Profile Warship 16 – HMS/S Upholder by Capt. M.L.C. Crawford

Wings of Fame: The Journal of Classic Combat Aircraft, Volume 18

DOCUMENTARY COLLECTIONS

Air Battle of Malta, The, HMSO, 1944

East of Malta, West of Suez, HMSO, 1943

Fleet Air Arm, HMSO, 1943

Naval Staff History Second World War, Submarines Volume II, Operations in the Mediterranean, 1955

Submarine Depot, Ships, Bases and Support Ships compiled by Leslie Honeywell, HMSO, 1972

OTHER PUBLISHED SOURCES

Alanbrooke, Field Marshal Lord. *War Diaries 1939–1945*, Weidenfeld & Nicolson, 2001

Allaway, Jim. *Hero of the Upholder*, Airlife, 1991

Attard, Joseph. *Britain and Malta: The Story of an Era*, Publishers Enterprises Group, 1988

Attard, Joseph. *The Battle of Malta: An Epic Story of Suffering and Bravery*, William Kimber, 1980

Barnett, Corelli. *Engage the Enemy More Closely*, Hodder & Stoughton, 1991

Barnham, Denis. *One Man's Window*, William Kimber, 1956

Beevor, Antony. *Crete: The Battle and the Resistance*, John Murray, 1991

Begg, Dr Richard Campbell & Liddle, Dr Peter. *For Five Shillings a Day: Personal Histories of World War II*, HarperCollins, 2000

Beurling, George & Roberts, Leslie. *Malta Spitfire: The Story of a Fighter Pilot*, The Military Book Society, 1973

Bierman, John & Smith, Colin. *Alamein: War Without Hate*, Viking 2002

Boffa, Charles J. *The Illustrious Blitz: Malta in Wartime 1940–41*, Progress Press Malta, 1995

Bowyer, Chaz. *Men of the Desert Air Force*, William Kimber, 1984

Bradford, Ernle. *Siege: Malta 1940–1943*, Penguin, 1987

Budiansky, Stephen. *Battle of Wits: The Complete Story of Codebreaking in World War II*, Viking, 2000

Caine, Philip D. *American Pilots in the RAF: The WWII Eagle Squadrons*, Brassey's, 1998

Caruana, Richard J. *Victory in the Air*, Modelaid International Publications, 1996

Chaplin, Lt.-Col. H.D. *The Queen's Own Royal West Kent Regiment 1920–1950*, Michael Joseph, 1954

Childers, James Saxon. *War Eagles: The Story of 71 Eagle Squadron*, Eagle Publishing Co., 1983

Churchill, Winston. *The Second World War, Volumes II, III, & IV*, Cassell, 1949

Ciano, Count Galeazzo. *Ciano's Diary 1938–1943*, William Heinemann, 1946

Coldbeck, Squadron Leader Harry. *The Maltese Spitfire: One Pilot, One Plane – Find Enemy Forces on Land and Sea*, Airlife, 1997

Coldman, Alfred. *Malta: An Aviation History*, Publishers Enterprises Group, 2001

Cull, Brian. *249 At War: The Authorised History of the RAF's Top-Scoring Fighter Squadron of WWII*, Grub Street, 1997

Cull, Brian & Galea, Frederick. *Hurricanes Over Malta June 1940–April 1942*, Grub Street, 2002

Cull, Brian, with Galea, Frederick & Malizia, Nicola. *Spitfires Over Sicily: The Crucial Role of the Malta Spitfires In The Battle of Sicily, January–August 1943*, Grub Street, 2000

Cunningham of Hyndhope, Viscount. *A Sailor's Odyssey*, Hutchinson, 1951

Davies, John. *Lower Deck*, Macmillan, 1945

Dobbie, Sybil. *Grace Under Fire*, Lindsay Drummond, 1944

Dobinson, Colin. *AA Command*, Methuen/English Heritage, 2001

Douglas-Hamilton, James. *The Air Battle For Malta: The Diaries of a Spitfire Pilot*, Airlife, 2000

Dugan, Sally. *Commando: The Elite Fighting Forces of the Second World War*, Channel 4 Books, 2001

Duncan Smith, Group Captain W.G.G. *Spitfire Into Battle*, John Murray, 1981

Dunning, Chris. *Courage Alone: The Italian Air Force 1940–1943*, Hakoki, 1998

Ellis, John. *The Sharp End: The Fighting Man in World War II*, Pimlico, 1993

Franks, Norman. *Buck McNair: Canadian Spitfire Ace*, Grub Street, 2001

Fussell, Paul. *Wartime: Understanding and Behaviour in the Second World War*, Oxford University Press, 1989

Galea, Frederick. *Call-Out: A Wartime Diary of Air/Sea Rescue Operations at Malta*, Malta At War Publications, 2002

Galea, Michael. *Malta Diary of a War 1940–1945*, Publishers Enterprises Group, 1992

Gibbs, Patrick. *Torpedo Leader*, Grub Street, 1992

Goddard, Isobel. *We Squeeze Them Like A Lemon: Childhood Memories of Malta Before and During World War Two*, Xpress Design & Print, 2000

Gunston, Bill. *Fighting Aircraft of World War II*, Salamander Books, 1988

Grech, Charles B. *Raiders Passed*, Midsea Books, 1998

Holloway, Adrian. *From Dartmouth to War: A Midshipman's Journal*, Buckland Publications Ltd, 1993

Horne, Alistair. *To Lose a Battle*, Macmillan, 1969

Jenkins, Roy. *Churchill*, Macmillan, 2001

Johnson, Air Vice Marshal J.E., & Lucas, Wing Commander P.B. *Winged Victory: The Recollections of Two Royal Air Force Leaders*, Stanley Paul, 1995

Johnston, Wing Commander Tim. *Tattered Battlements: A Fighter Pilot's Diary*, William Kimber, 1985

Keegan, John. *The Second World War*, Pimlico, 1997

Kesselring, Field Marshal. *The Memoirs of Field Marshal Kesselring*, William Kimber, 1953

Kyrle-Pope, Suzanne. *The Same Wife in Every Port*, Memoir Club, 1998

Lewin, Ronald. *Ultra Goes to War: The Secret Story*, Hutchinson, 1978

Liddell Hart, B.H. *The Other Side of the Hill*, Cassell, 1948

Lloyd, Air Marshal Sir Hugh. *Briefed To Attack: Malta's Part in African Victory*, Hodder & Stoughton, 1949

Lucas, Laddie. *Five Up*, Sidgwick & Jackson, 1978

Lucas, Laddie. *Malta, the Thorn in Rommel's Side: Six Months That Turned the War*, Penguin, 1993

Lucas, Laddie. Ed. *Thanks for the Memory: Unforgettable Characters in Air Warfare 1939–45*, Stanley Paul, 1989

Lukacs, John. *Five Days in London May 1940*, Yale University Press, 1999

Massimello, Giovanni and Apostolo, Giorgio. *Italian Aces of World War 2*, Osprey, 2000

Micallef, Josef. *When Malta Stood Alone (1940–1943)*, Malta, 1981

Mizzi, Laurence. *The People's War Malta: 1940/43*, Progress Press, 1998

Monsarrat, Nicholas. *The Kappilan of Malta*, Cassell, 1973

Moorehead, Alan. *African Trilogy: The Desert War 1940–1943*, Hamish Hamilton, 1944

Nesbit, Roy C. *Armed Rovers: Beauforts & Beaufighters Over the Mediterranean*, Airlife, 1995

Nesbit, Roy C. *Eyes of the RAF: A History of Photo-Reconnaissance*, Alan Sutton, 1996

Neil, Wing Commander T.F. *A Fighter in My Sights*, J&KH Publishing, 2001

Neil, Wing Commander T.F. *Onward to Malta*, Airlife, 1992

Newton, Don, & Hampshire, A Cecil. *Taranto*, New English Library, 1974

Niven, David. *The Moon's a Balloon*, Penguin 1994

Padfield, Peter. *War Beneath The Sea: Submarine Conflict 1939–1945*, John Murray 1995

Poolman, Kenneth. *Faith, Hope And Charity*, William Kimber, 1954

Price, Dr Alfred. *Spitfire Mark V Aces 1941–45*, Osprey, 1997

Oliver, David. *Fighter Command*, HarperCollins, 2000

Oliver, Leslie. *Malta At Bay: An Eye-Witness Account*, Hutchinson, 1942

Orange, Vincent. *Park: The Biography of Air Chief Marshal Sir Keith Park, GCB, KBE, MC, DFC, DCL*, Grub Street, 2001

Rinaldi, Nicholas. *The Jukebox Queen of Malta*, Bantam Press, 1999

Ritchie, Captain Lewis. *The Epic of Malta*, Odhams Press, 1944

Rogers, Anthony. *Battle Over Malta: Aircraft Losses and Crash Sites 1940–42*, Alan Sutton, 2000

Rollo, Denis. *The Guns and Gunners of Malta*, Mondial Publishers, 1999

Scott, Peggy. *They Made Invasion Possible*, Hutchinson, 1945

Scott, Stuart R. *Battle-Axe Blenheims: No. 105 Squadron RAF at War 1940–41*, Alan Sutton, 1996

Scutts, Jerry. *Bf 109 Aces of North Africa and the Mediterranean*, Osprey, 1995

Shankland, Peter, & Hunter, Anthony. *Malta Convoy*, Fontana, 1963

Shores, Christopher & Cull, Brian, with Malizia, Nicola. *Malta: The Hurricane Years, 1940–41*, Grub Street, 1987

Shores, Christopher & Cull, Brian, with Malizia, Nicola. *Malta: The Spitfire Year, 1942*. Grub Street, 1991

Simpson, Rear-Admiral G.W.G. *Periscope View: A Professional Autobiography*, Macmillan, 1972

Smith, Peter C. *Pedestal: The Convoy That Saved Malta*, William Kimber, 1970

Spick, Mike. *Allied Fighter Aces of World War II: The Air Combat Tactics and Techniques of World War II*, Greenhill Books, 1997

Spooner, Tony. *Clean Sweep: The Life of Air Marshal Sir Ivor Broom, KCB, CBE, DSO, DFC & Two Bars, AFC*, Crecy, 1994

Spooner, Tony. *Faith, Hope And Malta GC*, Newton, 1992

Spooner, Tony. *In Full Flight*, Wingham Press, 1991

Spooner, Tony. *Warburton's War: The Life of Wing Commander Adrian Warburton DSO & Bar, DFC & Two Bars, DFC (USA)*, Crecy Books, 1994

Spooner, Tony. *Supreme Gallantry: Malta's Role in the Allied Victory 1939–1945*, John Murray, 1996

Vella, Philip, *Malta: Blitzed But Not Beaten*, Progress Press, 1985

Warlimont, Walter. *Inside Hitler's Headquarters 1939–45*, Weidenfeld & Nicolson, 1964

Wellum, Geoffrey. *First Light*, Viking, 2002

Willmott, H.P. *The Great Crusade: A New Complete History of the Second World War*, Pimlico, 1992

Wingate, John. *The Fighting Tenth*, Leo Cooper 1991

Winton, John. *Cunningham: The Greatest Admiral Since Nelson*, John Murray, 1998

Winton, John. *The Submariners: Life in British Submarines 1901–1999*, Constable, 1999

Woodman, Richard. *Malta Convoys, 1940–1943*, John Murray, 2000

Young, Edward. *One of Our Submarines*, Wordsworth Editions, 1997

ACKNOWLEDGEMENTS

This book began with a conversation in a pub with former fighter pilot Geoff Wellum, and so I must thank him for that spark as well as for his subsequent help. However, it would never have been written were it not for the help and co-operation of a number of people, most obviously the veterans of the Siege of Malta themselves. The George Cross Island Association has been especially helpful and I must thank in particular Peter Rothwell for steering me in the right direction at the outset, and Frank Rixon for his tremendous support at every turn. I would also like to thank them for allowing me to interview them and for lending me numerous articles, books, photographs and documents. Enormous thanks must go to the other participants in the book, not just for allowing me to come and talk to them, but for putting up with numerous further calls, letters and other demands: Fraser Carlisle-Brown, Edward Fawcett, Bill 'Nat' Gold, Ken Griffiths, Fred Jewett, Suzanne Kyrle-Pope, Joe McCarthy, Michael Montebello, Tom Neil, Mary Rixon, Art Roscoe, Tommy Thompson, Frederick Treves, Meme Turner, and Elisabeth Young. Especial thanks go to John Agius, and Tubby and Margaret Crawford for their kindness and hard work on my behalf, all of which was well beyond the call of duty. I would also like to thank those who kindly gave me interviews and other help, particularly May Agius, Diana Barnham, Mary Bates, Antoine Pace Bonello, Anthony Buhagiar, Peter Cooper, Stan Fraser, Douglas Geer, the late Jack Hubbard, Malcolm Oxley, David Souter, Bob Spicer, Edward St George, Daryl Tutt, Robert Waxman, and especially Jim Gray and Ted Shute.

On Malta, I am hugely indebted to the National War Museum Association, especially its Honorary Secretary, Frederick Galea, who has given me tremendous help and support, not to say friendship. The National War Museum Association has been responsible for setting up the War Museum at Lower Fort St Elmo in Valletta, and, over the last twenty-six years, establishing an extensive library, and document and photographic archive. This has been the work of a few dedicated individuals, whose expertise – freely given – extends beyond the walls of any library; and so I would also like to also thank other NWMA members Henry De Marco, John Mizzi, and Alex Randon. Thanks also go to Ray Polidano, Director General of the Malta Aviation Museum, and Tony Spiteri, whose knowledge of the air warfare over Malta is considerable; both freely gave me the benefit of their knowledge. I would also like to Major Stanley Clews, the staff at the National Library in Valletta, and William Burridge for putting up with me for an entire week.

I am enormously grateful to the late Angela Daborn, sister of Raoul Daddo-Langlois, for safeguarding her brother's letters, papers and photographs, and to her daughter - Raoul's neice - Zoë Thomas, for her great support and for allowing me to come to her home and look through all the boxes of her uncle's papers.

I would also like to thank the following: Jim Allaway, Archie Barr, Peter Bell, Maggie Bidmead, Giles Bourne, Charlie Bryant, Brian Cull, Frank Dickinson, Dr Christopher Dowling, Patricia Evans, Jackie Freshfield, Eleo Gordon, Wendy Kyrle-Pope, Bradley Lander, Peter Lee, Richard Mason, Roy Nesbit, David Ross, Christopher Shores, Bill Simpson, Mark Souter, Rowland White, and especially Oliver Barnham, Emma Gardner, David Hindley, Lalla Hitchings, my father Martin Holland, and James Petrie.

Enormous thanks are also due to Emma Parry at Carlisle & Co; Chris Knutson, Jonathan Burnham and all who have helped at Talk Miramax; to Pandora White, Laura Meehan, Jo Carpenter, Richard Hussey, Erin Hussey, Helen Ewing, Lucie Stericker, Steve Dobell, Helen Richardson and everyone else at Orion; Sam North, Clare Conville, Ed Jespers, Nicola Gray, and Jo Cooke at Conville & Walsh. But I would particularly like to thank Trevor Dolby and Patrick Walsh for their friendship, help and guidance. Finally, I am indebted to Rachel for her unwavering support and patience.

INDEX